The Expert's Guide to SQL Server

Tuning, Security, and Cloud Migration

Venkata Reddy Pasam
Petchikumar Andiappan

Apress®

The Expert's Guide to SQL Server: Tuning, Security, and Cloud Migration

Venkata Reddy Pasam
Irving, TX, USA

Petchikumar Andiappan
Bengaluru, Karnataka, India

ISBN-13 (pbk): 979-8-8688-2450-0
https://doi.org/10.1007/979-8-8688-2451-7

ISBN-13 (electronic): 979-8-8688-2451-7

Managing Director, Apress Media LLC: Welmoed Spahr
Acquisitions Editor: Shaul Elson
Editorial Assistant: Gryffin Winkler

Cover designed by eStudioCalamar

Distributed to the book trade worldwide by Springer Science+Business Media New York, 1 New York Plaza, Suite 4600, New York, NY 10004-1562, USA. Phone 1-800-SPRINGER, fax (201) 348-4505, e-mail orders-ny@ springer-sbm.com, or visit www.springeronline.com. Apress Media, LLC is a California LLC and the sole member (owner) is Springer Science + Business Media Finance Inc (SSBM Finance Inc). SSBM Finance Inc is a **Delaware** corporation.

For information on translations, please e-mail booktranslations@springernature.com; for reprint, paperback, or audio rights, please e-mail bookpermissions@springernature.com.

Apress titles may be purchased in bulk for academic, corporate, or promotional use. eBook versions and licenses are also available for most titles. For more information, reference our Print and eBook Bulk Sales web page at http://www.apress.com/bulk-sales.

Any source code or other supplementary material referenced by the author in this book is available to readers on GitHub. For more detailed information, please visit https://www.apress.com/gp/services/source-code.

If disposing of this product, please recycle the paper

To my wonderful wife, whose love and partnership have been my greatest strength, and to my cherished daughters, Hitha and Sritha, who are my pride and joy. This work is a heartfelt tribute to my beloved parents and my brother, Gurava Reddy, for their unwavering guidance and support throughout my journey.

—Venkata Reddy Pasam

Table of Contents

About the Authors

Venkata Reddy Pasam has over 15 years of IT experience and has carved a remarkable career working with multinational organizations such as IBM, TCS, and multinational clients. His expertise spans a comprehensive range of database technologies, including SQL Server, Oracle, PostgreSQL, and multi-cloud platforms like AWS, Azure, and Google Cloud. Venkata has been instrumental in designing and implementing large-scale database solutions, driving successful migrations, and optimizing complex infrastructures. He has led critical projects, including the migration of over 1,500 SQL Servers across data centers, showcasing his technical acumen and leadership skills.

Renowned for his proficiency in cloud solution architecture, disaster recovery, high availability, and performance tuning, Venkata delivers robust and scalable solutions that align with modern IT demands. His ability to navigate diverse environments and resolve intricate challenges makes him a sought-after expert in the industry. In addition to his technical contributions, Venkata is an avid thought leader and mentor, actively providing insights on database technologies and cloud innovations. His experience extends to team leadership, project management, and client engagement, guaranteeing successful delivery of complex initiatives. He is passionate regarding pushing the boundaries of technology and is committed to empowering businesses to harness the full potential of databases and cloud technologies. His dedication to excellence and continuous innovation drives his mission to build resilient, future-ready IT systems.

Petchikumar Andiappan is a versatile technology leader with more than 20 years of experience in database architecture, cloud solutions, and software development. He has made significant contributions to renowned multinational organizations, playing a pivotal role in delivering transformative IT solutions. Petchikumar's expertise spans a wide range of database technologies, including SQL Server, Oracle, PostgreSQL, MySQL, and NoSQL solutions, along with in-depth knowledge of multi-cloud platforms such as AWS, Azure, and Google Cloud.

His technical skills extend beyond database management to application development, enabling him to design and deliver end-to-end, scalable solutions tailored to modern business needs. Petchikumar has led and executed complex projects, including cloud migrations, performance optimizations, and the implementation of high-availability architectures. His proficiency in DevOps practices and development expertise in programming languages such as Python, Java, and .NET guarantee seamless integration of database solutions with modern application frameworks.

As a thought leader and mentor, Petchikumar actively provides extensive knowledge through mentoring teams, conducting technical workshops, and delivering innovative solutions to challenging IT problems. His holistic approach to technology, combining a deep understanding of architecture, development, and operational processes, makes him a trusted advisor in the industry.

About the Technical Reviewers

Srujana Marupally With over 11 years of solid IT experience, **Srujana Marupally** has built a remarkable career as a SQL Server Architect and Team Lead at IBM India Pvt. Ltd., where she has spent most of her professional journey. She has successfully delivered numerous prestigious projects, showcasing her leadership and deep technical expertise in managing and architecting database solutions. Srujana's expertise spans on-premises database systems and diverse cloud platforms such as Amazon Web Services, Microsoft Azure, and Google Cloud Platform. She is adept at designing and implementing robust database solutions that meet the complex needs of modern IT landscapes. Her comprehensive knowledge and experience enable her to handle diverse challenges, making her a trusted leader in her field. Now extending her contributions to the literary world, Srujana brings her profound technical knowledge and passion for innovation to her role as a book reviewer. Her insights promise to enrich readers, offering them a blend of practical expertise and thought leadership in the ever-evolving world of technology.

Cintia Marin With over 20 years of extensive IT experience, **Cintia Marin** has established a distinguished career as a seasoned database architect and technology leader. She has delivered numerous high-impact projects, demonstrating exceptional leadership and technical acumen in designing, managing, and optimizing complex database solutions. By consistently managing high-achieving teams and driving critical initiatives, she has significantly contributed to advancing organizations' technology landscapes through visionary innovation and purposeful leadership.

CHAPTER 1

SQL Server Internals and Storage

This chapter serves as the foundational exploration into the core mechanisms that power SQL Server. Rather than focusing on the user-facing aspects, we will delve deep into the engine's inner architecture and its underlying storage systems. Our journey begins by dissecting the **protocol layer**, unveiling how SQL Server manages communication with external systems. We will then explore the **relational engine**, the cornerstone that implements the relational data model. Following this, we'll investigate the robust **storage engine**, the powerhouse responsible for data retrieval, storage, and manipulation. We'll delve into details surrounding the **page and extent architecture**, understanding the structures used to organize data. Finally, we'll examine the critical role of **locking and latching** in ensuring data consistency during concurrent operations, highlighting how these components safeguard data access. This comprehensive introduction is essential for readers, as it lays the groundwork for understanding the later sections of this guide and ensures a clear grasp of SQL Server's internal framework.

Microsoft SQL Server operates on a client-server model, where the client sends requests to the server, and the server processes and returns the relevant data. The following section will explore this architecture in depth.

The architecture can be divided into **three primary components**, as outlined in Figure 1-1.

© Venkata Reddy Pasam and Petchikumar Andiappan 2026

V. R. Pasam and P. Andiappan, *The Expert's Guide to SQL Server*, https://doi.org/10.1007/979-8-8688-2451-7_1

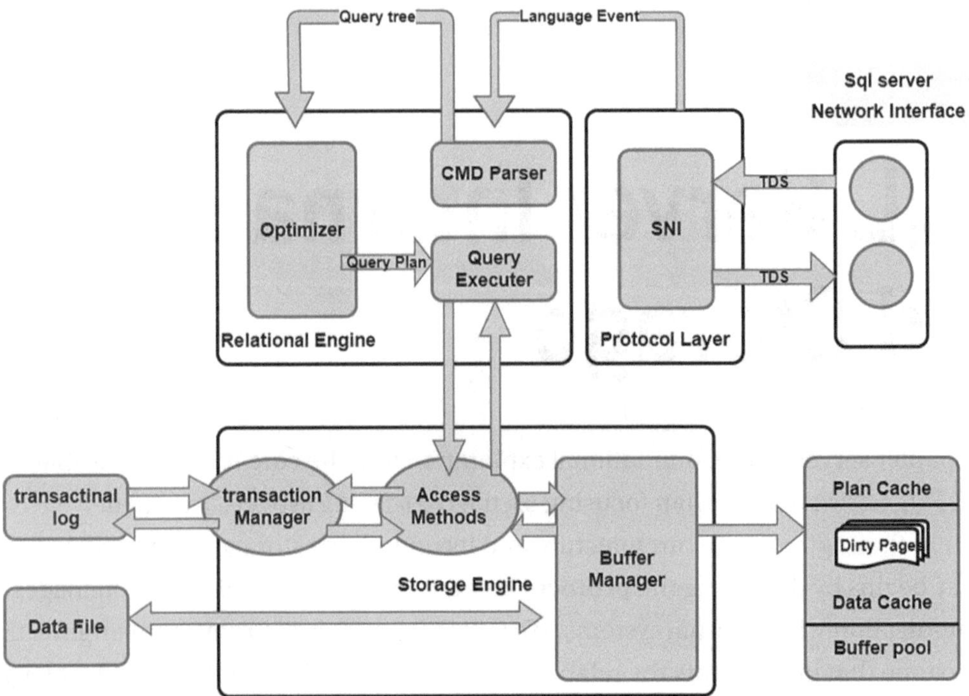

Figure 1-1. *SQL architecture*

Based on the illustration above, SQL Server architecture can be understood through its three core elements: (1) protocol layer, (2) relational engine, and (3) storage engine. Let's explore each of these fundamental layers, examining their roles and core functions to gain a comprehensive insight into how SQL Server operates.

Protocol Layer

The protocol layer is pivotal in supporting the client-server architecture and managing communication streams between clients and servers. It ensures seamless data exchange using various protocols. The main task of **the protocol layer** is to dialog between the SQL Server and the client software. As seen in Figure 1-1, the protocol layer facilitates communication between clients and the system by utilizing the tabular data stream (TDS) format. Within this layer, the SQL Server network interface is responsible for handling network-related operations.

SNI (SQL Server Network Interface)

- **Function**: Translates transact-SQL (T-SQL) commands and results into the appropriate protocol for communication.

  The SQL Server network interface (SNI) is an important intermediary when an application talks to a SQL Server. It makes sure that responses and queries in transact-SQL (T-SQL) are converted automatically to the format that can be transmitted over the network. This translation becomes crucial in the realization of interoperability between clients and SQL Server instances, irrespective of the platform or network protocol being utilized.

- **Supported Protocols:**

  - **TDS (Tabular Data Stream)**: SQL Server's protocol to send data over the network.

  - **TCP/IP**: TCP/IP is one of the most widely used transport protocols, enabling remote clients to access SQL Server over standard IP-based networks. Known for its stability and scalability, TCP/IP supports wide-area network (WAN) connectivity, making it highly suitable for production environments. It is stable and accommodates wide-area networking applications; thus, it is best suited for production environments.

  - **Named Pipes**: Named pipes are usually applicable in the local area network (LAN) configurations and offer client and server interaction using a common memory buffer. It tends to be more performant than TCP/IP in the circumstances of a tightly coupled network but not appropriate in distributed systems.

  - **Shared Memory**: This is the speediest method of communication, and it is limited to connections within the same machine. It completely bypasses the network stack and relies on memory-mapped files instead, making it particularly well-suited for simulated testing or development setups where both the client and SQL Server reside on the same machine.

Being informed about these underlying protocols guides the database administrators and the developers to make wise decisions relating to the performance tuning, the security settings, and the deployment architecture. The capacity of the SNI to apply this information in abstraction enables the applications to not become bound to low-level complexities of the network, illustrating the compatibility and maintainability all the more in cases of SQL Server. Below is a detailed process of how the protocol layer works.

Process

Receiving T-SQL Commands

The protocol layer acts as the primary gateway between the client application and SQL Server. It receives transact-SQL (T-SQL) commands over the network using the tabular data stream (TDS) protocol. These commands may involve data queries, such as SELECT, INSERT, or UPDATE, or administrative tasks like creating databases and managing users.

After their receipt, the next thing will be to ascertain what and why these orders came.

Command Interpretation and Forwarding

Upon receiving the commands, the protocol layer interprets their intent—whether related to data retrieval, modification, or metadata operations. It then forwards them to the relational engine, which is responsible for parsing, optimizing, and executing the query. Before doing so, the protocol layer ensures compliance with the TDS protocol and communication standards.

Once the query has been interpreted, it then has to undergo a series of stringent internal procedures before any action is performed on the data.

Processing by the Relational Engine

Once the relational engine takes control, it validates the syntax, optimizes the query, and prepares an execution plan. If the operation involves interacting with physical data on disk, the storage engine is called upon to manage the required input/output processes.

After the execution, it is time to concentrate and arrange the formatting of the server output.

Result Compilation and Formatting

After execution, the relational engine organizes the outcome, such as result sets or status messages, and formats them according to the TDS protocol. It converts internal SQL Server structures into a format that can be interpreted by the client application and passes them back to the protocol layer.

After formatting, the results can now be sent back to the client, which requested the result.

Returning Results to the Client

The protocol layer packages the formatted results or error messages into TDS packets and transmits them back to the client over the network. This ensures secure and reliable data delivery, allowing clients to display the results in a user interface, store them locally, or further process them as needed.

In addition to data transmission, the protocol layer has been central in the management of the complete session.

End-to-End Communication

Throughout the communication cycle, the protocol layer maintains seamless bidirectional interaction between the client and SQL Server. It manages connection persistence, session control, and error handling to ensure efficient and uninterrupted database access.

Collectively, these phases describe the ability of SQL Server to convert high-level commands into efficient data interactions that provide scalable, secure, and real-time access to both clients and applications.

After knowing the way SQL Server internally handles the request made by the client, it is also worth examining the different network protocols that can facilitate the communications in other types of deployment.

SQL Server Network Protocols

SQL Server utilizes the combination of several network protocols specially developed to serve various client-server interaction options and deployment conditions. So, let us make a closer inspection of the three major ones.

Shared Memory

It enables direct communication between client and server using shared system memory. First, the shared memory protocol becomes the most effective communication variant, yet only in the case when the client and the server belong to one and the same machine. A protocol that facilitates direct communication between processes on the same computer by sharing a memory section.

Purpose in SQL Server:

- Used for local connections where the client and SQL Server instance reside on the same machine.

- It is the fastest protocol because it bypasses network overhead.

Default protocol for local connections in SQL Server Management Studio (SSMS) or other local client applications.

This protocol is most appropriate to use in isolated development or testing situations in which speed and low latency are factors and the client and server are located in the same place.

TCP/IP

It facilitates communication between a client and a remote SQL Server, even when installed on different machines.

Then, we shift toward TCP/IP, which is the most popular remote database communication over network and internet protocol. TCP/IP is the most widely used network protocol for remote database communication over networks, especially across the internet and large intranets.

Purpose in SQL Server:

- Ideal for remote client connections across networks.

- It allows SQL Server to listen for and respond to requests on a specific port (default: **1433** for the default instance).

It is best suited for scenarios where SQL Server must communicate across multiple networks or with clients not on the same machine. Due to its flexibility and accessibility, TCP/IP has become the protocol of choice in the majority of enterprise and production SQL Server implementations.

Named Pipes

This method employs the local area network (LAN) for communication with SQL Server over the network.

The named pipes protocol is a different mechanism of communication, highly applicable in LAN-based systems and legacy Windows systems. A network protocol for interprocess communication allows one process to send data to another, either locally or over a network.

Purpose in SQL Server:

- Offers a channel of communication between clients and SQL Server through named channels (e.g., \\.\pipe\MSSQLSERVER\sql\query).

It is commonly used in older systems or when TCP/IP is unavailable. However, it is less widely used in modern deployments due to its reliance on Windows-only environments. As named pipes may be useful in certain applications, use of TCP/IP is becoming increasingly mainstream and the choice of best practice because of its platform independence and extended portability.

All these protocols have different, specific purposes, and knowing their nature will allow database professionals to apply the most appropriate communication method to a given environment and performance objectives.

How These Protocols Are Managed

These protocols can be configured using the **SQL Server configuration manager**. Administrators can turn on/off specific protocols based on requirements. Priority can also be assigned to the protocols, ensuring the most suitable one is used for client connections.

Relational Engine

The relational engine oversees how data is handled and coordinates with the storage engine. It plays a central role in handling SQL queries, managing their interpretation, optimization, and execution. This component is tasked with the logical control of database operations, ensuring that queries run in the most efficient way possible. A closer look at its three primary elements is provided below:

CMD Parser (Command Parser)

We can begin with the command parser, which is the initial interpretation process on the part of the SQL Server, which makes the query grammatically and logically correct.

The command parser translates the client-provided SQL query into a **query tree**, a logical representation of the SQL command. During the parsing phase, the SQL query is analyzed to detect both syntax and semantic errors. Syntax errors arise when the SQL command violates grammatical rules, for instance, a typo such as SELECT * FORM

TableName instead of FROM. Semantic errors, on the other hand, occur when the query references nonexistent tables or columns. The parser ensures that the structure and referenced objects of the SQL statement are valid before moving to the next step. Once parsing is complete, the query is transformed into a query tree, which serves as a logical representation of the operations required to execute the statement. This abstract structure outlines the sequence of tasks such as joins, filters, projections, and aggregations that SQL Server must perform to retrieve or manipulate the requested data. The CMD Parser ensures that the query is valid and prepares it for further processing by the optimizer.

Through the generation of this logical foundation, the CMD Parser prepares the grounds to the next important challenge, optimization of query.

Optimizer

Based on the query tree, which has been constructed by the parser, the optimizer comes in to devise the most optimal plan for executing queries.

The optimizer takes the query tree generated by the CMD Parser and creates an **optimized query plan**, ensuring the query is executed with minimal resource usage. The optimizer evaluates the query tree, identifying **joins, filters, indexes**, and **statistics** associated with querying tables and columns. If there are multiple ways to join two tables (e.g., nested loops and hash joins), it will evaluate which method is most efficient. The optimizer calculates the **cost** of different execution strategies using metrics like **CPU usage, I/O operations**, and **memory consumption**. A full table scan may be more efficient for small tables or when queries require retrieving a large proportion of rows from a bigger table. The optimizer produces an **execution plan** that details the best strategy for retrieving or modifying the requested data. It decides the **order of joins**, **index usage**, and **sequence of operations**. The optimizer ensures that the query is executed with the **fewest resources** while returning the correct results.

When the process of optimization is already finished, the implementation plan, which is the result of optimization, will be sent to the query executor, which in turn will perform the actual data operations using this blueprint.

Query Executor

The query executor gets to execute the actual commands required to execute the request of the client with a well-determined execution plan.

The query executor takes the **execution plan** from the optimizer and performs the actual operations to retrieve or manipulate the data. The query executor carries out the steps outlined in the execution plan, which was previously generated by the optimizer. Depending on the plan, this may involve operations such as index seeks, table scans, or joins. Each action is performed in the specified sequence to ensure efficient data retrieval or modification. To fulfill data operations, the executor interacts with the storage engine, which is responsible for accessing the actual data. For read operations, the storage engine retrieves the required data pages from memory or disk and delivers them to the executor. For write operations, it ensures that the necessary updates are applied to the data storage structures. Once the execution is complete, the query executor compiles the results, whether rows of data or a confirmation message, and sends them back to the client application through the protocol layer, concluding the query lifecycle. The query executor ensures the logical steps outlined in the execution plan are carried out accurately, interacting with the storage engine to handle data retrieval or modification.

This is the last step where everything, including parsing and execution, goes harmoniously to provide the correct, efficient, and reliable query results to a final user.

Storage Engine

This engine is in charge of overseeing the actual storage and data retrieval from the underlying storage systems, such as disks or a **storage area network (SAN)**. It ensures efficient data management while maintaining the integrity and consistency of the database. Below is a more detailed explanation of its key components and processes.

Access Methods

It provides the interface between the relational engine and the storage layer, handling **physical read/write operations** on data. It retrieves data pages from the **buffer pool** if they are cached. If the requested data is not in the buffer pool, it fetches it from the disk. It performs **write operations** by marking pages in memory as **dirty** and scheduling them for eventual write-back to disk. It works closely with the **transaction manager** to ensure data modifications adhere to **ACID properties**. For example, if a transaction is rolled back, the access methods layer ensures that no uncommitted data is written to disk.

Transaction Manager

It ensures that all database operations comply with **ACID (atomicity, consistency, isolation, and durability)** properties, guaranteeing reliable transaction processing. **Transactional log** records every change made to the database, including insert, update, and delete operations, to enable recovery and rollback. It logs each transaction step to ensure **durability** in case of failures like power outages. It is used for **point-in-time recovery** and replaying transactions during database restoration. **Lock manager** manages locks to control concurrency in a multi-user environment. It implements **row-level** or **page-level locks** to ensure multiple transactions do not conflict or corrupt data. It ensures proper isolation by preventing dirty reads and maintaining transactional integrity.

Buffer Manager

It manages memory allocation for SQL Server operations to optimize performance by reducing **disk I/O operations**. A **buffer pool** acts as a memory cache for frequently accessed data pages. It stores recently accessed data pages in memory, allowing faster access than reading from disk. It minimizes disk I/O by serving read requests directly from memory whenever possible. The **plan cache** stores **execution plans** of previously executed queries to avoid repetitive query optimization. When a query is executed, the relational engine checks the **plan cache** for an existing execution plan. If found, it reuses the plan, saving time and resources. **Data cache** temporarily holds data retrieved from the disk to serve ongoing queries. Data pages fetched from the disk are placed in the data cache for reuse by other queries accessing the same data. **Dirty pages** are the pages in the buffer pool pages that have been altered but have not yet been written back to the storage medium. SQL Server manages **checkpoint operations** to write modified pages to storage, maintaining data integrity and persistence.

Additional Storage Engine Elements

Data Files

It is the physical repository for storing data. It is the physical location on disk where the database stores its data files. The **primary data file (MDF)** is the main storage file that contains the primary database objects (tables, views, stored procedures). **Secondary data files (PDF)** are the optional files that are used to split storage across multiple files or drives to improve performance or manageability. Data is read from and written to these files as required during query execution or transaction processing.

Transactional Log File (LDF)

It tracks all changes made to the database, ensuring durability and enabling recovery. The transactional log sequentially logs every operation (e.g., insert, update, and delete), including committed and uncommitted transactions. The log ensures that changes survive system crashes by replaying logged operations during recovery. The LDF file is used to restore the database to a specific point by replaying or rolling back transactions.

The **storage engine** is the backbone of SQL Server's data storage and retrieval system, working with the **relational engine**. It ensures that data is stored, retrieved, and managed efficiently while adhering to ACID principles. Its major components, like the access methods, transaction manager, and buffer manager, work seamlessly to provide high performance, reliability, and data consistency. The data files (MDF and NDF) and transactional logs (LDF) further ensure the data's physical and logical integrity, making SQL Server a robust relational database management system.

Page and Extent Architecture

SQL Server organizes data storage using **pages and extents**, which form the foundation of the **SQL Server storage engine**. This architecture is crucial for database performance optimization, indexing, and space management.

Pages in SQL Server

A page is the fundamental data storage unit in SQL Server, with a standard size of 8 KB (8192 bytes). Each page includes a 96-byte header that stores crucial metadata. This header captures information such as the page type (e.g., data page, index page), the page number, allocation details, the availability of free space, and the transaction log sequence number (LSN), which is vital for recovery and maintaining transactional integrity.

Types of Pages

SQL Server supports several types of pages, each designed to handle specific data structures. Data pages (Type 1) store the actual rows of user table data, excluding large object (LOB) types. Index pages (Type 2) maintain B-Tree structures that facilitate efficient data lookups and sorting. For LOB data such as VARCHAR(MAX), TEXT, or IMAGE, SQL Server uses text/image pages (Type 3). To manage allocation, index allocation map (IAM) pages (Type 10) record the extents allocated to database objects, while page free space (PFS) pages (Type 11) track the usage and availability of space on each page. Global allocation map (GAM) pages (Type 8) keep track of allocated extents across the database, and shared global allocation map (SGAM) pages (Type 9) identify mixed extents that still have free space available for further allocations.

Extents in SQL Server

An **extent consists of eight consecutive pages (64 KB)** allocated together to improve efficiency.

Types of Extents

Uniform extents are all eight pages belonging to a single object. In **mixed extents**, each page may belong to different objects (used for small tables). SQL Server efficiently tracks pages and extents using specialized tracking pages:

- **PFS (Page Free Space) Pages:** Track allocated pages and free space.

- **GAM (Global Allocation Map) Pages:** Track extent allocation.

- **SGAM (Shared Global Allocation Map) Pages:** Track mixed extent usage.

It **avoids fragmentation** by using appropriate fill factors. It **monitors PFS, GAM, and SGAM contention** in high-transaction environments. It **optimizes index storage** to reduce page splits and I/O overhead.

Understanding SQL Server's **page and extent architecture** helps optimize storage, improve query performance, and efficiently manage space in large-scale enterprise databases.

Locking and Latching Internals

SQL Server ensures data consistency and concurrency control using **locking** and **latching** mechanisms. While **locking** is a **logical mechanism** to control access to data, **latching** is a **physical mechanism** to maintain consistency during read/write operations in memory.

Locking in SQL Server

Locking is a concurrency control mechanism that prevents several transactions from concurrently changing the same data inconsistently.

Lock Granularity

In SQL Server, locks are mechanisms used to control concurrent access to data and ensure transactional consistency. These locks can be applied at various levels depending on the scope of the operation. A row identifier (RID) lock targets a single row in a heap structure, while a key lock applies to a specific index key in indexed tables. Page locks are used for 8-KB data or index pages, offering a balance between granularity and performance. For broader operations, SQL Server can place a table lock, affecting all rows within a table, or even a database lock, which restricts access to the entire database during critical operations.

Lock Modes

SQL Server implements several lock modes to manage concurrent data access and avoid conflicts. A shared (S) lock allows multiple transactions to read data simultaneously but blocks any write operations. An exclusive (X) lock ensures that no other transaction can read or write the locked data. The update (U) lock is a hybrid that helps prevent deadlocks by initially reserving the right to update, without blocking shared access. Intent locks (such as IS, IX, and IU) serve as signals to the system about intended locking behavior at lower levels, helping SQL Server manage hierarchical locking efficiently. A schema modification (Sch-M) lock is acquired during structural changes like ALTER TABLE, ensuring no access interferes during DDL operations. For high-performance data loading, a bulk update (BU) lock is used when performing bulk inserts with the TABLOCK option.

Lock Escalation

SQL Server automatically escalates row/page locks to table locks when a query locks **5,000+** rows/pages or the server is under memory pressure.

You can **control lock escalation** with

SQL

```
ALTER TABLE TableName SET (LOCK_ESCALATION = AUTO | TABLE | DISABLE);
```

Deadlocks and Resolution

Deadlocks occur when two transactions wait on each other to release resources. SQL Server detects and resolves deadlocks by **terminating the least expensive transaction** (victim).

You can monitor deadlocks using

SQL

```
SET DEADLOCK_PRIORITY HIGH; -- Lowers the chance of being chosen as a victim
```

Or capture deadlock graphs using **extended events**.

Latching in SQL Server

Latches are lightweight synchronization primitives that protect **in-memory** structures (like buffer pages and index trees) from corruption when multiple threads access them.

Types of Latches

- **Buffer Latches:** Protect data pages in memory (e.g., read/write buffers).

- **Non-Buffer Latches:** Protect internal structures (e.g., locks and caches).

- **I/O Latches:** Protect data during disk-to-memory transfers.

Latch Modes

Latches work similarly to locks but are managed internally by SQL Server:

- **SH (Shared):** Allows multiple reads

- **UP (Update):** Acquired before modifying a page

- **EX (Exclusive):** Prevents all other access

Latch Contention

Heavy contention on latches can slow down workloads. Causes can be **high concurrent read/write workloads** (causing buffer latch contention), **index hot spots** (frequent updates to a single index page), and **heavy tempdb usage** (causing PAGELATCH_* waits).

Ways to reduce latch contention are to optimize indexing to avoid frequent updates on the same page, **use multiple tempdb files** to reduce PAGELATCH_UP waits, and **monitor wait types** using:

SQL

```
SELECT * FROM sys.dm_os_wait_stats WHERE wait_type LIKE 'PAGE%';
```

Table 1-1. *Locking vs. latching: key differences*

Feature	Locking	Latching
Purpose	Controls concurrent access to data	Protects in-memory structures
Scope	Transactions	Internal SQL Server operations
Types	Shared, Exclusive, Update, Intent, Schema	Shared, Update, Exclusive
Performance Impact	Can cause blocking/deadlocks	It can cause contention but is lightweight
Resolution	Deadlock detection, lock escalation	Optimize indexing, reduce hot spots

Summary

This chapter has laid the groundwork for understanding SQL Server's internal architecture. We explored its multi-layered design, starting with the protocol layer, which establishes client connections. The relational engine then processes database structures and queries, while the storage engine handles data retrieval and management. Within this storage framework, the page and extent architecture ensures efficient data organization at the physical level. Additionally, locking and latching mechanisms play a vital role in maintaining data consistency, especially in multi-user environments.

By working together, these components create a robust and efficient system for data storage and retrieval. Gaining insight into these foundational elements is essential for delving deeper into SQL Server's architecture and operations, as discussed in the following chapters.

CHAPTER 2

Backup and Recovery Strategies

This chapter provides a detailed exploration of backup and recovery strategies within a SQL Server environment. We begin by establishing the fundamental importance of backups in safeguarding against data loss, corruption, or damage caused by a range of threats, from hardware failures to cyberattacks. This chapter categorizes the primary types of backups in MS SQL Server, including full, differential, and transaction log backups, which are at the core of any strong recovery plan. Beyond these foundational backups, we will delve into other specialized types, such as tail-log backups, file and filegroup backups, copy-only backups, mirror backups, and compressed backups. The chapter will further explore incremental and differential backups and discuss the benefits of each approach. We will also review the concepts and application of transaction log backups, including the more specialized use of tail-log backups. More advanced backup and recovery strategies, such as file and filegroup backups as well as mirror backups, will be reviewed. Finally, the role of compression in backups will be considered, and special considerations for large environments will be discussed. By the end of this chapter, readers will have a thorough understanding of the various backup options available in SQL Server, along with the strategies and techniques necessary to build a robust and effective data protection and recovery plan for both simple and complex environments.

Backup refers to creating a duplicate copy of data, ensuring it is recoverable in unintentional loss, corruption, or damage. In the context of MS SQL Server, backing up a database is a critical aspect of data protection and recovery planning. It helps safeguard against data loss caused by hardware failures, software issues, cyberattacks, or human errors.

© Venkata Reddy Pasam and Petchikumar Andiappan 2026

V. R. Pasam and P. Andiappan, *The Expert's Guide to SQL Server*, https://doi.org/10.1007/979-8-8688-2451-7_2

MS SQL Server backups are broadly categorized into three main types: The primary types of backups available in SQL Server include

- Full

- Differential

- Transaction log

There are other backup types available as well:

- Tail-log backup

- File and filegroup backups

- Copy-only backup

- Mirror backups

- Compress backups

Full Backup

A full backup captures the entire database, including all data files and enough of the transaction log to ensure that the database can be recovered to a consistent state at the time the backup was taken. This makes it the foundation of most backup strategies and essential for restoring the entire database. You can perform a full backup either with T-SQL or through SQL Server Management Studio (SSMS). The examples below illustrate how to create a full backup.

backup database testdb to disk = 'C:\Program Files\Microsoft SQL Server\ MSSQL16.MSSQLSERVER\MSSQL\Backup\testdb_full.bak' with stats=20, as shown in Figure 2-1.

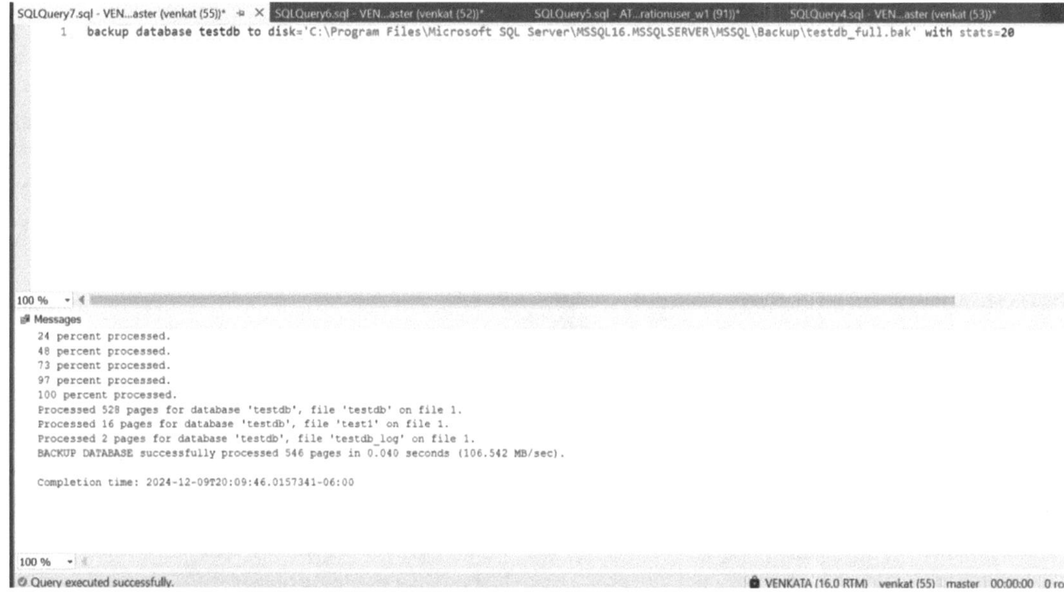

Figure 2-1. *T-SQL starting server*

Using SQL Server Management Studio

- Right-click Choose Tasks ➤ Backup under the database name.

Right-click the database name, choose Tasks, and then select Back Up… as shown in Figure 2-2.

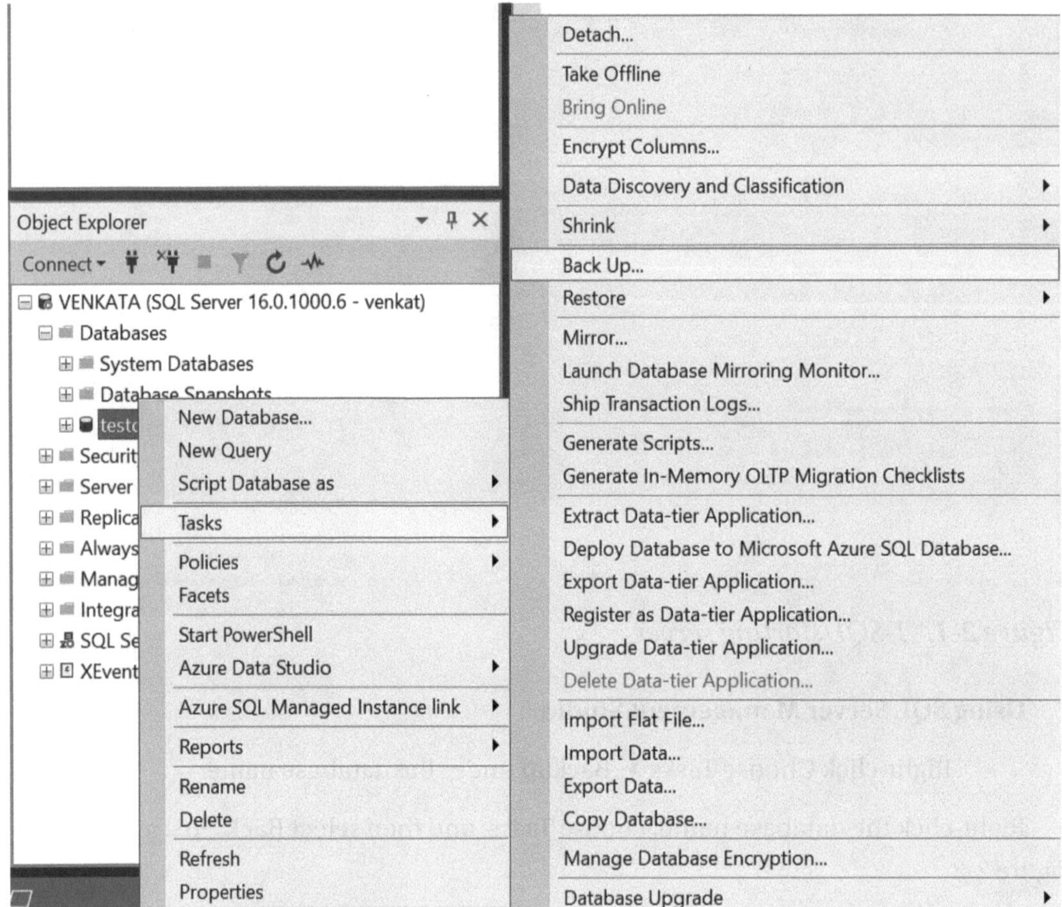

Figure 2-2. *Back up the tasks*

- Make "Full" your backup type

- selection

- "Disk" should be chosen as the destination

- To add a backup file, click "Add…" and enter "Path\testdb.BAK" and click "OK"

Specify the backup destination and file name, as shown in Figure 2-3.

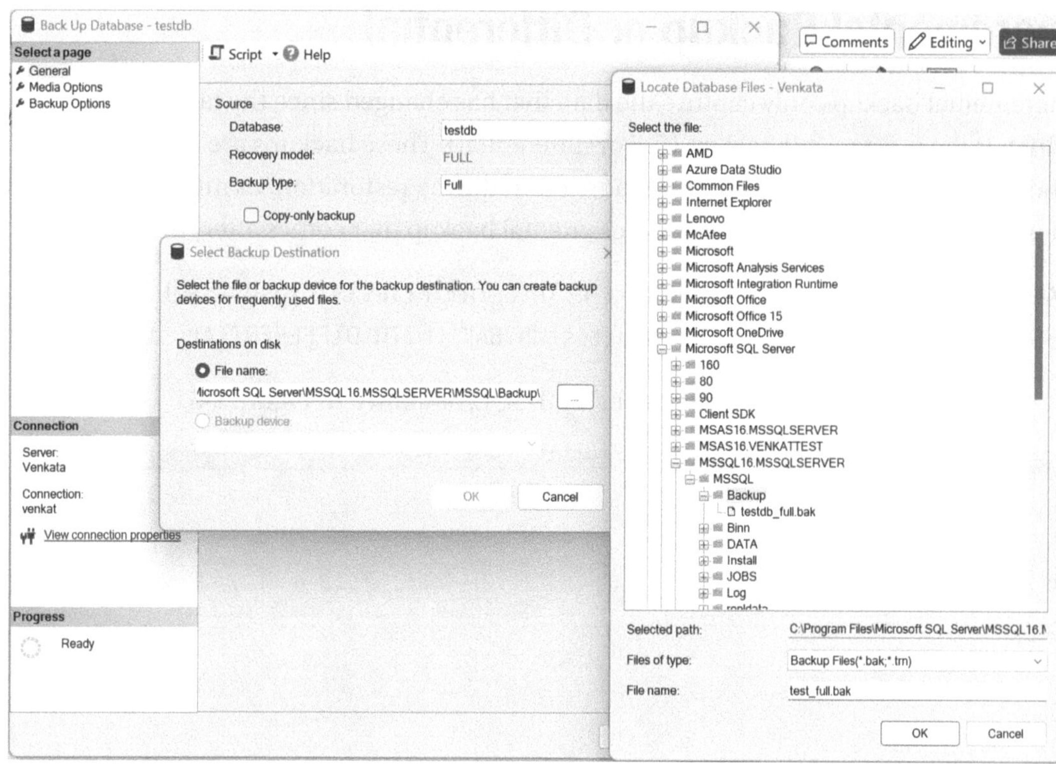

Figure 2-3. *Creating backup*

- Click "OK" again to create the backup.

- The entire backup file is in the location below. An extension ending in BAK indicates that the backup is a complete database backup.

After the backup completes, you can verify the .bak file in the SQL Server backup directory, as shown in Figure 2-4.

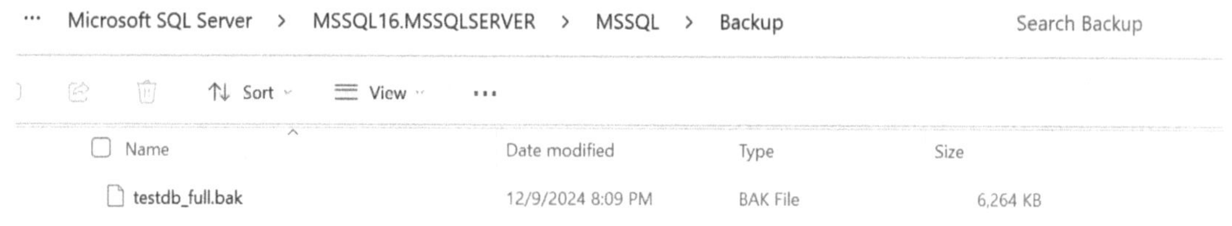

Figure 2-4. *Location of backup file*

Incremental Backup or Differential

Incremental backups only capture the data that has changed since the last backup, which is the most recent backup (full or differential). These backups are even smaller and faster to create but may require more effort during restoration, as multiple backup files (the last full backup and every incremental backup that comes after) must be used.

```
BACKUP DATABASE testdb TO DISK = 'C:\Program Files\Microsoft SQL Server\
MSSQL16.MSSQLSERVER\MSSQL\Backup\testdb.BAK' WITH DIFFERENTIAL,stats=50
```

You can also perform the backup using T-SQL, as shown in Figure 2-5.

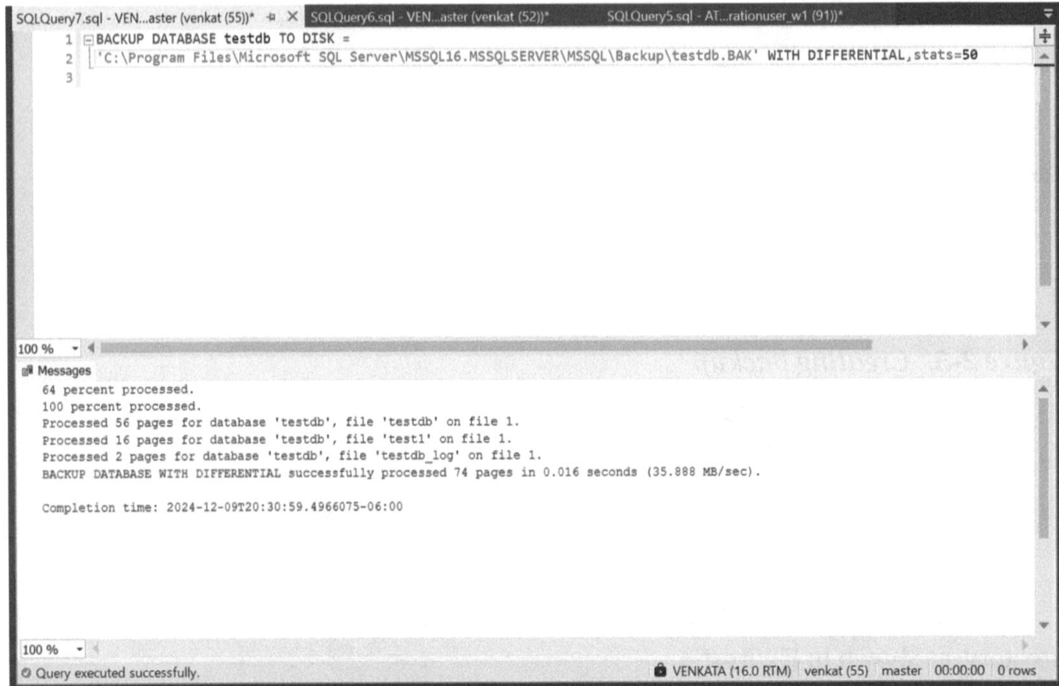

Figure 2-5. *SQL Server Management Studio*

Using SQL Server Management Studio

- Right-click on the database name

- Select Tasks ➤ Backup

To create a differential backup using SQL Server Management Studio, right-click the database, choose Tasks, and select Back Up, as shown in Figure 2-6.

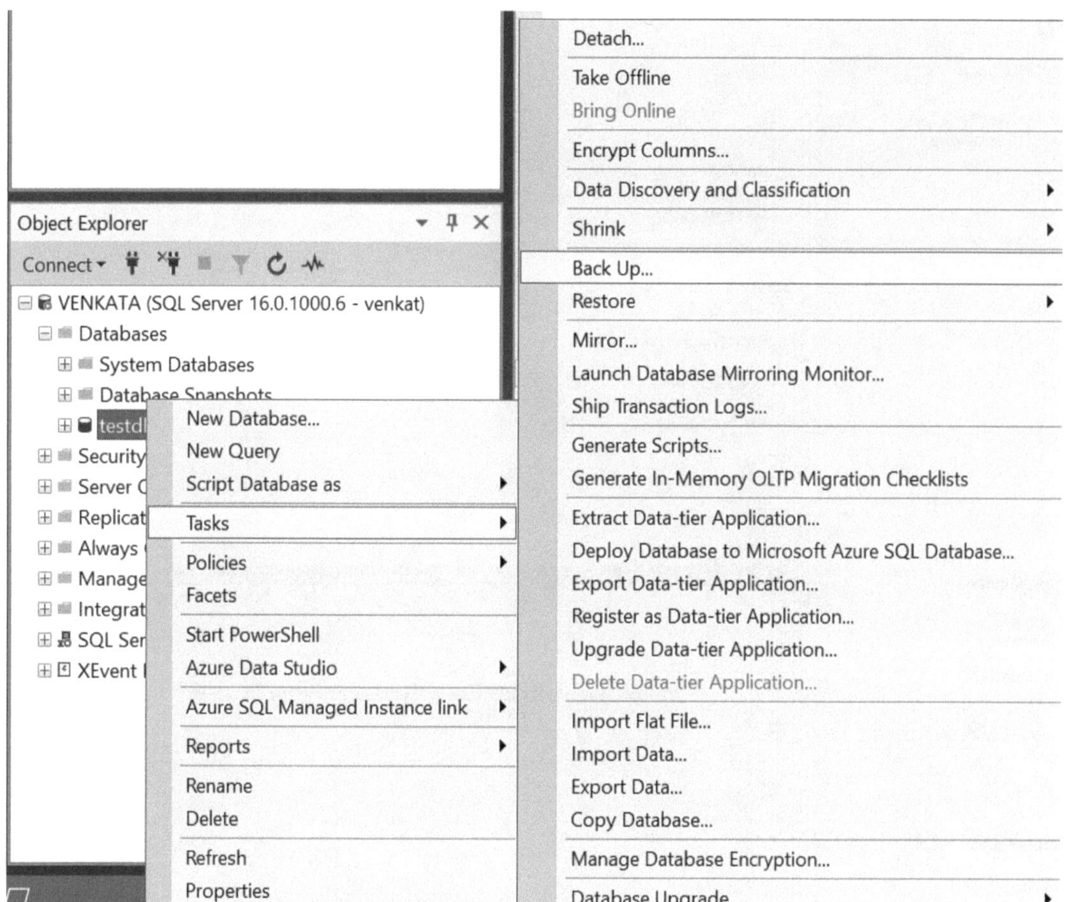

Figure 2-6. *Backup of differential tasks*

- Select "Differential" as the backup type.

Configure the backup type as Differential and review the destination settings, as shown in Figure 2-7.

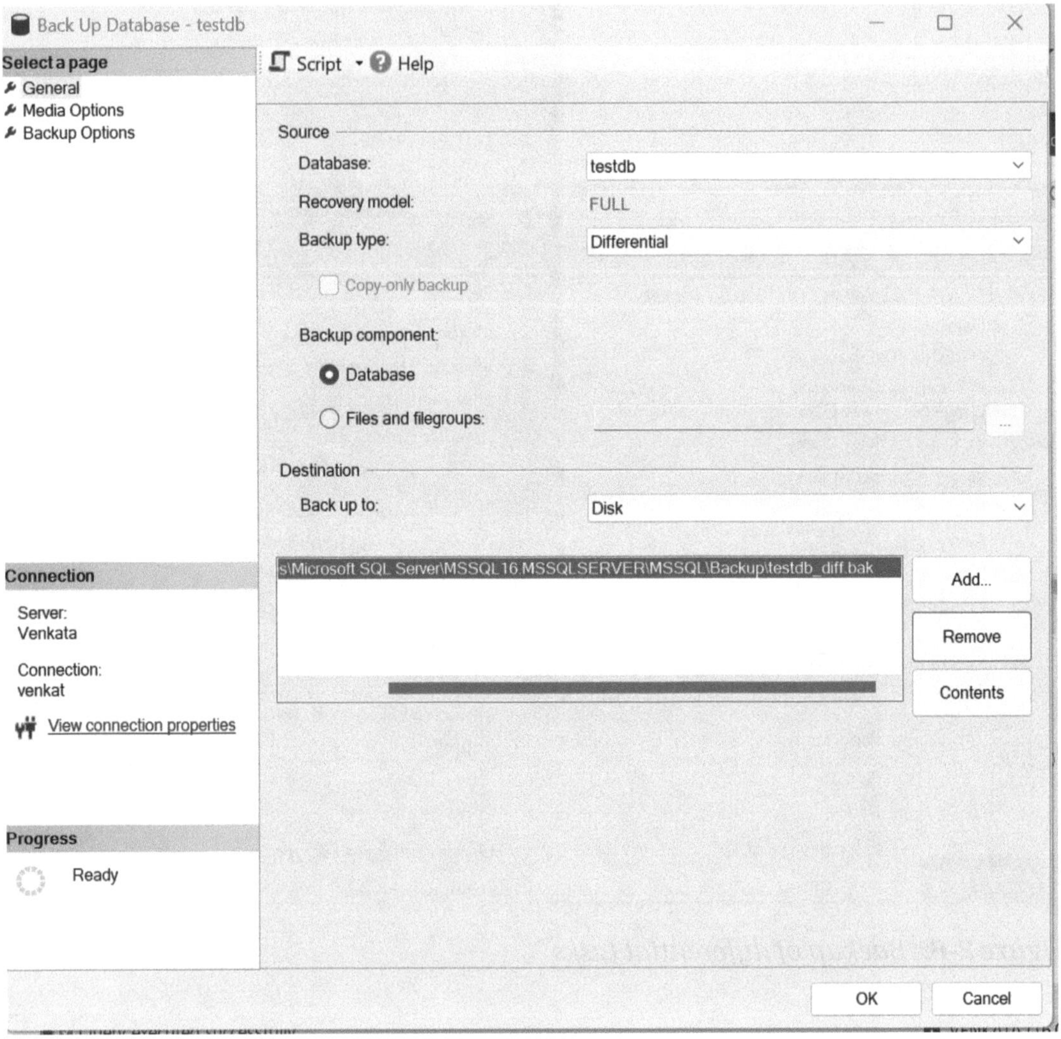

Figure 2-7. *Back up database*

- Select "Disk" as the destination.

  Click on "Add..." to add a backup file, type "Path:\testdb_diff.bak"
  and click "OK".

After the differential backup completes, SQL Server displays a confirmation message,
as shown in Figure 2-8.

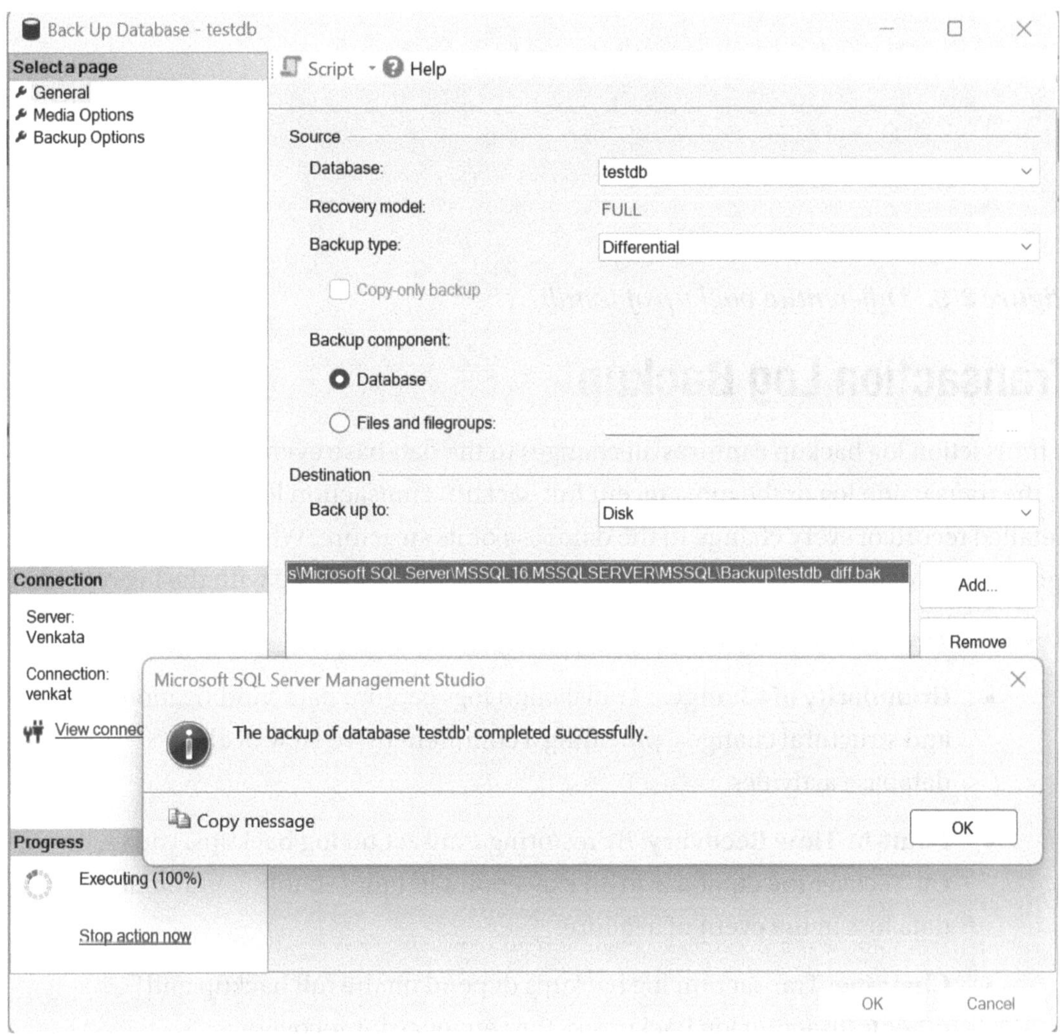

Figure 2-8. Backup completed successfully

- You can see that the differential backup was completed. Click OK.

You can verify the differential backup file in the SQL Server backup directory, as shown in Figure 2-9.

Microsoft SQL Server > MSSQL16.MSSQLSERVER > MSSQL > Backup			Search Backup
⮤ 🗑 ↑↓ Sort ˅ ≡ View ˅ •••			
☐ Name	Date modified	Type	Size
▢ testdb.BAK	12/9/2024 9:21 PM	BAK File	2,168 KB

Figure 2-9. *Differential backup of testdb*

Transaction Log Backup

A transaction log backup captures all changes to the database ever since the last backup
of the transaction log or the most recent full backup. Transaction logs (T-logs) are a
detailed record of every change to the database or its structure. Whenever an operation
modifies the database, a corresponding transaction log is updated with the log record.

Key Features of Transaction Logs

- **Granularity of Changes**: Transaction logs capture data modifications
  and structural changes, providing a comprehensive view of all
  database activities.

- **Point-in-Time Recovery**: By restoring transaction log backups, you
  can recover the database to an exact point in time, enabling minimal
  data loss in the event of a failure.

- **Chaining**: Transaction log backups depend on the full backup and
  other transaction log backups in the sequence for recovery.

Transaction log backups are typically saved with a .TRN extension to distinguish
them from other types of backups.

T-SQL Command for Transaction Log Backup

Use the following T-SQL command to create a transaction log backup:

T-SQL Code

```
BACKUP LOG testdb
TO DISK
'C:\Program Files\Microsoft SQL Server\MSSQL16.MSSQLSERVER\MSSQL\Backup\
testdb.TRN'
GO
```

The T-SQL syntax for performing a transaction-log backup is shown in Figure 2-10.

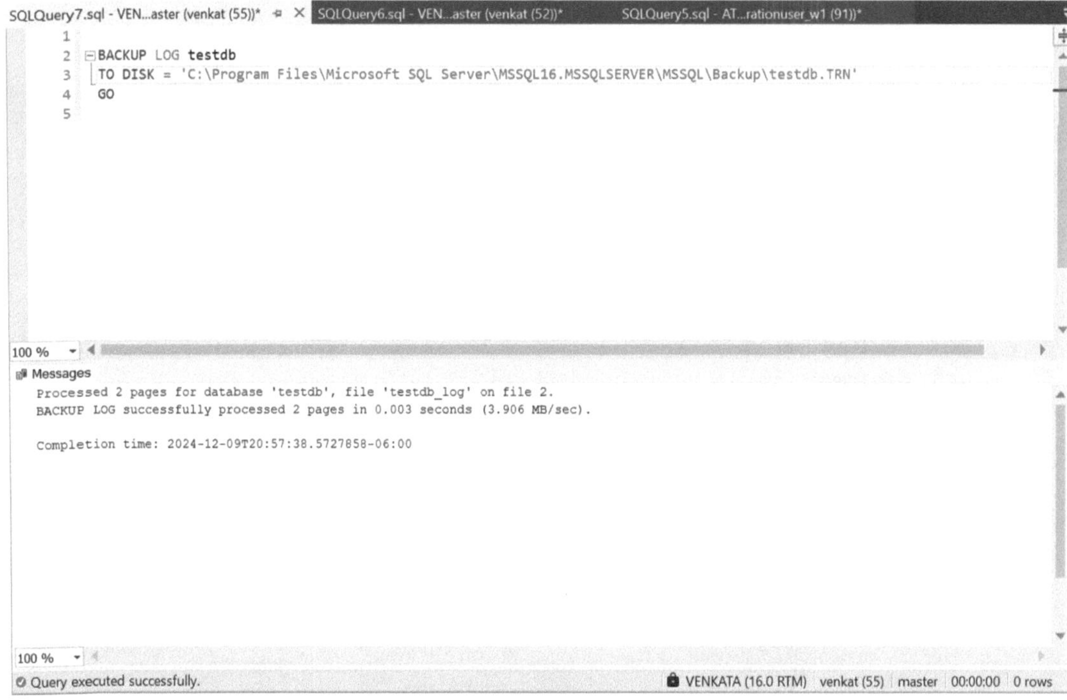

Figure 2-10. *SQLQuery server*

- To add a backup file and type, right-click on the database name.

- Select Tasks ➤ Backup.

The menu path for initiating a transaction log backup in SQL Server Management Studio is shown in Figure 2-11.

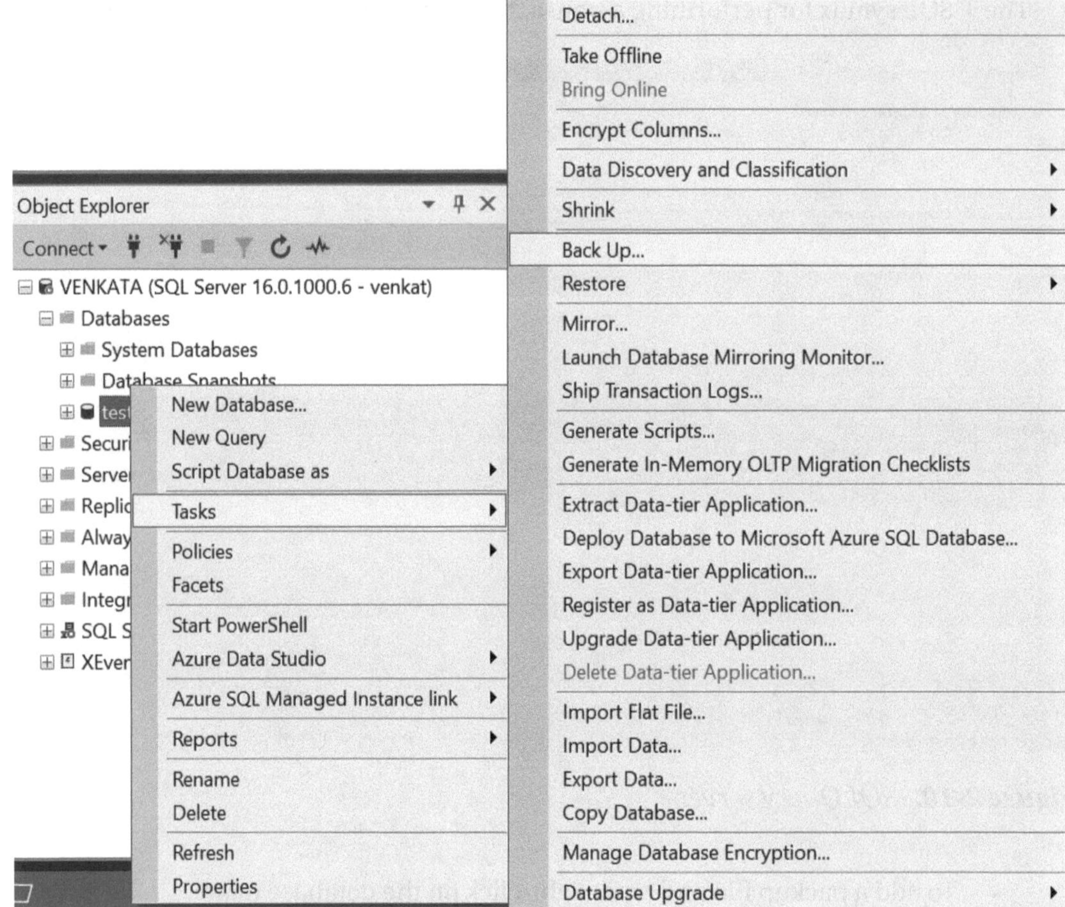

Figure 2-11. *Transaction log backup*

- Choose "Transaction Log" as the backup type.

- "Path\testdb.TRN" and click "OK".

Figure 2-12 shows the dialog used to choose the transaction-log backup location.

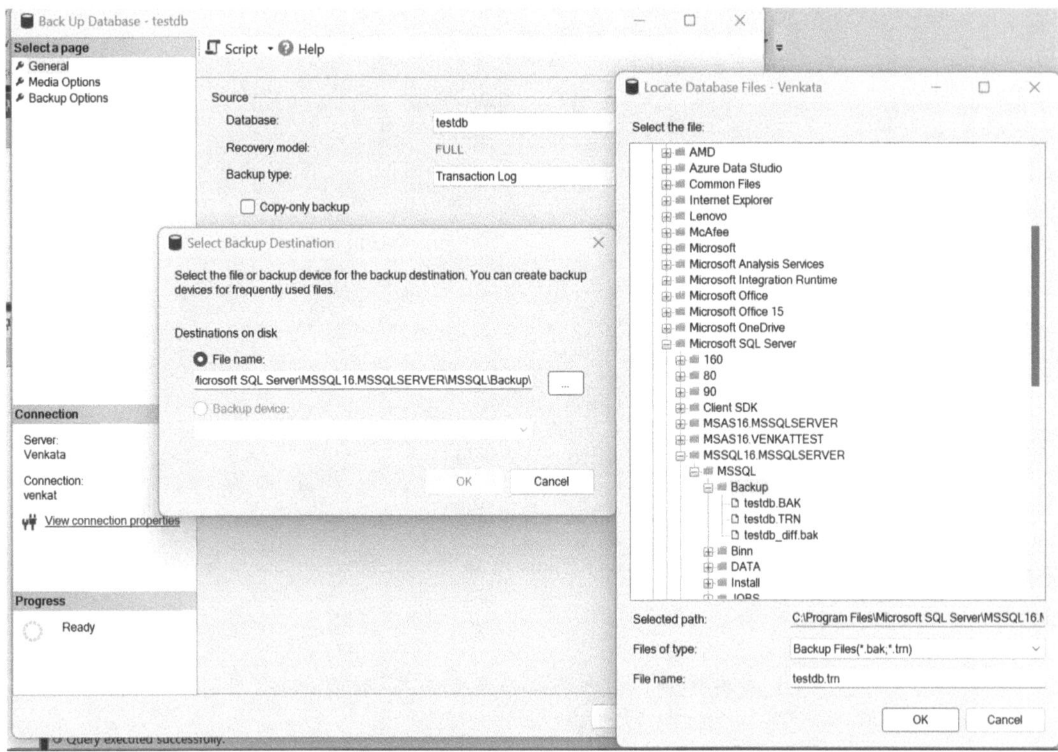

Figure 2-12. *Backing file in a specific location*

- Click "OK" again to create the backup.

Figure 2-13 shows the successful transaction-log backup confirmation.

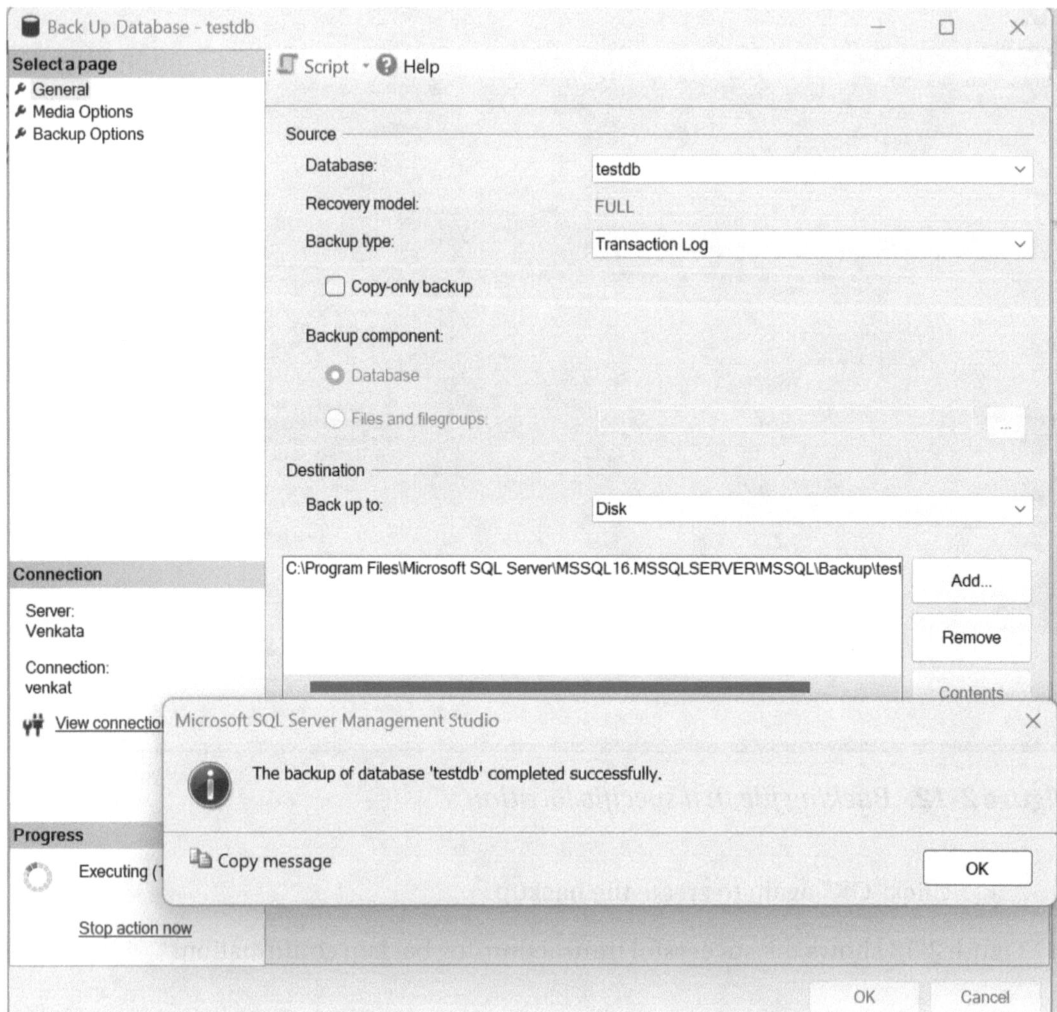

Figure 2-13. *Backup of a transaction file*

- Once done, you can see the transactional backup file.

Figure 2-14 shows the transaction-log backup file.

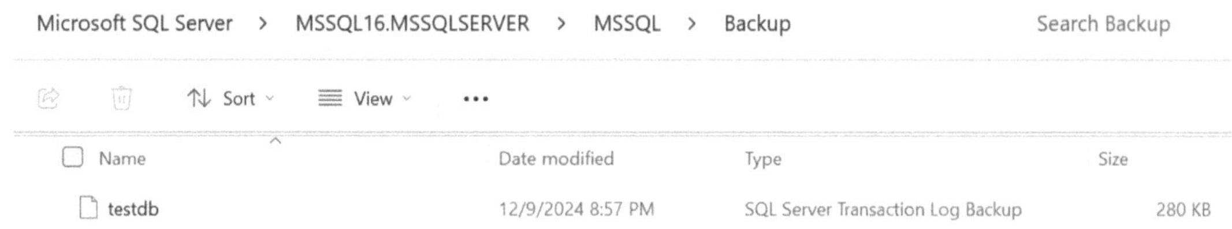

Figure 2-14. *Transaction backup file*

Tail-Log Backup

A **tail-log backup** is a backup of the active portion of the transaction log taken **just before a restore operation** or when a database becomes damaged. It ensures no data loss by capturing all log records that have not yet been backed up, including those generated since the last transaction log backup.

Tail-log backups are commonly used in disaster recovery scenarios to recover to the most recent point.

Prerequisites:

- The database must be set to either the **FULL** or **BULK_LOGGED** recovery model.

- If the database is damaged, the tail-log backup can still be attempted using the NO_TRUNCATE option.

Using T-SQL

To take a tail-log backup for the database testdb, use the following command:
SQL

```
BACKUP LOG testdb TO DISK ='C:\ProgramFiles\Microsoft SQLServer\MSSQL16.
MSSQLSERVER\MSSQL\Backup\testdb_tail_log.trn'WITH NO RECOVERY;
GO
```

Figure 2-15 shows the tail-log backup command.

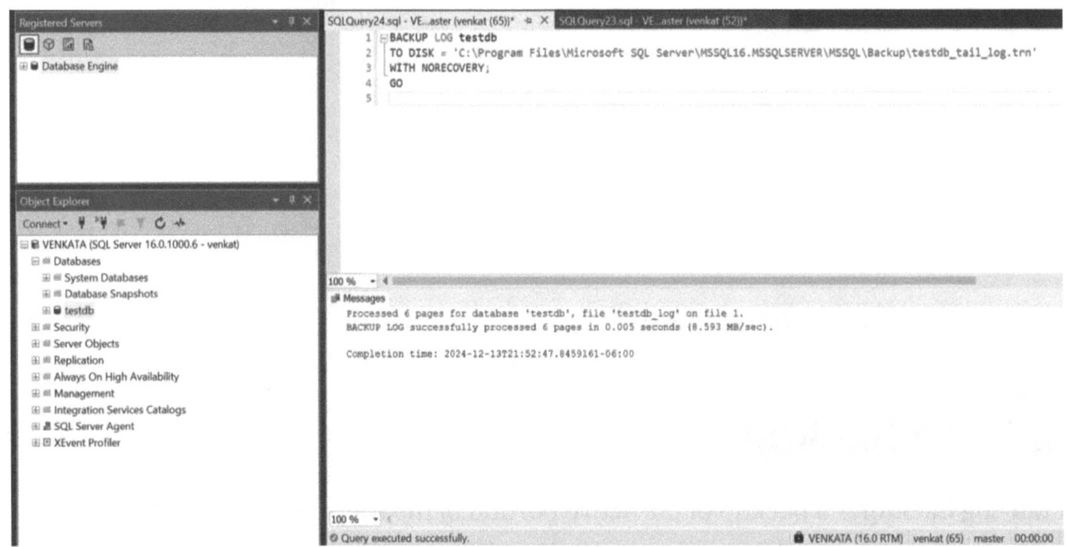

Figure 2-15. *Tail log server*

- TO DISK: Specifies the location and name of the backup file.

- WITH NORECOVERY: Prepares the database for restore operations, ensuring no additional changes are made.

- If the database is damaged, add the NO_TRUNCATE option:

T-SQL

```
BACKUP LOG testdb TO DISK = 'C:\ProgramFiles\Microsoft SQLServer\MSSQL16.
MSSQLSERVER\MSSQL\Backup\testdb_tail_log.trn'WITH NO_TRUNCATE; GO
```

Using the GUI (SSMS)

Connect to the SQL Server instance in SSMS. Right-click the **testdb** database, navigate to **Tasks**, and select **Back Up**. In the **Backup Database** dialog:

- Set **Backup Type** to transaction log.

- Specify the destination path and file name (e.g., C:\Program Files\ Microsoft SQL Server\MSSQL16.MSSQLSERVER\MSSQL\Backup\ testdb_tail_log.trn).

Figure 2-16 shows the SQL Server database backup configuration window.

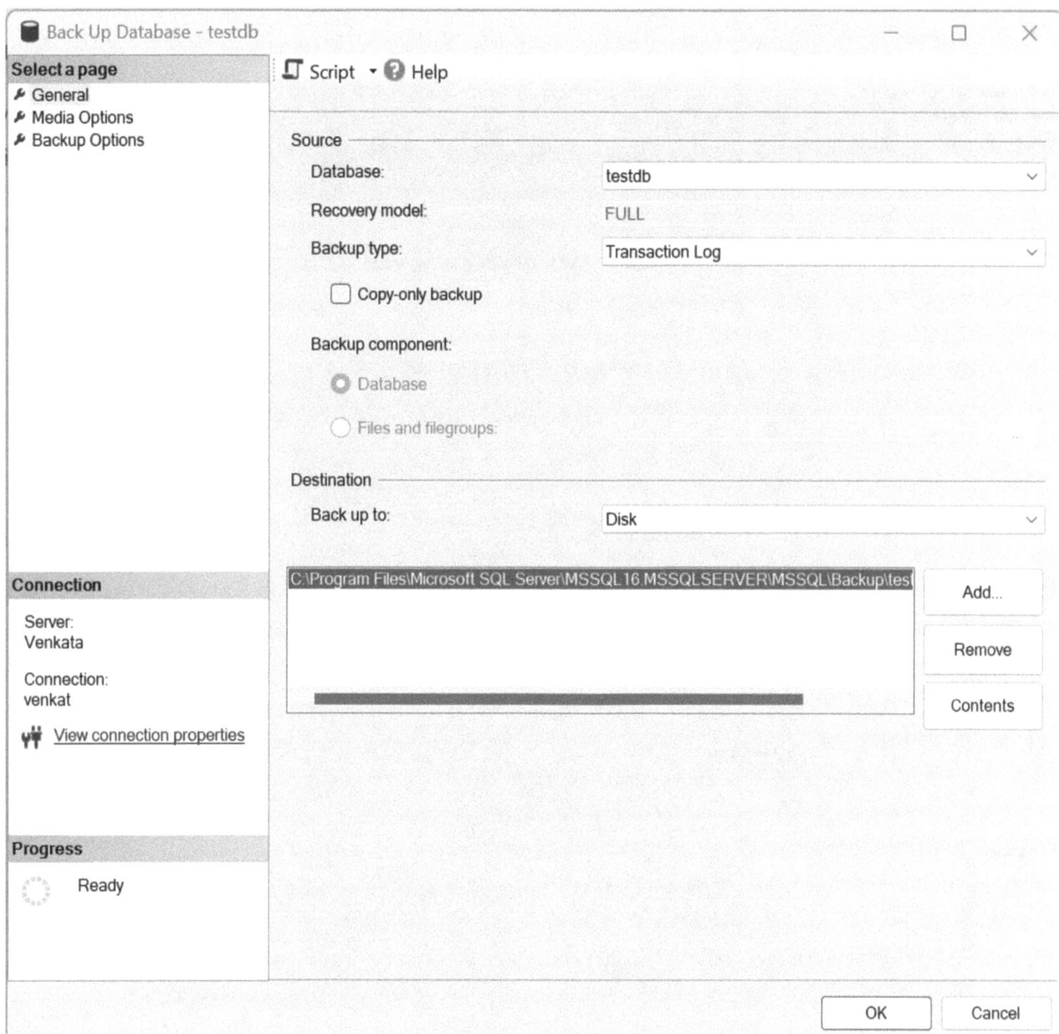

Figure 2-16. *Location for tail log file*

- Go to the **Options** page.

- Check the **Copy Only Backup** option if needed.

- Enable the **Truncate transaction log** or **NORECOVERY** option to leave the database ready for restoration.

Figure 2-17 shows the SQL Server backup options configuration window.

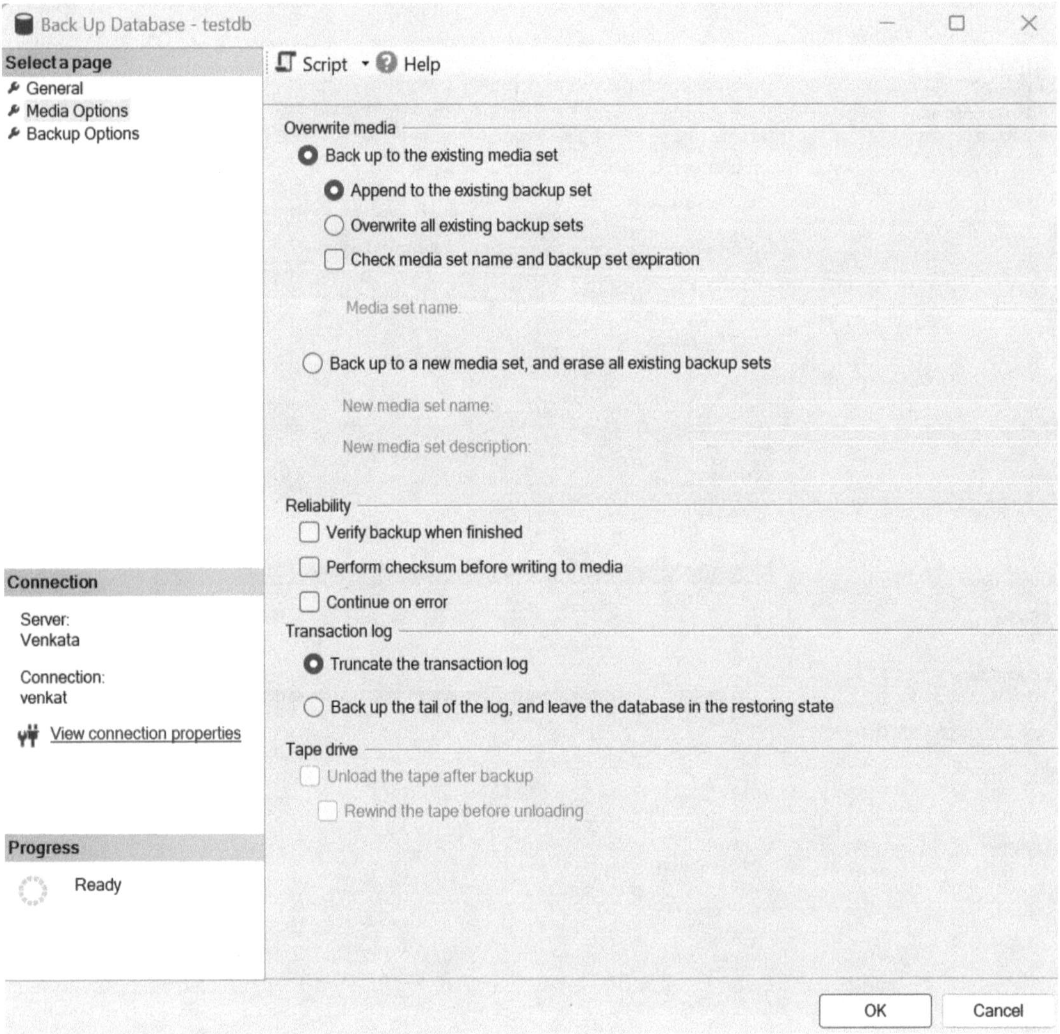

Figure 2-17. *Finalizing the tail log server*

- Click **OK** to take the backup.

Advantages of Tail-Log Backups

It captures all transaction log records since the last backup, ensuring data consistency. It supports restoring the database to the precise moment of failure. It enables recovery of transactions even if the primary data files are damaged or inaccessible. A tail-log backup is required before restoring a database to a specific point in time.

Use Cases

- When performing a **RESTORE** operation at a specific point in time.

- Before restoring from a failure, ensure all committed transactions are backed up.

- During **log shipping** or database mirroring transitions.

File and Filegroup Backup Strategies

It focuses on backing up specific files or filegroups, which is helpful for large databases where full backups are time-consuming. SQL Server allows for the backing up of individual files and filegroups, which is particularly useful for large databases or when only specific files require recovery. You can accomplish this using **SQL Server Management Studio (SSMS)** or **Transact-SQL (T-SQL)**.

Using SQL Server Management Studio (SSMS)

- **Connect to the Database Engine**:

- Connect to the SQL Server instance by opening SSMS.

- **Navigate to the Database**:

- Expand the server tree, and right-click the database you want to back up.

- Select **Tasks➤Back Up**.

- **Configure the Backup Options**:

- In the **Backup Database** dialog, set the following:

- **Backup type**: Select **Files and Filegroups**.

- **Select files and filegroups**: Click the **Files and Filegroups** button and select the files or filegroups you want to back up.

Figure 2-18 shows the SQL Server interface for configuring a full database backup of file.

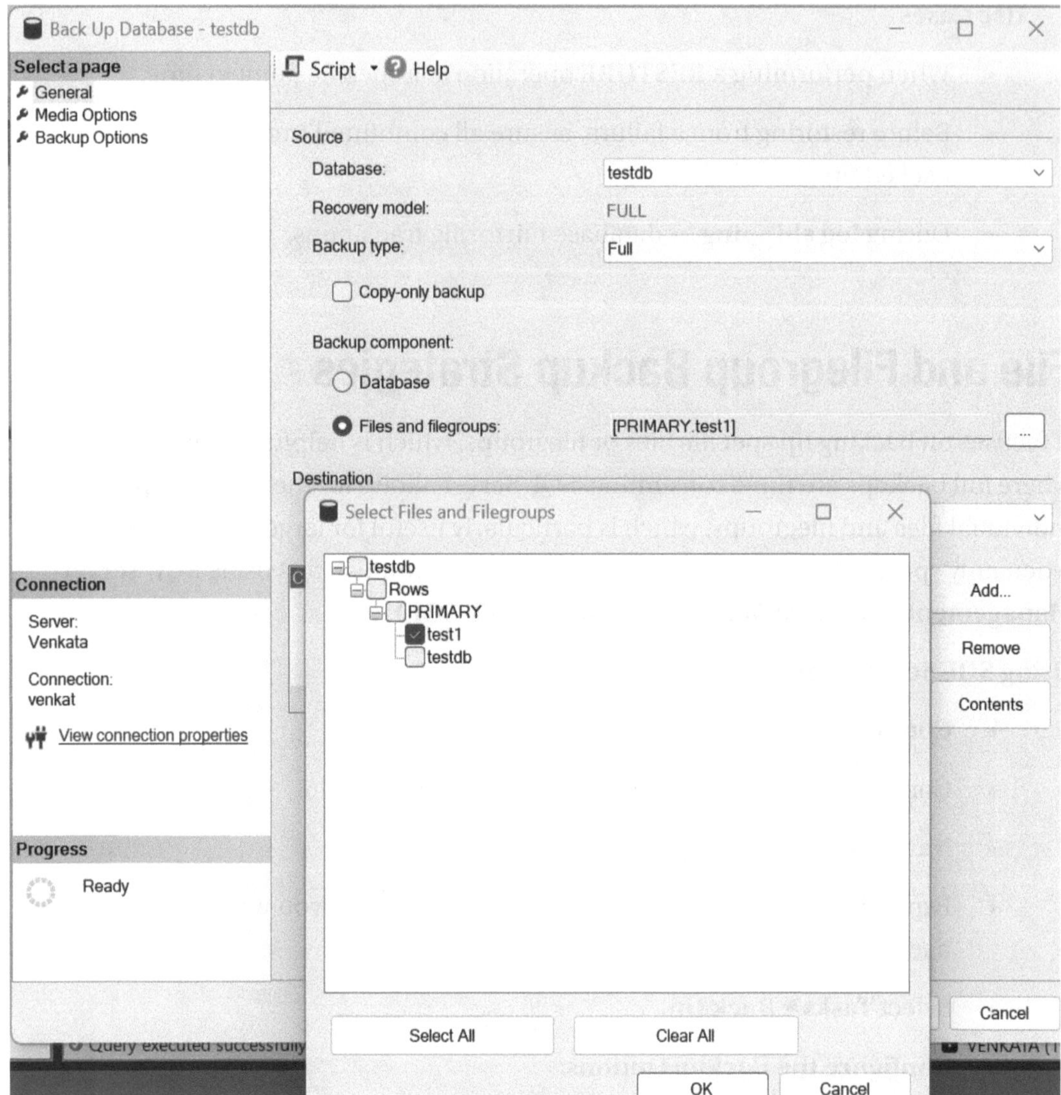

Figure 2-18. *Backing up of file*

- **Specify the Backup Destination**:

- In the **Destination** section, specify the location for the backup file (e.g., a disk file).

- **Perform the Backup**:

- Click **OK** to start the backup operation.

Using Transact-SQL (T-SQL)

The BACKUP DATABASE command allows for the backing up of specific files and filegroups.

Syntax:

T-SQL

Examples:

Back Up a Specific File: To back up a file named **File1**:

T-SQL

```
BACKUP DATABASE testdb
FILE = 'File1'
TO DISK = 'C:\Backups\File1_Backup.bak';
GO
```

Back Up a Specific Filegroup: To back up a filegroup named **Primary**:

T-SQL

```
BACKUP DATABASE Testdb
FILEGROUP = 'Primary'
TO DISK = 'C:\Backups\Primary_Filegroup_Backup.bak';
GO
```

Considerations

Ensure a recent **full database backup** is available before initiating file or filegroup backups. File and filegroup backups rely on the full backup for recovery. If using the **Full Recovery Model**, ensure regular transaction log backups are taken to maintain the chain of log backups needed for point-in-time recovery. Restoring files and filegroups requires restoring the full database backup, the file or filegroup backup, and subsequent transaction log backups. SSMS or T-SQL can efficiently back up files and filegroups to meet your recovery and storage needs.

Copy-Only Backup and Mirror Backups

Running a combination of **full**, **differential**, and **transaction log** backups in SQL Server is common to preserve data security and save downtime during recovery. However, there are scenarios where you may need to take an additional backup—such as creating a full backup for a test environment—without disrupting your regular backup sequence. The COPY_ONLY option is specifically designed for such cases.

Backup Sequence Example

Suppose you follow this backup schedule for your production database:

- **Full backup**: Midnight.

- **Differential backups**: Every 3 hours (3:00 AM, 6:00 AM, 9:00 AM, etc.).

- **Transaction log backups**: Every 30 minutes throughout the day.

Now, taking an **additional full backup** for a special purpose, such as loading data into a test server, disrupts the backup sequence. The reason is that **differential backups** rely on the most recent full backup. Without the COPY_ONLY option, subsequent differential backups will reference this new full backup instead of the regular one.

This disruption complicates recovery because you would need to use the latest full backup, any differentials after it, and transaction log backups that followed. Alternatively, you could use the original full backup and only the transaction log backups. However, this approach negates the advantages of differential backups, increasing recovery time.

COPY_ONLY Option

The COPY_ONLY option ensures the backup is independent and does not affect the **Log Sequence Numbers (LSNs)** or alter the regular backup sequence. A **COPY_ONLY full backup** does not reset the differential base, so subsequent differential backups still reference the regular full backup. A **COPY_ONLY transaction log backup** does not interrupt the log chain or sequence.

Examples

Scenario: Full Backup with COPY_ONLY

Suppose you must take a complete backup for testing without impacting the differential backup sequence.

T-SQL

```
BACKUP DATABASE testdb
TO DISK = 'C:\Backups\testdb_COPY_ONLY_FULL.bak'
WITH COPY_ONLY, INIT;
GO
```

This complete backup is standalone and does not reset the differential backup base. Differential backups continue to rely on the original full backup.

Scenario: Transaction Log Backup with COPY_ONLY

Suppose you must take an additional transaction log backup for auditing or temporary data protection without breaking the log sequence.

T-SQL

```
BACKUP LOG testdb
TO DISK = 'C:\Backups\testdb_COPY_ONLY_LOG.trn'
WITH COPY_ONLY;
GO
```

This log backup is independent and does not affect the transaction log chain. You can still restore using the regular full and transaction log backups without referencing this COPY_ONLY backup.

Including a COPY_ONLY Backup

If a COPY_ONLY backup was taken, you can safely ignore it during the restore process, as it does not alter the sequence.

Benefits of COPY_ONLY

It ensures regular backups remain consistent. This feature allows you to create testing, reporting, or auditing backups without interfering with production workflows. For transaction log backups, the sequence remains intact, avoiding potential recovery issues.

Best Practices

Use the COPY_ONLY option whenever you need a backup for a purpose other than the regular backup and recovery plan. Clearly label and organize COPY_ONLY backups separately to avoid confusion. Regularly test your restore strategy, ensuring all backup types (regular and COPY_ONLY) integrate seamlessly.

Leveraging the COPY_ONLY option allows you to address special backup requirements without compromising your regular backup and recovery processes.

SQL Server Mirrored Backups

Mirrored backups in SQL Server allow you to create multiple identical copies of a database backup on different destinations. This feature ensures redundancy and enhances the reliability of backups. Mirrored backups are made simultaneously, ensuring that all mirrors are identical.

Uses of Mirrored Backups

It provides multiple backup copies, reducing the risk of backup failure. It ensures backup availability in case one destination is corrupted or inaccessible. It satisfies requirements for data protection by storing backups in multiple locations. It enables backups stored on multiple disks, reducing I/O contention on a single drive.

Disadvantages of Mirrored Backups

It requires multiple storage locations, increasing resource consumption. Simultaneous writing to multiple destinations can affect database performance. It requires precise setup and maintenance for multiple storage paths. Mirrored backups are only available in SQL Server Enterprise Edition and Developer Edition.

How to Create Mirrored Backups

Using T-SQL

To create a mirrored backup for the testdb database to multiple locations (C:\ Program Files\Microsoft SQL Server\MSSQL16.MSSQLSERVER\MSSQL\Backup, D:\ Backups, and D:\Backups1), execute the following command:

```
BACKUP DATABASE testdb
TO DISK = 'C:\Program Files\Microsoft SQL
Server\MSSQL16.MSSQLSERVER\MSSQL\Backup\testdb.bak'
MIRROR TO DISK = 'D:\Backups\testdb.bak'
MIRROR TO DISK = 'D:\Backups1\testdb.bak' WITH FORMAT
Go
```

Figure 2-19 shows the SQL command used to create a mirrored database backup.

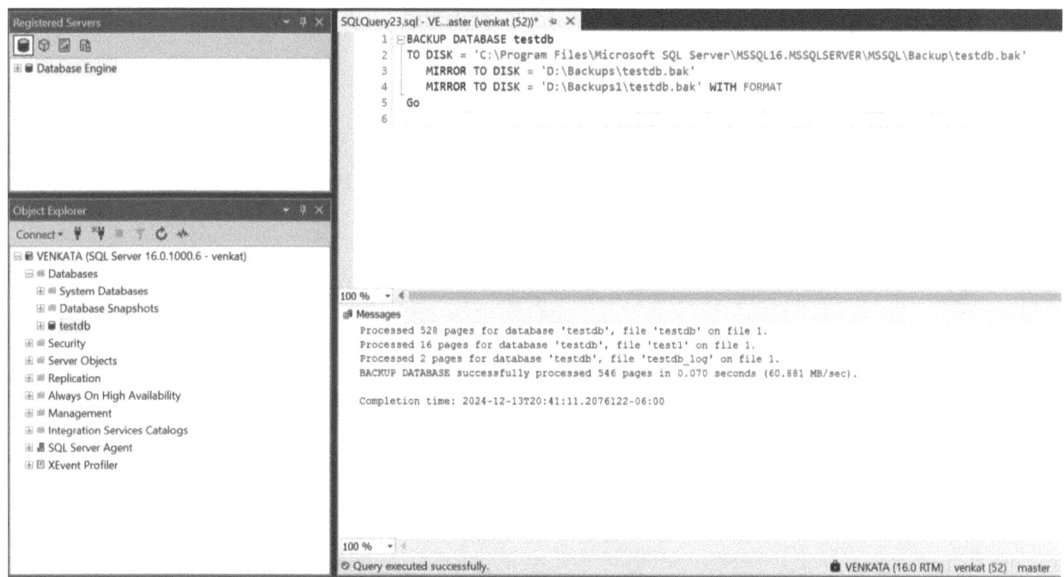

Figure 2-19. *Mirrored backup server*

You may see backup files on all mentioned locations.

TO DISK specifies the primary backup destination. MIRROR TO DISK adds mirror locations. WITH FORMAT initializes the backup media.

Using the GUI (SSMS)

- **Connect** to the database engine in SQL Server Management Studio (SSMS).

- Expand the **Databases** node and locate the testdb database.

- Right-click the database, select **Tasks**, and then click **Back Up**.

- In the **Backup Database** dialog:

- Choose full as the backup type.

- Specify the backup component as a database.

- Under the **Destination** section, click **Add** and specify the first backup location (e.g., C:\Program Files\Microsoft SQL Server\MSSQL16.MSSQLSERVER\MSSQL\Backup).

- Click **Add** again to specify the second and third backup locations (D:\Backups and D:\Backups1).

- In the **Options** page, check **Enable Mirroring** and add mirrored destinations for each primary location.

- Click **OK** to start the backup process.

Figure 2-20 shows the SQL Server interface used to perform a full database backup.

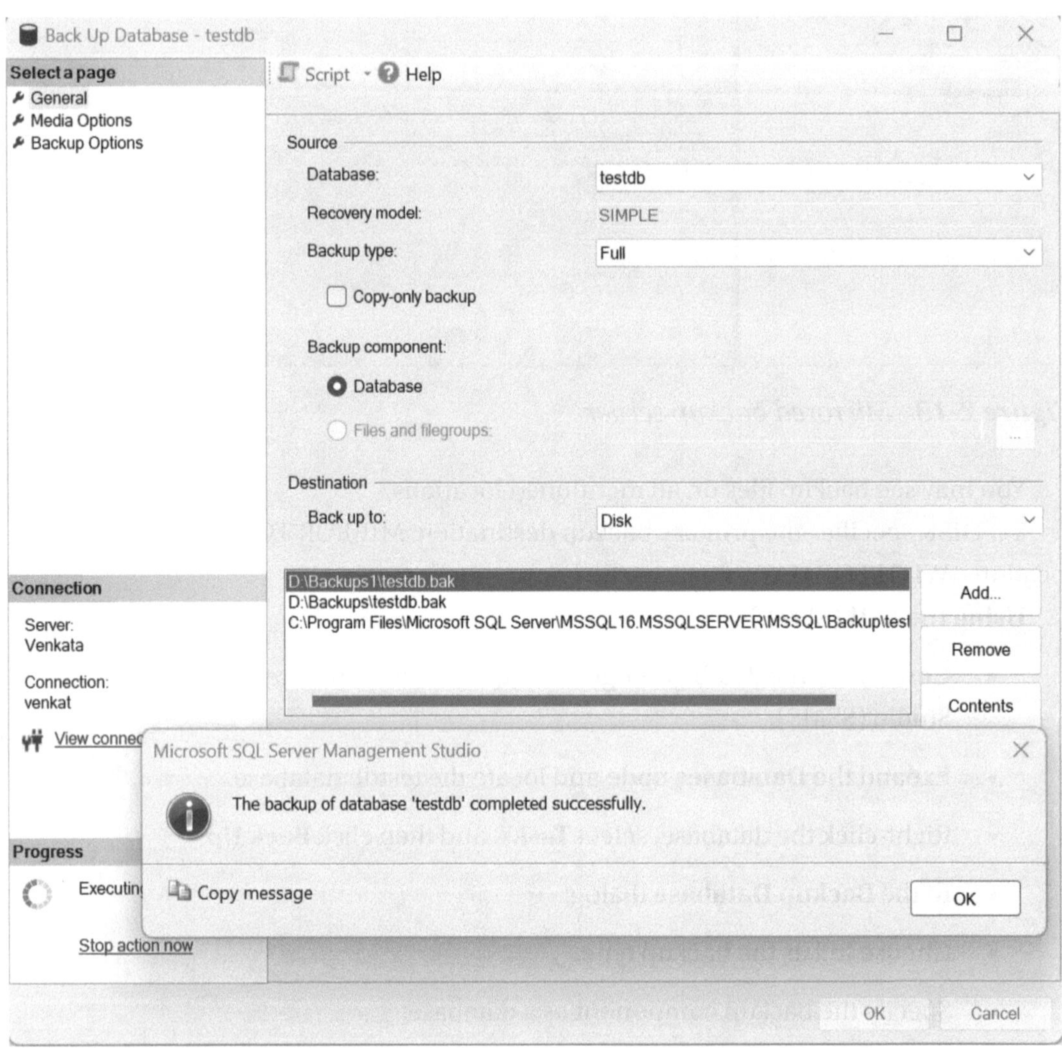

Figure 2-20. *Mirroring process*

Advanced Backup Compression and Encryption

Compressed backups in SQL Server reduce the size of backup files by using compression techniques during the backup process. This feature decreases storage requirements and speeds up backup and restore operations. Compression works by eliminating redundant data, resulting in smaller backup files.

Uses of Compressed Backups

It saves disk space by reducing the size of backup files. Backup operations are more rapid due to more minor data being written to disk. Smaller files are quicker to copy or transfer to other locations. Faster backup and restore times enhance recovery time objectives (RTOs).

How to Take a Compressed Backup

Using T-SQL

To create a compressed backup of the testdb database at the specified location, execute the following command:

SQL

```
BACKUP DATABASE testdb TO DISK = 'C:\Program Files\Microsoft SQL Server\
MSSQL16.MSSQLSERVER\MSSQL\Backup\testdb_compressed.bak' WITH COMPRESSION, INIT;
GO
```

Figure 2-21 shows the SQL command used to create a compressed database backup.

Figure 2-21. *Compressed backup server*

TO DISK specifies the backup file's location and name. WITH COMPRESSION enables backup compression. INIT overwrites any existing backup file with the same name.

Using the GUI (SSMS)

- **Connect** to the database engine in SQL Server Management Studio (SSMS).

- Navigate to **Databases**, locate the testdb database, right-click it, and select **Tasks ➤ Back Up**.

- In the **Backup Database** dialog box:

- Select the **Backup Type** as Full.

- Set the **Destination** by clicking **Add** and specifying the backup file's location (C:\Program Files\Microsoft SQL Server\MSSQL16. MSSQLSERVER\MSSQL\Backup\testdb_compressed.bak).

Figure 2-22 shows the SQL Server interface used to configure database backup settings.

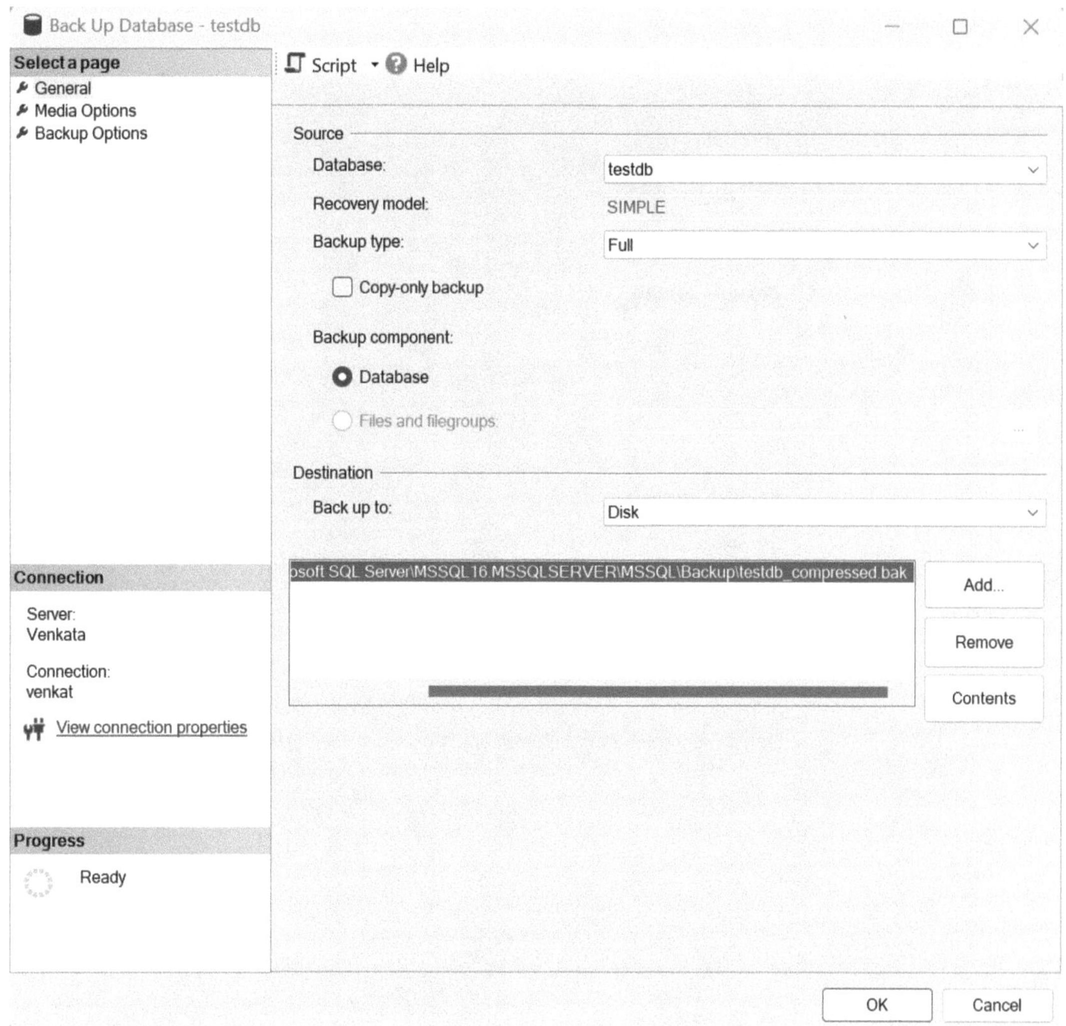

Figure 2-22. *Compressed backup process*

- Go to the **Options** page:

- Under the **Compression** section, select **Compress Backup**.

Figure 2-23 shows the SQL Server interface used to configure backup set options.

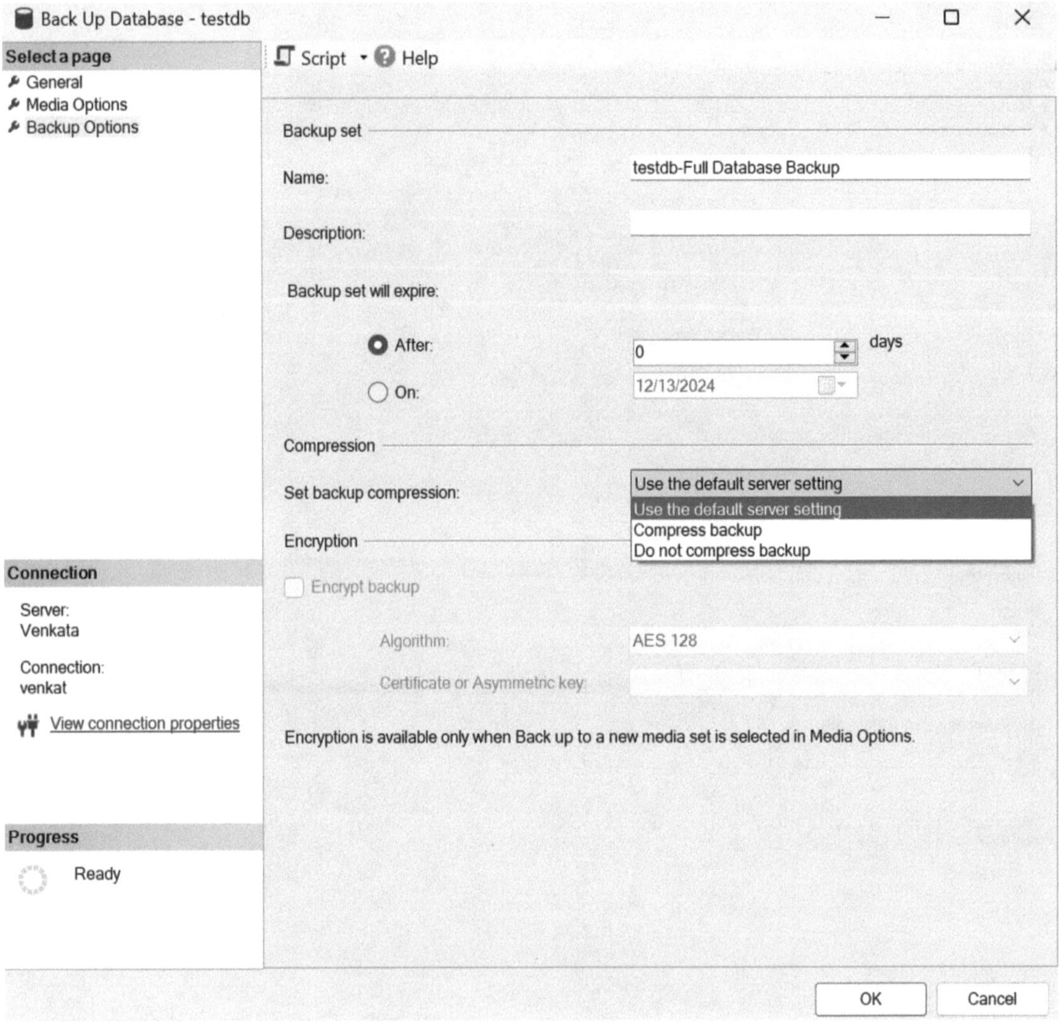

Figure 2-23. *Finalization of compressed backup*

- Click **OK** to start the backup process.

Benefits and Considerations

Benefits

It significantly reduces backup file size, saving storage costs. It decreases backup and restore times due to smaller files.

Considerations

Compression consumes additional CPU resources during the backup process. This could affect other workloads on the server. Backup compression is available in SQL Server Standard and Enterprise editions (SQL Server 2008 and later). It ensures the backup destination supports the file size and format.

Backup Operations and Restrictions

Backups can be performed while the database is online and in use, but some limitations apply during the backup process. It is impossible to back up data in an offline database. Some operations, such as file-management tasks (e.g., adding or removing files) and shrink operations, cannot run simultaneously with a database or transaction log backup.

Best Practices for SQL Server Backups

Always store database backups in a separate physical location or device from the primary database files. This ensures data recoverability in case of hardware failures or drive malfunctions. Cloud storage or offsite locations can provide additional security. The recovery model of a database determines the types of backups supported and influences recovery scenarios. The **Simple Recovery Model** is suitable for scenarios where transaction log management is not required, but it limits recovery options to the last full or differential backup. The **Full Recovery Model** provides comprehensive recovery options by enabling transaction log backups, minimizing work-loss exposure, and supporting point-in-time recovery. Periodically test your backup strategy by restoring backups to a test environment. This validates the integrity of the backups and ensures that the restoration process works as expected during an actual recovery scenario.

By adhering to these best practices and understanding the operations and limitations of backups, you can develop a strong backup strategy to safeguard your SQL Server databases, ensure data security by preventing data loss, and improve data dependability and availability.

Using SQL Server's Encryption to Secure the Database

The job of a database administrator is crucial to the operation of large databases since managing them entails managing millions of transactions and terabytes of data. In addition to making sure that the system is available, administrators also need to protect data security and integrity and be able to recover data in case of an outage with the least amount of disturbance to company operations.

While on-premises database management presents fewer security concerns, storing backups off-site or in the cloud introduces additional risks. Since externally stored data is housed on third-party infrastructure, unlawful access may result in restoring the entire database on a different system. Traditional security methods, including limiting access to internal systems, lose their effectiveness if that occurs.

To reduce these risks, backup plans must apply security best practices. Data protection procedures should be incorporated into the backup procedure to guarantee that sensitive data is safe even if the backup files end up in the wrong hands.

In earlier versions of SQL Server, native encryption was unavailable for backups, requiring third-party solutions to secure and compress backup files. Starting with SQL Server 2014, Microsoft incorporated built-in **backup encryption** capabilities. This feature allows database administrators to encrypt data during the backup process using multiple encryption algorithms; with the release of SQL Server 2014, security saw substantial improvements. This article delves into how backup encryption operates its implementation in recent SQL Server versions, and best practices for safeguarding backups. We'll also cover essential topics like **certificate recovery, database restoration, asymmetric key encryption, and integration with Extensible Key Management (EKM) providers**.

Requirements for Backup Encryption

To enable database backup encryption in SQL Server, the following prerequisites must be met:

- **SQL Server 2014 or Later** (Enterprise or Standard Edition)

- **Write Access to a Local or Remote Storage System**

- **Sufficient Storage Capacity for Encrypted Backups**

Benefits of Backup Encryption in SQL Server

It protects sensitive data against unauthorized access. It ensures backups remain unchanged and secure. It works alongside existing database encryption mechanisms. It prevents unauthorized restoration outside the organization's infrastructure. It allows selection of encryption algorithms based on security and compliance requirements. It strengthens key management and access control.

In the following sections, we will walk through the step-by-step process of configuring backup encryption in SQL Server, demonstrating how to **encrypt, restore, and recover backups using certificates and keys**.

By implementing **backup encryption**, organizations can ensure their database backups remain secure when stored on-premises, off-site, or in the cloud.

Creating an Encrypted Database Backup

Let's walk through setting up an encrypted backup for off-site storage. We'll begin by setting up a **new database**, inserting sample data, and implementing encryption before taking the backup.

```
CREATE DATABASE SecureDB;
GO
USE SecureDB;
GO
-- Create a sample table
CREATE TABLE SecureData (
RecordID INT IDENTITY(100,10) PRIMARY KEY,
DataValue INT NOT NULL
);
GO
-- Create a procedure to populate the table with sample data
CREATE PROCEDURE PopulateSecureData
AS
BEGIN
DECLARE @count INT = 1;
WHILE @count <= 50
    BEGIN
        INSERT INTO SecureData (DataValue) VALUES (@count * 2);
        SET @count = @count + 1;
END;
END;
GO
-- Execute the procedure to insert sample records
EXEC PopulateSecureData;
GO
-- Verify the inserted records
SELECT * FROM SecureData;
GO
```

Figure 2-24 shows the SQL script used to create and execute sample database records.

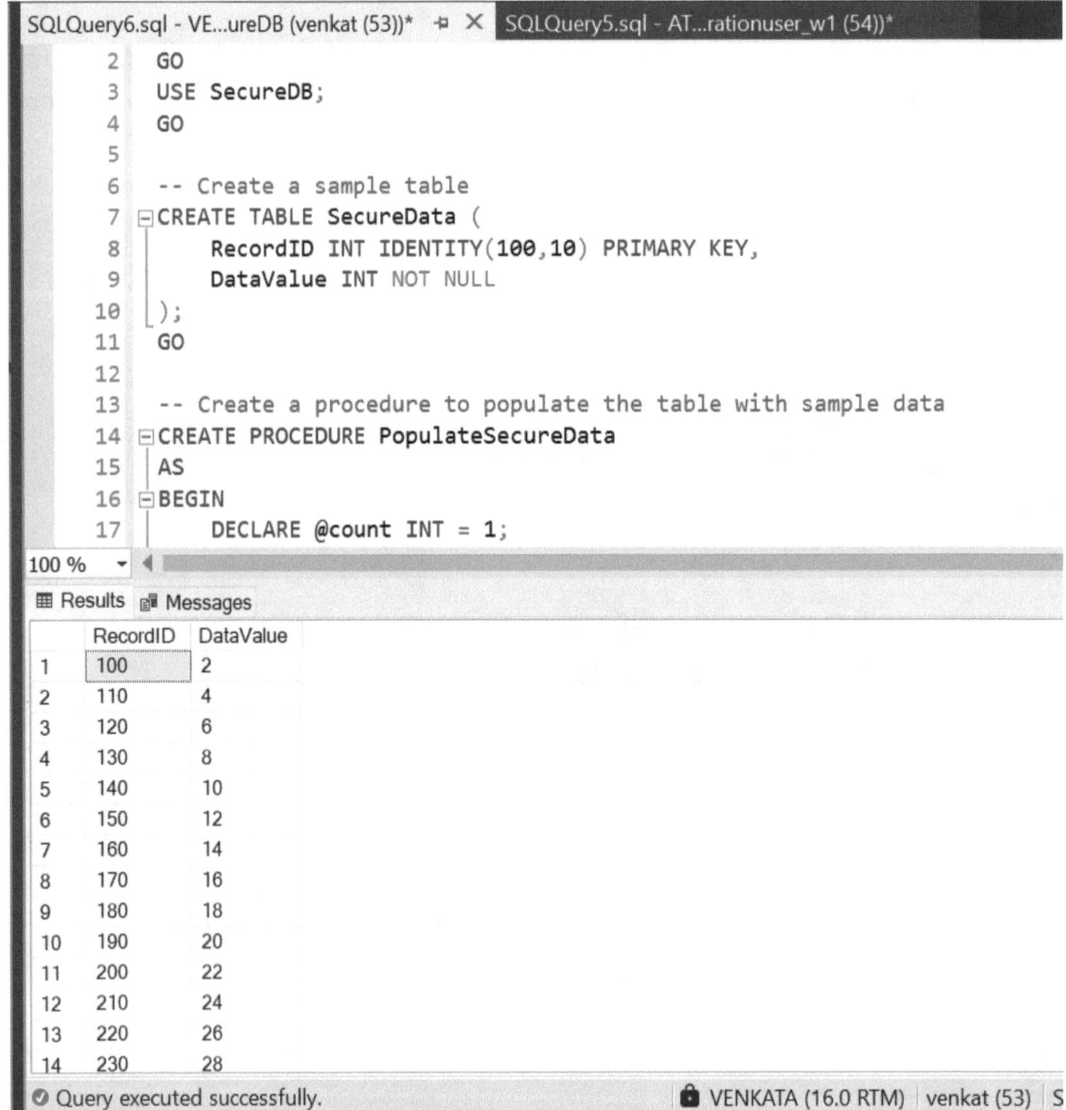

Figure 2-24. *Query execution of sample records*

Generating a Master Key and Certificate for Encrypted Backups

We need to encrypt our backups using a **certificate** to enhance database security. Before creating a certificate, we must generate a **master key** to manage encryption within the SQL Server.

Step 1: Create the Master Key

First, we switch to the **master database** and create a **master key**, which a strong password will protect.

```
USE master;
GO
-- Create a master key with a secure password
CREATE MASTER KEY ENCRYPTION BY PASSWORD = 'Str0ngP@ssw0rd_2025!';
GO
```

Figure 2-25 shows the SQL command used to create a master encryption key.

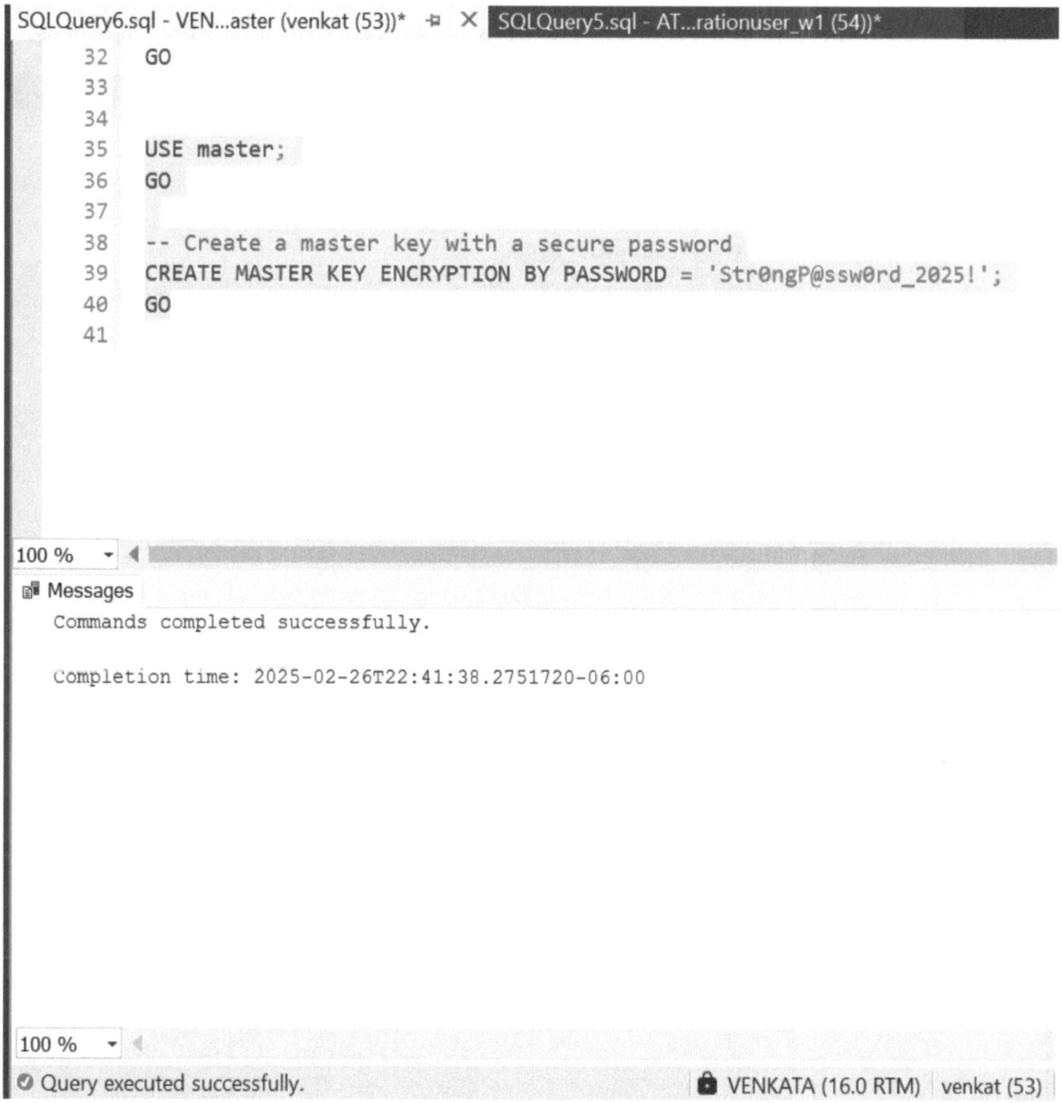

Figure 2-25. *Query execution of master key encryption*

Step 2: Create a Certificate for Backup Encryption

Now, we generate a **certificate** called SecureDB_Cert to encrypt our backups. The certificate includes a **subject description** that helps identify its purpose in system metadata.

```
-- Create a certificate for backup encryption
CREATE CERTIFICATE SecureDB_Cert
    WITH SUBJECT = 'SecureDB Backup Encryption Certificate';
GO
```

Figure 2-26 shows the SQL command used to create a backup encryption certificate.

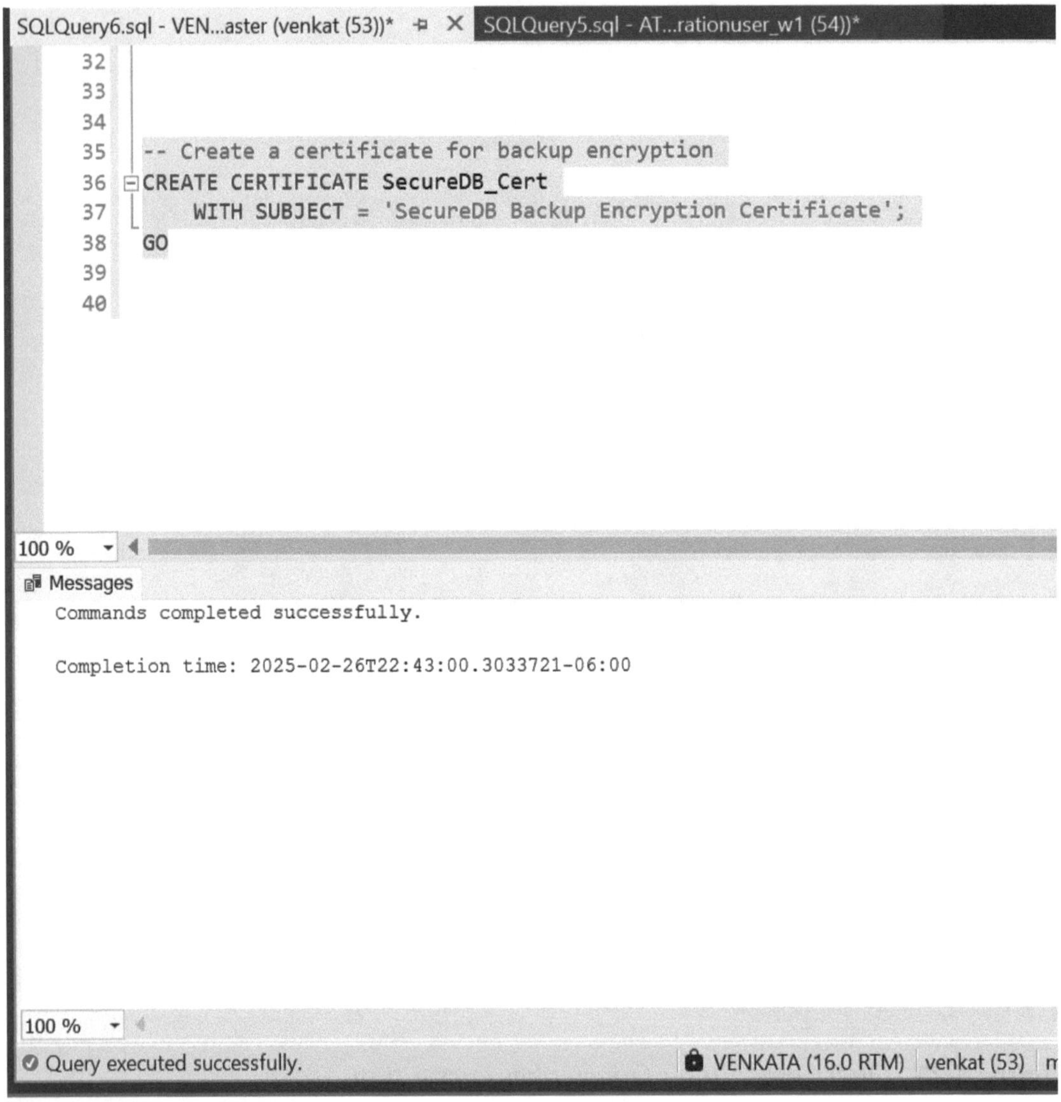

Figure 2-26. *Query execution of creating certificate*

Once the certificate is created, it is stored in the **system database** under the **master security certificates folder**. You can verify its existence using **SQL Server Management Studio (SSMS)** by navigating to:

Object Explorer ➤ Databases ➤ System Databases ➤ Master ➤ Security ➤ Certificates

Step 3: Back Up the Certificate for Recovery

To prevent data loss in case of a system failure, it's crucial to back up the certificate to an **external secured location**. This ensures that we can restore encrypted backups if needed.

```
-- Backup the certificate and save it securely
BACKUP CERTIFICATE SecureDB_Cert
    TO FILE = 'C:\Backup\SecureDB_Cert.bak'
    WITH PRIVATE KEY (
        FILE = 'C:\Backup\SecureDB_Key.pvk',
        ENCRYPTION BY PASSWORD = 'CertPrOtect!2025'
    );
GO
```

Figure 2-27 shows the backup files for the encryption certificate and private key.

Name	Date modified	Type	Size
SecureDB_Cert.bak	2/26/2025 10:48 PM	BAK File	1 KB
SecureDB_Key.pvk	2/26/2025 10:48 PM	PVK File	2 KB

Figure 2-27. *Backup of certificate for recovery*

You cannot restore encrypted backups if the certificate is lost or corrupted. Always store a copy of the certificate and its private key in a **safe and secure location**.

Database Backup with Encryption

To ensure the safety of our database, we will create an encrypted backup using **AES_256 encryption**, a highly secure algorithm. The encryption will be applied using the **SecureDB_Cert** certificate that we created earlier.

Step 1: Perform an Encrypted Database Backup

```
-- Backup the Database with encryption enabled
BACKUP DATABASE SecureDB
TO DISK = 'C:\Backup\SecureDB_Encrypted.bak'
WITH ENCRYPTION (ALGORITHM = AES_256, SERVER CERTIFICATE = SecureDB_Cert);
GO
```

Figure 2-28 shows the SQL command used to perform an encrypted database backup.

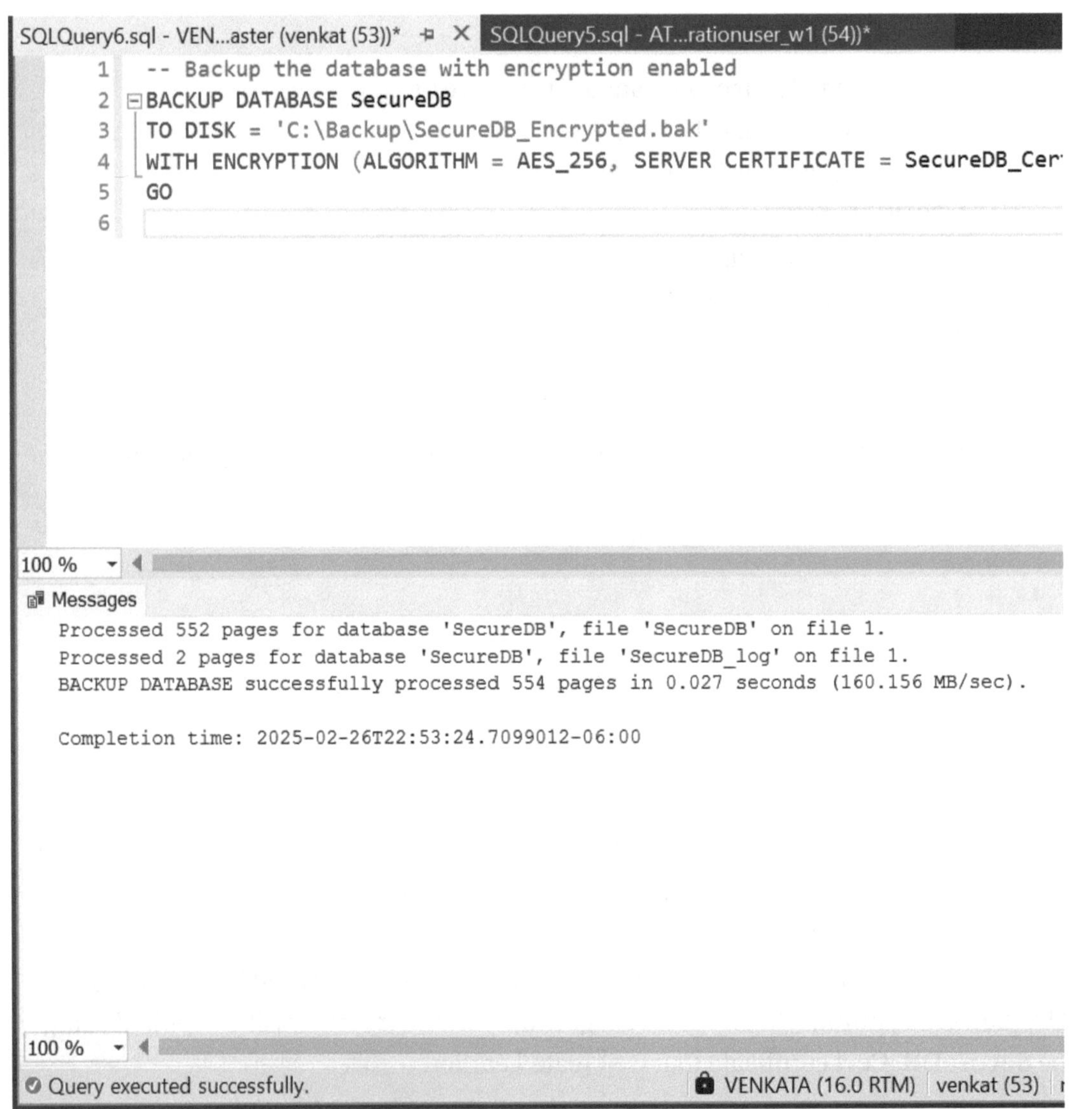

Figure 2-28. *Encrypted database backup*

Database Recovery and Tail Log Backup

Now, let's simulate a **disaster recovery scenario** in which we assume the database has been accidentally deleted or corrupted or that we deleted it.

Figure 2-29 shows the SQL commands used to remove the encrypted database and related security components.

```
10
11    DROP DATABASE [SecureDB];
12    GO
13    DROP CERTIFICATE SecureDB_Cert;
14    GO
15    DROP MASTER KEY;
16    GO
100 %

Messages
    Commands completed successfully.

    Completion time: 2025-02-26T23:01:02.1702238-06:00
```

Figure 2-29. *Database recovery*

Restoring an Encrypted Database

To successfully restore the **SecureDB** database, we must **recreate the master key** and **fix the certificate** before proceeding with the database restoration process.

Step 1: Recreate the Master Key and Restore the Certificate

Since our backup is encrypted, we must **restore the certificate** from the exported file rather than create it from scratch.

```
-- Recreate the master key
CREATE MASTER KEY ENCRYPTION BY PASSWORD = 'Secure@DB#2025!';
GO
-- Restore the certificate from the previously backed-up files
CREATE CERTIFICATE SecureDB_Cert
FROM FILE = 'C:\Backup\SecureDB_Cert.cert'
```

```
WITH PRIVATE KEY (FILE = 'C:\Backup\SecureDB_Cert.key',
DECRYPTION BY PASSWORD = 'Secure@DB#2025!')
GO
```

Why Is This Necessary?

The certificate is required to **decrypt the backup** during restoration. Without this step, SQL Server cannot restore the encrypted database.

Step 2: Restore the Encrypted Database

Now that we have restored the certificate, we can restore the **SecureDB** database using the **RESTORE DATABASE** command.

```
RESTORE DATABASE SecureDB
FROM DISK = 'C:\Backup\SecureDB_Encrypted.bak'
WITH RECOVERY,
MOVE 'SecureDB_Data' TO 'D:\SQLData\SecureDB_Data.mdf',
MOVE 'SecureDB_Log' TO 'D:\SQLLogs\SecureDB_Log.pdf',
REPLACE,
STATS = 10;
GO
```

The database has been recovered from the backup file.

The **MOVE** option ensures the MDF and LDF files are placed correctly.

The **REPLACE** option forces restoration even if a database with the same name exists.

The **STATS = 10** option provides progress updates every 10%.

Following these steps, we can **restore an encrypted database** to a SQL Server, either a new or old instance. Ensuring the **certificate is restored first** is critical for decrypting the backup.

Restoring in Large-Scale Environments

Use Cases for Large-Scale Database Restoration

Use Case 1: Disaster Recovery After Storage Failure

Scenario

A financial institution's primary storage system crashes, leading to data corruption in the production SQL Server instance. A disaster recovery plan is initiated.

Solution

Restore the latest full database backup. Apply differential and transaction log backups to recover the most recent data. If the database is TDE-encrypted, restore the encryption certificate before initiating the recovery.

Key Takeaways

Maintaining offsite encrypted backups ensures quick recovery. SAN replication or Always On Availability Groups can reduce downtime.

Use Case 2: Restoring a Multi-Terabyte Database on a New Server

Scenario

A global e-commerce platform must migrate its 15 TB SQL Server database to a new data center with minimal downtime.

Solution

Use striped backups across multiple disks to optimize restoration speed. Apply WITH NORECOVERY to allow further log restores. Use instant file initialization to speed up MDF and LDF allocation.

```
RESTORE DATABASE SalesDB
FROM DISK = 'E:\Backup\SalesDB_Part1.bak',
            'F:\Backup\SalesDB_Part2.bak'
WITH NO RECOVERY,
MOVE 'SalesDB_Data' TO 'D:\SQLData\SalesDB_Data.mdf',
MOVE 'SalesDB_Log' TO 'D:\SQLLogs\SalesDB_Log.pdf',
BUFFERCOUNT = 1024, MAXTRANSFERSIZE = 4194304,
STATS = 10;
```

Apply transaction logs to bring the database online.

Key Takeaways

Parallel processing speeds up extensive database restorations. Using multiple backup files reduces I/O bottlenecks. Instant file initialization reduces MDF/LDF file allocation time.

Use Case 3: Recovering from Ransomware Attack

Scenario

A healthcare provider's SQL Server database is compromised by ransomware, and attackers encrypt production data.

Solution

Take the affected database offline immediately. Restore a full database backup from a secure, isolated backup server. Apply point-in-time recovery using transaction log backups. Validate restoration using checksum-based integrity checks.

SQL

```
RESTORE DATABASE HealthDB
FROM DISK = 'C:\SecureBackup\HealthDB_Full.bak'
WITH CHECKSUM, VERIFY ONLY;
```

Key Takeaways

Offsite, immutable backups prevent ransomware data loss. Backup validation prevents corrupted restores. Point-in-time recovery minimizes data loss.

Use Case 4: Automating Large-Scale Restorations for DevOps Pipelines

Scenario

A software development company must refresh its testing environment daily with a copy of the production database.

Solution

Use a PowerShell or SQL Agent Job to automate the backup and restore process. Restore the database to a non-production server and apply masking for sensitive data.

```
PowerShell
Invoke-Sqlcmd -Query "RESTORE DATABASE DevDB FROM DISK = 'E:\Backup\ProdDB.
bak' WITH REPLACE, RECOVERY"
```

Key Takeaways

Automated restore pipelines reduce manual effort. Data masking protects sensitive information in non-production environments.

Restoring databases in large-scale environments requires strategic planning, high-speed recovery techniques, and automation to minimize downtime. Organizations can ensure a seamless restoration process by implementing best practices, even in critical failure scenarios.

Summary

This chapter meticulously explored the diverse landscape of SQL Server backup and recovery strategies, emphasizing their crucial role in data integrity and business continuity. We examined various approaches, including incremental and differential backups, transaction log backups, tail-log backups, file and filegroup strategies, and copy-only and mirror backups, understanding how each caters to different needs. The chapter also delved into advanced concepts like compression and encryption for efficiency and security, culminating in a discussion of restoring large-scale environments with minimal downtime. Ultimately, the key takeaway is that a robust backup strategy requires selecting the appropriate methods and testing them rigorously, allowing us to effectively respond to data loss and ensure the continuous availability of our SQL Server databases.

CHAPTER 3

Restorations

This chapter delves into the critical realm of database restoration, a fundamental process for ensuring data integrity and business continuity. We begin by exploring common scenarios that necessitate database restoration, encompassing issues such as accidental data loss, system failures, and large-scale disasters. Understanding these triggers allows for proactive planning and strategic restoration implementation. We then move to an essential series of preparatory steps, focusing on necessary pre-restoration tasks vital for a smooth and efficient recovery. The chapter further provides a step-by-step guide for executing the database restore utilizing SQL Server Management Studio (SSMS) and with the RESTORE command. Finally, we discuss post-restoration best practices, emphasizing verification techniques and continuous monitoring, which ensure that the restored database functions optimally and reliably. Throughout this chapter, we emphasize the importance of meticulous planning, diligent execution, and consistent verification as fundamental components of a sound database restoration strategy.

Database restoration is recovering a database from a backup file to maintain data integrity and reliability, particularly during system failures or accidental data loss. This procedure is essential for restoring a database to a specific state, whether to recover from a failure, migrate to another server, or replicate it in a different environment. Depending on recovery needs, the restoration process may involve full backups, differential backups, or transaction log backups. It necessitates an organized approach to guarantee success in data recovery.

The process typically starts with creating a reliable backup of the database, followed by selecting the appropriate restore option based on the specific requirements. The backup file is then specified as the source for restoration, and the final step involves verifying the success of the restoration process. By understanding these steps and adhering to best practices, database administrators and users can protect their data effectively and ensure the continuity of operations.

© Venkata Reddy Pasam and Petchikumar Andiappan 2026
V. R. Pasam and P. Andiappan, *The Expert's Guide to SQL Server*, https://doi.org/10.1007/979-8-8688-2451-7_3

Common Scenarios for Database Restoration

Recovering a database after hardware malfunctions, server crashes, or operating system failures. Restoring data due to unintended deletions, overwrites, or corruption caused by human errors or software issues. Rebuilding a database after catastrophic events like power outages, fires, or natural disasters. Rolling back to a specific moment to undo undesired transactions or changes. Moving a database to a new server, environment, or platform while retaining all data and configurations. Creating a copy of the database in a non-production environment for testing, debugging, or development purposes. Restoring historical data to review past transactions for compliance or security investigations. Rebuilding a fragmented or underperforming database by restoring it from a clean and optimized backup.

These scenarios emphasize the critical role of database restoration in maintaining operational continuity and data reliability.

Essential Pre-restoration Preparations

Verify backup files by using the RESTORE VERIFYONLY command. This step prevents issues during the restoration process.

```
RESTORE VERIFYONLY FROM DISK = 'C:\Backups\MyDatabaseBackup.bak';
```

Output: The backup set on file one is valid.

Confirm that the target server has sufficient disk space to accommodate the restored database files. Identify the purpose of restoration (e.g., full recovery, point-in-time recovery, or migration) and the specific data or time frame required. To avoid conflicts, ensure no active connections to the target database. To terminate existing connections, configure the database to SINGLE_USER mode.

SQL

```
ALTER DATABASE [DBNAME] SET SINGLE_USER WITH ROLLBACK IMMEDIATE;
```

If restoring an existing database, a backup of the current/target database should be taken as a precautionary measure. Always understand and decide on the restore options (e.g., overwrite existing database, point-in-time restore, or relocating files). If restoring a database incrementally, ensure all necessary transaction logs and differential backups are in sequence. Confirm that the account performing the restoration has the required permissions to execute the restore process on the target database. Inform relevant teams about the restoration process on the target database, especially if it involves downtime or impacts active systems. Prepare a clear step-by-step restoration plan to minimize errors and ensure a smooth process.

By following these preparations, database administrators can significantly minimize the likelihood of errors and guarantee a successful and efficient restoration process.

Step-by-Step Guide to SQL Server Database Restoration

Restoring a database in SQL Server involves systematically executing steps to recover data from a backup. Follow this guide for a successful restoration process:

A database can be restored using backups through either the graphical user interface (GUI) in SQL Server Management Studio (SSMS) or transact-SQL (T-SQL) commands. Both methods offer effective restoration, and we can demonstrate both processes here.

Below is the step-by-step process for restoring a database using T-SQL commands:

Restore a Full Backup

This step lays the foundation by restoring the full backup.

```
RESTORE DATABASE [testdb] FROM DISK = 'D:\Backups1\testdb_full.bak'
WITH MOVE 'testdb' TO 'D:\DBFILES\testdb.mdf', MOVE 'test1' TO 'D:\DBFILES\
test1.ndf',
MOVE 'testdb_log' TO 'D:\DBFILES\testdb_log.ldf',NORECOVERY,stats=2
```

NORECOVERY: Keeps the database in a restoring state for additional backups to restore (e.g., differential or transaction logs). During the restoring state of the database, no one can connect to the database.

WITH MOVE: The **WITH MOVE** option in SQL Server relocates the database files (data and log) to a new directory or path during the database restoration process. This is particularly useful when the original paths specified in the backup are unavailable, or you need to restore the database to a different environment or server. **Logical Names** come from the below RESTORE FILELISTONLY command.

```
RESTORE FILELISTONLY FROM DISK = 'D:\Backups1\testdb_full.bak';
```

New Paths specify the new physical file locations for the .mdf (data file) and .ldf (log file).

The STATS option in SQL Server is used during the database restoration process to display progress information. It provides feedback about the percentage of the restoration that has been completed, which is particularly useful for large databases, where the restoration process might take a significant time **percentage**. It specifies how often progress is reported. For example, if you specify **STATS = 10**, the system will report progress every 10% of the restore operation.

Figure 3-1 shows the SQL command used to restore a database from a backup file.

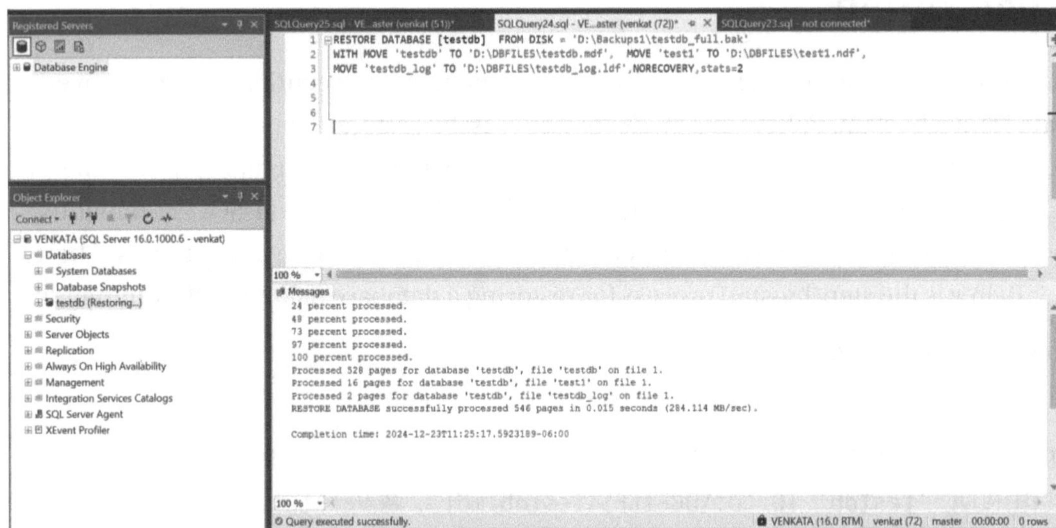

Figure 3-1. *STATS in SQL Server*

If the database status remains in a "restoring" state, it indicates that additional backups (such as differential or transaction log backups) need to be restored to complete the process.

Restore a Differential Backup (If Applicable)

Apply the differential backup, which contains changes made since the last full backup.

T-SQL

```
RESTORE DATABASE [testdb]
FROM DISK = ' D:\Backups1\testdb.BAK'
WITH NO RECOVERY;
```

If the database status remains in a "restoring" state, it indicates that additional backups (such as backups of transaction logs) must be restored to complete the process.

Restore Transaction Logs (If Applicable)

To recover data up to a specific point in time, apply transaction log backups sequentially:

T-SQL

```
RESTORE LOG [testdb] FROM DISK = 'D:\Backups1\testdb.TRN'withRECOVERY;
```

Figure 3-2 shows the SQL command used to restore transaction logs.

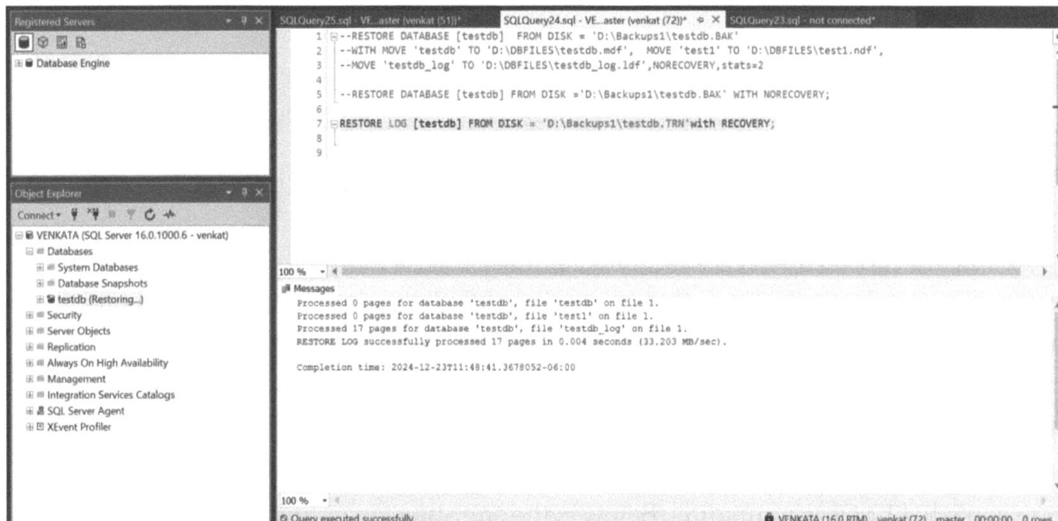

Figure 3-2. *Restore transaction logs*

Verify the Restoration

Check the database state to confirm it has been successfully restored:

```
SELECT name, state_desc FROM sys.databases WHERE name = 'testdb';
```

Figure 3-3 shows the SQL query used to verify the successful database restoration.

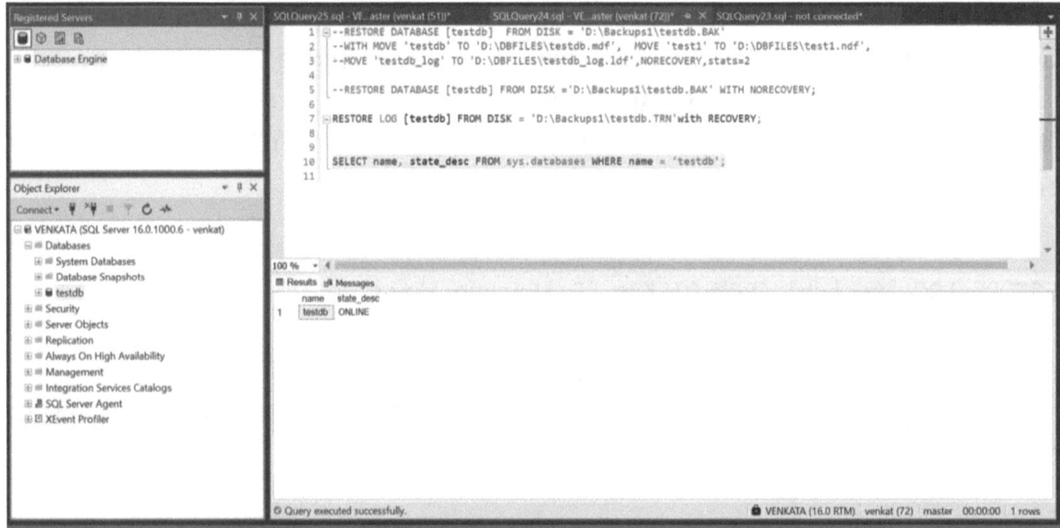

Figure 3-3. *Verification of restoration*

Using the **WITH RECOVERY** option signifies that no pending backups will be restored for the database. Once this option is applied, the database is brought online immediately, making it ready for regular operations and allowing users to connect.

Restoring a Database Using the Graphical User Interface (GUI) in SQL Server Management Studio (SSMS)

The SSMS GUI provides a user-friendly way to restore a database without requiring transact-SQL (T-SQL) commands. Below is the step-by-step guide:

Step 1: Open SQL Server Management Studio (SSMS)

Connect to the SQL Server instance where the database needs to be restored. In the **Object Explorer**, expand the server node.

Step 2: Launch the Restore Wizard

Right-click on the **Databases** node. Select **testdb…** from the context menu. Right-click on the Database ➤ Tasks ➤ Restore ➤ Database.

Figure 3-4 shows the SQL Server interface used to initiate the database restoration wizard.

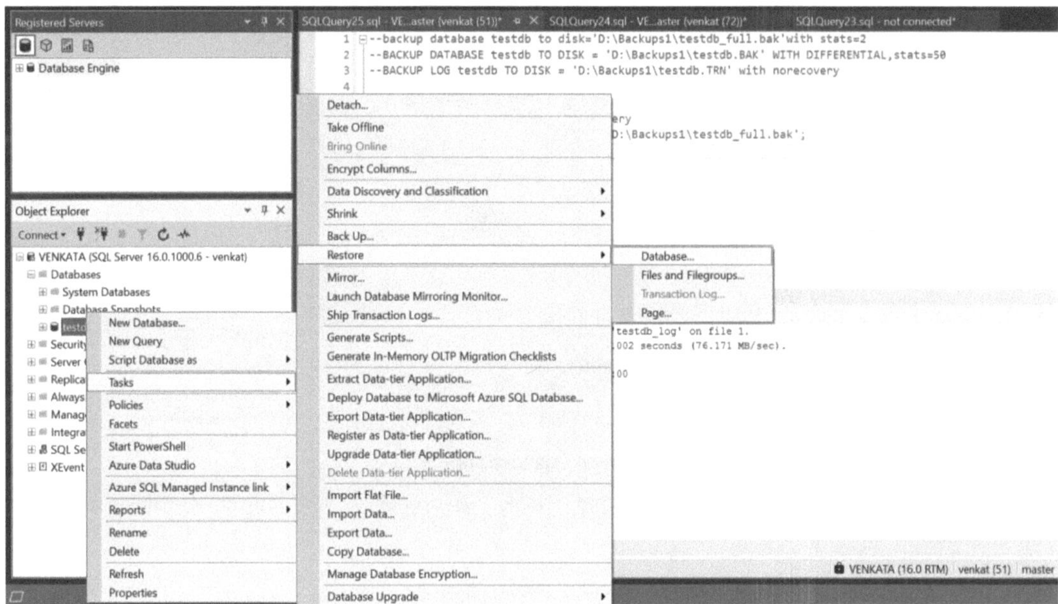

Figure 3-4. *Restoring wizard*

Step 3: Select the Device and Click On … (Ellipsis)

Figure 3-5 shows the interface used to select a backup device during database restoration.

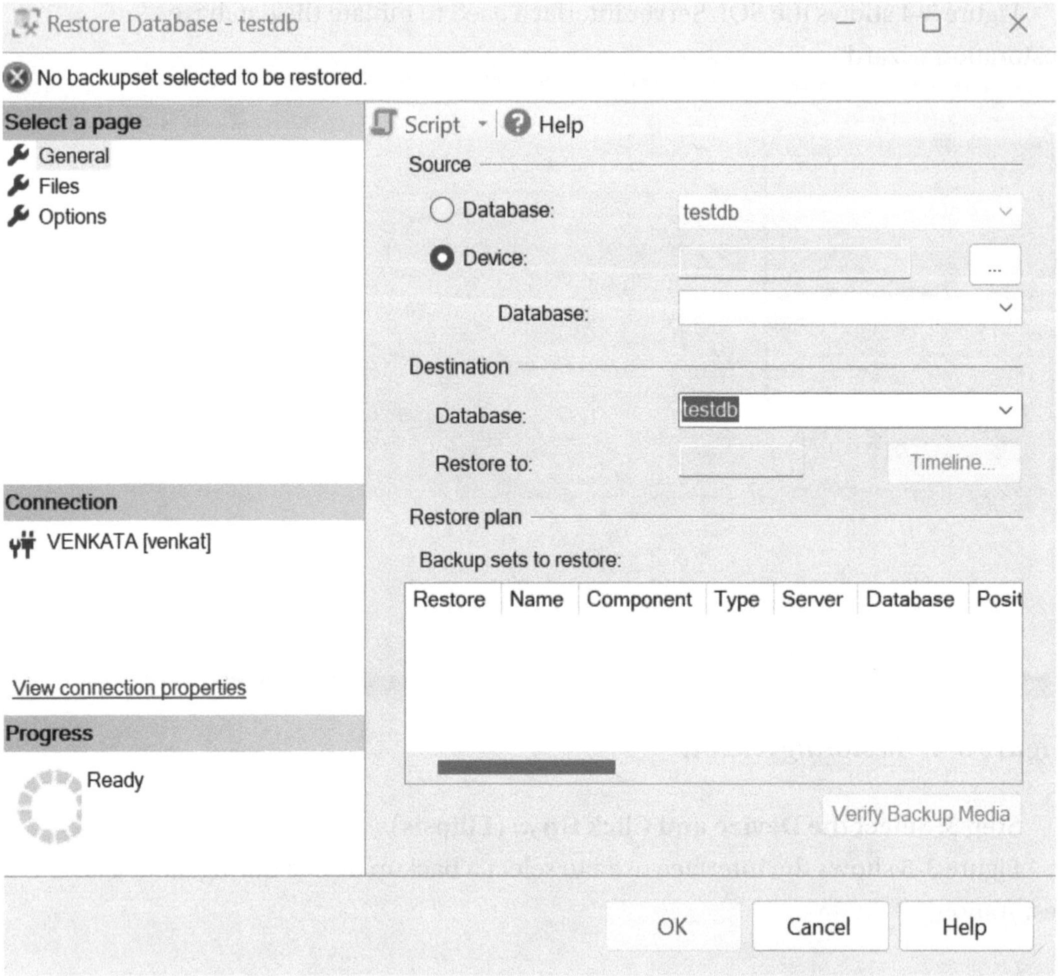

Figure 3-5. *Device for restoring database*

Step 4: Click on Add to Attach a Backup File

Figure 3-6 shows the interface used to add a backup media file during database restoration.

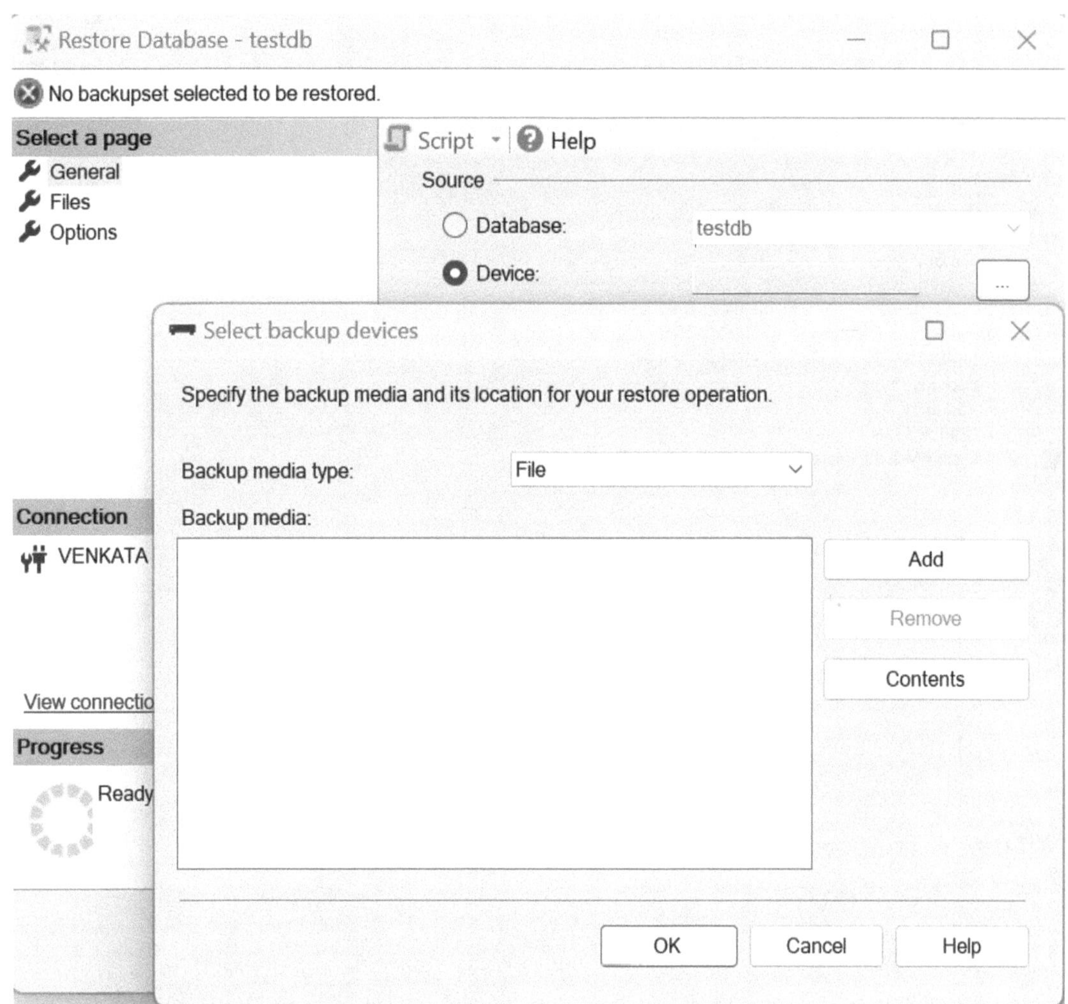

Figure 3-6. *Backup media file selection*

Step 5: Select a Database Fullback Backup Already in the System

Figure 3-7 shows the interface used to select the full database backup file for restoration.

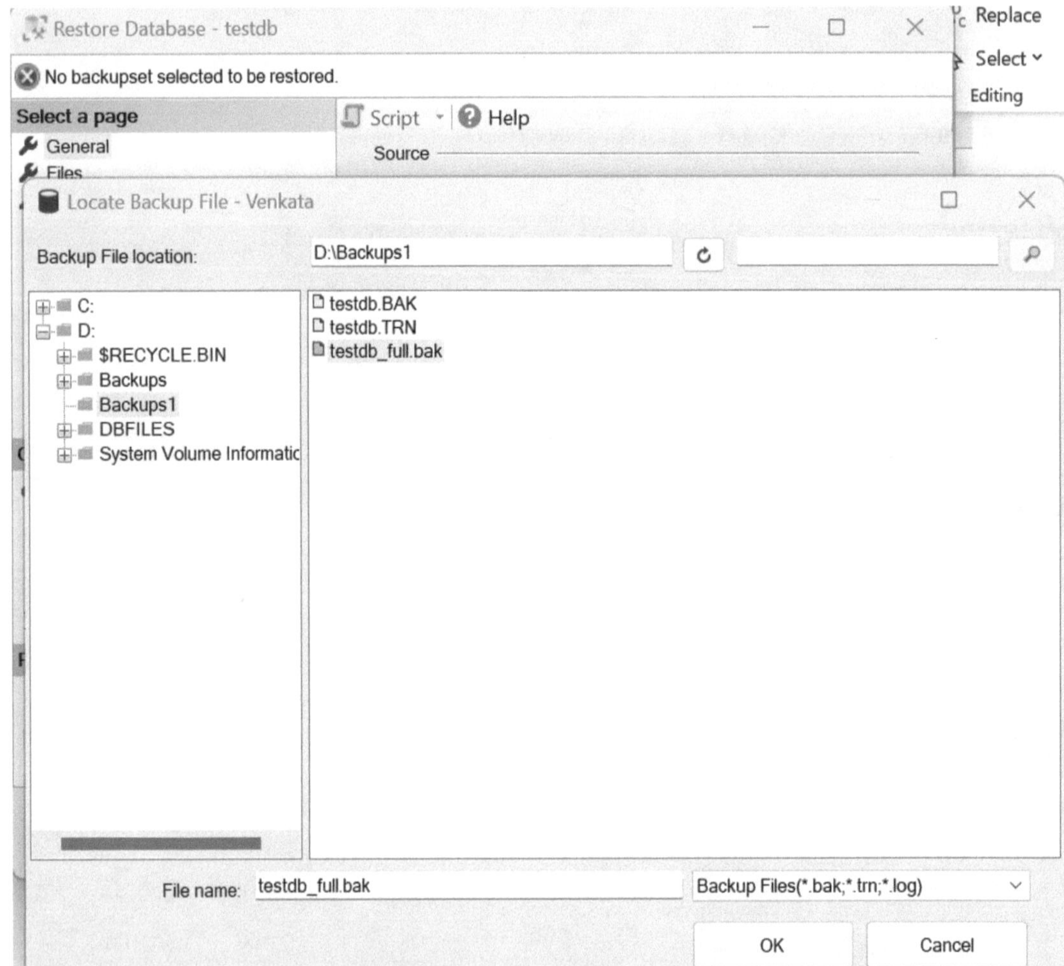

Figure 3-7. *Database fullback*

STEP 6: Switch to the Options Page

Restore Options: Select options such as overwriting the existing database (WITH REPLACE) if restoring over an existing database.

Recovery State:

RESTORE WITH NORECOVERY: To keep the database in a restoring state for additional backups.

Figure 3-8 shows the restore options and recovery state configuration during database restoration.

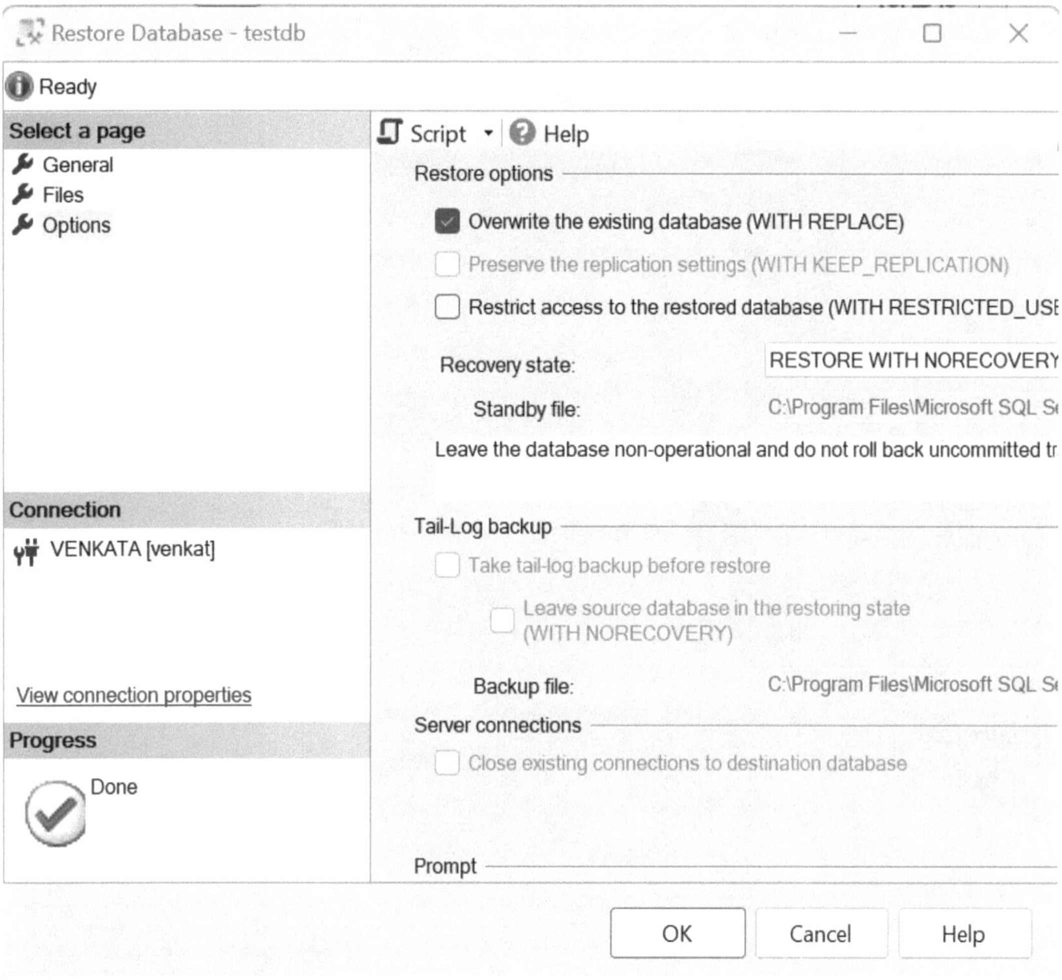

Figure 3-8. *Recovery state*

STEP 7: Start the Restore Process

Click **OK** to start the restore operation. Monitor the progress in the **Messages** window.

See the image below. The restoration process was completed.

Figure 3-9 shows the progress of the database restoration process.

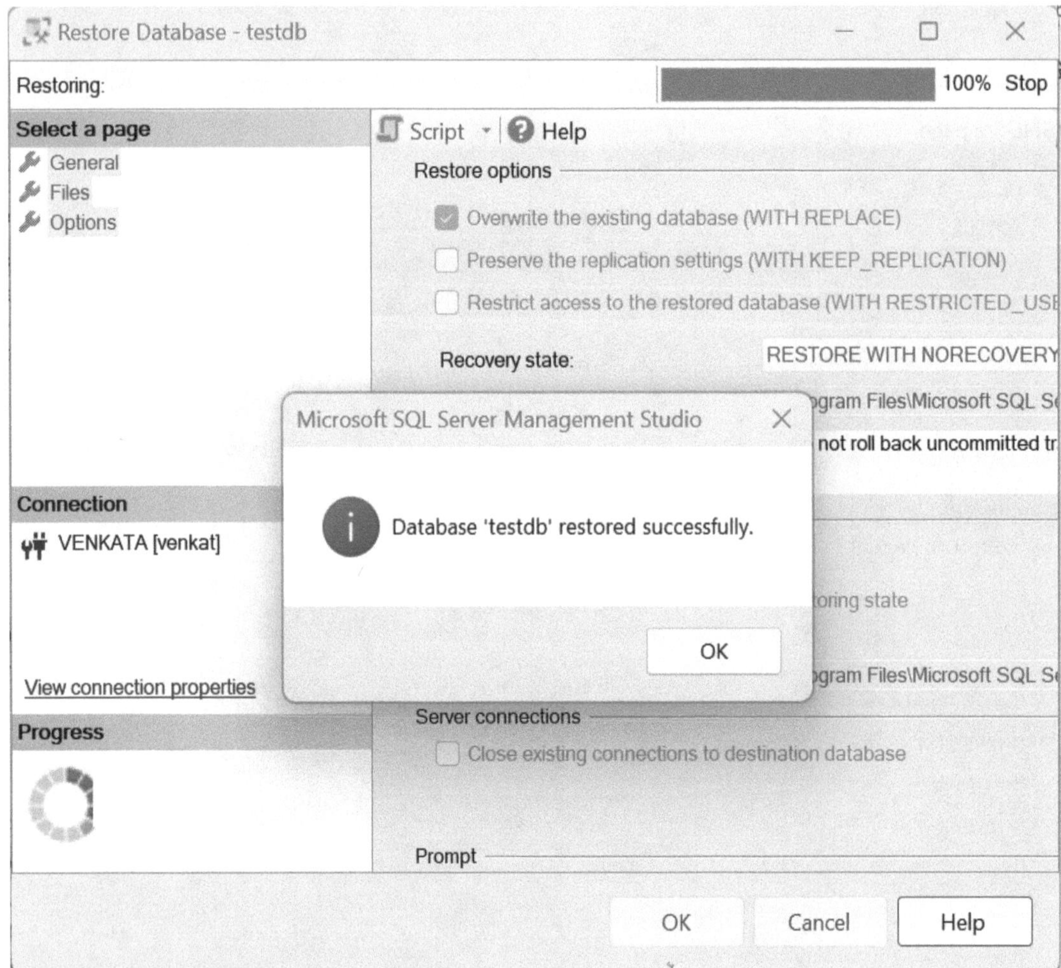

Figure 3-9. *Restoring process*

Step 8: If you see database status even after completing the full backups, it is still in the restoring state, i.e., a few backups are pending to restore against the database

Figure 3-10 shows the database status displayed in the Object Explorer during restoration.

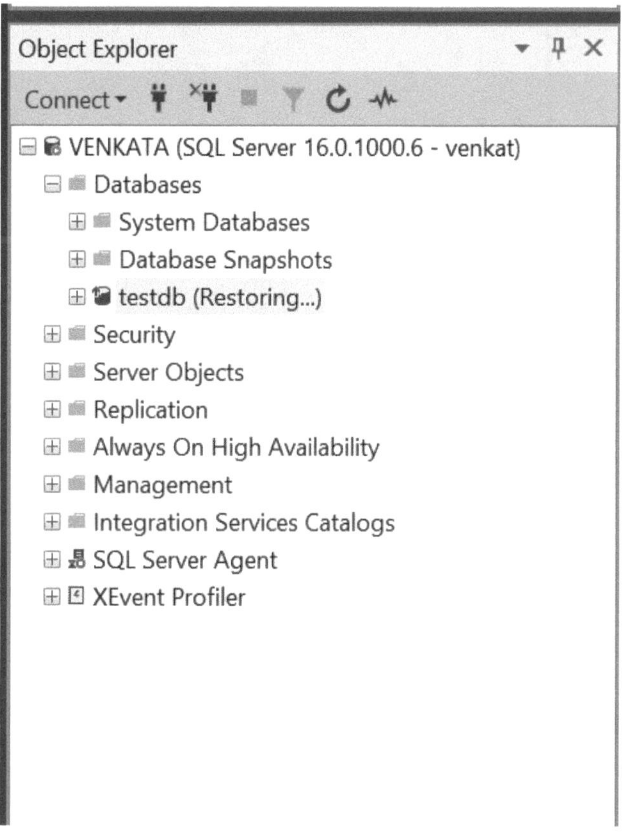

Figure 3-10. *Pending backups*

Restoring Differential Backups Against the Same Database (Where DB Is Restoring)

Step 1: Launch SQL Server Management Studio (SSMS).

Establish a connection to the SQL Server instance where the database needs to be restored. In the **Object Explorer**, expand the server node.

Step 2: Launch the Restore Wizard

Right-click on the **Databases** node. Select **testdb...** from the context menu. Right-click on the Database ➤ Tasks ➤ Restore ➤ Database.

Figure 3-11 shows the interface used to access the database restore wizard.

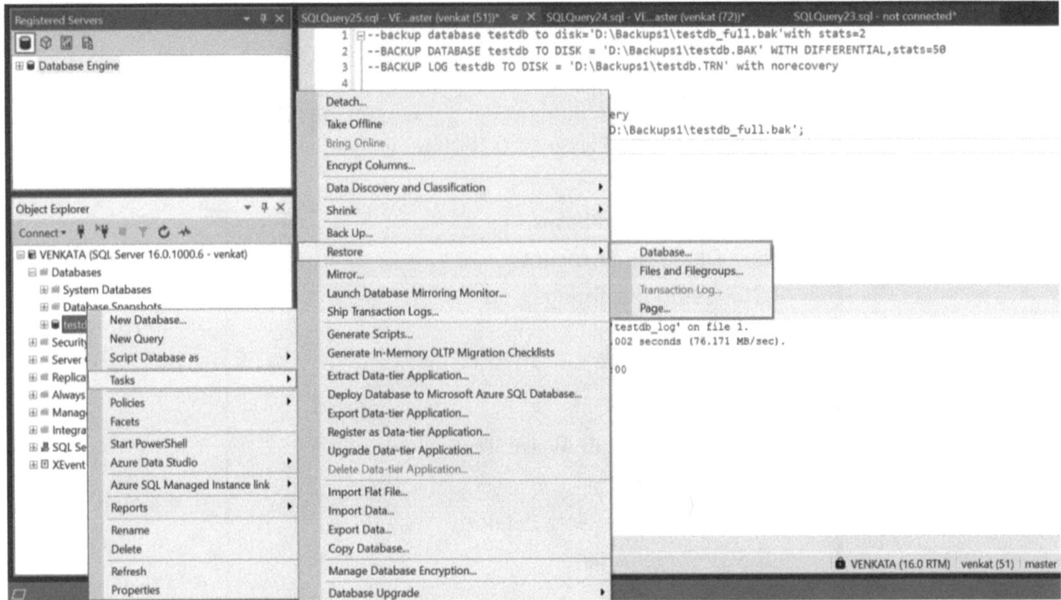

Figure 3-11.   *Restoring wizard*

Step 3: Select the Device and Click On … (Ellipsis)

Figure 3-12 shows the interface used to select a backup device during database restoration.

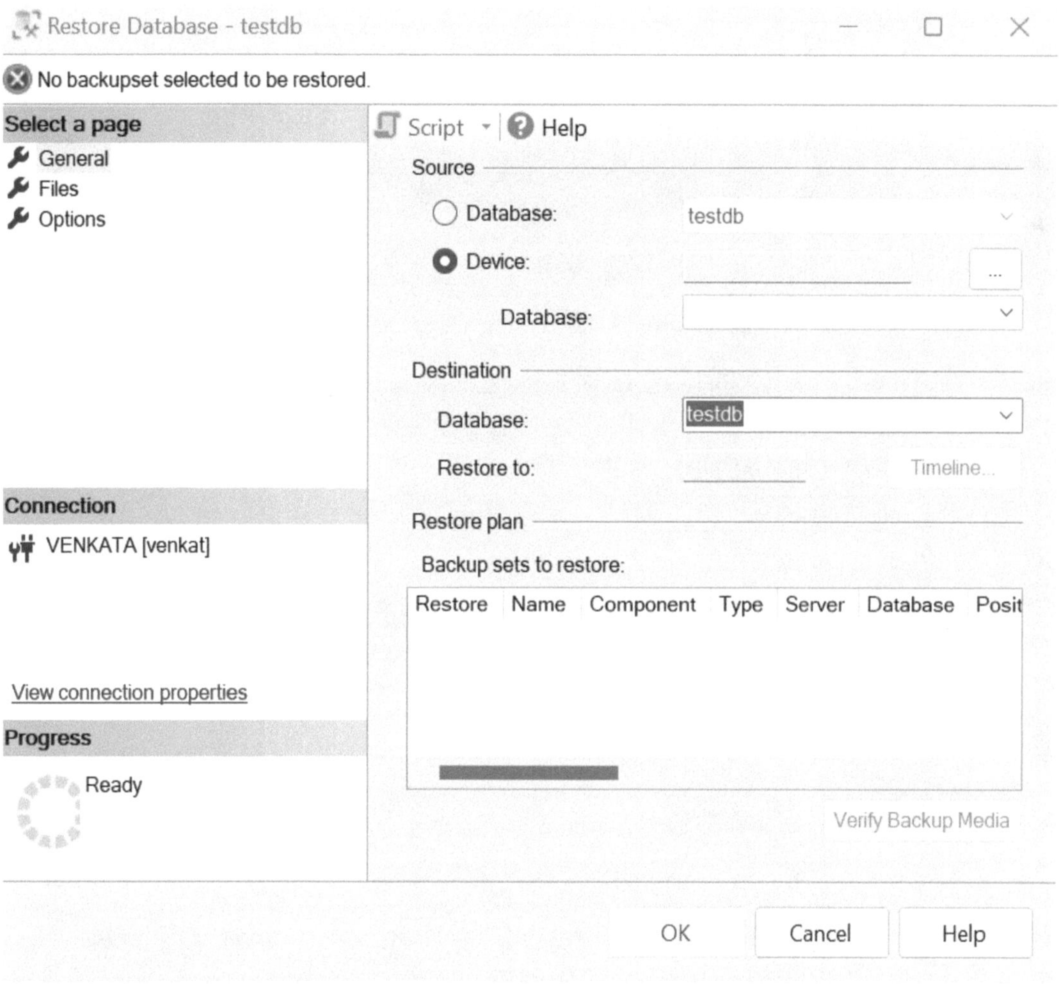

Figure 3-12. *Device for backup database*

Step 4: Click on Add to Attach a Backup File

Figure 3-13 shows the interface used to attach a backup file during database restoration.

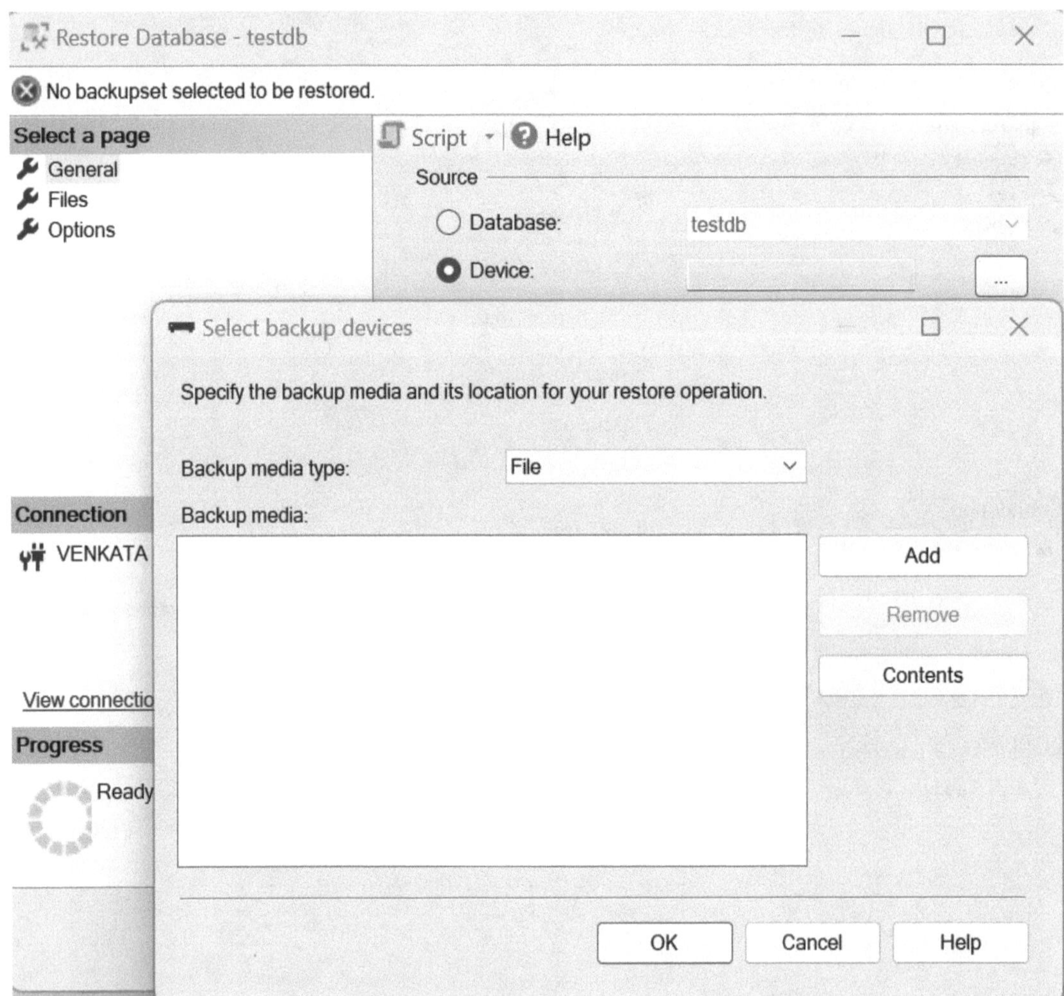

Figure 3-13. *Backup file attachment*

Step 5: Select a Database Differential Backup Already in the System.

Figure 3-14 shows the dialog box used to select a differential backup file.

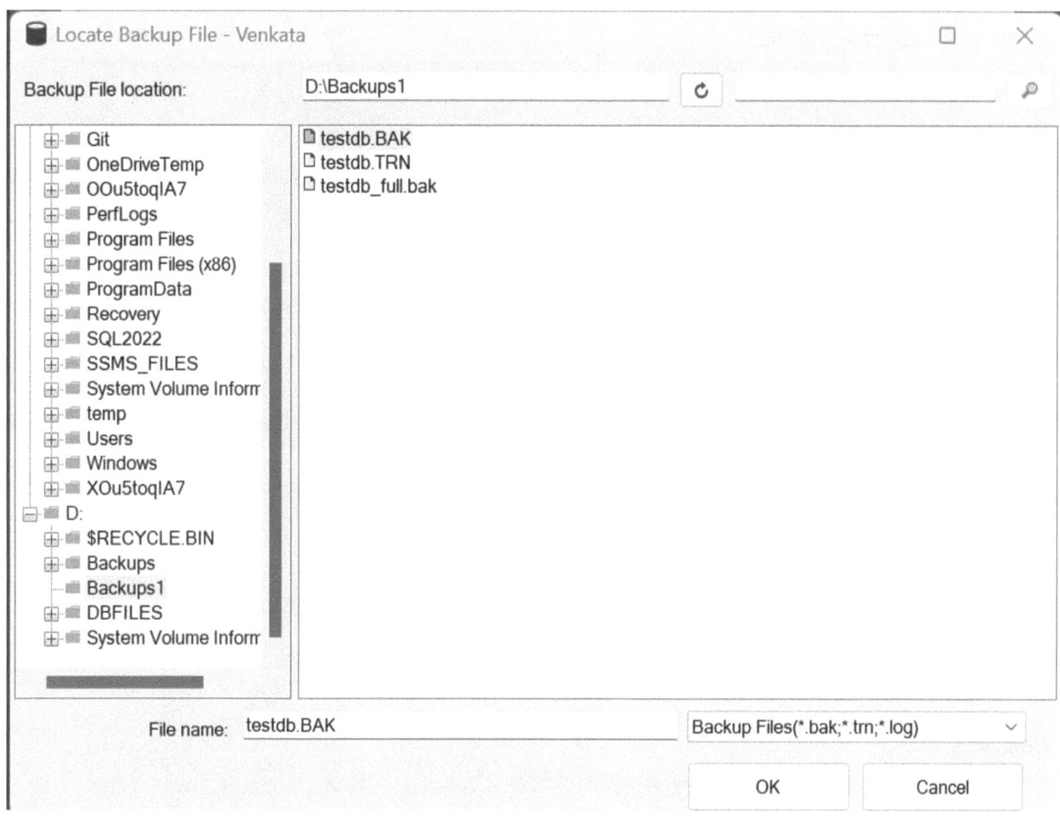

Figure 3-14. *Differential backup*

STEP:6 Switch to the Options Page

SQL Server Restoration Options and Techniques

Select options such as: Overwrite the existing database (WITH REPLACE): If restoring over an existing database.

Recovery State:

RESTORE WITH NORECOVERY: To keep the database in a restoring state for additional backups.

Figure 3-15 shows the recovery state configuration options during database restoration.

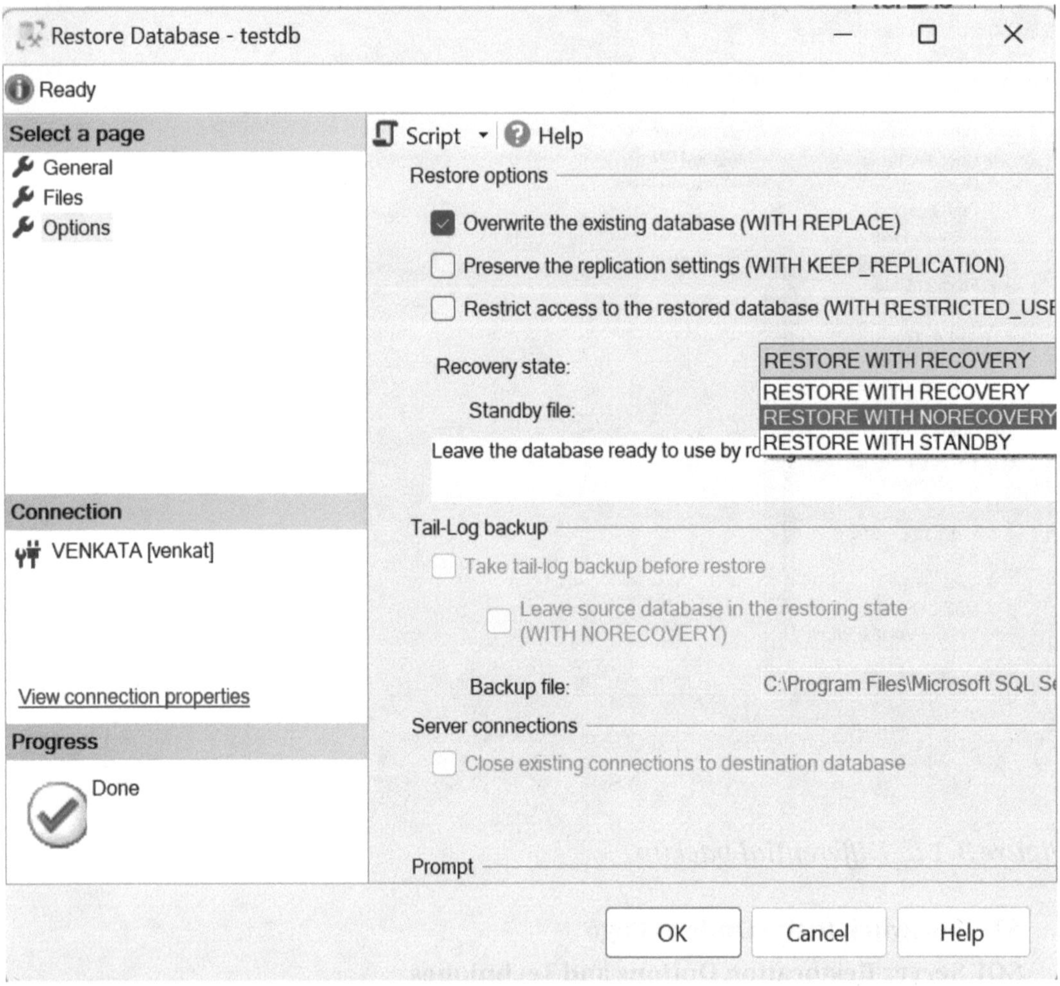

Figure 3-15. *Recovery state*

STEP 7: Start the Restore Process

1. Click OK to start the restore operation.

2. Monitor the progress in the Messages window.

See below. Assume that the restore process is completed.

Figure 3-16 shows the database restoration process in progress.

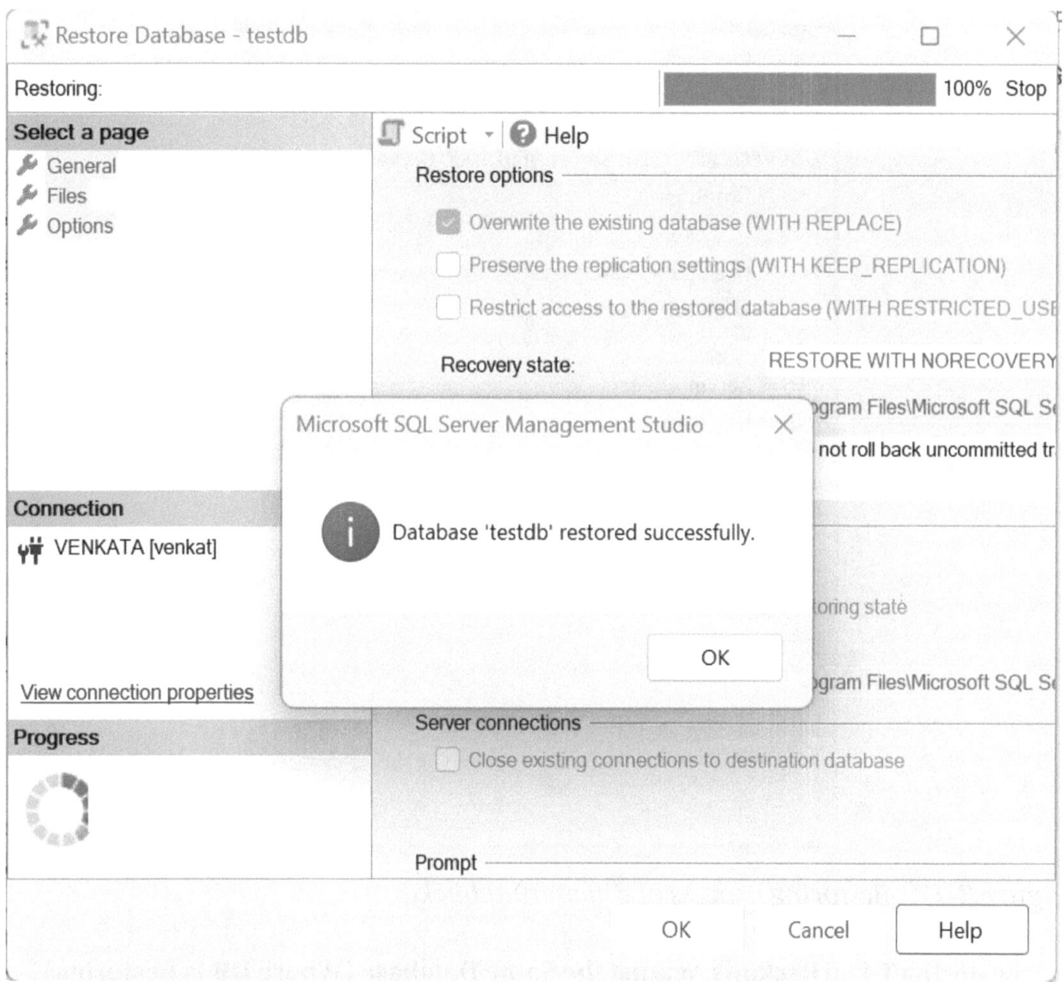

Figure 3-16. *Restore process initiation*

Step 8: If the database status remains in the "restoring" state even after completing the differential backup restoration, it indicates that additional backups must be restored.

Figure 3-17 shows the database status during the differential restoration process.

Figure 3-17. *Restoring process of differential backup*

Restoring T Log Backups Against the Same Database (Where DB Is Restoring)
Step 1: Open SQL Server Management Studio (SSMS)
Connect to the SQL Server instance where the database needs to be restored. In the
Object Explorer, expand the server node.

Step 2: Launch the Restore Wizard
Right-click on the **Databases** node. Select **testdb…** from the context menu. Right-
click Database ➤ Tasks ➤ Restore ➤ Database. So, a full backup has been completed,
and we are yet to restore another backup like differential backups and transactional
backups.

Figure 3-18 shows the interface used to open the database restore wizard.

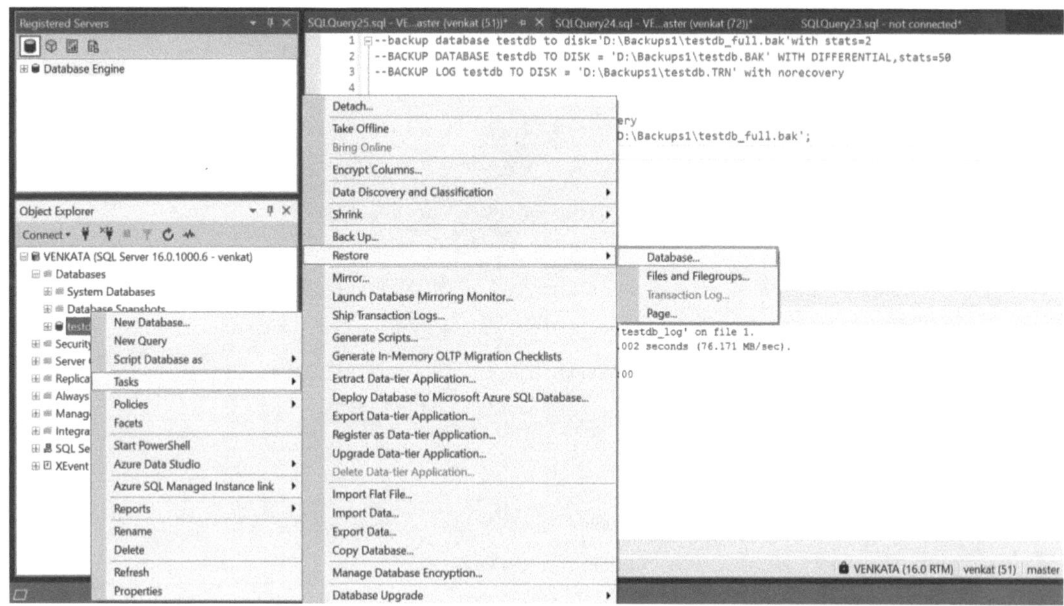

Figure 3-18. *Restore wizard*

Step 3: Select the Device and Click On … (Ellipsis)

Figure 3-19 shows the interface used to select a backup device for database restoration.

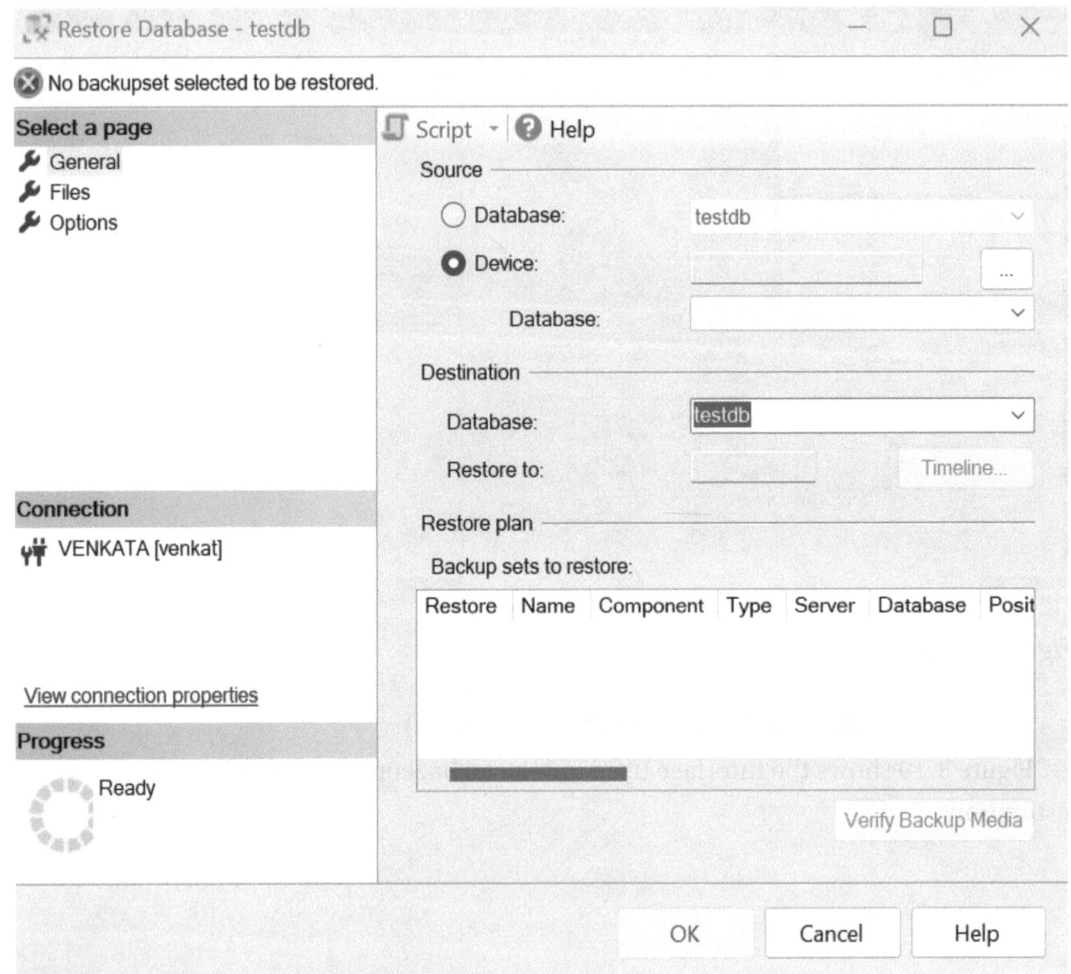

Figure 3-19. *Selecting device for backup*

Step 4: Click on Add to Attach a Backup File

Figure 3-20 shows the interface used to attach a backup file during database restoration.

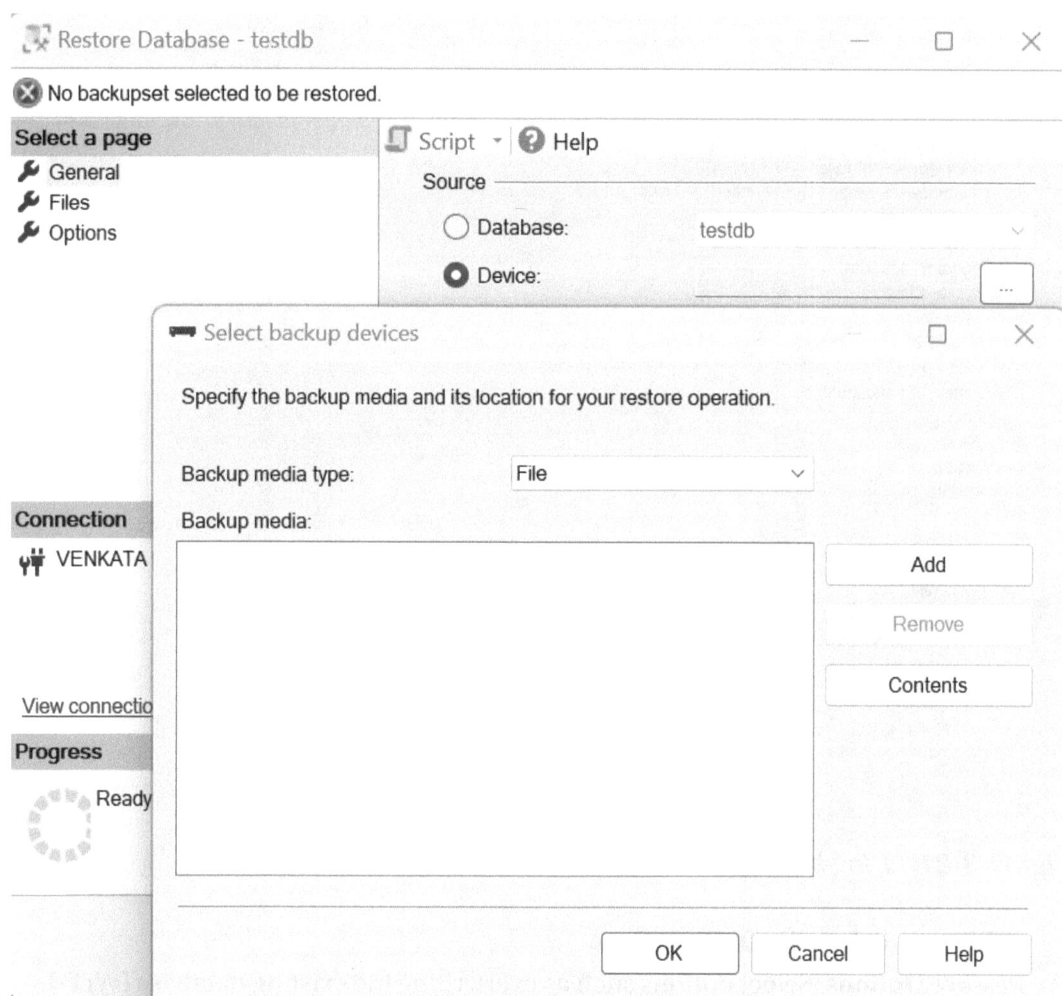

Figure 3-20. *Attaching a backup file*

Step 5: Select a Database T Log Backup That Is Already in the System

Figure 3-21 shows the selection of the transaction log backup file for database recovery.

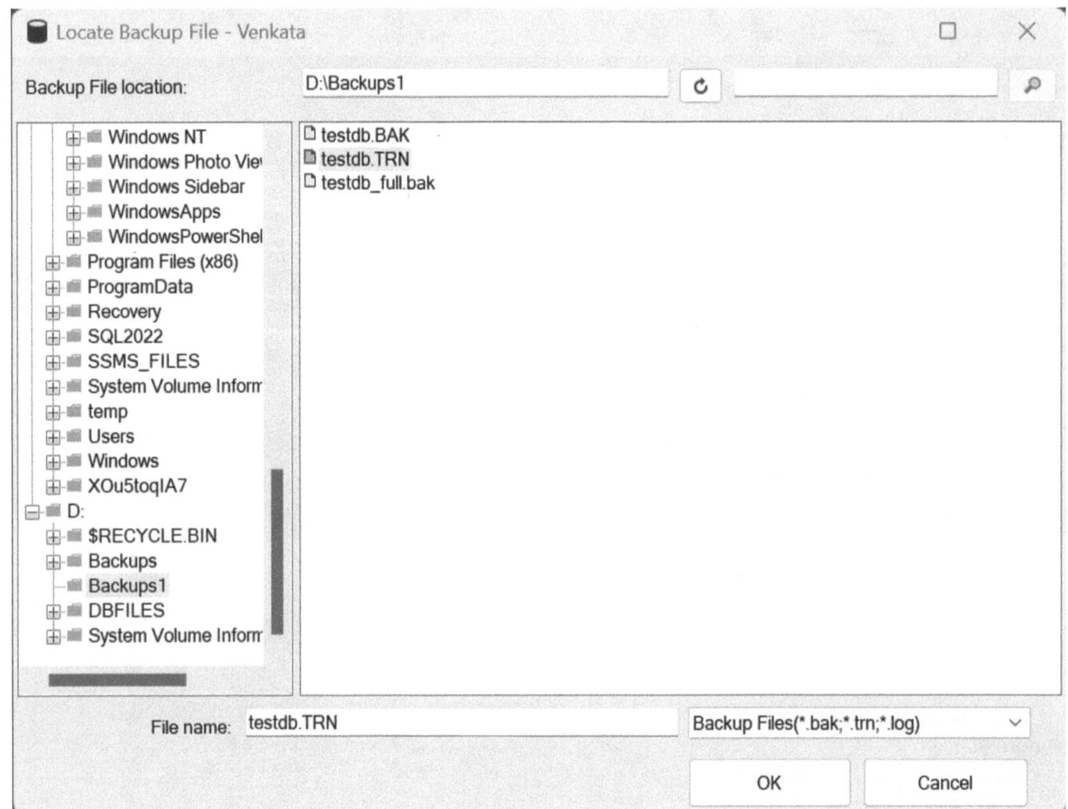

Figure 3-21. *T log backup*

STEP 6: Switch to the Options Page

Restore Options: Select options such as overwriting the existing database (WITH REPLACE) if restoring over an existing database.

Recovery State:

RESTORE WITH RECOVERY: To keep the database in an online state

Figure 3-22 shows the Options page used to configure restore settings during database restoration.

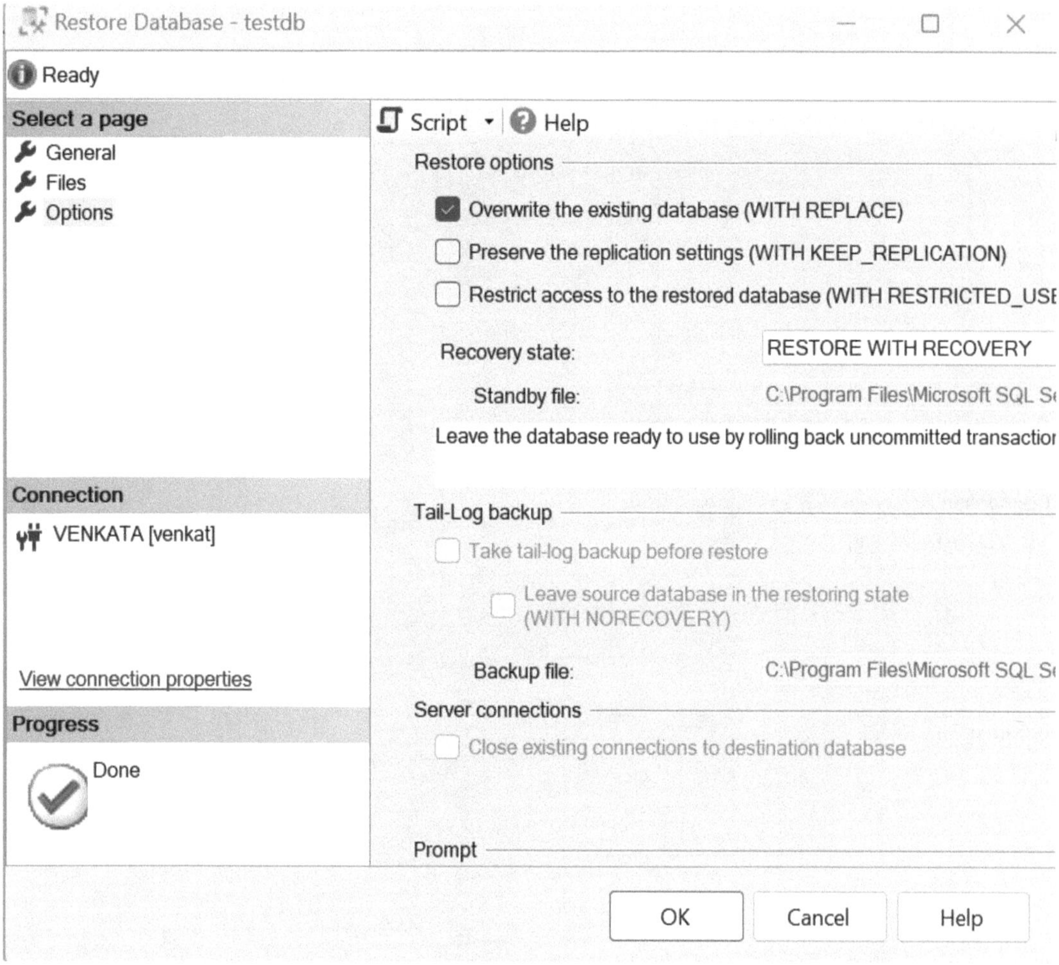

Figure 3-22. *Options page*

STEP 7: Start the Restore Process

1. Click OK to start the restore operation.

2. Monitor the progress in the Messages window.

See below. Imagine the restore process got completed.
Figure 3-23 shows the successful completion of the database restore process.

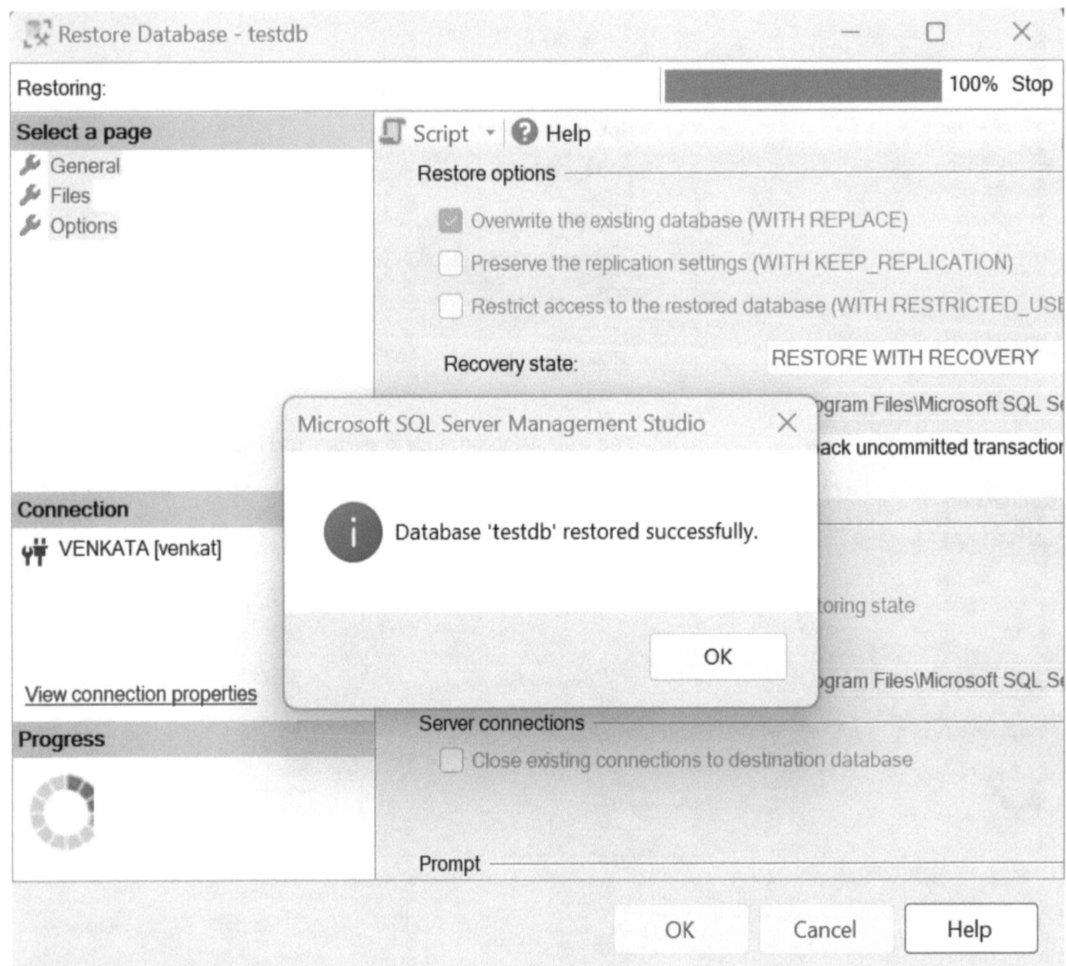

Figure 3-23. *Restore process*

Step 8: The database is now in an "online" status, indicating it is ready for normal operations.

Figure 3-24 shows the database in an online state after the restore operation.

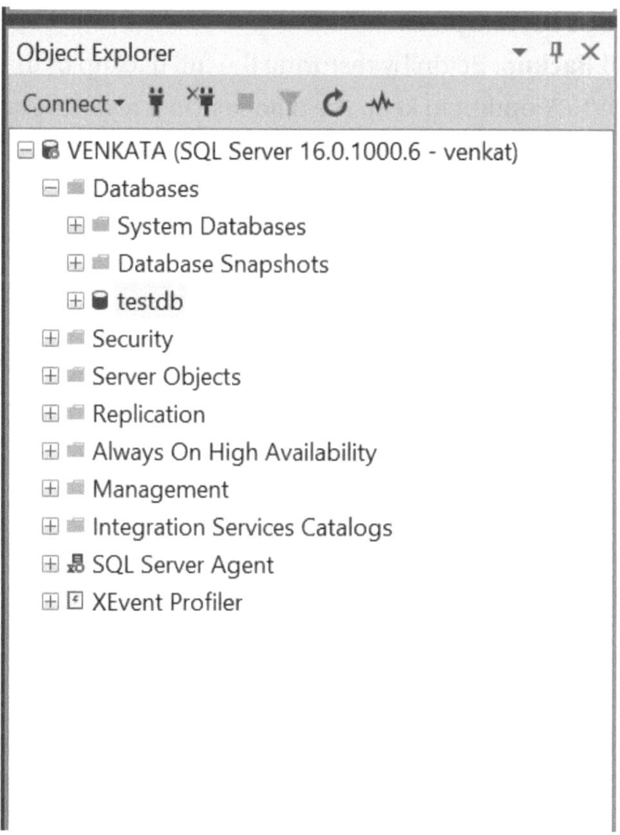

Figure 3-24. *Online status of database*

Key Benefits of GUI Restoration

- Intuitive and easy for beginners.

- Eliminates the need to memorize complex T-SQL commands.

- Provides a visual overview of backup files and restore options.

Using the SSMS GUI ensures a straightforward process for database restoration, especially for users who prefer visual tools over scripting.

Restore with STOPAT Option in SQL Server

The STOPAT option is used during a database restoration process to restore the database to a specific point in time. This is particularly useful for point-in-time recovery, allowing you to restore data just before an undesirable incident, like unintentional data corruption or erasure.

Steps to Use the STOPAT Option

Restore the Full Backup. Begin by restoring the full backup of the database using the WITH NORECOVERY option to keep the database in a restoring state.

```
RESTORE DATABASE [testdb]
FROM DISK = 'FullBackup.bak'
WITH NO RECOVERY;
```

Restore Transaction Log Backup

Apply the transaction log backup with the STOPAT option to specify the date and time you want to restore the database.

T-SQL

```
RESTORE LOG [testdb]
FROM DISK = 'TransactionLog.bak'
WITH STOPAT = '2024-12-20 15:30:00', RECOVERY;
```

Ensure the STOPAT date and time match the format and timezone of the SQL Server instance. The point in time specified must fall within the range of the transaction log backups available. The database is rolled back to the state at the specified time, and any uncommitted transactions are not applied. Use the WITH RECOVERY option in the final step to bring the database online.

Practical Use Cases

Restore the database to a time just before critical data was accidentally deleted. Recover the database to a known good state before the corruption. Restore data for a specific event or transaction.

Using the STOPAT option gives database administrators precise control over recovery, ensuring minimal data loss during critical situations.

Post-restoration Best Practices

Run the DBCC CHECKDB command to ensure the restored database is corrupt or error-free.

T-SQL

```
DBCC CHECKDB ('DatabaseName');
```

Check the database status to ensure it is online and available for use. Validate that all required backups (full, differential, and transaction logs) have been applied. Confirm settings such as recovery model, compatibility level, and collation to match the source database or desired configuration. Restore user access by mapping logins and verifying permissions using sp_change_users_login or ALTER USER. Test application connectivity to the restored database once you have added logins/users. Rebuild indexes to improve performance after the restoration. Update statistics to ensure query optimization.

T-SQL

```
EXEC sp_updatestats;
```

Run queries to verify critical data in the restored database. Compare data with the source or backup to ensure accuracy. Re-enable any jobs, replication tasks, or maintenance plans associated with the database. If the database uses full-text indexing, rebuild or re-enable the full-text catalogs. Create a new full backup of the restored database to establish a fresh recovery point.

T-SQL

```
BACKUP DATABASE [DatabaseName]
TO DISK = 'BackupFilePath.bak';
```

Use tools like SQL Server profiler or query store to ensure the restored database performs as expected. Record details of the restoration process, including the backup file used, date and time, and any changes made post-restoration.

By following these best practices, you can ensure a smooth transition to regular operations and maintain the dependability and functionality of your SQL Server database.

Summary

This chapter provided an in-depth exploration of SQL Server database restoration, focusing on various recovery scenarios and the necessary preparations to prevent potential issues. We walked through detailed restoration procedures, including using the **STOPAT** option for precise point-in-time recovery.

Beyond the restoration itself, we emphasized crucial post-restoration steps, such as verifying data integrity, adjusting user permissions, rebuilding indexes, and confirming database functionality. Additionally, we addressed the importance of reconfiguring scheduled jobs and full-text indexes to restore full operational capacity.

Ultimately, effective database restoration is more than just restoring files—it requires **strategic planning, accurate execution, and thorough validation** to maintain data reliability, optimize performance, and support seamless business continuity.

CHAPTER 4

Security and Compliance

This chapter shifts the focus to the crucial area of security and compliance within SQL Server databases. Recognizing that sensitive data requires robust protection, this chapter explores a range of security measures that businesses can employ. We begin by examining the core layers of SQL Server authentication, starting with the foundational concepts of logins and database users, and then diving into the specifics of Windows and SQL Server authentication. The chapter moves on to cover different ways to manage user access, including server-level roles. We will examine Transparent Data Encryption (TDE), which allows data protection at rest. Then we will explore data protection during transmission using Always Encrypted. Finally, we will discuss Row-Level Security (RLS), a feature that allows for granular access controls. This chapter emphasizes that building a strong security posture requires a multi-faceted approach involving both administrative controls and features built into SQL Server.

SQL Server security is essential for businesses that rely on the platform to store sensitive and confidential data. Without proper security measures, SQL Server databases can become vulnerable to data breaches, unauthorized access, and the theft of critical information, potentially exposing a company to significant operational and reputational risks.

Security in SQL Server involves implementing robust measures and practices to safeguard databases and their components from misuse, vulnerabilities, and unauthorized access. This guarantees the security, accuracy, and accessibility of the data, aligning with broader organizational and compliance requirements. By adhering to best practices and keeping up with the latest security advancements, businesses can protect their data and ensure a secure operational environment.

© Venkata Reddy Pasam and Petchikumar Andiappan 2026
V. R. Pasam and P. Andiappan, *The Expert's Guide to SQL Server*, https://doi.org/10.1007/979-8-8688-2451-7_4

SQL Server supports the two layers of authentication: login and database user. Login is the first layer of security to access and connect to the SQL Server. A login has nothing to do with the databases. Instead, login is mapped to a user in a database to read or write to a particular database.

You can use two authentication modes to log in and connect to SQL Server.

Windows authentication

SQL Server authentication

Windows Authentication

Windows authentication mode allows users to log in to SQL Server using their local Windows credentials.

For instance, the following example demonstrates how a Windows credential is used to connect to SQL Server, where the user is in... VENKATA\venka, the local user account on Windows. VENKATA is the database server's name. To log in with these credentials and establish a connection to the VENKATADDatabase

As shown in Figure 4-1, the SQL Server connection window uses Windows Authentication.

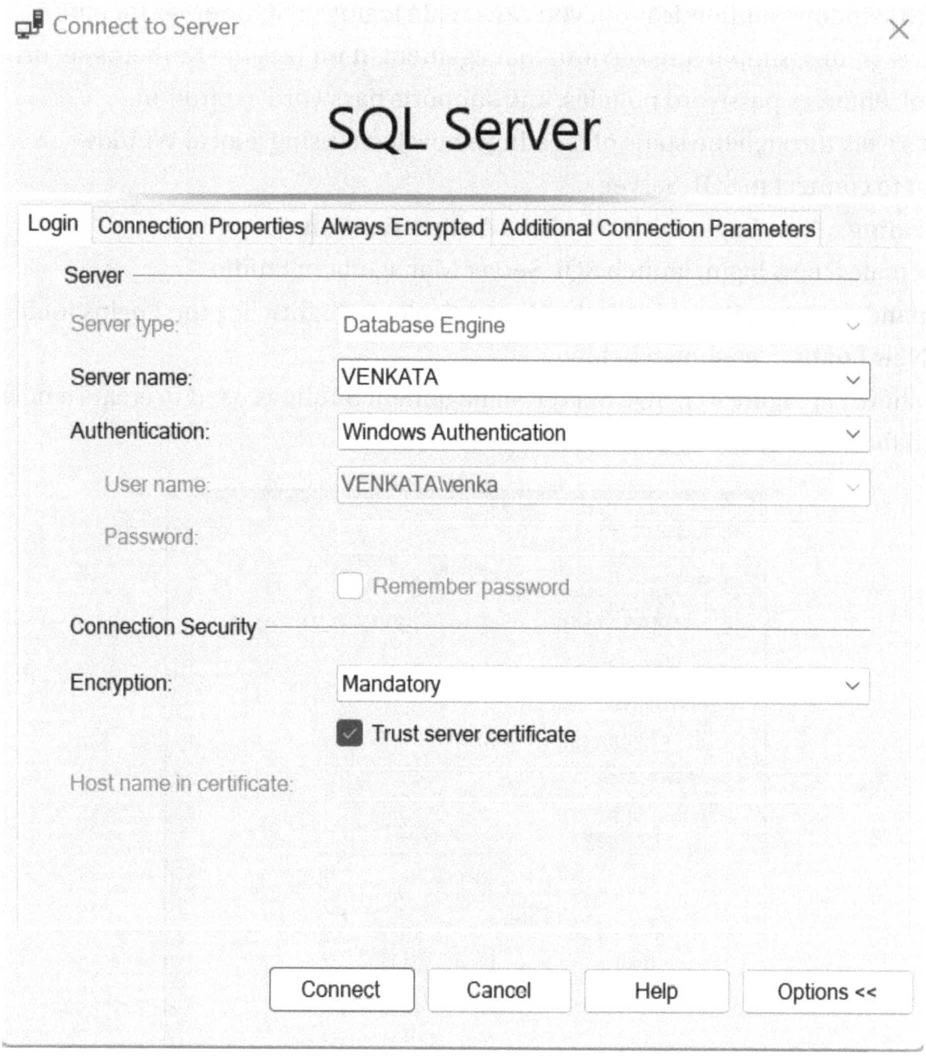

SQL Server

Login   Connection Properties   Always Encrypted   Additional Connection Parameters

Server

Server type: Database Engine

Server name: VENKATA

Authentication: Windows Authentication

User name: VENKATA\venka

Password:

☐ Remember password

Connection Security

Encryption: Mandatory

☑ Trust server certificate

Host name in certificate:

Connect   Cancel   Help   Options <<

Figure 4-1. *Windows authentication*

Server:

Windows authentication is the default mode and is considered more secure than SQL Server authentication. It is often called integrated security, as it is closely tied to Windows. Users already authenticated by Windows don't need to provide additional credentials when connecting to SQL Server. This is a trusted connection where Windows verifies the user account.

With Windows authentication, you can create logins in SQL Server for entire Windows groups, simplifying account management. It utilizes the Kerberos security protocol, enforces password policies, and supports password expiration.

Let's walk through the steps of creating a new login using a local Windows user account to connect to SQL Server.

Creating a New Login with Windows Authentication

To create a new login, launch SQL Server Management Studio.

Expand the **Security** folder in the Object Explorer. Right-click the Logins folder and select **New Login**…, as shown below.

As shown in Figure 4-2, SQL Server Management Studio is used to create a new login through the Security ➤ Logins folder.

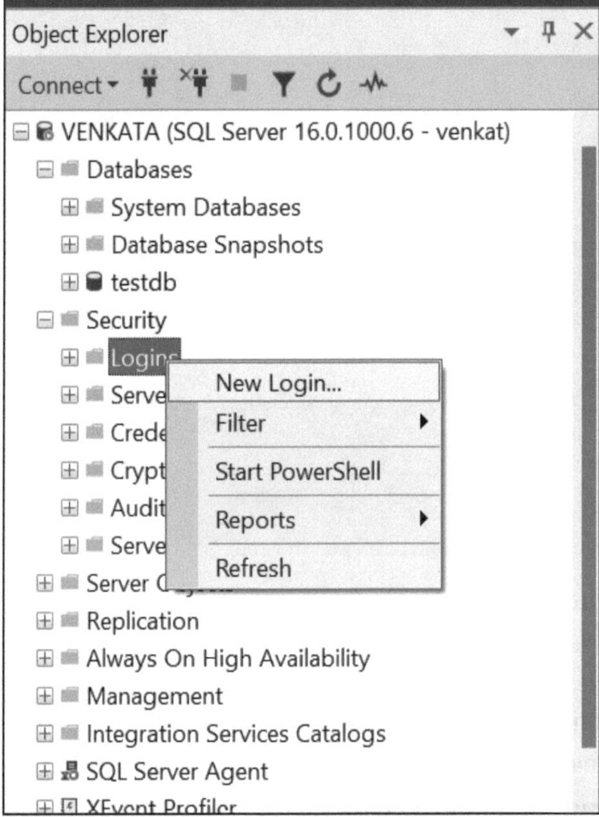

Figure 4-2. *SQL Server Management Studio: Creating a new login*

In the New Login window, input the Windows username. Username. An error will occur if the username is not a valid Windows user. You may locate a Windows user using the Search button below.

As shown in Figure 4-3, the Login – New window is used to configure user login settings and authentication options in SQL Server.

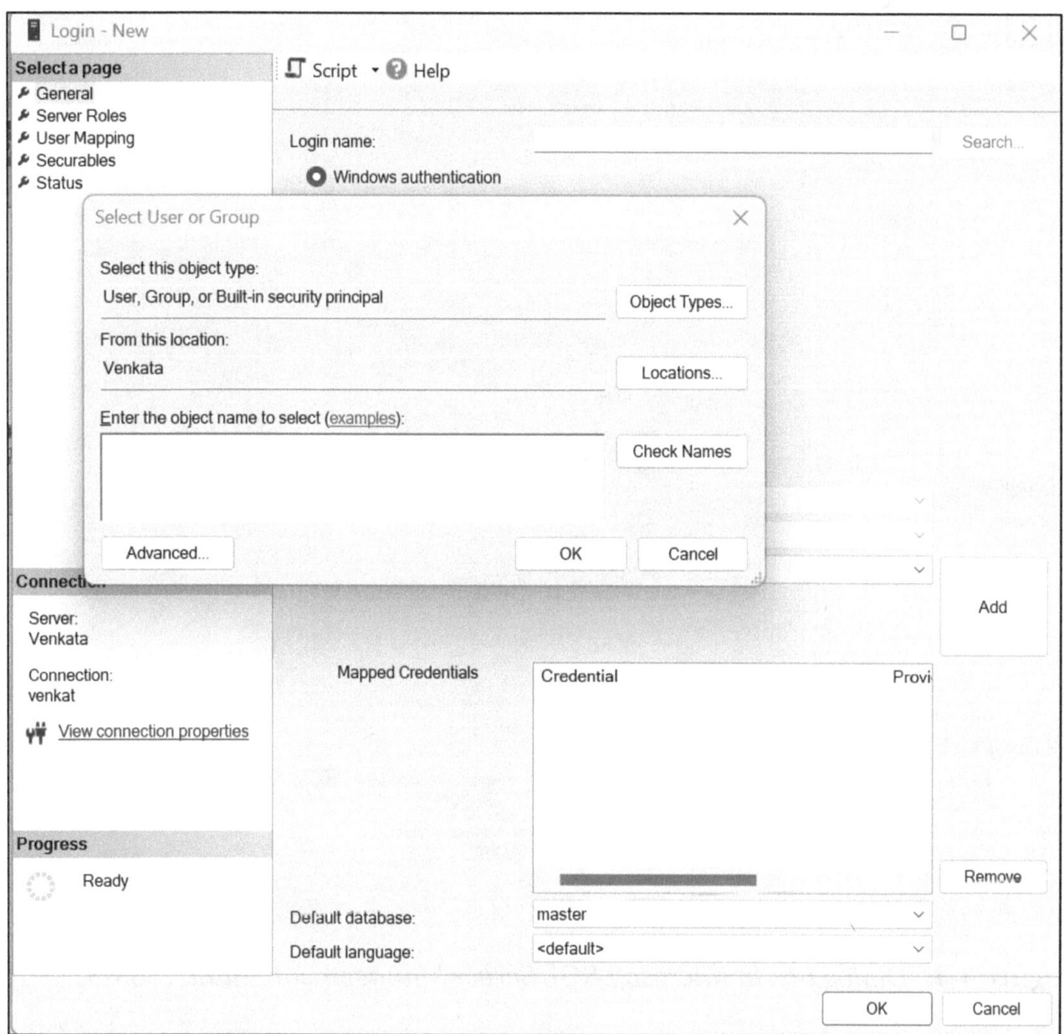

Figure 4-3. *The login*

After entering the login name, you must choose Windows or SQL Server authentication. If you select Windows authentication, the password field and policy options will be disabled, as Windows credentials are used.

As shown in Figure 4-4, the Login – New dialog box in SQL Server Management Studio (SSMS) is used to configure login credentials and authentication methods.

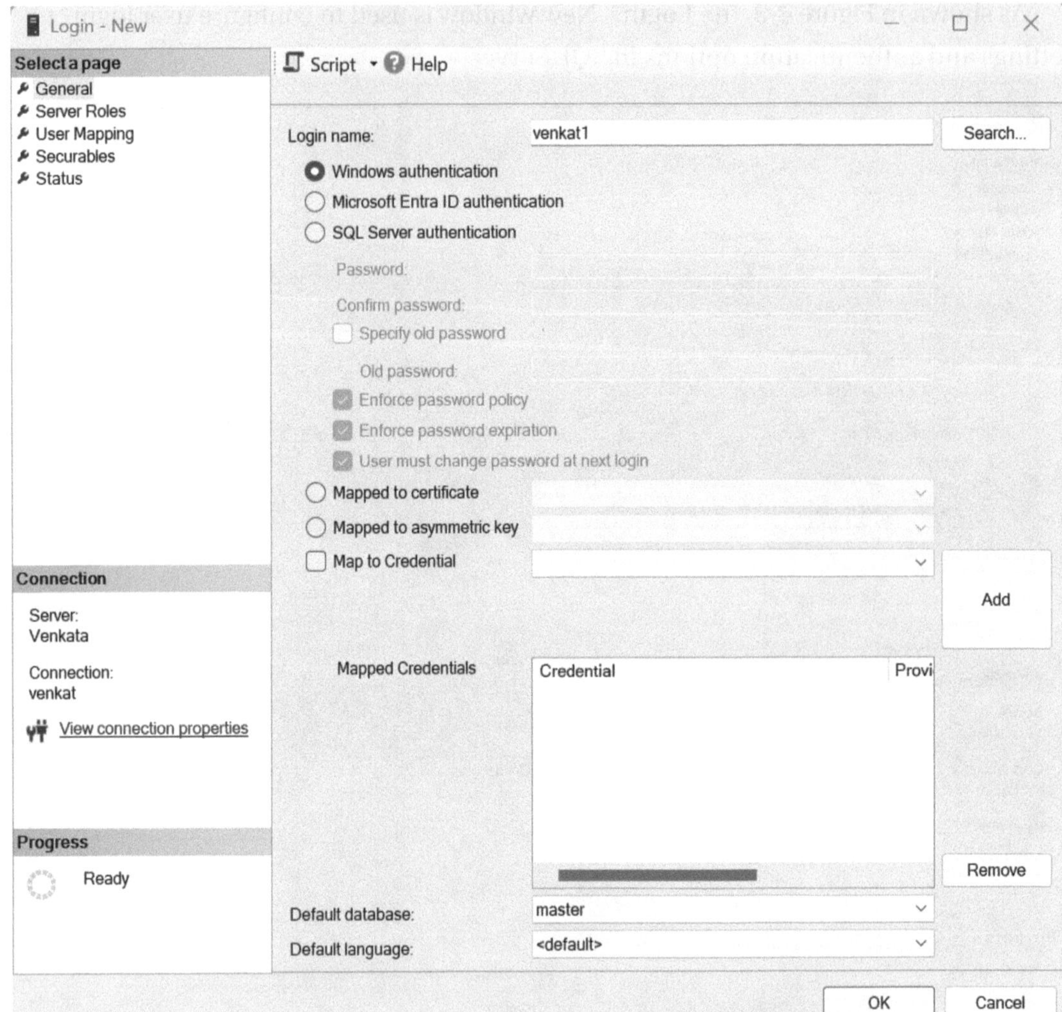

Figure 4-4. *Dialog box in Microsoft SQL Server Management Studio (SSMS)*

Go to the Server Roles tab to assign roles and permissions to the new login. You can assign a server-level role on this page by checking the box next to the role. By default, the public role is assigned to the new login. To assign the sysadmin role, check the box next to sysadmin. Users with this role have complete control and can perform any action on the server.

As shown in Figure 4-5, the Login – New window in SQL Server Management Studio (SSMS) is used to assign server roles, such as sysadmin, to a user during login configuration.

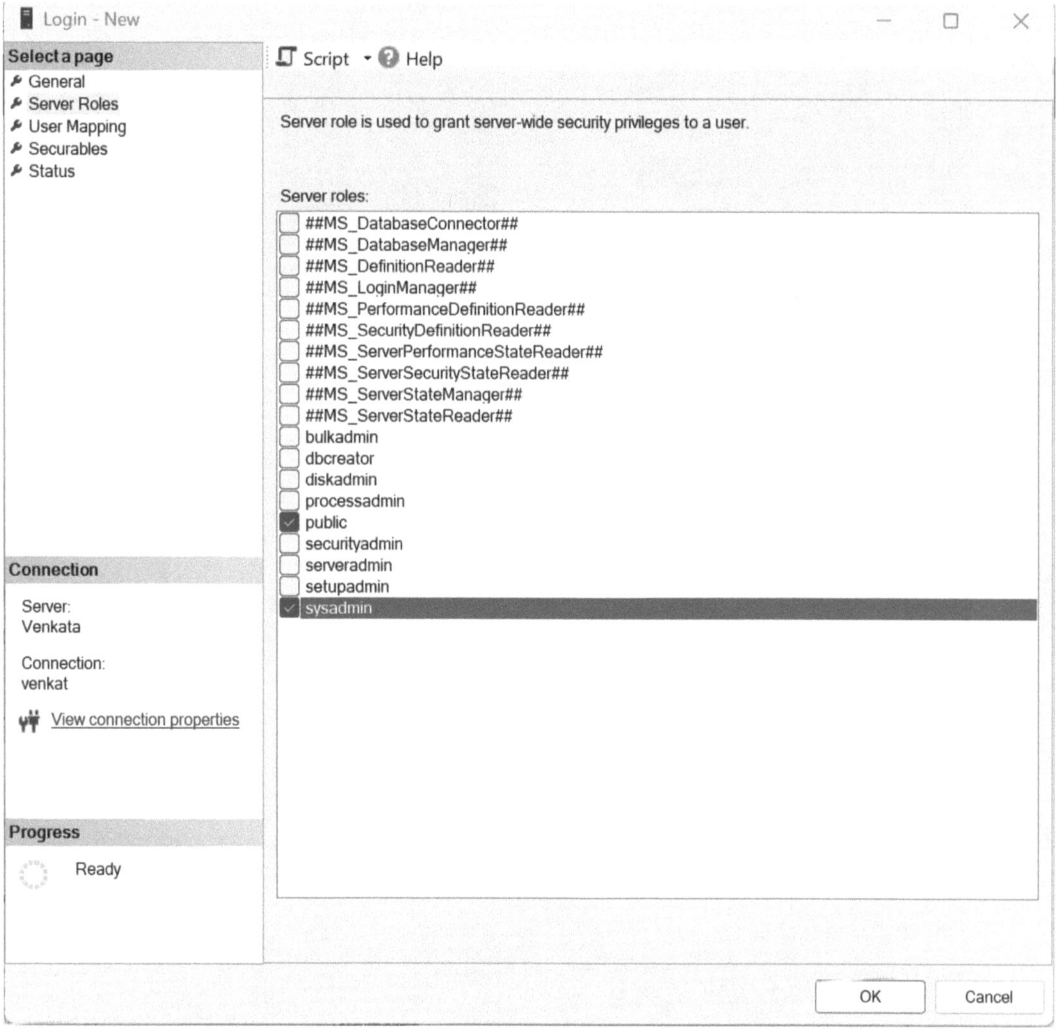

Figure 4-5. *Select a page*

Next, click the User Mapping tab. Here, you can map the new Windows login to a
database user.

This tab displays all databases on the server. To map the login to a database select
the checkboxes next to the databases that the login should access. The testdb database is
selected, and the user column now displays the updated login for testdb.

As shown in Figure 4-6, the Login – New window in SQL Server Management Studio
(SSMS) displays the user mapping configuration, where the login is mapped to the testdb
database and assigned database roles.

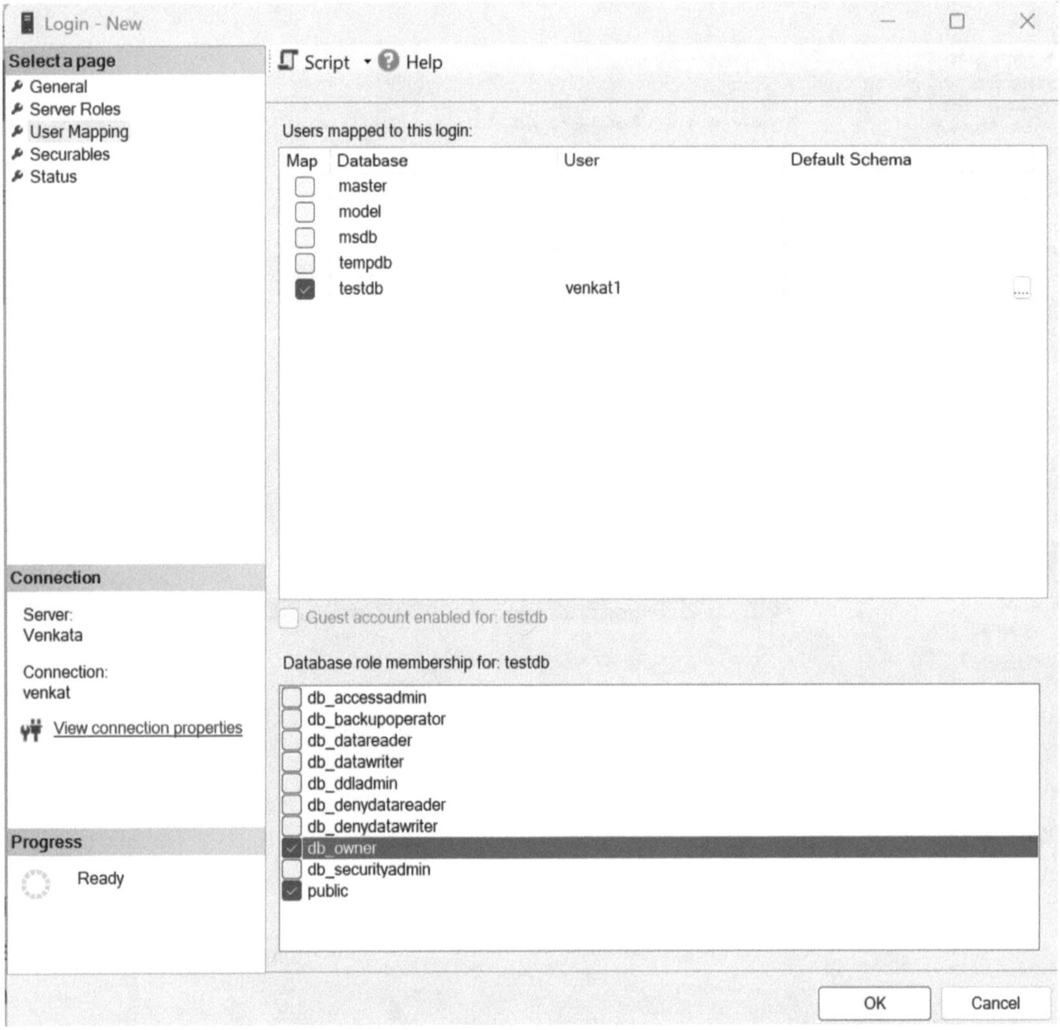

Figure 4-6. *Login configuration window in SQL Server Management Studio*

Select the Securables tab now. SQL server resources, known as securables, are accessible through a login you create. On the Securable tab, select the Search button. Choose the server "<Your Server name>" and click "OK." This will display all explicit permissions available on the server; select Grant, With Grant, or Deny based on the required access privileges.

This step is optional and can be skipped based on your needs. Securable: Configure the settings during login creation or adjust them later.

As shown in Figure 4-7, the Securables tab displays the login permission settings in SQL Server Management Studio (SSMS).

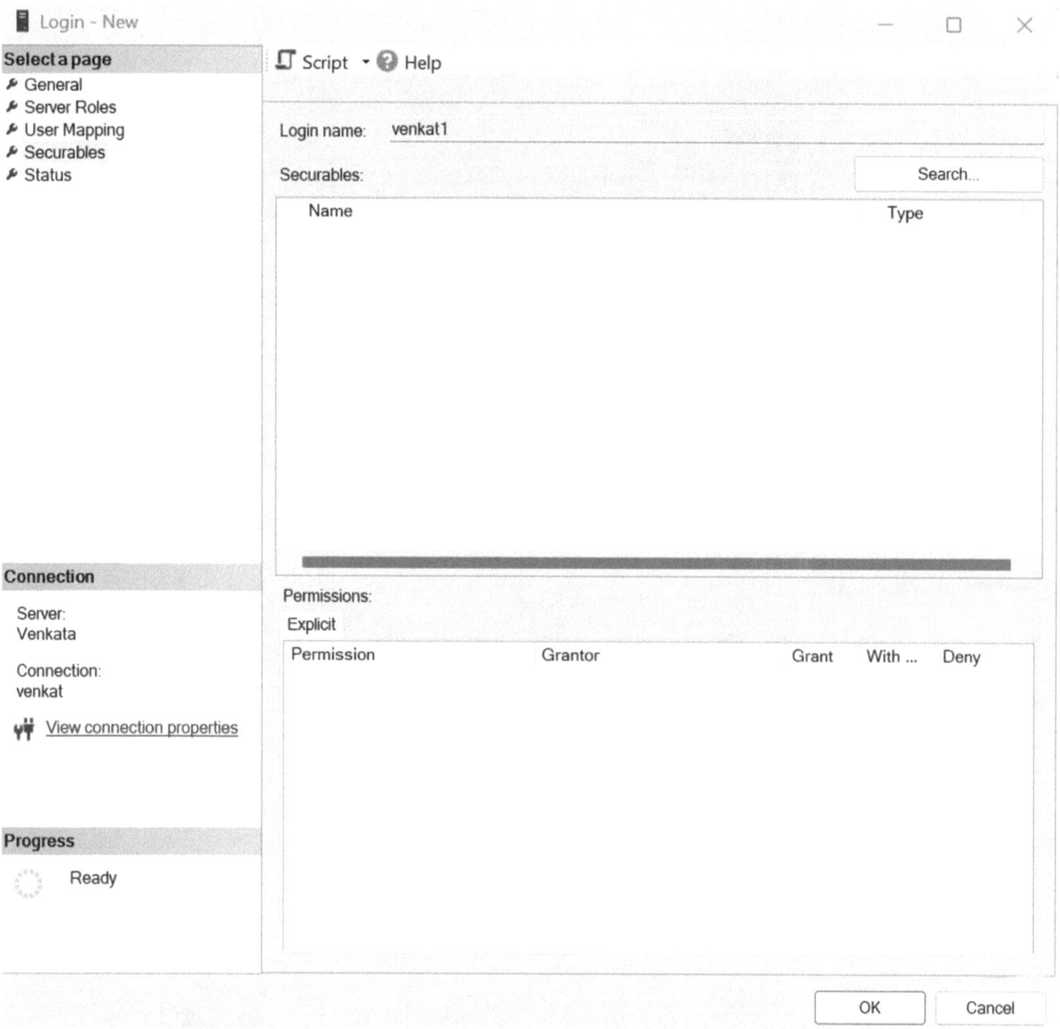

Login - New
Select a page
General
Server Roles
User Mapping
Securables
Status
Script   Help
Login name: venkat1
Securables: Search...
Name   Type
Connection
Permissions:
Explicit
Permission   Grantor   Grant   With ...   Deny
Server:
Venkata
Connection:
venkat
View connection properties
Progress
Ready
OK   Cancel

Figure 4-7. *Securables tab showing login permissions in SSMS*

Next, navigate to the Status tab, select the Grant option for permission to connect to the database engine, and enable the login, as illustrated below.

As shown in Figure 4-8, the Status tab displays options to grant or deny login access to the SQL Server database engine.

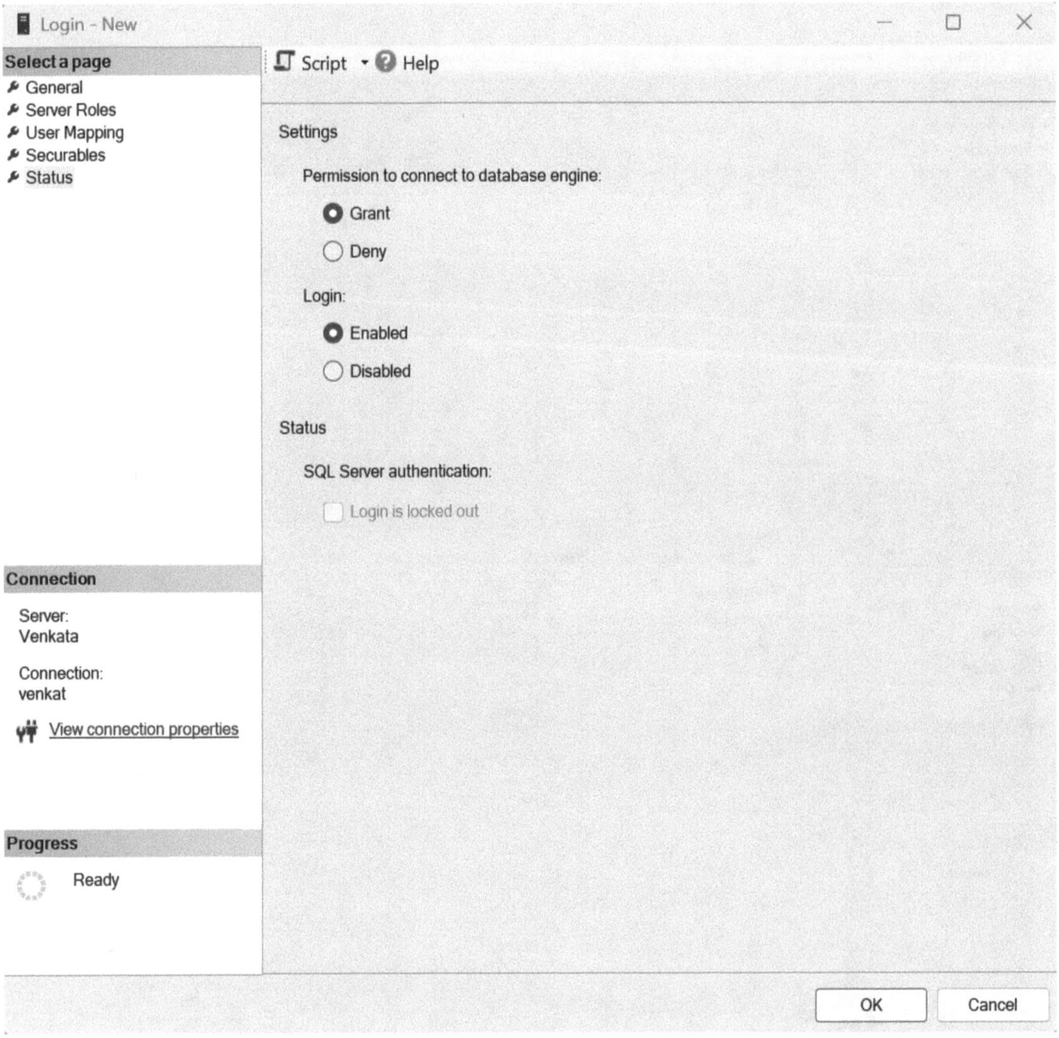

Figure 4-8. *"Status"*

Click "OK" to finalize the login creation. A new login will be added to the resultant Logins node.

In this way, you can add your local Windows user account to access the database server using Windows authentication.

Advantages

> **Enhanced Security**: Windows authentication mode integrates with Active Directory, allowing centralized user management and enforcing strong password policies, account lockout, and other security measures.

Single Sign-On (SSO): Allows users to authenticate once. By connecting to their Windows domain, users can access SQL Server without entering extra credentials, enhancing convenience and minimizing the risk of password reuse.

Centralized Management: User accounts and permissions are handled through Active Directory, streamlining user management and lowering the chances of errors within SQL Server.

Strong Authentication Protocols: Windows authentication uses Kerberos, NTLM, or both, offering stronger security than SQL Server authentication.

Audit and Monitoring: Integration with Windows Event Logs allows for better tracking of user activities, improving monitoring and compliance capabilities.

Reduced Attack Surface: Eliminating the need for SQL Server-specific credentials minimizes the attack surface by avoiding weak or hardcoded passwords commonly associated with SQL Server authentication.

Disadvantages

Dependency on Active Directory: Operation requires an Active Directory domain, which can be a limitation in standalone environments or non-Windows-based infrastructures.

Limited Cross-Platform Support: Windows authentication may not be ideal for applications or users outside the Windows environment, as they may lack integration with Active Directory.

Complexity in Mixed Environments: Configuring Windows authentication can be challenging when users or applications need to connect from non-domain or external networks.

Scalability Issues: Handling a high volume of users. Active Directory may introduce complexity if not structured properly, especially in organizations with extensive group policies and permissions.

Dependency on Windows Security: Windows or Active Directory vulnerabilities could compromise the authentication process, making the entire system susceptible.

Not Ideal for Public-Facing Applications: Windows authentication is less suitable for applications accessed by external users, such as web apps with a wide variety of users who do not belong to the domain.

SQL Server Authentication

This section will teach you how to create a login using a SQL Server user.

If you choose Mixed Mode authentication during SQL Server installation, you must set a password for the built-in System Administrator (sa) account. Create a secure password for the SA account; otherwise, consider deactivating it. Since this account is linked to the sysadmin server role and has full administrative privileges over the server, it can be a potential target for hackers.

Creating a New Login with SQL Server Authentication

A login created with SQL Server authentication operates independently of Windows user accounts. The username and password are among the login credentials. They are stored in the sys login table within the master database, and the passwords are not in straightforward text.

To establish a fresh login with SQL Server authentication, adhere to these steps:

Open SQL Server Management Studio. In the Object Explorer, expand the "Security" node, right-click on the "Logins" node, and select "New Login."

As shown in Figure 4-9, SQL Server Management Studio (SSMS) Object Explorer displays the server structure and the Logins folder under the Security section.

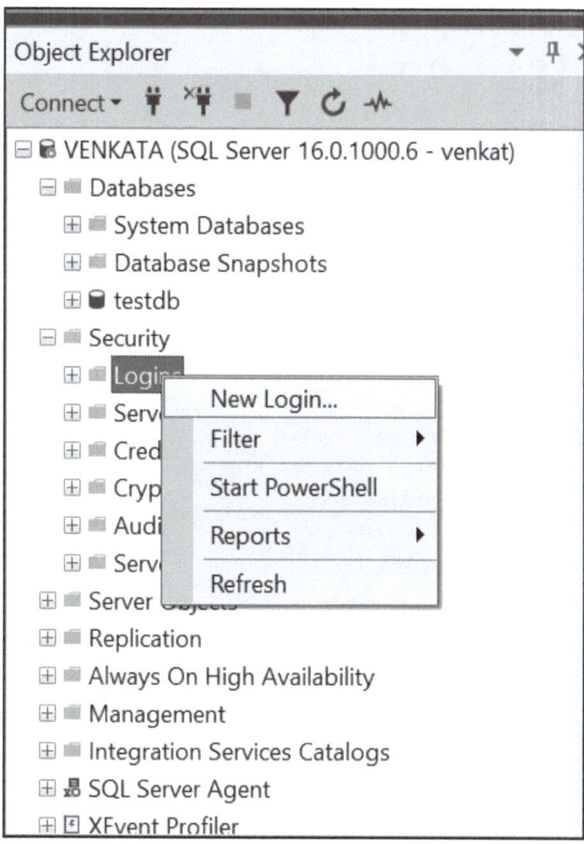

Figure 4-9. *SQL Server Management Studio (SSMS)*

In the "Login – New" window, enter a new username. Select the "SQL Server authentication" option, set a password, then enter it again to verify it in the "Confirm password" field.

There are three optional password policies you can apply:

Enforce Password Policy: Enforces Windows password policies on SQL Server logins.

Enforce Password Expiration: Enforces the computer's maximum password age policy.

Users Must Update Their Password Upon the Next Login: This mandates them to change their password the next time they log in.

As shown in Figure 4-10, the General tab of the Login – New window is used to configure login authentication and credential settings in SQL Server Management Studio (SSMS).

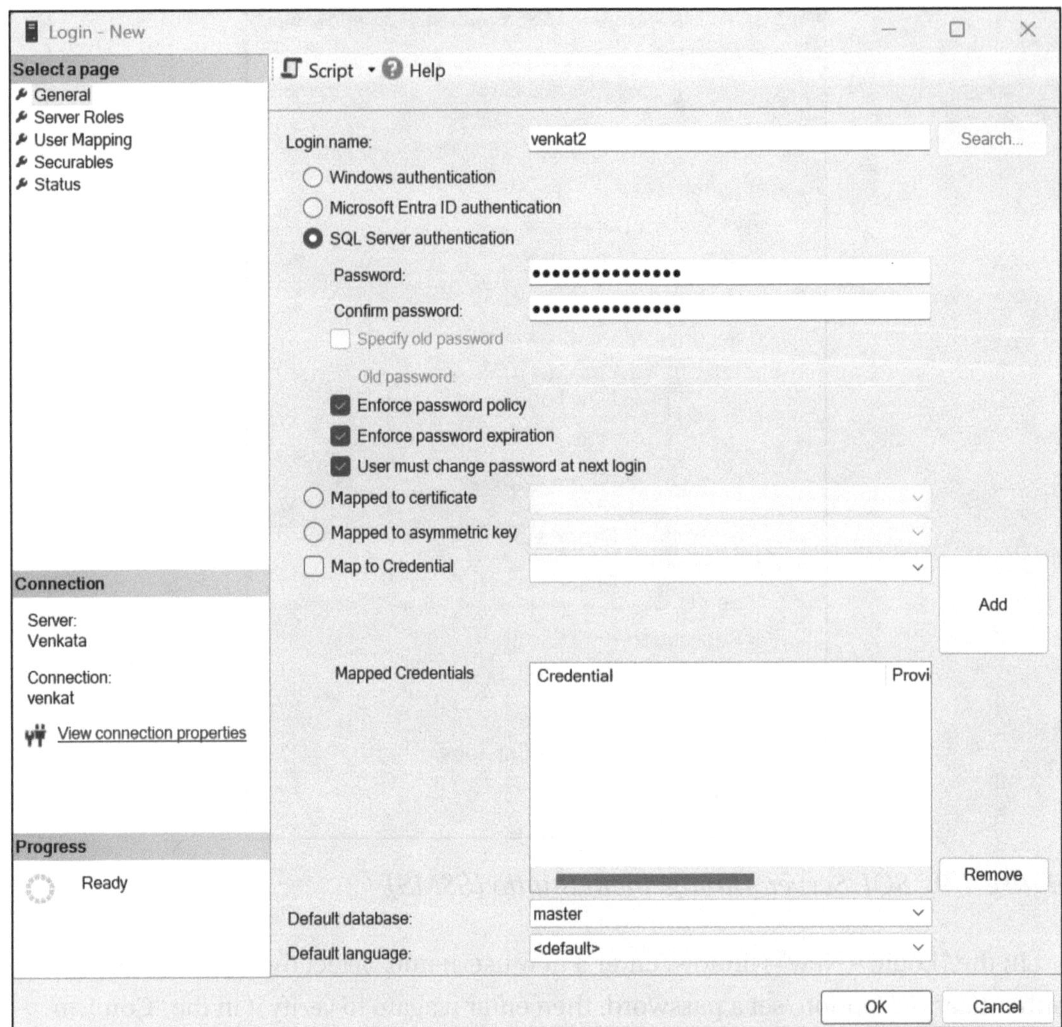

Figure 4-10. *General tab of the Login – New window in SSMS*

Select the "Server Roles" tab. In the new window, assign a server-level role to the login. By default, "public" is selected. You can add roles by selecting the checkbox next to the desired role. For example, selecting the "sysadmin" role will give the user complete control and the ability to perform any activity on the server.

As shown in Figure 4-11, the Server Roles tab displays the available roles that can be assigned to a SQL Server login.

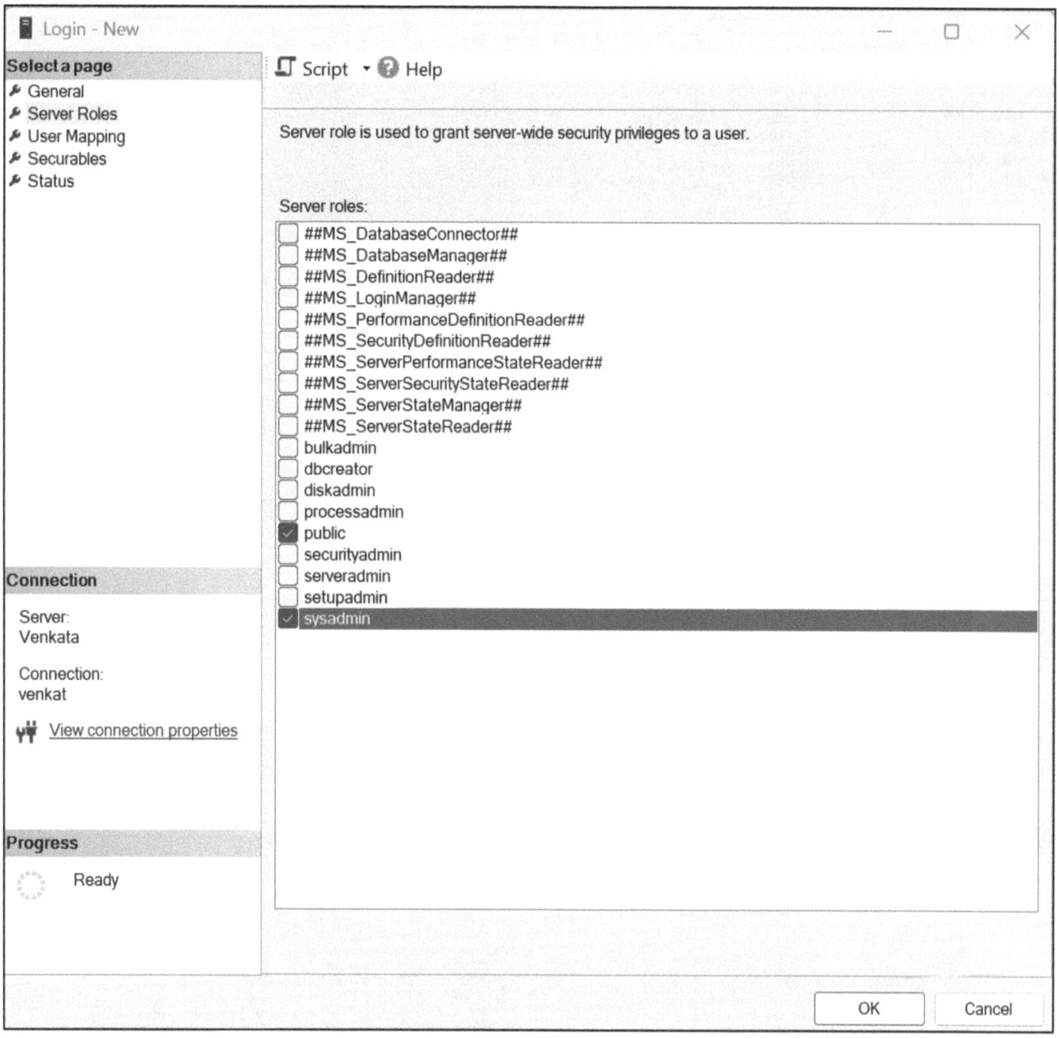

Figure 4-11. *Login SQL Server*

Click on the "User Mapping" tab. Here, you can associate the new login with a database. The window will show a list of all databases on the server instance. Select the checkbox next to the database(s) to map the login to a database. The login name will appear next to the chosen database(s).

As shown in Figure 4-12, the User Mapping tab displays the databases that the login can access in SQL Server Management Studio (SSMS).

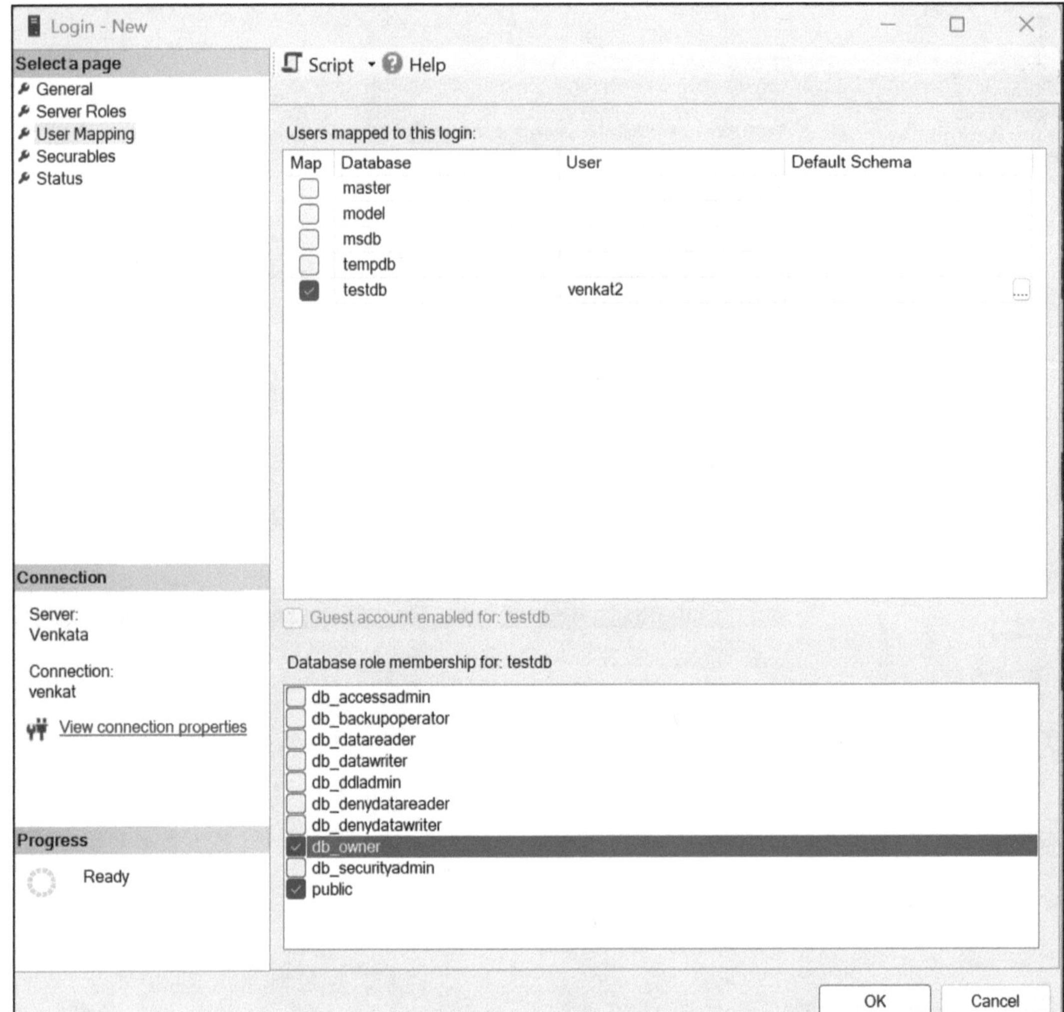

Figure 4-12. *User Mapping tab showing database access in SSMS*

Click on the "Securable" tab. In this window, click the "Search" button, choose "The Server <Your Server Name>," and click "OK." This step is optional and can be skipped. Permissions can be set at a later time.

As shown in Figure 4-13, the Status tab displays the login permission settings where Grant and Enabled options are selected in SQL Server Management Studio (SSMS).

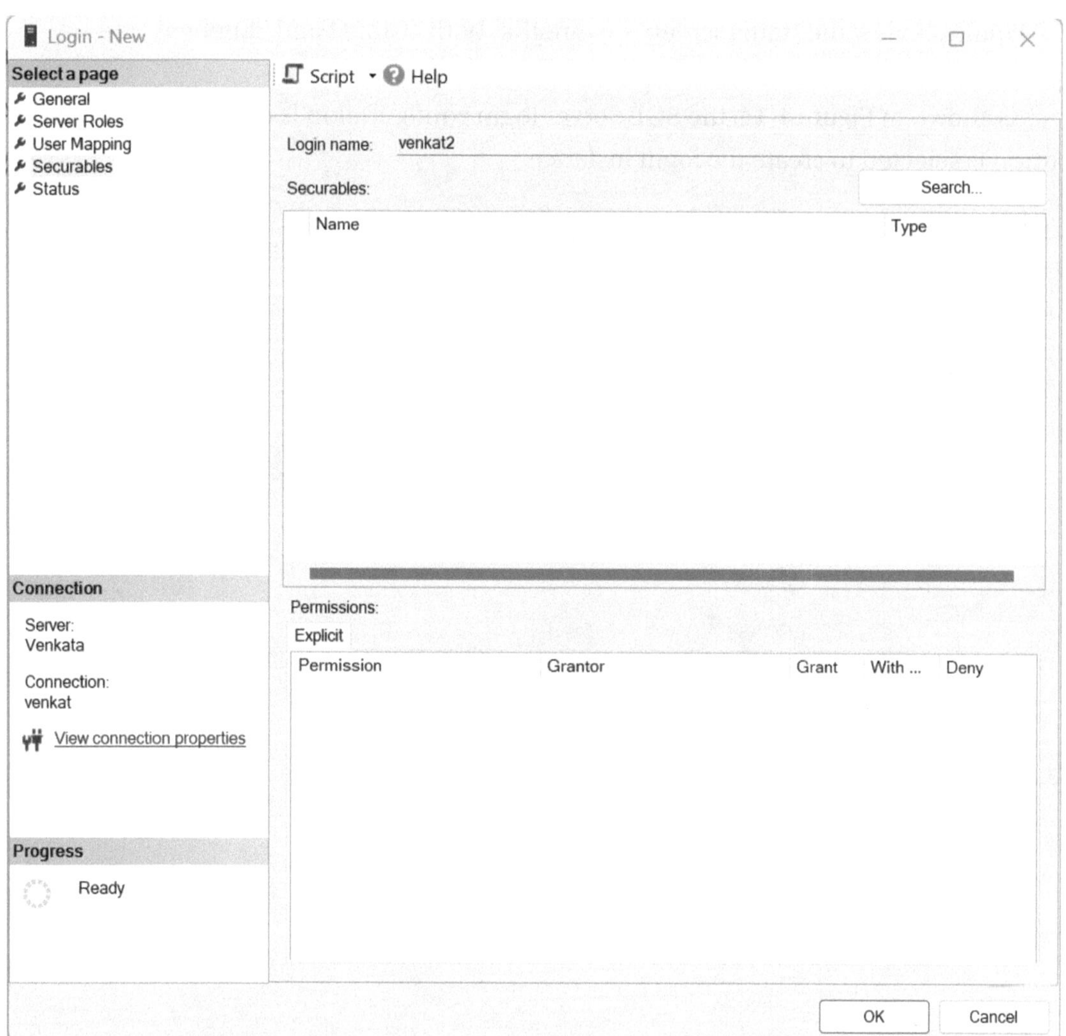

Figure 4-13. *"Grant" and "Enabled" are selected*

Finally, review the status screen. Ensure that both "Grant" and "Enabled" are selected.

As shown in Figure 4-14, the SQL Server login configuration is completed and the OK button is selected to create the login instance.

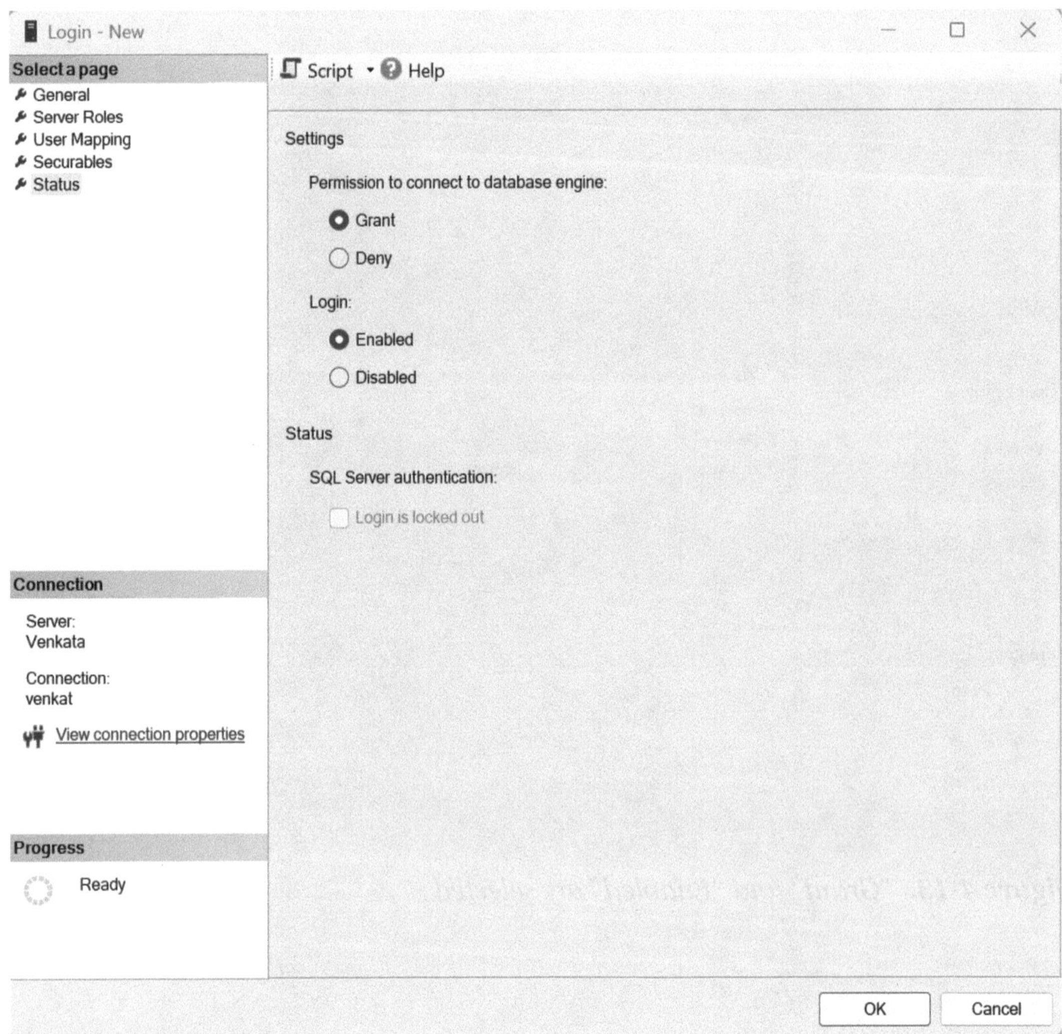

Figure 4-14. SQL Server instance login, click "OK"

To create a new SQL Server instance login, click "OK." The new login will be added to the "Logins" node in SQL Server Management Studio.

As shown in Figure 4-15, SQL Server Management Studio (SSMS) Object Explorer displays the server structure, databases, and available login accounts.

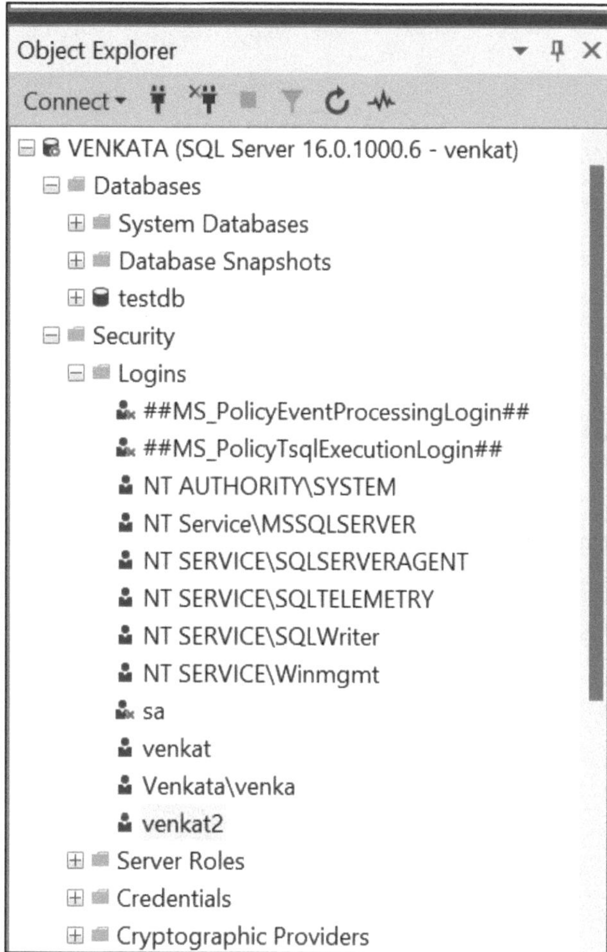

Figure 4-15. *SQL Server Management Studio*

You can now use this new login to access SSMS.

As shown in Figure 4-16, the Connect to Server dialog box in SQL Server Management Studio (SSMS) is used to connect to the database engine using SQL Server Authentication.

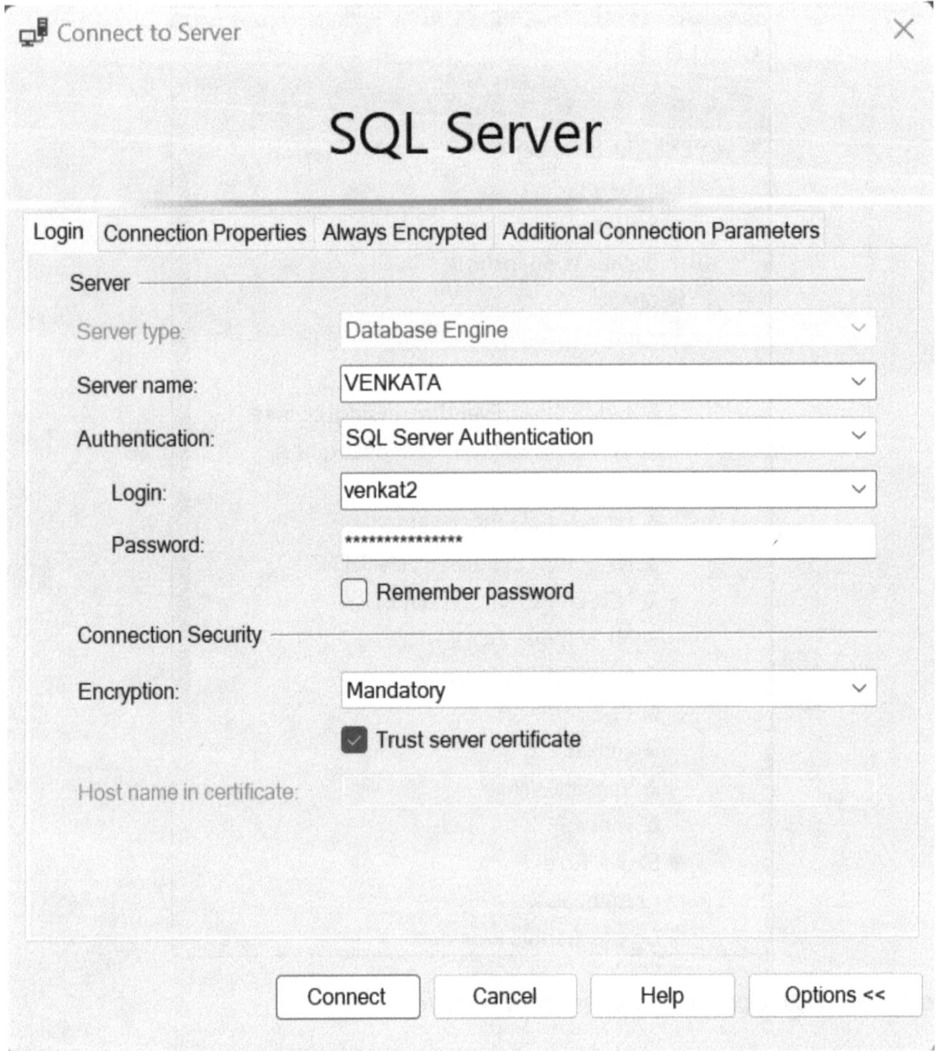

Figure 4-16. *Connect to server*

Advantages of SQL Server Authentication:

Supports older applications and those built on mixed operating systems.

Allows access to web-based applications where users can create their own identities.

Enables connections from unknown domains.

Disadvantages of SQL Server Authentication:

Users must provide an additional login and password when using Windows authentication.

SQL Server authentication does not support the Kerberos security protocol.

SQL Server logins lack the additional password policies available in Windows.

Login credentials are transmitted over the network during database server connection, posing a potential security risk despite encryption.

Some applications store the encrypted password on the client side, providing an additional layer of security.

Vulnerability.

Creating Logins in SQL Server Using T-SQL

1. **Create a Windows Authentication Login**

   Windows authentication uses Active Directory credentials to log into SQL Server. To create a login using Windows authentication:

   Syntax:

   T-SQL

   ```
   CREATE LOGIN [Domain\UserName] FROM WINDOWS;
   ```

   Example:

   T-SQL

   ```
   CREATE LOGIN [CORP\JohnDoe] FROM WINDOWS;
   ```

   This creates a Windows login for the user JohnDoe in the domain CORP.

   Permissions can then be assigned at the server or database level.

2. **Create a SQL Server Authentication Login**

   Passwords and usernames are needed for SQL Server authentication. To create such a login:

   Syntax:

   T-SQL

   ```
   CREATE LOGIN [LoginName]
   WITH PASSWORD = 'YourSecurePassword';
   ```

Example:

T-SQL

```
CREATE LOGIN [TestLogin]
WITH PASSWORD = 'StrongP@ssw0rd!';
```

This creates a SQL Server login named TestLogin with the
password StrongP@ssw0rd!.

Assigning the Login to a Database User

After creating a login, you must map it to a database user to provide access to specific
databases.

Example:

T-SQL

```
USE [YourDatabase];
CREATE USER [TestLoginUser] FOR LOGIN [TestLogin];
```

This creates a database user, TestLoginUser, mapped to the TestLogin.

Granting Permissions

Assign specific permissions to the user based on requirements.

Grant Database Role Membership:

T-SQL

```
EXEC sp_addrolemember 'db_datareader', 'TestLoginUser';
EXEC sp_addrolemember 'db_datawriter', 'TestLoginUser';
```

This assigns the db_datareader and db_datawriter roles to the TestLoginUser.

Grant Explicit Permissions:

T-SQL

```
GRANT SELECT ON [YourTable] TO [TestLoginUser];
GRANT INSERT ON [YourTable] TO [TestLoginUser];
```

This grants SELECT and INSERT permissions on a specific table.

Database-Level Roles in SQL Server

In SQL Server, **database-level roles** are predefined and user-defined collections of
permissions that simplify the management of user access within a database. They allow

administrators to assign a set of permissions to users or groups without having to grant individual permissions explicitly.

Built-In Database Roles

SQL Server provides several built-in database roles, each with specific permissions tailored to everyday tasks. These roles are database-specific and exist in every database. Here are the built-in database roles.

As shown in Figure 4-17, the built-in database roles available in SQL Server are displayed, including roles such as db_owner, db_datareader, and public.

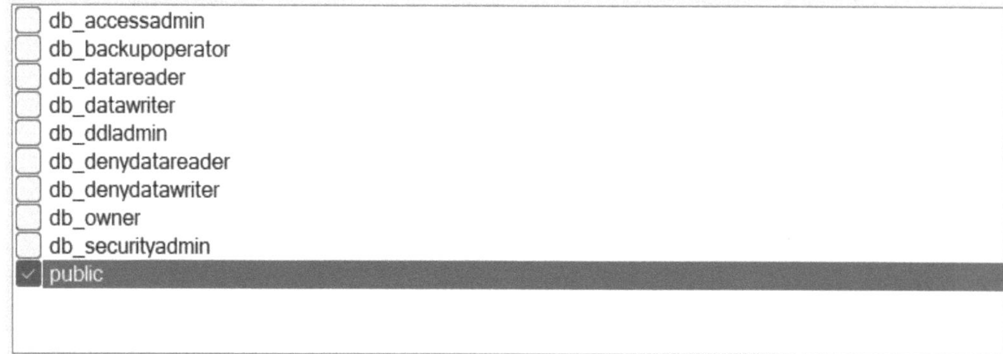

Figure 4-17. *Built-in database roles*

Fixed Database Roles in SQL Server

Fixed database roles come with predefined permissions that cannot be changed. They provide **essential security management** and **access control** for various database operations.

Role	Description
db_owner	Full control over the database.
db_securityadmin	Manages security policies, users, and roles.
db_accessadmin	Controls database user access.
db_backupoperator	Grants permission to back up the database.
db_ddladmin	Allows executing **DDL commands** (CREATE, ALTER, DROP).
db_datawriter	Grants permission to insert, update, and delete data.
db_datareader	Allows read-only access to tables.
db_denydatawriter	Prevents users from modifying data.
db_denydatareader	It prevents users from reading data.

1. **db_owner (Database Owner Role)**

   Members of this role have **complete control** over the database.

   Can **create, alter, and drop** database objects.

   It can **manage permissions, back up, restore**, and even drop the database.

   It should be **assigned cautiously** to prevent unauthorized actions.

   Example: Granting db_owner role to a user

   SQL

   ```
   ALTER ROLE db_owner ADD MEMBER JohnDoe;
   ```

   Use Case:

   Used for **administrators** managing the database.

   It is best suited for **DBAs or senior developers** who need
   full access.

2. **db_securityadmin (Security Administrator Role)**

   Manage **security policies** inside the database.

   They can **modify permissions for users and roles** but **cannot grant themselves higher access**.

   Example: Adding a user to the db_securityadmin role

   SQL

   ```
   ALTER ROLE db_securityadmin ADD MEMBER JaneDoe;
   ```

   Use Case:

   It is ideal for **security teams** managing database access.

   Helps in **auditing and compliance enforcement**.

3. **db_accessadmin (Database Access Administrator)**

   Controls **who can access the database**.

   Can **add or remove database users** but cannot modify objects.

   Example: Granting access to a new user

SQL

```
ALTER ROLE db_accessadmin ADD MEMBER TestUser;
```

Use Case:

Suitable for **user management teams** controlling access.

Used in **organizations where database access must be regulated**.

4. **db_backupoperator (Backup Operator)**

Grants permission to **back up the database** but **not restore it**.

Cannot modify tables, views, or other objects.

Example: Assigning backup permission

SQL

```
ALTER ROLE db_backupoperator ADD MEMBER BackupUser;
```

Use Case:

Ideal for **database maintenance teams** handling scheduled backups.

Ensures **separation of duties** between backup and restore tasks.

5. **db_ddladmin (DDL Administrator Role)**

- Can execute DDL operations such as **CREATE**, **ALTER**, and **DROP** on database objects.

- Cannot grant permissions, assign roles, or manage security configurations.

- **Privilege Elevation Note:** Although db_ddladmin does not provide direct security-management rights, it can be used for indirect privilege escalation. A user may create or alter stored procedures, functions, or views that run under elevated ownership chains, potentially accessing objects they otherwise wouldn't. Because of this, the role should be assigned only to trusted users and monitored carefully.

Example: Granting db_ddladmin role

SQL

```
ALTER ROLE db_ddladmin ADD MEMBER DevUser;
```

Use Case:

Best for **developers** managing schema changes.

Used in environments where **developers need control over table structures but not security.**

6. **db_datawriter (Data Writer Role)**

   allowed to add, edit, and remove data from tables.

   Cannot **read data or modify schema.**

   Example: Assigning data writer permissions

   SQL

   ```
   ALTER ROLE db_datawriter ADD MEMBER AnalystUser;
   ```

   Use Case:

   Ideal for **ETL developers, application services**, and **data entry teams.**

   Ensures **data modifications without exposing schema changes.**

7. **db_datareader (Data Reader Role)**

   Grants **read-only** access to tables and views.

   Cannot modify, insert, or delete data.

   Example: Granting read-only access

   SQL

   ```
   ALTER ROLE db_datareader ADD MEMBER ReportUser;
   ```

   Use Case:

   Best for **business analysts, reporting teams, and auditors.**

   Useful when **users need query access but should not alter data.**

8. **db_denydatawriter (Deny Data Writer Role)**

   - Explicitly **prevents users from inserting, updating, or deleting** records.

   Example: Denying data modifications

   SQL

   ```
   ALTER ROLE db_denydatawriter ADD MEMBER ReadOnlyUser;
   ```

   Use Case:

   - Ideal for users who should never modify data but may have other permissions.

   - Used in **compliance-sensitive environments**.

9. **db_denydatareader (Deny Data Reader Role)**

   - Explicitly **prevents users from reading data** from tables and views.

   Example: Preventing data reads

   SQL

   ```
   ALTER ROLE db_denydatareader ADD MEMBER RestrictedUser;
   ```

   Use Case:

   - Suitable for users who should not access sensitive data.

   - Used in cases where **access needs to be explicitly blocked**.

Server-Level Roles

Server-level roles manage access and permissions at the server level. They apply to the entire instance of SQL Server.

As shown in Figure 4-18, the server fixed roles in SQL Server are displayed, including roles such as sysadmin, securityadmin, and serveradmin.

> bulkadmin
> dbcreator
> diskadmin
> processadmin
> public
> securityadmin
> serveradmin
> setupadmin
> sysadmin

Figure 4-18. *Server fixed server roles*

Understanding SQL Server Fixed Server Roles

SQL Server provides **fixed server roles** to manage administrative tasks at the **server level**. These roles help delegate responsibilities while ensuring security and efficiency in database management.

List of fixed server roles

Server Role	Purpose
Sysadmin	Complete control over SQL Server.
server admin	Manages server settings and configurations.
security admin	Controls login security and permissions.
process admin	Manages system processes and queries.
setup admin	Configures linked servers and sets up tasks.
disk admin	Handles disk space management for databases.
Dbcreator	Can create, modify, and drop databases.
bulk admin	Can perform bulk data imports.
Public	The default role is assigned to all logins.

1. **sysadmin (System Administrator Role)**

   - Has **unrestricted access** to SQL Server.

   - Can **manage all server configurations, databases, and logins**.

   - Members of this role **bypass all security restrictions**.

Use Case:

- Assigned to **database administrators (DBAs)** who manage the entire SQL Server instance.

- Used in **emergencies** where full access is required for troubleshooting.

SQL

```
ALTER SERVER ROLE sysadmin ADD MEMBER DBAUser;
```

2. **server admin (Server Administrator Role)**

- Manages **server-wide settings**, including configurations and shutdowns.

- Can **change system-level options** and **restart the SQL Server instance**.

Use Case:

- Suitable for **IT administrators** who need access to **server configuration settings**.

SQL

```
ALTER SERVER ROLE server admin ADD MEMBER ITAdmin;
```

3. **security admin (Security Administrator Role)**

- Controls **server-level security policies**.

- Can **create, modify, or delete logins and server permissions**.

- They cannot **grant themselves higher privileges like a sysadmin**.

Use Case:

- Used by **security teams** to **enforce access control policies**.

- Ensures that **only authorized users gain database access**.

SQL

```
ALTER SERVER ROLE security admin ADD MEMBER SecurityUser;
```

4. **process admin (Process Administrator Role)**

- Manages **server processes and queries**.

- Can **terminate sessions that cause performance issues**.

Use Case:

- Helps **DBAs monitor system performance**.

- **It helps resolve deadlocks and kill long-running queries**.

SQL

```
ALTER SERVER ROLE process admin ADD MEMBER PerformanceUser;
```

5. **setup admin (Setup Administrator Role)**

- Manages **linked servers** and other setup configurations.

- Can **install and configure server-wide settings**.

Use Case:

- It is best for **system administrators** who manage **distributed database environments**.

SQL

```
ALTER SERVER ROLE setup admin ADD MEMBER SetupUser;
```

6. **disk admin (Disk Administrator Role)**

Manages **disk-related tasks** within SQL Server.

Can **allocate storage and configure database file locations**.

Use Case:

Assigned to **storage management teams** handling **database files**.

SQL

```
ALTER SERVER ROLE disk admin ADD MEMBER StorageUser;
```

7. **dbcreator (Database Creator Role)**

   Can **create, alter, drop, and restore databases**.

   Cannot **manage server-wide security or configurations**.

   Use Case:

   Used by **application teams and developers** who need **database management access**.

   SQL

   ```
   ALTER SERVER ROLE dbcreator ADD MEMBER DevTeamUser;
   ```

8. **bulk admin (Bulk Data Administrator Role)**

   Can **import large amounts of data using BULK INSERT operations**.

   Cannot **modify schema or manage security**.

   Use Case:

   Best for **ETL developers and data migration teams** handling **bulk data loads**.

   SQL

   ```
   ALTER SERVER ROLE bulk admin ADD MEMBER ETLUser;
   ```

9. **public (Default Role for All Users)**

   Every login in SQL Server is automatically assigned the **public** role.

   The **permissions assigned to the public apply to all users** unless overridden by another role.

   Use Case:

   Used to define **default access for all users** in a SQL Server environment.

Transparent Data Encryption (TDE)

Transparent Data Encryption (TDE) in SQL Server: A Comprehensive Guide

Overview

Ensuring data security is a fundamental component of database management, and SQL Server provides several features to ensure data protection. **Transparent Data Encryption (TDE)** is one feature that encrypts data at rest. This blog post explores TDE, its benefits, the setup process, and how to manage it in an Always On Availability Group.

What Is Transparent Data Encryption (TDE)?

TDE is a feature in SQL Server that encrypts the entire database, including data files, log files, and backups. It ensures that data at rest remains protected from unauthorized access. Introduced in SQL Server 2008, TDE was initially an **Enterprise Edition** feature but became available in **Standard Edition** starting from SQL Server 2019.

Key Features of TDE:

1. Encrypts the entire database, including log files and backups.

2. Uses a hierarchical encryption model.

3. Transparent to applications and users.

4. Minimal performance overhead.

5. Helps meet compliance requirements.

6. Compatible with SQL Server's high availability features.

Setting Up TDE in SQL Server

Below is a step-by-step guide to configuring TDE on a database and ensuring its security.

The DMK protects certificates and symmetric keys stored in the master database.

When creating it, SQL Server requires:

Step 1: Create a Database Master Key

The **Database Master Key (DMK)** is the root of the encryption hierarchy and is stored in the **master database**.

```
USE master;
GO
CREATE MASTER KEY ENCRYPTION BY PASSWORD = 'YourStrongPasswordHere';
GO
```

Explanation: What Does "ENCRYPTION BY PASSWORD" Mean?

- SQL Server stores the DMK encrypted two ways:

  By the service master key (SMK) for automatic opening

  By the password you specify as a backup method

- The password does not need to be used every day.

- It provides an extra layer of protection if the DMK ever needs to be restored manually.

```
-- Verify the creation
SELECT * FROM sys.symmetric_keys;
```

Step 2: Create a Certificate Protected by the DMK

TDE uses a certificate stored in the master database. The DMK automatically encrypts the certificate's private key.

TDE uses a **certificate** to encrypt the database encryption key.

```
CREATE CERTIFICATE TDECertificate
WITH SUBJECT = 'TDE Certificate',
EXPIRY_DATE = '2100-12-31';
GO
-- Verify the certificate
SELECT name, pvt_key_encryption_type_desc, issuer_name, subject, expiry_
date FROM sys.certificates WHERE name = 'TDECertificate';
```

Explanation: How the Certificate Is Protected

- The certificate's private key is encrypted using the DMK.

- When SQL Server starts, it can automatically decrypt the certificate because the DMK is automatically opened by the SMK.

- This allows SQL Server to decrypt the database encryption key (DEK) when needed.

Step 3: Create the Database Encryption Key (DEK)

The **database encryption key (DEK)** is a symmetric key to encrypt database contents.

```
USE AdventureWorks;
GO
CREATE DATABASE ENCRYPTION KEY
WITH ALGORITHM = AES_256
ENCRYPTION BY SERVER CERTIFICATE TDECertificate;
GO
```

Explanation: What Happens Here.

- The DEK is generated inside the database.

- SQL Server encrypts that DEK using the certificate created in Step 2.

- This means the certificate must always be available to open the database.

Step 4: Enable TDE on the Database

Once the encryption key is created, enable TDE on the database.

```
ALTER DATABASE AdventureWorks SET ENCRYPTION ON;
GO
```

Step 5: Verify Encryption Status

Monitor the encryption process with the following query:

```
SELECT db.name, DB.is_encrypted, dm.encryption_state, dm.percent_complete,
dm.key_algorithm, dm.key_length
FROM sys. databases db
LEFT JOIN sys.dm_database_encryption_keys dm
ON db.database_id = dm.database_id;
```

Setting Up TDE for Databases in an Availability Group

For databases in an **Always On Availability Group**, follow these additional steps on **secondary replicas**:

Step 1: Back Up the Certificate

```
BACKUP CERTIFICATE TDECertificate
TO FILE = 'C:\Temp\TDECertificate.cer'
WITH PRIVATE KEY (FILE = 'C:\Temp\TDECertificate.pvk',
ENCRYPTION BY PASSWORD = 'YourStrongPasswordHere');
GO
```

Step 2: Copy the Certificate to Secondary Replicas

Manually copy the .cer and .pvk files to all secondary replicas.

Step 3: Create the Master Key on Secondary Replicas

```
USE master;
GO
CREATE MASTER KEY ENCRYPTION
BY PASSWORD = 'YourStrongPasswordHere';
GO
```

Note   The certificate cannot be restored unless a DMK already exists.

Step 4: Restore the Certificate on Secondary Replicas

```
USE master;
GO
CREATE CERTIFICATE TDECertificate
FROM FILE = 'C:\Temp\TDECertificate.cer'
WITH PRIVATE KEY (FILE = 'C:\Temp\TDECertificate.pvk',
DECRYPTION BY PASSWORD = 'YourStrongPasswordHere');
GO
```

Step 5: Enable TDE on the Database

```
ALTER DATABASE AdventureWorks SET ENCRYPTION ON;
GO
```

Removing TDE from a Database

To disable TDE, follow these steps:

```
ALTER DATABASE AdventureWorks SET ENCRYPTION OFF;
GO
```

Backing Up and Restoring a TDE-Encrypted Database

Step 1: Back Up the Encrypted Database

```
BACKUP DATABASE AdventureWorks TO DISK = 'C:\Temp\AdventureWorks_
Encrypted.bak';
```

Step 2: Restore on Another Server

Before restoring, ensure the certificate is present. If missing, import it using the .cer and .pvk files. Then restore:

```
RESTORE DATABASE AdventureWorks FROM DISK = 'C:\Temp\AdventureWorks_
Encrypted.bak'
WITH MOVE 'AdventureWorks_Data' TO 'C:\Temp\AdventureWorks_Data.mdf',
MOVE 'AdventureWorks_Log' TO 'C:\Temp\AdventureWorks_Log.ldf',
REPLACE;
```

Conclusion

Transparent Data Encryption (TDE) is a powerful feature in SQL Server that ensures **data-at-rest protection** with minimal performance impact. Implementing TDE correctly, especially in **high-availability environments**, requires careful planning, including managing **certificates and encryption keys**. Following these steps, you can secure your databases while complying with data protection regulations.

Always Encrypted

Introduction

Organizations have serious concerns about data security.

Handling sensitive information such as personally identifiable data, financial records, or healthcare data. Microsoft SQL Server provides Always Encrypted, a robust feature intended to prevent unwanted access to sensitive data by encrypting it at the column level. Unlike Transparent Data Encryption (TDE), which secures data at rest, Always Encrypted ensures that data remains encrypted at rest and in transit, even from database administrators.

This article provides a comprehensive guide to Always Encrypted in SQL Server, including its key benefits and step-by-step implementation.

How Always Encrypted Works

Always Encrypted leverages client-side encryption, meaning the encryption and decryption processes occur outside the SQL Server environment. The client application handles cryptographic operations using an Always Encrypted-enabled driver rather than the database engine.

It employs a key hierarchy that includes:

1. **Column Encryption Key (CEK)**: Encrypts the data within the column.

2. **Column Master Key (CMK)**: This key protects the CEK and is stored externally, such as in Azure Key Vault, Windows Certificate Store, or Hardware Security Modules (HSMs).

This separation ensures that even database administrators (DBAs) cannot directly access or decrypt sensitive data without encryption keys.

Benefits of Always Encrypted

1. **Improved Data Security**: Prevents unwanted access to private information by keeping it encrypted throughout storage and transmission.

2. **Separation of Roles**: Ensures database administrators and system operators do not have direct access to plaintext data.

3. **Minimal Performance Overhead**: Since encryption and decryption occur on the client side, the database engine does not experience a significant load.

4. **Regulatory Compliance**: Helps organizations meet compliance requirements such as GDPR, HIPAA, PCI-DSS, and others.

5. It supports multiple key stores and can integrate with secure external key management solutions, such as Azure Key Vault or HSMs.

Always Encrypted vs. Transparent Data Encryption (TDE)

Feature	Always Encrypted	Transparent Data Encryption (TDE)
Scope	Column-level encryption	Database-level encryption
Encryption Method	Client-side	Server-side
Protects Data At Rest?	Yes	Yes
Protects Data In Transit?	Yes	No
Prevents DBA Access?	Yes	No
Performance Impact	Low (client-side)	Moderate (database-side)

Always Encrypted is ideal for securing sensitive data at the column level, whereas TDE primarily focuses on encrypting the entire database at rest.

Implementing Always Encrypted in SQL Server

Step 1: Configure the Column Master Key (CMK)

The CMK protects the column encryption keys. It is stored externally in a keystore such as the Windows Certificate Store or Azure Key Vault.

```
CREATE COLUMN MASTER KEY CMK_Example WITH ( KEY_STORE_PROVIDER_
NAME = 'MSSQL_CERTIFICATE_STORE', KEY_PATH = 'CurrentUser/My/
ABC12345ABCDE1234567890ABCDE1234567890' );
```

Explanation

- KEY_STORE_PROVIDER_NAME tells SQL Server which external store contains the key.

- KEY_PATH is the certificate thumbprint (Windows Certificate Store in this example).

- The CMK itself is not stored in SQL Server, only its pointer is.

Step 2: Create the Column Encryption Key (CEK)

SQL Server encrypts the CEK automatically using the CMK.

```
CREATE COLUMN ENCRYPTION KEY CEK_Example WITH VALUES ( COLUMN_MASTER_KEY =
CMK_Example, ALGORITHM = 'RSA_OAEP' );
```

Step 3: Encrypt a Column in a Table

Modify an existing column or create a new table with encrypted columns.

```
CREATE TABLE Customers
CustomerID INT PRIMARY KEY,
SSN VARBINARY(100) COLLATE Latin1_General_BIN2 ENCRYPTED WITH (
COLUMN_ENCRYPTION_KEY = CEK_Example,
ENCRYPTION_TYPE = RANDOMIZED,
ALGORITHM = 'AEAD_AES_256_CBC_HMAC_SHA_256' );
```

Explanation

- Randomized encryption gives the strongest protection (no pattern detection).

- The CEK now encrypts the column data.

Step 4: Configure the Client Application

Ensure the client application uses an Always Encrypted-enabled driver (e.g., .NET Framework 4.6+ or JDBC with Always Encrypted support).

```
SqlConnectionconn = new SqlConnection("Data Source=server;Initial
Catalog=database;Integrated Security=True; Column Encryption
Setting=Enabled");
```

Step 5: Query Encrypted Data

To query encrypted columns, the client application must include the Column Encryption Setting in the connection string.

```
SELECT CustomerID, SSN FROM Customers;
```

If configured correctly, SQL Server will return the decrypted data to the authorized client application.

Limitations of Always Encrypted

1. **Limited Operations on Encrypted Data**: Only equality comparisons (=) work with deterministic encryption. Other operations (e.g., LIKE, ><, SUM) are not supported.

2. **Indexing Restrictions**: Encrypted columns cannot be used in indexed searches unless deterministic encryption is enabled.

3. **Application Dependency**: The client side's encryption and decryption processes require compatible drivers and configurations.

4. **Increased Storage Requirements**: Encrypted values require more storage than plaintext values.

5. **Limited ALTER Operations**: Modifying an encrypted column's encryption type or keys requires dropping and recreating the column.

Best Practices for Always Encrypted

1. **Use Deterministic Encryption for Indexing**: If searching or filtering on encrypted data is required, choose deterministic encryption.

2. **Secure Column Master Keys (CMK)**: Store CMKs in Azure Key Vault or HSMs for better security.

3. **Use Secure Application Connections**: Enable TLS/SSL for additional security when transmitting encrypted data.

4. **Test Performance Impact**: Always Encrypted can affect performance due to increased client-side processing.

5. **Periodically Rotate Encryption Keys**: Refresh CEKs and CMKs regularly to improve security.

Conclusion

Always Encrypted is a robust feature in SQL Server that guarantees sensitive data stays encrypted throughout its lifecycle. Encrypting data at the column level and ensuring decryption only occurs on authorized client applications provides enhanced security and helps meet compliance requirements.

Organizations handling sensitive data should combine Always Encrypted with other security features, such as TDE, TLS, and row-level security (RLS), to build a robust data protection strategy.

Row-Level Security (RLS)

Understanding Row-Level Security (RLS) in SQL Server

Introduction

Securing sensitive information is a top priority in modern database systems. Row-level security (RLS) in SQL Server allows administrators to manage access to table rows according to the user's identity or role. This feature helps enforce fine-grained security at the data level without requiring application changes.

Introduced in SQL Server 2016, RLS enables organizations to restrict access dynamically and transparently, ensuring users can only see data relevant to them.

How Row-Level Security Works

RLS uses security predicates (filter predicates and block predicates) that control access to rows based on specific conditions.

1. **Security Predicates**

   Filter predicates define which rows a user can access in SELECT and DELETE operations. Unauthorized rows are automatically filtered out.

   Block predicates prevent unauthorized INSERT, UPDATE, or DELETE operations, ensuring users cannot modify or delete rows they should not access.

   These predicates are applied via inline table-valued functions (TVFs) that determine the access rules dynamically.

Benefits of Row-Level Security

Centralized Access Control: Security policies are defined at the database level rather than in the application, reducing complexity.

Improved Data Security: This feature ensures that users can only view the data they can view, preventing unauthorized data exposure.

Seamless Implementation: Since RLS is managed within SQL Server, applications remain unchanged.

Minimal Performance Impact: RLS operates efficiently using indexed views, maintaining query performance.

Regulatory Compliance: Enforcing access policies at the database level helps organizations comply with GDPR, HIPAA, and other data privacy regulations.

Implementing Row-Level Security in SQL Server

Step 1: Create a User Table with Access Control

Create a sample table where access will be restricted based on user roles.

SQL

```
CREATE TABLE EmployeeRecords (
    EmployeeID INT PRIMARY KEY,
    EmployeeName NVARCHAR(100),
    Department NVARCHAR(50),
    ManagerName NVARCHAR(100)
);
```

Step 2: Create a Security Predicate Function

Define a function that filters rows based on the user's role.

SQL

```
CREATE FUNCTION dbo.fn_RLS_FilterPredicate(@ManagerName NVARCHAR(100))
RETURNS TABLE
WITH SCHEMABINDING
 AS
 RETURN SELECT 1 AS AccessResult
WHERE @ManagerName = USER_NAME();
```

Explanation:

- USER_NAME() returns the name of the SQL user executing the query.

- Because your test users are named "Alice" and "Bob," this aligns correctly.

Step 3: Create a Security Policy

Apply the filter predicate to enforce row-level access.

SQL

```
CREATE SECURITY POLICY EmployeeRLS_Policy
ADD FILTER PREDICATE dbo.fn_RLS_FilterPredicate(ManagerName)
ON dbo.EmployeeRecords
WITH (STATE = ON);
```

This ensures users only access rows where their user name matches the ManagerName.

Testing Row-Level Security

To verify the implementation, create test users and check their access:

SQL

```
CREATE USER Alice WITHOUT LOGIN;
CREATE USER Bob WITHOUT LOGIN;

EXECUTE AS USER = 'Alice';
SELECT * FROM EmployeeRecords;
REVERT;
```

```
EXECUTE AS USER = 'Bob';
SELECT * FROM EmployeeRecords;
REVERT;
```

Users will only see records assigned to their respective roles.

Modifying and Removing RLS Policies

To Disable RLS:

SQL

```
ALTER SECURITY POLICY EmployeeRLS_Policy
WITH (STATE = OFF);
```

To Remove RLS:

SQL

```
DROP SECURITY POLICY EmployeeRLS_Policy;
DROP FUNCTION dbo.fn_RLS_FilterPredicate;
```

Best Practices for Using RLS

Use RLS in combination with other security features like Always Encrypted and Transparent Data Encryption (TDE) for complete data protection.

Minimize performance impact by ensuring the filter function is efficient and indexes are used effectively.

Consistently review access controls to verify adherence to security policies.

Test RLS implementations thoroughly before deployment to avoid unintended access restrictions.

Conclusion

Row-level security (RLS) in SQL Server is a powerful feature that enhances data protection and access control by restricting visibility at the row level. With centralized security policies, minimal performance overhead, and regulatory compliance benefits, RLS is essential for organizations handling sensitive and classified data.

This chapter has explored essential security measures for SQL Server, starting with Windows authentication, a fundamental aspect of secure access control. We then examined server-level roles, delving into the importance of appropriate user permissions for maintaining least privilege and adhering to compliance requirements. We investigated the value of transparent data encryption (TDE) and Always Encrypted technologies, which provide robust encryption at rest and in use, thus safeguarding sensitive data. Finally, the chapter discussed row-level security (RLS), which allows for dynamic and fine-grained control over data access based on user context. The core takeaway is that a multi-layered approach, combining authentication methods, access control roles, various encryption techniques, and data-specific security measures like RLS, is paramount to establishing a comprehensive security posture for SQL Server databases, ensuring confidentiality, integrity, and adherence to regulatory standards.

CHAPTER 5

Advanced SQL Server Upgrades and Migrations

This chapter delves into the intricate world of advanced SQL Server upgrades and migrations, moving beyond simple installations to explore strategies and considerations crucial for modern database environments. In today's dynamic technological landscape, databases need to be not only reliable but also adaptable to changing business needs. This chapter will guide you through crucial planning, execution, and post-migration steps involved in advanced SQL Server scenarios. We also consider how built-in security capabilities like always encrypted and row-level security factor into upgrade and migration planning. We will then explore a variety of upgrade approaches, from side-by-side methodologies to in-place upgrades, evaluating the pros and cons of each. We will also analyze migration strategies from on-premises environments to Azure Cloud, considering the benefits and trade-offs for each. Finally, we will focus on SQL Server to Babelfish for Aurora PostgreSQL migrations and all that it entails. Ultimately, this chapter will equip you with the knowledge and tools to ensure successful, secure, and efficient database upgrades and migrations.

Migration in SQL Server refers to transferring databases from one environment to another. This could involve moving databases between servers, migrating to newer versions of SQL Server, switching to different database platforms, or transitioning to cloud-based solutions. The primary goals of migration are to ensure better performance, scalability, cost efficiency, or compliance with organizational requirements.

Types of SQL Server Migrations

Side-by-Side and In-Place Upgrade Strategies

This involves setting up a new SQL Server environment alongside the existing one. Once the new environment is ready, databases, configurations, and applications are migrated.

© Venkata Reddy Pasam and Petchikumar Andiappan 2026

V. R. Pasam and P. Andiappan, *The Expert's Guide to SQL Server*, https://doi.org/10.1007/979-8-8688-2451-7_5

As shown in Figure 5-1, side-by-side and in-place strategies are used for upgrading SQL Server during the migration process.

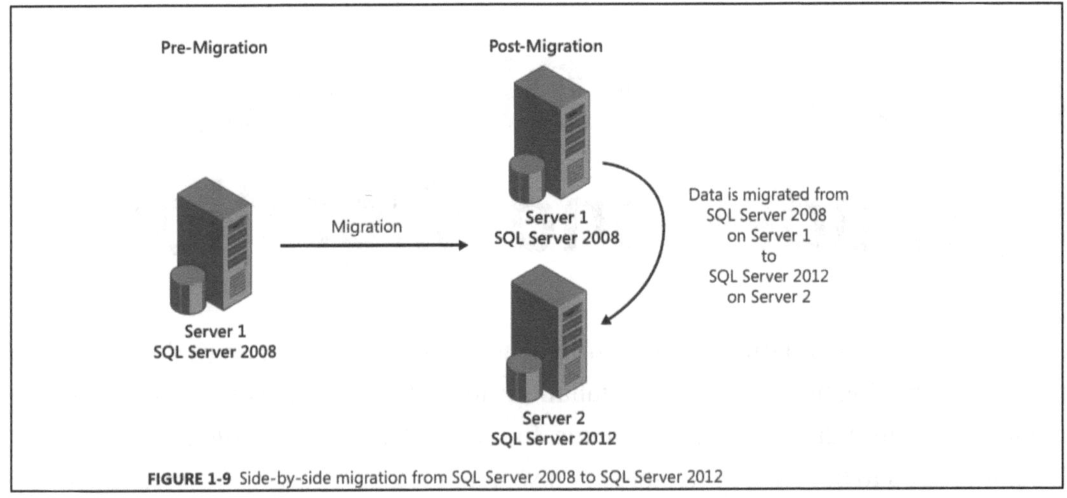

FIGURE 1-9 Side-by-side migration from SQL Server 2008 to SQL Server 2012

Figure 5-1. *Side-by-side and in-place upgrade strategies*

Key Features:

Ideal for major version upgrades.

There is minimal risk to the existing environment, as the old server remains intact during migration.

Ensures minimal downtime if appropriately planned.

Steps for Side-by-Side Migration:

Pre-Migration Steps:

> **Assess the Environment:** The first step in a database migration is to assess the environment and gather information about the current database and its application dependencies, along with any possible risks or problems during migration.

> **Choose the New SQL Server Version:** Determine the version of the SQL Server to which the database will be migrated. It's essential to check the compatibility of the existing database with the new version.

> **Arrange the Migration:** Create a migration plan that details the required actions and timelines for the migration process. Considerations include data backup strategy, application downtime, and testing procedures.

Back Up the Existing Database: Before initiating the migration, creating a full backup of the existing database is essential to ensure that data is not lost during the process.

Turn Off Any Constraints or Triggers: Disable any constraints or triggers that may interfere with the migration process.

Prepare the New SQL Server: Configure the latest SQL Server, including security settings, compatibility level, server-level settings, and any other necessary configurations.

Migration Steps:

1. **Migrate the Database Schema**: Move the database schema from the old SQL Server to the new SQL Server. This includes tables, views, stored procedures, and other database objects.

2. **Migrate the Data**: Once the database schema has been migrated, the next step is to migrate the data. This can be done using various tools such as SQL Server Integration Services (SSIS), database backup restore, log shipping, availability groups, or third-party migration tools.

3. **Test the Migrated Database**: After migrating the database, it's essential to test it to ensure that data has been migrated correctly and that all functionality is working as expected.

Post-migration Steps:

1. **Enable Constraints and Triggers**: Once the database has been successfully migrated and tested, enable any constraints or triggers that were previously disabled.

2. **Update Application Connection Strings**: Update any application connection strings to point to the new SQL Server.

3. **Decommission the Old SQL Server**: Once the new SQL Server is operational and the migrated database is verified, decommission the old SQL Server.

4. **Monitor and Maintain the New SQL Server**: Monitor the latest SQL Server to ensure that it performs as expected and perform regular maintenance tasks such as backups and index maintenance.

In summary, migrating a database from an old SQL Server to a new version involves several steps, including assessing the environment, planning the migration, backing up the existing database, migrating the database schema and data, testing the migrated database, enabling constraints and triggers, updating application connection strings, decommissioning the old SQL Server, and monitoring and maintaining the new SQL Server. Adequate preparation, testing, and observation ensure a successful database migration.

In-Place Upgradation

Here's a comprehensive guide for **In-Place Upgradation** in SQL Server covering the requested topics.

Key Features:

Same Hardware: Upgrades the existing SQL Server instance on the same hardware.

Cost-Effective: No need to procure additional servers or resources.

Quick Setup: Faster than side-by-side migration, as no data transfer is needed.

Risk of Downtime: The entire process requires planned downtime since the existing instance is updated.

Steps for In-Place Upgradation

1. **Pre-Migration Steps:**

    1. **Assess the Existing Environment:**
       Run the SQL Server Data Migration Assistant (DMA) to identify potential compatibility issues.

       Review the SQL Server version, edition, and service pack level using

       ```
       SELECT @@VERSION;
       ```

       Check database compatibility levels and features that may be deprecated or discontinued.

2. **Backup All Data:**

   Take full backups of all user and system databases (master, msdb, model).

   Perform transaction log backups for point-in-time recovery. Validate the backup files by restoring them in a test environment.

3. **Verify Pre-requisites:**

   Ensure that the operating system and hardware meet the requirements of the target SQL Server version.

   Download the latest SQL Server installation media and cumulative updates.

4. **Notify Stakeholders:**

   Communicate the planned downtime to stakeholders and get approval for the maintenance window.

5. **Stop Dependent Applications:**

   Shut down all applications or services using the SQL Server instance to prevent data changes during the upgrade.

2. **Migration Steps:**

   1. **Launch SQL Server Installation Wizard:**

      Start the SQL Server setup executable and **select the option to upgrade from an earlier version of SQL Server.**

   2. **Select Instance to Upgrade:**

      Choose the existing SQL Server instance that you want to upgrade.

   3. **Feature Selection:**

      Ensure that the required features and services are selected for the upgrade.

      Review any warnings or errors in the **Upgrade Rules** step.

4. **Perform Upgrade:**

Allow the installer to complete the in-place upgrade process.

Monitor progress for any interruptions or failures.

5. **Install Latest Updates:**

Once the upgrade is complete, install the latest cumulative updates and service packs for the target SQL Server version.

3. **Post-Migration Steps:**

1. **Verify the Upgrade:**

Confirm the SQL Server version and edition using:

SQL

Copy code

```
SELECT @@VERSION;
```

2. **Test Application Connectivity:**

Verify that applications can connect to the upgraded instance and function as expected.

3. **Validate Databases:**

Check the status of all databases and ensure they are accessible.

Update the compatibility level of databases if necessary:

SQL

```
ALTER DATABASE [DatabaseName] SET COMPATIBILITY_LEVEL =
[TargetLevel];
```

4. **Reconfigure SQL Server Settings:**

Review and reapply custom server-level and database-level configurations (e.g., MAXDOP and memory settings).

5. **Monitor Performance:**

Track CPU, memory, and disk utilization to detect and resolve post-upgrade performance issues.

6. **Document Changes:**

   Record all changes made during the upgrade process for future reference.

7. **Notify Stakeholders:**

   Inform stakeholders that the upgrade is complete and share relevant details or next steps.

Steps for Side-by-Side Migration (For Comparison)

If needed, the previous response outlines steps for side-by-side migration in detail. It focuses on setting up a new environment and migrating data to it while keeping the old instance intact as a fallback.

The plan outlines straightforward and actionable steps for performing an in-place upgrade of SQL Server. Feel free to ask if you need more details or scripts for specific tasks!

Migrating from On-Premises to Azure Cloud

Migrating SQL Server databases from an on-premises setup to Microsoft Azure can be challenging. However, with careful preparation and implementation, it can be achieved seamlessly. This guide offers a systematic method to guarantee a smooth transition while maintaining data accuracy and enhancing performance in the cloud.

Step 1: Assess Your Existing SQL Server Environment

Before initiating the migration process, a thorough assessment of the current SQL Server environment is essential. This involves:

Evaluating Database Size and Complexity:

Identify the total size of databases, tables, and indexes.

Assess stored procedures, triggers, functions, and complex queries.

Analyzing Dependencies:

Determine any interdependencies between databases.

Identify linked servers, external integrations, and application dependencies.

Assess the impact of the migration on data-driven applications.

Performing a Compatibility Check:

Use tools like the Azure Data Migration Assistant (DMA) to analyze compatibility issues.

Check for unsupported SQL Server features in Azure SQL Database or Azure SQL Managed Instance.

Determine whether schema modifications are required for a successful migration.

Step 2: Select the Right Migration Strategy

Choosing an appropriate migration method is critical for ensuring minimal downtime and a seamless transition. The following options are commonly used:

Azure Database Migration Service (DMS):

A fully managed tool that simplifies large-scale migrations.

Supports online (minimal downtime) and offline (longer downtime) migration methods.

Azure Data Migration Assistant (DMA):

It is ideal for assessing compatibility and migrating smaller databases.

Provides recommendations for schema adjustments.

SQL Server Integration Services (SSIS):

Suitable for organizations using ETL (Extract, Transform, Load) processes.

Allows customization for complex data transformations.

Backup and Restore Method:

It involves creating a full database backup and restoring it in Azure.

Recommended for noncritical databases where downtime is acceptable.

Step 3: Prepare for Migration

Preparation is crucial to prevent unexpected issues during migration. Key steps include:

Performing Full and Incremental Backups:

Take a full backup of all databases to ensure data is not lost.

Implement log backups to capture changes made after the full backup.

Setting Up an Azure Subscription:

Create an Azure account if not already available.

Configure necessary resources like Azure SQL Database, managed instance, or virtual machines.

Configuring Network and Security Settings:

Set up virtual network (VNet) and firewall rules for secure database connections.

Ensure that authentication and role-based access control (RBAC) are correctly configured.

Step 4: Execute the Migration

After thorough preparation, the migration process can be executed using one of the chosen methods:

Using Azure DMS:

Set up a migration project in the Azure portal.

Select the source SQL Server and destination Azure SQL instance.

Choose an online or offline migration mode based on downtime requirements.

Using Data Migration Assistant (DMA):

Run a pre-migration assessment.

Fix any identified schema or compatibility issues.

Use the migration wizard to transfer data efficiently.

Using SSIS for Advanced Data Transfers:

Develop SSIS packages to extract and load data into Azure.

Apply necessary transformations during the data transfer process.

Step 5: Validate the Migration

Once the migration is complete, validation is essential to ensure data integrity and application compatibility:

Data Integrity Checks:

Compare row counts between the source and destination databases.

Verify schema, indexes, constraints, and stored procedures.

Application Testing:

Conduct functional testing to ensure applications interact correctly with the Azure database.

Run performance tests to compare query execution times and optimize where necessary.

Step 6: Optimize and Secure the Azure Environment

Post-migration, optimizing, and securing the database ensures long-term efficiency and protection.

Performance Optimization:

Rebuild indexes and update statistics to enhance query performance.

Monitor resource utilization and adjust performance tiers accordingly.

Use Azure SQL database's built-in performance recommendations to improve efficiency.

Security Best Practices:

Implement Azure Defender for SQL to detect potential security threats.

Enable transparent data encryption (TDE) for data protection.

Set up firewall rules, access control lists (ACLs), and multi-factor authentication (MFA) to enhance security.

Configure Azure Monitor and Alerts for proactive database monitoring.

Conclusion

Migrating SQL Server databases to Azure can significantly enhance scalability, performance, and security while reducing infrastructure costs. By following a structured migration approach that assesses the current environment, selects the right strategy, effectively prepares, executes the migration, validates results, and optimizes security, you can guarantee a smooth cloud migration. Azure provides a robust platform for managing SQL workloads efficiently, enabling businesses to leverage cloud-native benefits seamlessly.

SQL Server to Babelfish for Aurora PostgreSQL

Comprehensive Guide to Migrating SQL Server to Babelfish for Aurora PostgreSQL

Migrating from SQL Server to Amazon Aurora PostgreSQL using Babelfish can be transformative. It enables cost savings and enhanced scalability while maintaining SQL Server compatibility. This guide outlines a structured approach to ensure a seamless migration process.

Step 1: Assess Your SQL Server Environment

Before initiating the migration, a thorough evaluation of the existing SQL Server setup is crucial. This assessment includes:

Database Size and Structure:

Determine the size and complexity of databases.

Identify tables, indexes, views, and stored procedures that need to be migrated.

Feature Compatibility:

Use **Babelfish Compass** to analyze SQL Server feature compatibility with Babelfish.

Identify any unsupported features and determine alternatives.

Application Dependencies:

Assess connections between SQL Server and external applications.

Ensure that linked servers, triggers, and functions align with Babelfish's capabilities.

Step 2: Choose the Right Migration Strategy

Selecting the appropriate migration method is essential to ensure efficiency and minimize downtime. Options include:

Babelfish Compass for Pre-Migration Analysis:

Runs compatibility checks and identifies necessary modifications before migration.

AWS Database Migration Service (DMS):

Facilitates schema and data migration with minimal downtime.

Supports full load and ongoing replication for a smooth transition.

Manual Migration:

Best suited for smaller databases or scenarios requiring extensive customization.

It involves exporting and modifying schema, then loading data manually.

Step 3: Prepare for Migration

Proper preparation prevents migration failures and minimizes risks. Key steps include:

Schema Conversion:

Adjust the SQL Server schema to align with Babelfish-supported features.

Modify data types and constraints where necessary.

Database Backup and Testing:

Create complete backups of SQL Server databases.

Set up a test environment in Babelfish to validate schema compatibility.

Network and Security Configuration:

Configure **Amazon RDS for Aurora PostgreSQL with Babelfish**.

Set up security groups, IAM roles, and firewall rules for access control.

Step 4: Execute the Migration

With preparations complete, the migration process can be carried out using one of the selected methods:

Using AWS DMS:

Set up a replication instance.

Define source (SQL Server) and target (Babelfish) endpoints.

Choose full load or ongoing replication for minimal downtime.

Using Manual Export and Import:

Export the SQL Server schema and transform it for Babelfish.

Load schema and migrate data using tools such as **pgloader** or **native PostgreSQL commands**.

Step 5: Validate Migration and Optimize Performance

After migration, validation ensures data integrity and application functionality:

Data Integrity Checks:

Compare row counts and table structures between SQL Server and Babelfish.

Validate stored procedures and functions for correct execution.

Application Testing:

Test application connections and query performance.

Optimize indexes and queries to enhance performance.

Step 6: Secure and Optimize Babelfish Environment

Post-migration, focus on optimizing and securing the database for efficient operation:

Performance Tuning:

Adjust indexes and partitioning for PostgreSQL optimization.

Monitor query execution plans and optimize where necessary.

Security Best Practices:

Implement role-based access control (RBAC).

Enable encryption and auditing for data protection.

Set up monitoring and alerting for database health.

Conclusion

Migrating from SQL Server to Babelfish for Aurora PostgreSQL provides flexibility and cost-efficiency while retaining compatibility with SQL Server-based applications. By following a structured approach—assessing the environment, selecting the proper migration method, preparing effectively, executing the migration, validating results, and optimizing security—you can promote a seamless shift to the AWS cloud while leveraging the power of PostgreSQL.

This chapter has provided a detailed overview of advanced SQL Server upgrade and migration strategies, moving beyond simple installations. It began by examining side-by-side and in-place upgrade strategies, assessing their suitability based on different scenarios and environments. The chapter then explored the complexities of migrating SQL Server databases to cloud platforms, including on-premises to Azure Cloud migrations, which require careful planning for network configuration and data migration. Finally, it tackled a more complex migration scenario: transitioning from SQL Server to Babelfish for Aurora PostgreSQL, offering a comprehensive approach to ensure compatibility and functionality during such migrations. The key takeaway is that successful SQL Server upgrades and migrations require a strategic understanding of various options, comprehensive planning, rigorous testing, and the use of appropriate tools and techniques, enabling seamless transitions while minimizing risks and ensuring database continuity.

CHAPTER 6

Clustering

This chapter embarks on an in-depth exploration of SQL Server Clustering, a critical technology for ensuring high availability and resilience in database environments. In today's world, where uninterrupted access to data is crucial, clustering stands out as a key solution. This chapter will guide you through the essential aspects of understanding, implementing, and managing SQL Server clusters. We will begin by establishing a fundamental understanding of the architecture of SQL Server clusters, including the underlying concepts of failover clustering. We will then delve into the various components of a SQL Server cluster, exploring how these components work in harmony to provide continuous availability. Further, we will analyze the advantages and benefits that a cluster can provide, as well as the various types of cluster models that are available. We will then examine SQL Server cluster scenarios and look at testing SQL Server 2019 failover clusters. Finally, we will explore failover methodologies. Ultimately, this chapter is designed to equip you with the knowledge to deploy and maintain reliable and robust SQL Server clusters.

Understanding the Architecture of a SQL Server Cluster

In the world of data management, high availability is of utmost importance. Companies rely on their databases to store and retrieve critical information, and any downtime can result in significant financial losses. One solution to ensure continuous operations is the implementation of a SQL Server cluster architecture.

A SQL Server cluster architecture is a configuration that provides redundancy and failover capabilities for SQL Server instances. By leveraging multiple servers, a cluster guarantees that if one server fails, another can seamlessly assume control. This ensures that database operations can continue uninterrupted.

© Venkata Reddy Pasam and Petchikumar Andiappan 2026
V. R. Pasam and P. Andiappan, *The Expert's Guide to SQL Server*, https://doi.org/10.1007/979-8-8688-2451-7_6

At the heart of a SQL Server cluster is the failover cluster instance (FCI). This virtual server represents the whole cluster rather than individual servers. Clients connect to the FCI, which handles routing requests to the appropriate server within the cluster. This enables clients to access the database without knowing the specific server they are connecting to.

Each server within the cluster, known as a node, has a SQL Server instance installed. These instances are kept in sync using a unified storage solution, like a storage area network (SAN) or a network-attached storage (NAS). This shared storage ensures that data is available to all nodes within the cluster, regardless of which node it resides on.

Components of SQL Server Cluster Architecture?

A SQL Server cluster architecture refers to the configuration and setup of a cluster in Microsoft SQL Server. A cluster is a group of servers connected to act as a single unit, providing provides database operations with high availability and resilience to faults.

Different components and layers in a SQL Server cluster architecture work together to ensure continuous availability of the database. These components include:

> **Clustered Instances:** These are SQL Server instances configured to work together in a cluster. Each instance runs on a separate server, referred to as a node, and they share the same data stored on shared storage.

> **Failover Cluster:** This is the foundational layer of the cluster architecture, providing the infrastructure for the cluster. It manages the node communication and handles the failover process when a node becomes unavailable.

> **Shared Storage:** Shared storage is a key SQL Server cluster architecture component. It is a storage medium, such as a Storage Area Network (SAN), accessible by all the nodes in the cluster. The shared storage holds the database files, such as data files and log files, that are accessed by the clustered instances.

> **Network:** The network layer in a SQL Server cluster architecture connects the nodes and enables communication between them. It ensures that the clustered instances can communicate with each other and with clients or applications that access the database.

Overall, a SQL Server cluster architecture provides high availability and fault tolerance by allowing multiple server instances to work together as a cluster. This ensures that the database remains accessible even if one of the nodes fails, providing a reliable and robust infrastructure for critical business applications.

The Basics of SQL Server Cluster Architecture

The architecture of a SQL Server cluster is essential in upholding fault tolerance and ensuring high availability for an organization's database systems. A cluster is a server group that provides clients with a single, highly available database service. In a SQL Server cluster, multiple server nodes are connected through shared storage, allowing them to share the same database and maintain data consistency.

One crucial component of a SQL Server cluster architecture is the failover cluster instance (FCI). An FCI consists of multiple server nodes configured to provide failover support for each other. If one node fails, another node can continue serving client requests without interruption. This ensures that the database service remains accessible even in the case of hardware or software failures.

Another key element of a SQL Server cluster architecture is shared storage. Shared storage enables all nodes in the cluster to access the same data set, allowing for synchronized updates and ensuring consistency across the cluster. Shared storage can be implemented using storage area networks (SAN) or network-attached storage (NAS).

In addition to the failover cluster instance and shared storage, a SQL Server cluster architecture also includes network connectivity, which enables client applications to access the database and establish a connection with the cluster service. The network architecture should be built to withstand high workloads and ensure stable connectivity between the cluster nodes.

In summary, a SQL Server cluster setup integrates multiple server nodes, shared storage, and network connections to deliver a highly available, fault-tolerant database service. This structure allows organizations to minimize downtime and ensure continuous access to critical data, making it an essential component of a robust database infrastructure.

Components of SQL Server Cluster Architecture

A SQL Server cluster architecture consists of several key components that work together to provide high availability and fault tolerance for database systems. These components include:

Cluster Nodes: Cluster nodes are physical servers or virtual machines participating in the SQL Server cluster. Each node runs an instance of SQL Server and shares the workload of processing database requests.

Quorum Disk: The quorum disk is a shared storage device that maintains cluster coordination and data integrity. It holds the cluster configuration information and helps determine its overall health.

Clustered Shared Volume (CSV): A clustered shared volume is a storage volume shared by all cluster nodes. It allows multiple nodes to read and write data simultaneously, providing high performance and scalability for the cluster.

Failover Cluster Instance (FCI): A failover cluster instance logically represents a SQL Server instance within the cluster. It includes one active node and multiple passive nodes. If a failure occurs, the active node fails over to one of the passive nodes, ensuring continuous database availability.

Windows Server Failover Clustering (WSFC): WSFC is the underlying technology that enables the SQL Server cluster. It provides the infrastructure for managing and monitoring cluster resources, coordinating failover, and ensuring high cluster availability.

Network Shared Storage: In a SQL Server cluster, network shared storage stores database files and other data. It is accessible to all cluster nodes and allows for seamless failover and recovery in case of node or hardware failures.

These components work together to create a highly reliable and scalable architecture for SQL Server clusters. By distributing the workload across multiple nodes and providing automatic failover capabilities, clusters ensure that databases remain available and performant even in the face of hardware or software failures.

How Does SQL Server Cluster Architecture Work?

A SQL Server cluster architecture, also known as a failover cluster, is a configuration that combines several real servers into one logical server. This architecture guarantees high availability and dependability for Microsoft SQL Server, allowing continuous access to databases in the case of software or hardware malfunctions. The main components of a SQL Server cluster architecture include two or more physical servers (nodes), a shared storage subsystem, and a network interconnect. The nodes are connected, and the shared storage through a network works together to provide a highly available cluster. Each node runs an instance of SQL Server, and these instances are configured to failover to another node in the cluster if one node becomes unavailable.

When a SQL Server cluster is set up, the specified active node handles client connections and processes database requests. The other nodes in the cluster are passive, ready to take over the active node's responsibilities if it fails. The passive nodes continuously monitor the active node's status and can quickly assume its role to minimize downtime.

In the event of a failure on the active node, the cluster detects the failure and automatically fails over to one of the passive nodes. This failover process ensures minimal disruption to the client applications connected to the SQL Server cluster. The failover process typically involves transitioning the current active node to a passive role and bringing up the failed node as the new active node.

The shared storage subsystem plays a crucial role in the cluster architecture. It provides a shared storage space accessible to all the cluster nodes. This shared storage allows active and passive nodes to access duplicate database files consistently, ensuring data integrity. In failover, the new active node takes control of the shared storage and continues processing database requests without interruption.

In summary, a SQL Server cluster architecture utilizes multiple physical servers, shared storage, and network connectivity to provide high availability and reliability for SQL Server databases. It allows seamless failover between nodes in the event of failures, ensuring continuous access to databases and minimizing downtime for client applications.

Benefits or Advantages of SQL Server Cluster Architecture

SQL Server cluster architecture offers several benefits and advantages for organizations looking for high availability and scalability in their database infrastructure.

One of the main benefits of fault tolerance is the ability of SQL Server cluster architecture to provide fault tolerance. By deploying SQL Server in a cluster, organizations can ensure that their database remains accessible even in the case of software or hardware malfunctions. The cluster architecture enables automatic failover to a standby node, minimizing downtime and ensuring continuous access to critical data.

> **Scalability:** SQL Server cluster architecture allows organizations to scale their database infrastructure to handle increasing workloads quickly. By adding nodes to the cluster, organizations can spread the workload across several servers, boosting performance and accommodating growing data requirements. This scalability feature ensures the database can meet the organization's evolving needs.

> **Load Balancing:** With SQL Server cluster architecture, organizations can achieve load balancing by distributing the incoming database requests throughout the cluster's numerous nodes. This makes the workload more equally distributed and keeps any one node from becoming overloaded, ensuring optimal performance across the entire cluster.

> **High Availability:** SQL Server cluster architecture provides high availability for organizations by reducing the risk of downtime. In the event of a failure, the cluster automatically detects the issue and fails over to a standby node, minimizing user impact and preventing data loss. This ensures that critical applications relying on the database remain accessible and operational.

> **Cost-Effective:** SQL Server cluster architecture offers a cost-effective solution for businesses seeking high availability and scalability. By utilizing commodity hardware and distributing the workload across multiple nodes, organizations can maximize the utilization of their resources and achieve greater cost efficiency compared to deploying standalone servers.

SQL Server Clustering Modes

Clustering in SQL Server is based on Windows Server Failover Clustering (WSFC) and is used to ensure high availability (HA) and disaster recovery (DR) for SQL Server instances. Below is a detailed explanation of Active-Active and Active-Passive cluster configurations:

1. **Active-Passive Cluster**

   Definition:

   An Active-Passive cluster involves one active node (hosting the SQL Server instance) and one or more passive nodes (idle and waiting to take over in case of failure).

   Only one SQL Server instance is active at a time across the cluster.

   Architecture:

   The SQL Server instance is installed on all nodes but only runs on the active node.

   A shared storage (e.g., SAN or SMB) is used for database files, accessible only by the active node.

   How It Works:

   1. The active node processes all client requests.

   2. Upon failure of the active node, the passive node takes over (failover).

   3. The failover process is automatic and usually takes a few seconds to a few minutes.

   Advantages:

   Simple configuration.

   Complete resources of the passive node are available during failover.

   Easy to manage and maintain.

Disadvantages:

The passive node remains idle during normal operations, leading to underutilization of resources.

Requires shared storage, which can be a single point of failure unless redundantly configured.

Use Case:

Organizations prioritize reliability over resource utilization, where one server can be dedicated for failover purposes.

2. **Active-Active Cluster**

Definition:

An Active-Active cluster involves multiple active nodes, each hosting a SQL Server instance and actively processing workloads simultaneously.

Each node in the cluster hosts its own SQL Server instance, but both share the same cluster resources.

Architecture:

Two or more nodes are active and serve their respective SQL Server instances.

Shared storage is used, and each SQL Server instance uses its own set of database files.

How It Works:

Both (or all) nodes are active, running separate SQL Server instances.

Each instance handles its workloads independently.

If one node fails, its workload is moved to another active node (failover).

Advantages:

Efficient use of server resources since both nodes are active.

Provides load balancing between SQL Server instances.

Reduced hardware underutilization.

Disadvantages:

It is more complex to configure and manage than Active-Passive.

Failover can lead to resource contention if the remaining node(s) become overloaded.

Requires proper resource planning to avoid performance degradation during failover.

Use Case:

Scenarios requiring load balancing between SQL Server instances.

Organizations aiming to maximize server resource utilization while maintaining high availability.

Key Differences: Active-Active vs. Active-Passive

Considerations for Choosing a Cluster Mode

Workload:

For light workloads, Active-Passive is more straightforward and sufficient.

For heavy workloads, Active-Active provides better resource utilization.

Resource Availability:

If resources are limited, Active-Passive may waste hardware capacity.

Active-Active ensures better utilization but needs more planning.

Complexity:

Active-Passive is less complex and easier to troubleshoot.

Active-Active requires more advanced setup and monitoring.

Budget:

Active-Passive may be more cost-effective for small or medium businesses.

Active-Active is suitable for larger enterprises with critical workloads.

Installing a SQL Server 2019 Failover Clustered Instance (FCI)

Follow the steps below to install a default SQL Server 2019 Failover Clustered Instance (FCI). Select a server within the Windows Server Failover Cluster (WSFC) to start the installation.

Run **setup.exe** from the SQL Server 2019 installation media to open the **SQL Server Installation Center**. On the left-hand side, click the **Installation** link.

Choose the new SQL Server failover cluster installation Option to initiate the SQL Server 2019 Setup wizard.

As shown in Figure 6-1, the SQL Server Installation Center provides the option to install a SQL Server 2019 Failover Clustered Instance (FCI).

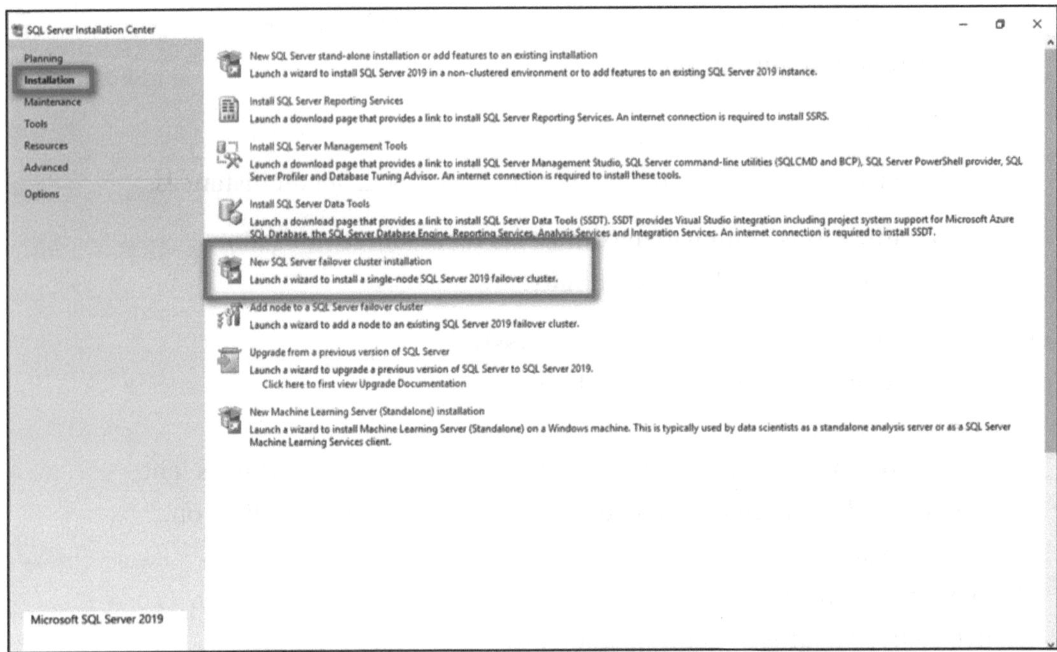

Figure 6-1. *Installing a SQL Server 2019 failover clustered instance (FCI)*

Product Key

1. In the **Product Key** dialog box, enter the product key provided with your installation media, then click **Next**.

As shown in Figure 6-2, the Product Key page is used to enter or select the edition during the SQL Server Failover Cluster installation.

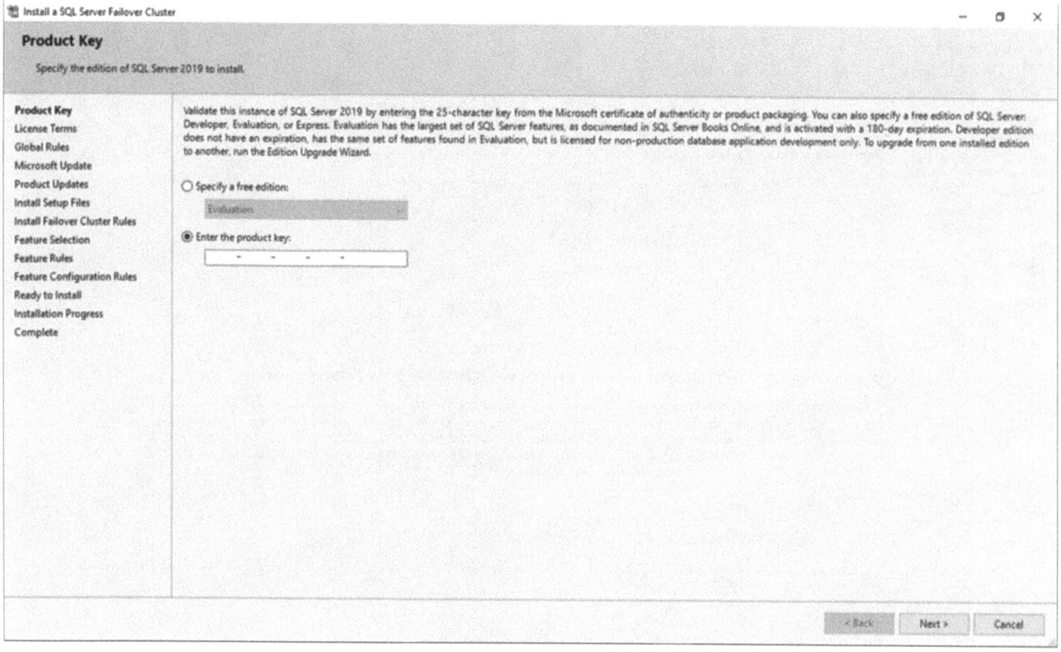

Figure 6-2. *Product key*

License Terms

2.   Select the **"I accept the license terms"** checkbox and click **Next**

As shown in Figure 6-3, the License Terms page requires users to accept the SQL Server license agreement before proceeding with the installation.

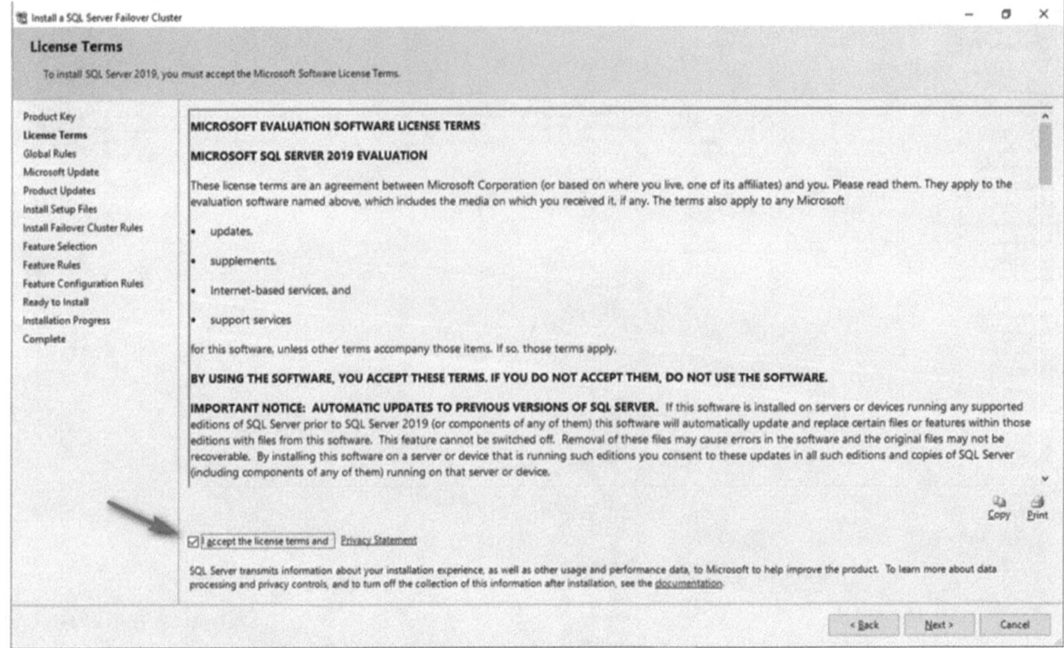

Figure 6-3. *License terms*

3. **In the License Terms dialog box, accept the license terms and click Next** dialog box.

4. Global Rules

5. Ensure all checks pass successfully in the Global Rules dialog box, then click **Next**.

As shown in Figure 6-4, the Global Rules page verifies that all prerequisite checks are passed before continuing with the SQL Server installation.

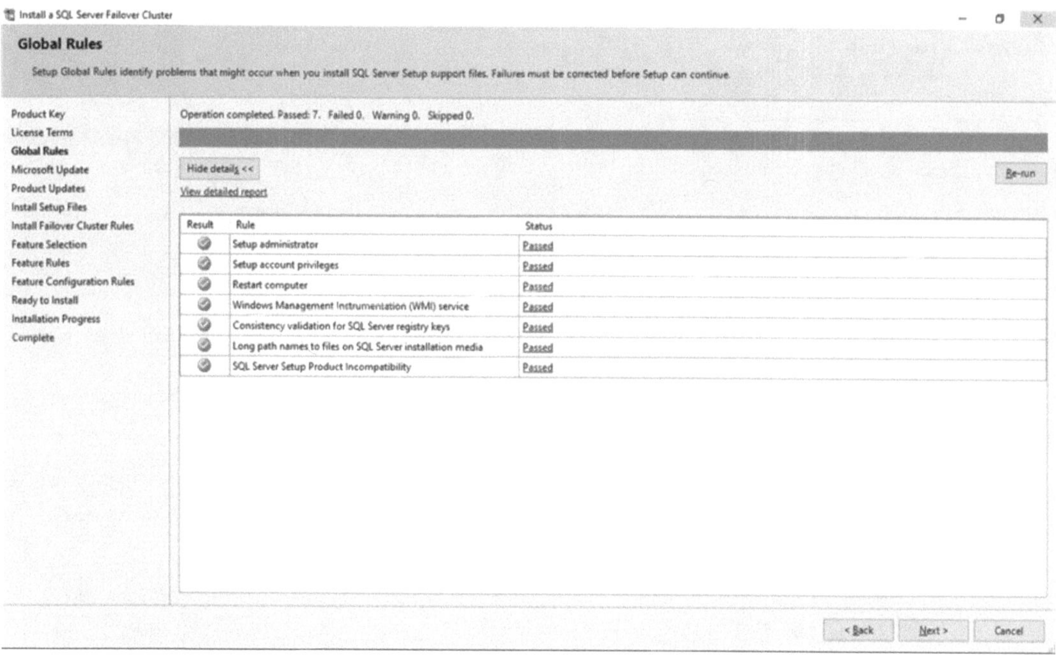

Figure 6-4. *Global rules*

Microsoft Update

6. In the **Microsoft Update** dialog box, you can include SQL Server
    product updates during installation. By default, it will search
    for updates online via the Microsoft Updates service, assuming
    the server has internet connectivity. If the server has no internet
    access, you can manually download updates and place them
    in a network-shared folder. Installing a SQL Server FCI with the
    latest cumulative update will be covered in the section *titled
    Installing a SQL Server 2019 Failover Clustered Instance (FCI) with
    Slipstreamed Updates*. Click **Next**.

Install Failover Cluster Rules

7. Ensure the checks return successful results in the Install Failover
    Cluster Rules dialog box. If any warnings appear, address them
    before continuing with the installation. Click **Next**. Due to the
    direct storage spaces (S2D) checks, you may receive a warning
    regarding Microsoft Cluster Service (MSCS) cluster verification
    (As shown in Figures 6-5 and 6-6).

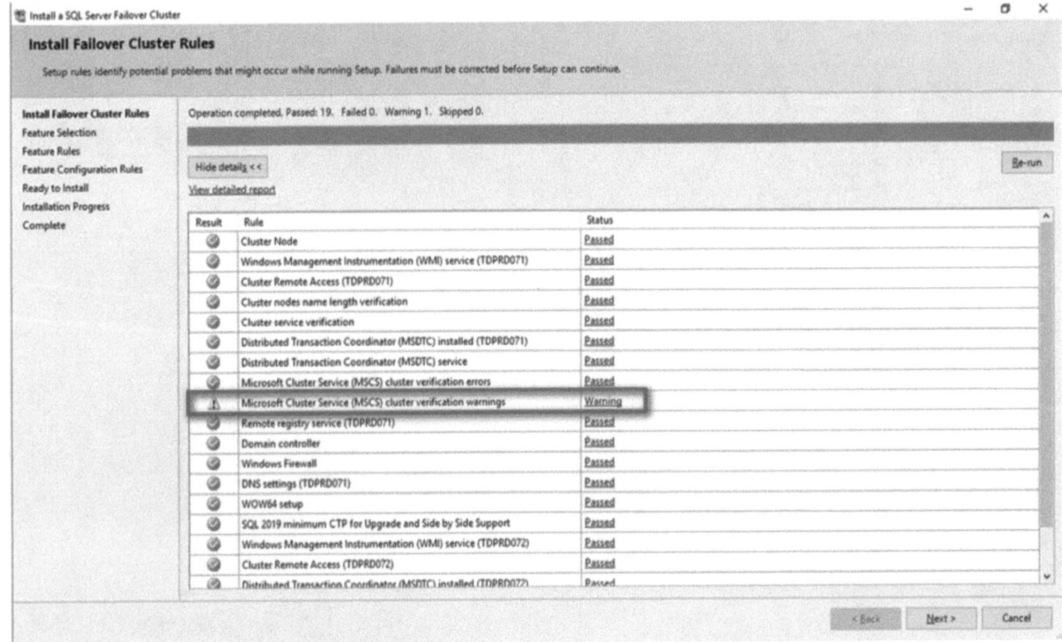

Figure 6-5. *Install failover cluster rules*

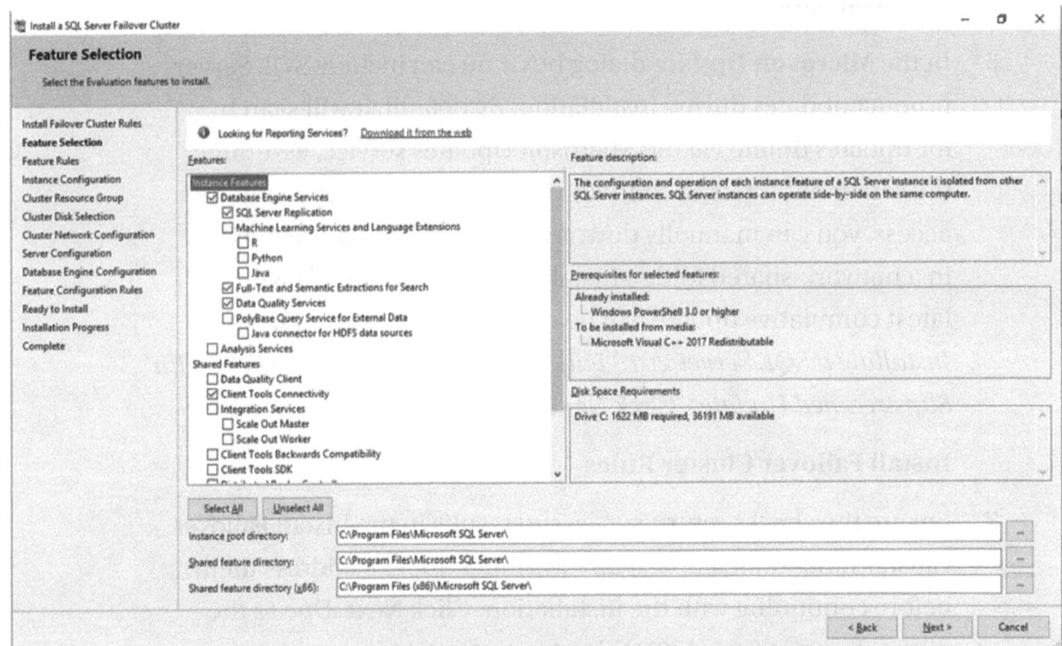

Figure 6-6. *Feature selection*

Feature Rules

8. Verify that all the rules have passed in the Feature Rules dialog box. If any warnings appear during the rules check, address them before installing.

9. Then, click **"Next"** (As shown in Figure 6-7).

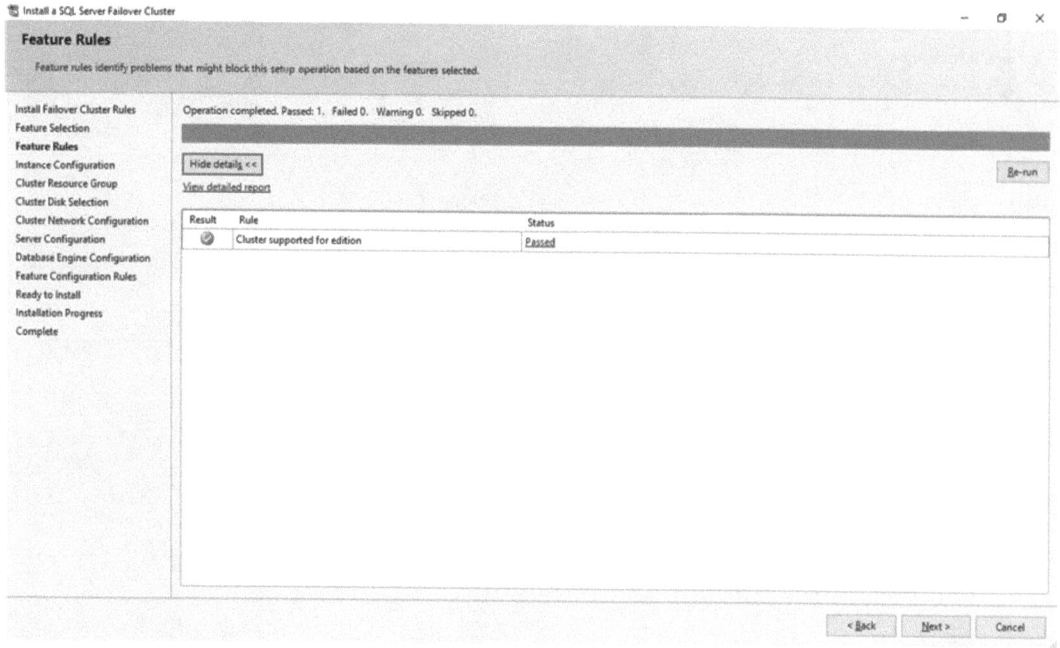

Figure 6-7. *Feature rules*

Configuration

10. In SQL Server Network Name

11. Enter a value for the SQL Server Network Name in the Instance Configuration dialogue box. The client apps will use this name to connect with this server. This name will be produced in Active Directory as a virtual computer object (VCO).

There are a few essential points to note in this section. By default, the instance name is assigned as the **Instance ID**. This identifier is used for the installation paths and registry entries associated with this particular SQL Server instance. It's beneficial when managing multiple instances within a WSFC environment. This applies to both default and named instances. In the case of a default instance, both the instance name and instance ID are set to **MSSQLSERVER** for the default instance. To use a non-default instance ID, enter a value in the **Instance ID** field, then click **Next** (As shown in Figure 6-8).

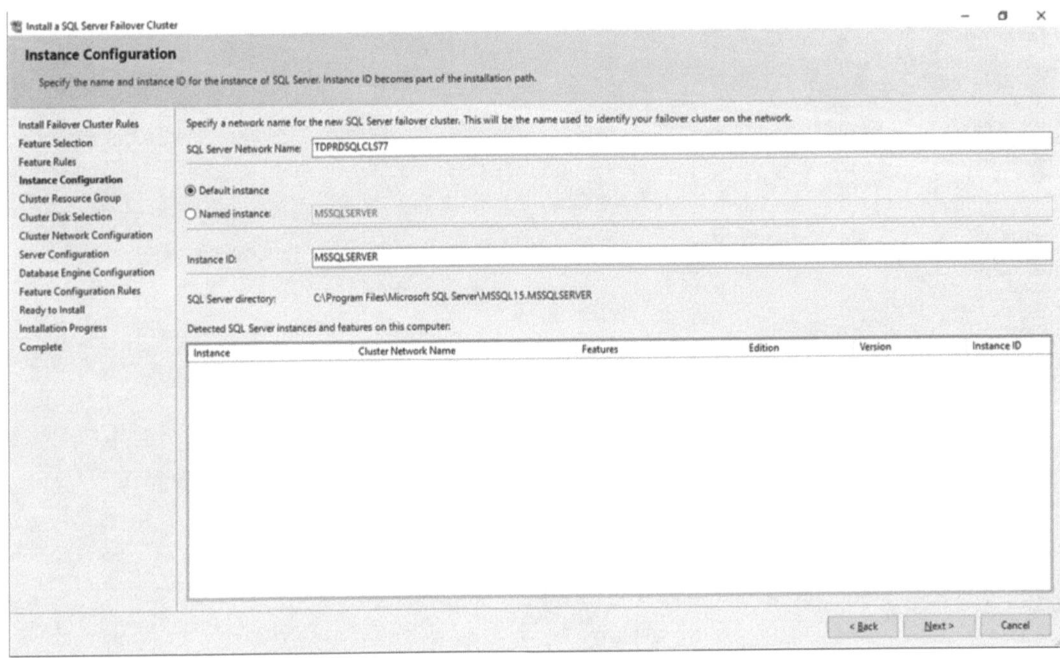

Figure 6-8. *Instance configuration*

Cluster Resource Group Configuration

12. Review the resources available within your WSFC in the **Cluster Resource Group** window. This indicates that a new resource group will be created in your Windows Server Failover Cluster (WSFC) specifically for the SQL Server FCI. To define the name of the SQL Server cluster resource group, select it from the drop-down menu. Choose an existing group from the list or enter a new group name to create one. Then, click **Next** (As shown in Figure 6-9).

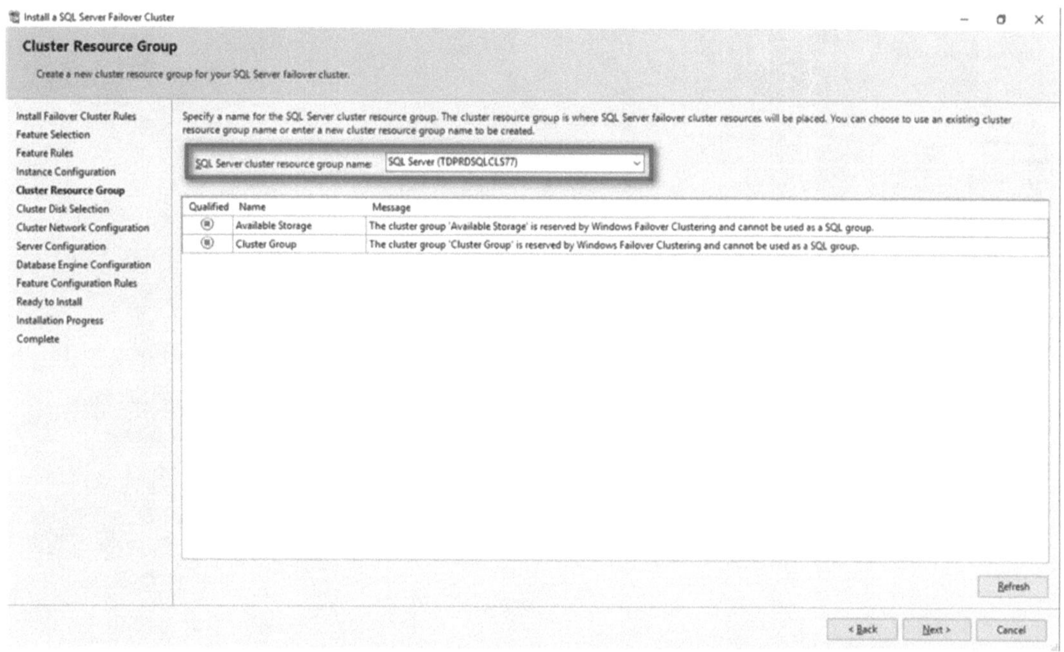

Figure 6-9. *Cluster resource group*

Disk Selection Options

13. In the Cluster Disk Selection window, choose from the available
     disk groups within the WSFC that the SQL Server FCI will use.
     The disks shown here vary based on how you have configured
     the shared storage resources in your WSFC setup. Click **Next** to
     continue (As shown in Figure 6-10).

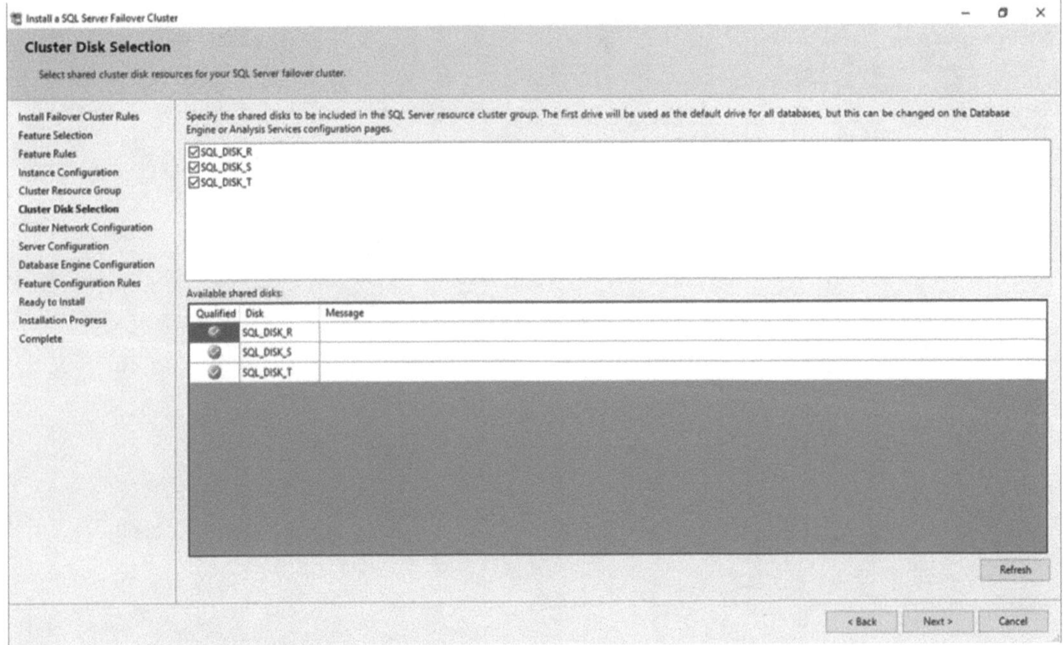

Figure 6-10. *Cluster disk selection*

Network Configuration Settings

14. Your SQL Server FCI's IP address and subnet mask should be entered in the Cluster Network Configuration dialog box. Since you will use a static IP address, tick the IPv4 option in the IP Type column. Press Next. This virtual IP address will establish an entry in your DNS server for the SQL Server Network Name (As shown in Figure 6-11).

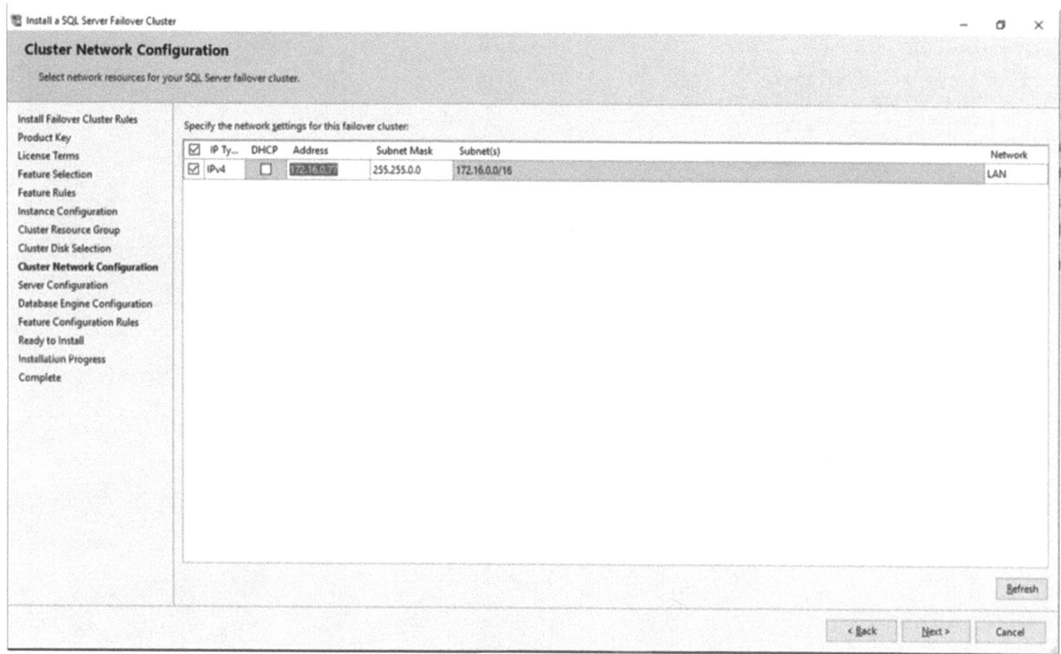

Figure 6-11. *Cluster network configuration*

Server Configuration

15. In the **Server Configuration** window, enter the credentials for
the SQL Server service accounts under the **Service Accounts** tab.
Ensure that both the SQL Server Agent and SQL Server Database
Engine services are set to start manually. The WSFC will manage
the starting and stopping of these services. Check the box **to grant
the "Perform Volume Maintenance Task" privilege to the SQL
Server Database Engine Service** (As shown in Figure 6-12).

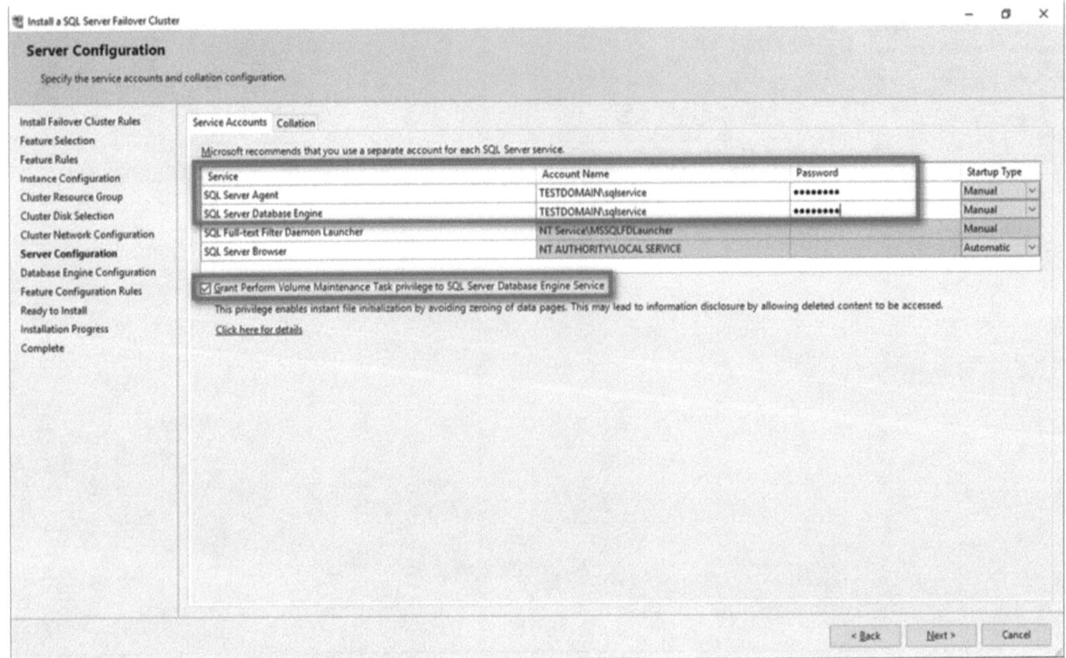

Figure 6-12. *Server configuration*

Database Engine Configuration

16.   In the **Database Engine Configuration** dialog box, under the
      Server Configuration tab. **In the Authentication Mode section,
      select Windows authentication** mode. You can change it later
      after the installation is complete if necessary.

17.   Click the Add Current User button in the Specify SQL Server
      Administrators section to add the currently logged-on user to
      the **SQL Server administrators** group. You may also include
      Active Directory domain accounts or security groups as needed
      (As shown in Figure 6-13).

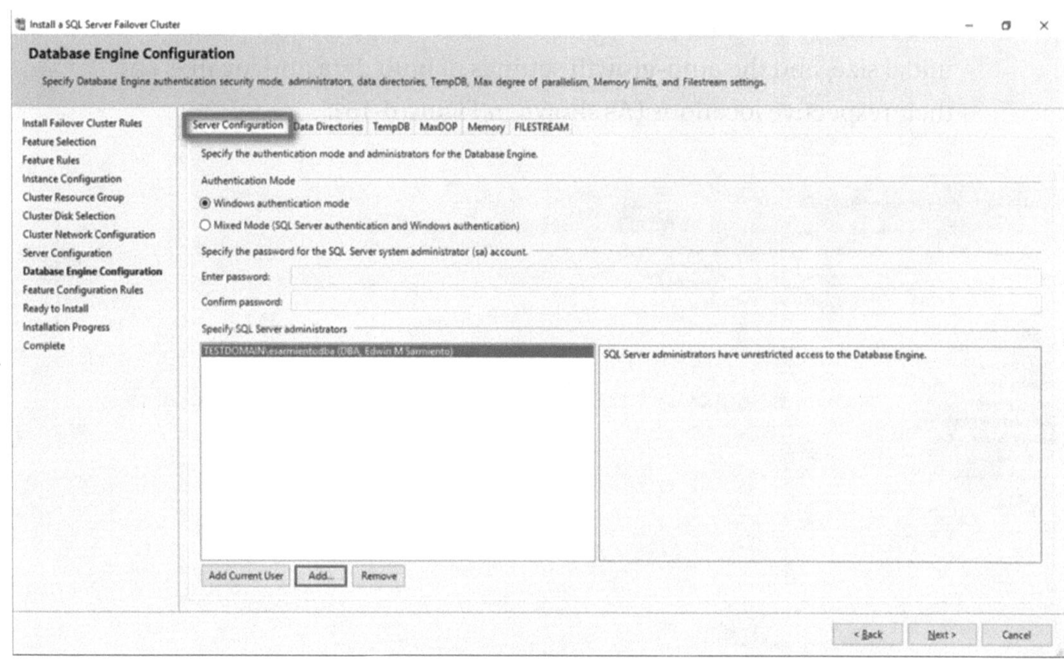

Figure 6-13. *Database engine configuration*

The **Data Directories** tab enables you to define the paths for the data, log, and backup files (As shown in Figure 6-14).

Figure 6-14. *Database engine configuration*

The **TempDB** tab configures the number of tempdb data files, their initial size, and the auto-growth settings of both data and log files and their respective locations (As shown in Figure 6-15).

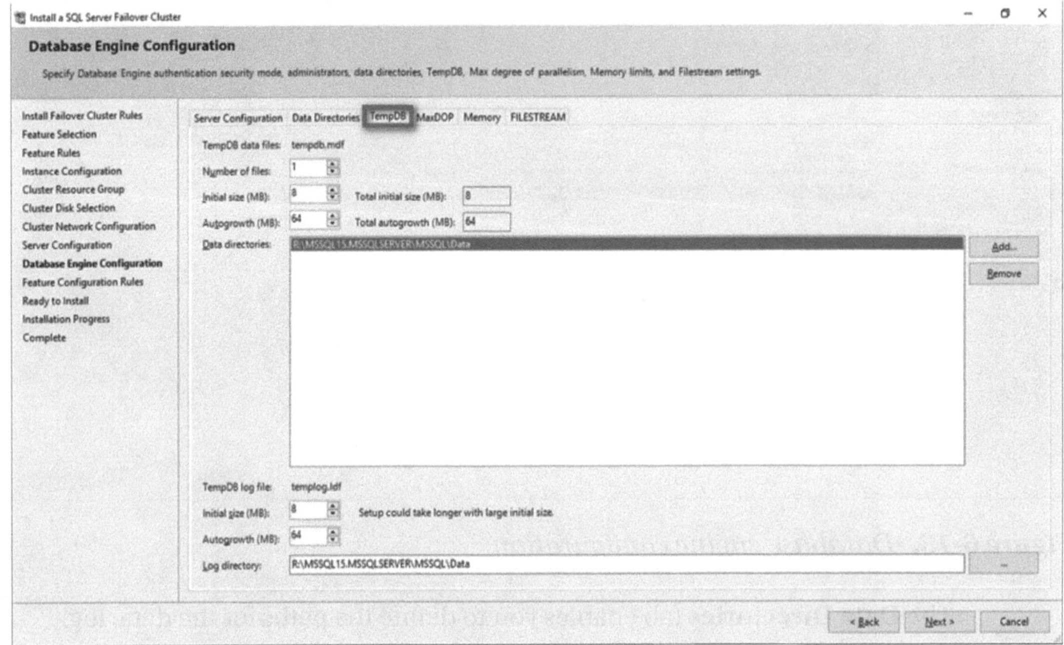

Figure 6-15. *Database engine configuration*

Note   In a WSFC environment, you can place your tempdb database files on a local drive.

Alternatively, as demonstrated in this example, you can store the tempdb on shared storage. Suppose you locate tempdb on a local drive. In that case, you will be prompted to ensure that all the WSFC nodes maintain an identical folder structure and make sure the SQL Server service account possesses the required permissions to read. Access and write access for those folders (As shown in Figure 6-16).

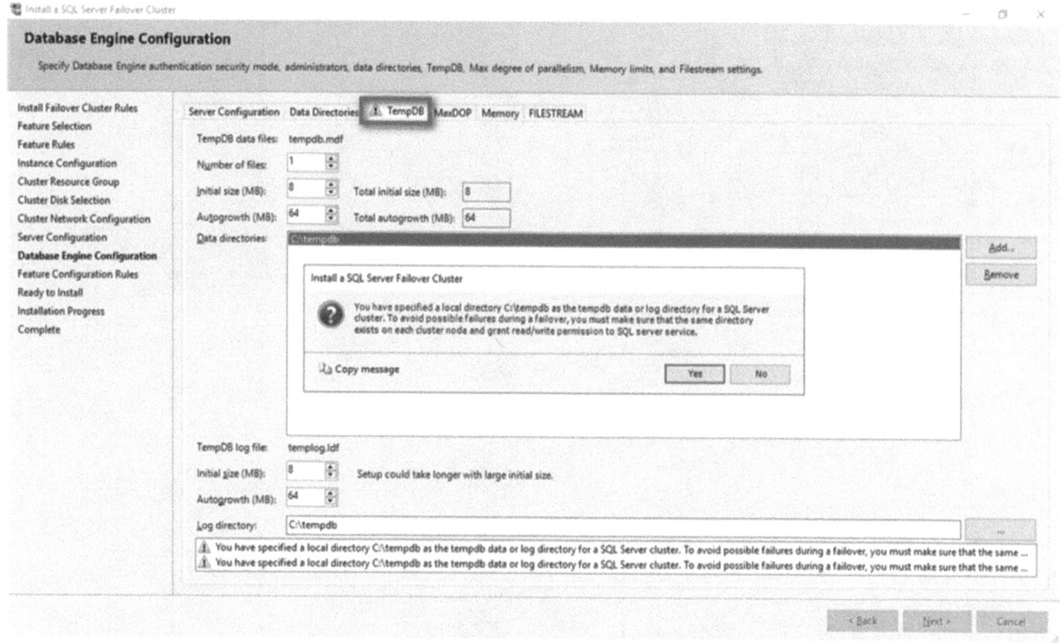

Figure 6-16. *Database engine configuration*

The new SQL Server 2019 has the **MaxDOP** tab, which presents
automatic suggestions for the MAXDOP server configuration option
setting during installation, which are determined by the number of
logical CPU cores on the server. Once you run your workload tests,
you can accept the default recommendations and make modifications
(As shown in Figure 6-17).

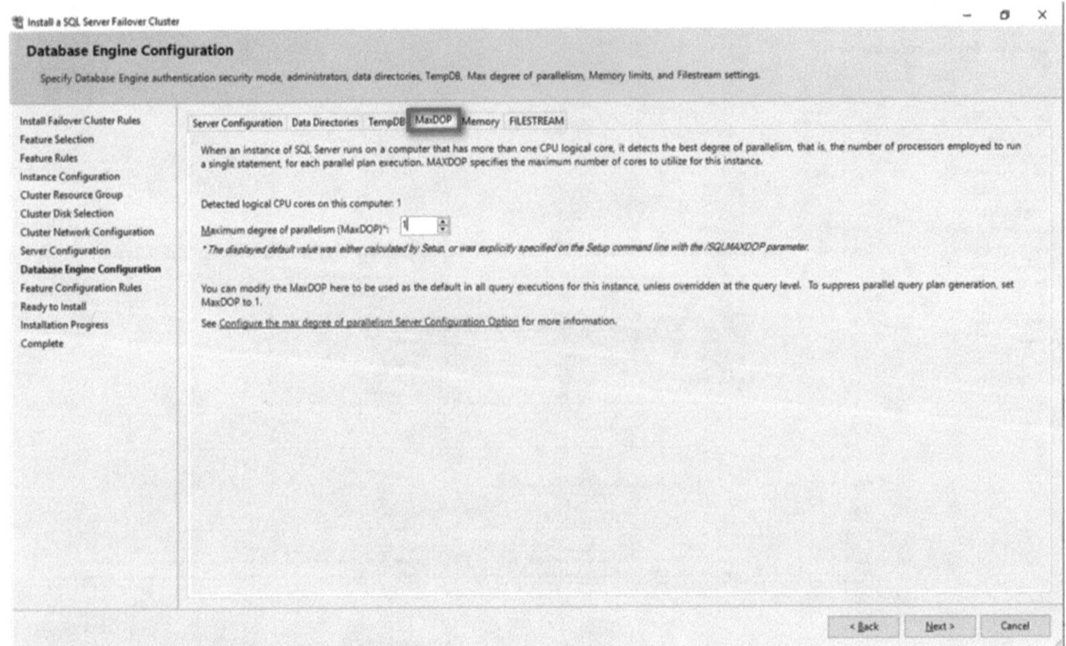

Figure 6-17. *Database engine configuration*

Another addition in SQL Server 2019 is the **Memory** tab, which allows
you to define the minimum and maximum server memory limits
during installation—similar to configuring them later with
sp_configure (As shown in Figure 6-18).

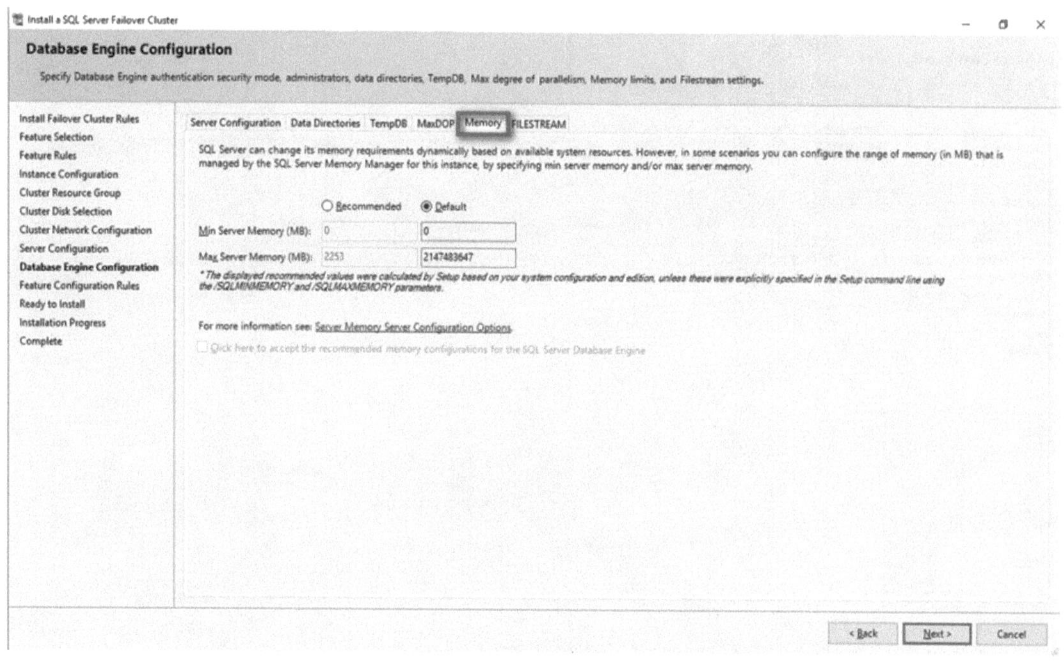

Figure 6-18. *Feature configuration rules window*

Click **Next**.

Feature Configuration Rules

18. Ensure that all validations pass in the **Feature Configuration Rules** window. Then, click **Next** to continue (As shown in Figure 6-19).

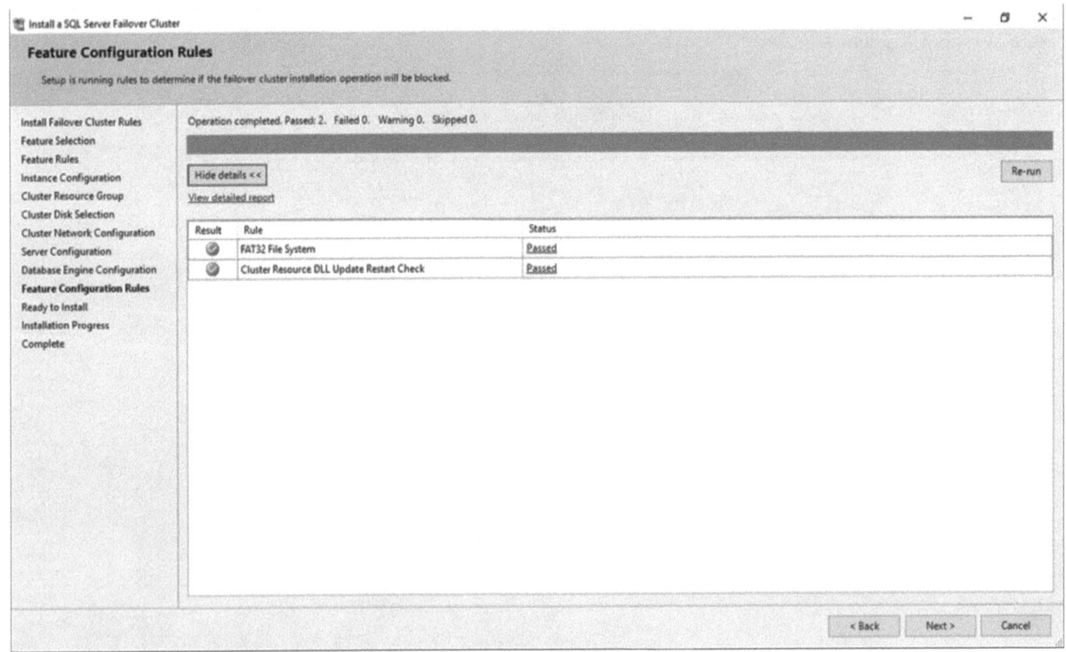

Figure 6-19. *The configuration settings*

Ready to Install

19.   Before proceeding, review the **configuration settings on the Ready to Install** page and verify that all configuration settings are correct. Then, click **Install** to proceed with the installation (As shown in Figure 6-20).

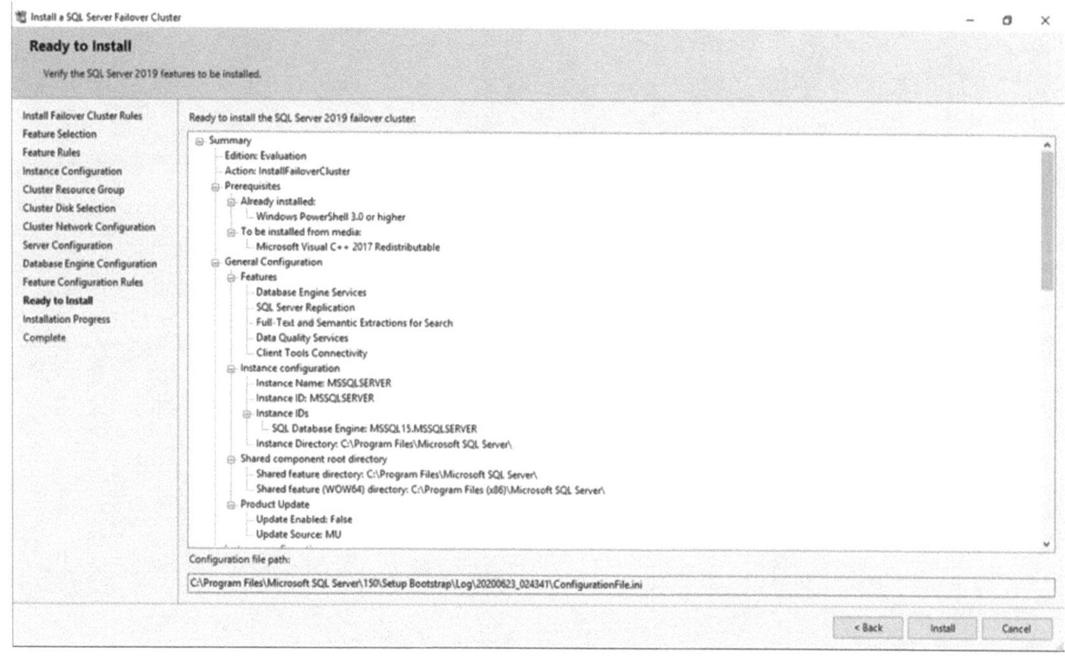

Figure 6-20. *Ready to install*

Complete

20. In the **Complete** dialog box, click **Close**. This concludes the installation of a SQL Server 2019 FCI (As shown in Figure 6-21).

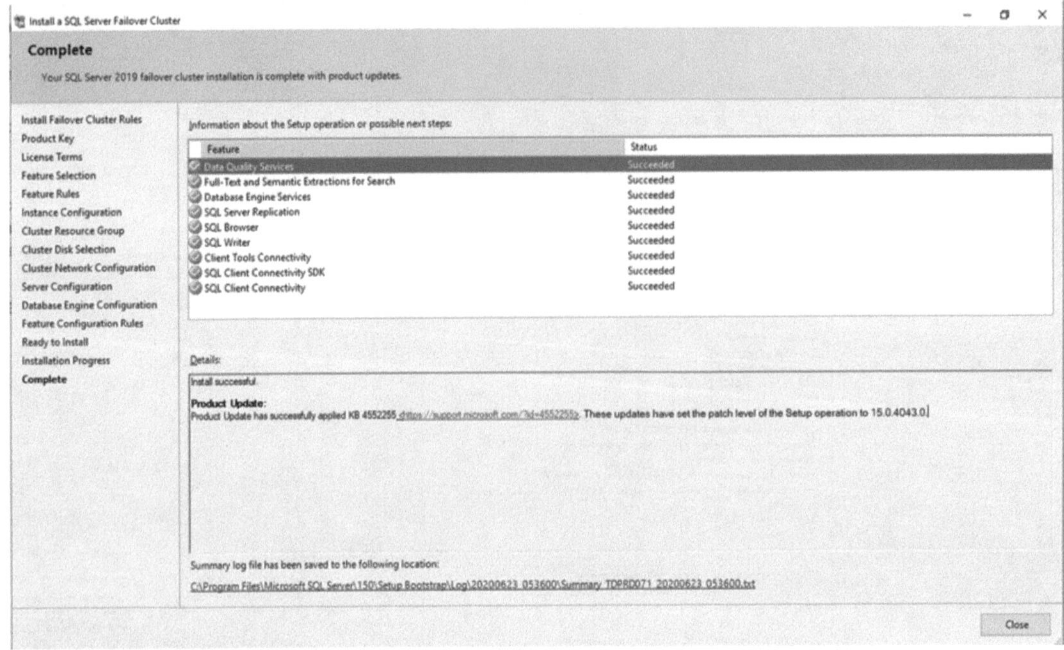

Figure 6-21. *Complete*

Once the node has been installed and configured, you will have a fully operational SQL Server 2019 FCI. To confirm its status, launch the **Failover Cluster Manager** console. Click on **SQL Server (<NAME>)** under **Roles** and ensure all dependencies are online (As shown in Figure 6-22).

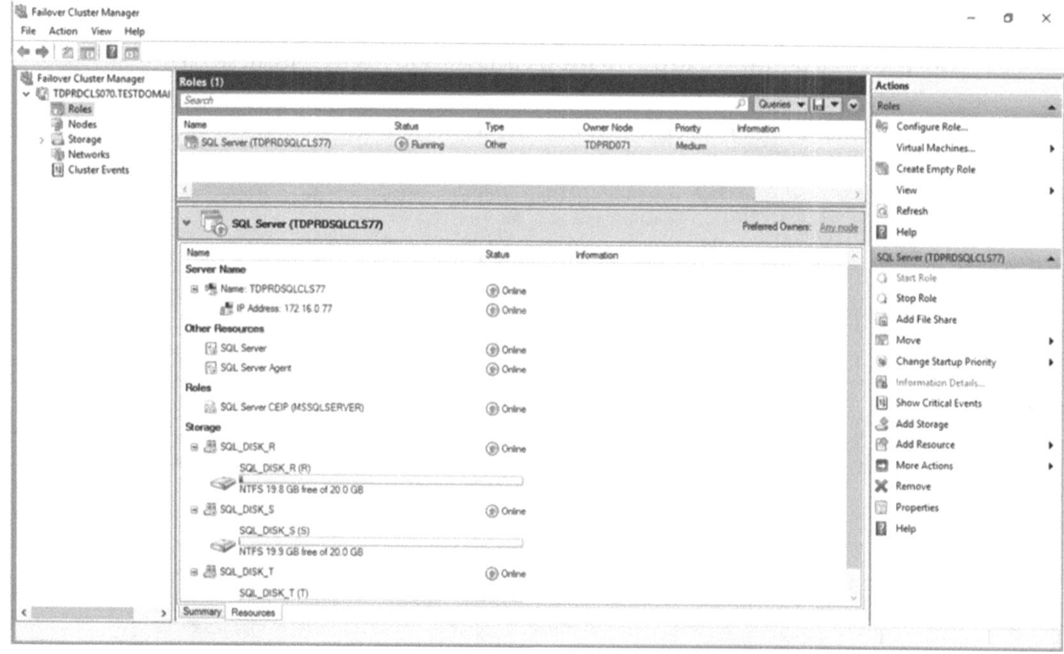

Figure 6-22. *Failover cluster manager*

While your SQL Server 2019 FCI is operational, it isn't yet highly available because the SQL Server binaries are only installed on one node of the WSFC. To achieve high availability, you must add the second node of the WSFC to the SQL Server FCI.

SQL Server 2019 Setting Up a Secondary (Failover) Cluster Node

for a SQL Server 2019 Failover Cluster Instance (FCI) setup

Now that your SQL Server is operational

2019 To make an FCI highly available, you add additional nodes. TTo add a node to an existing SQL Server 2019 Failover Cluster Instance (FCI), follow these steps

21. Run **setup.exe** from the SQL Server 2019 installation media to launch **the SQL Server Installation Center**. Click on the **Installation** link on the left-hand side.

22. Click the **Add node to a SQL Server failover cluster** link. The SQL
    Server 2019 Setup wizard will then run (As shown in Figure 6-23).

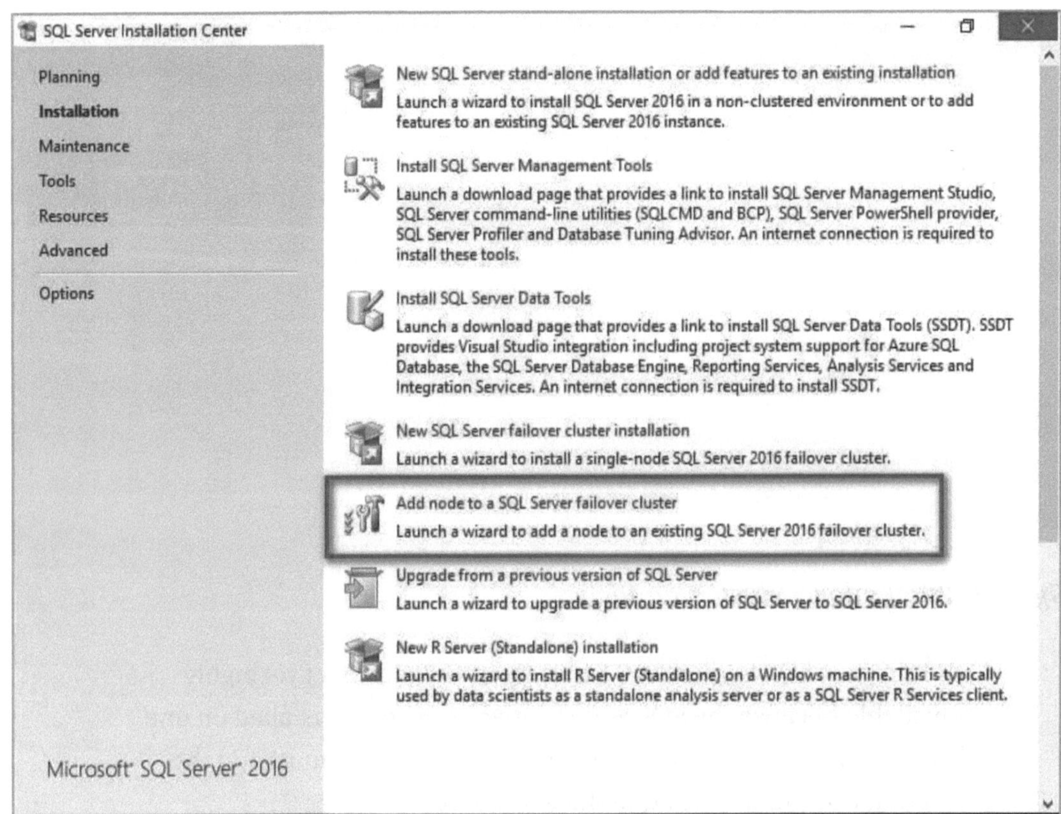

Figure 6-23. *SQL Server installation center*

23. In the **Product Key** dialog box, enter the product key
that came with your installation media and click **Next**
(As shown in Figure 6-24).

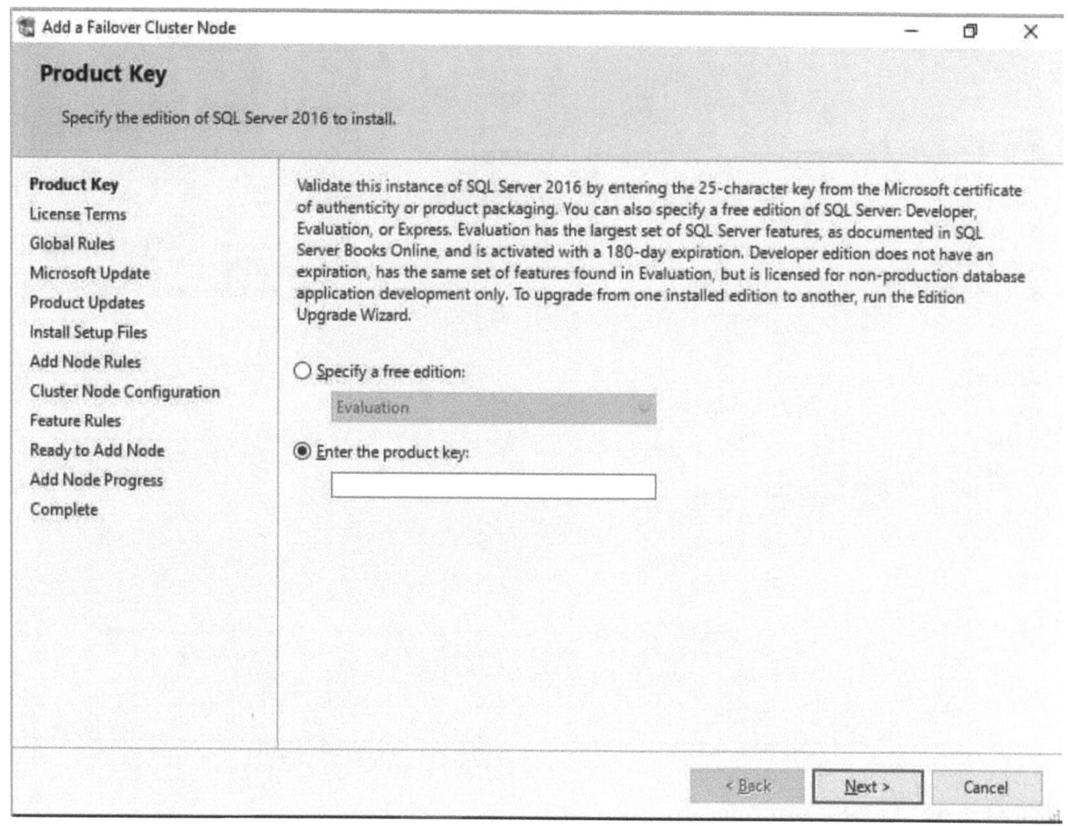

Figure 6-24. *Add a failover cluster node*

24. In the **License Terms** dialog box, click the **I accept the license terms** check box and click **Next** (As shown in Figure 6-25).

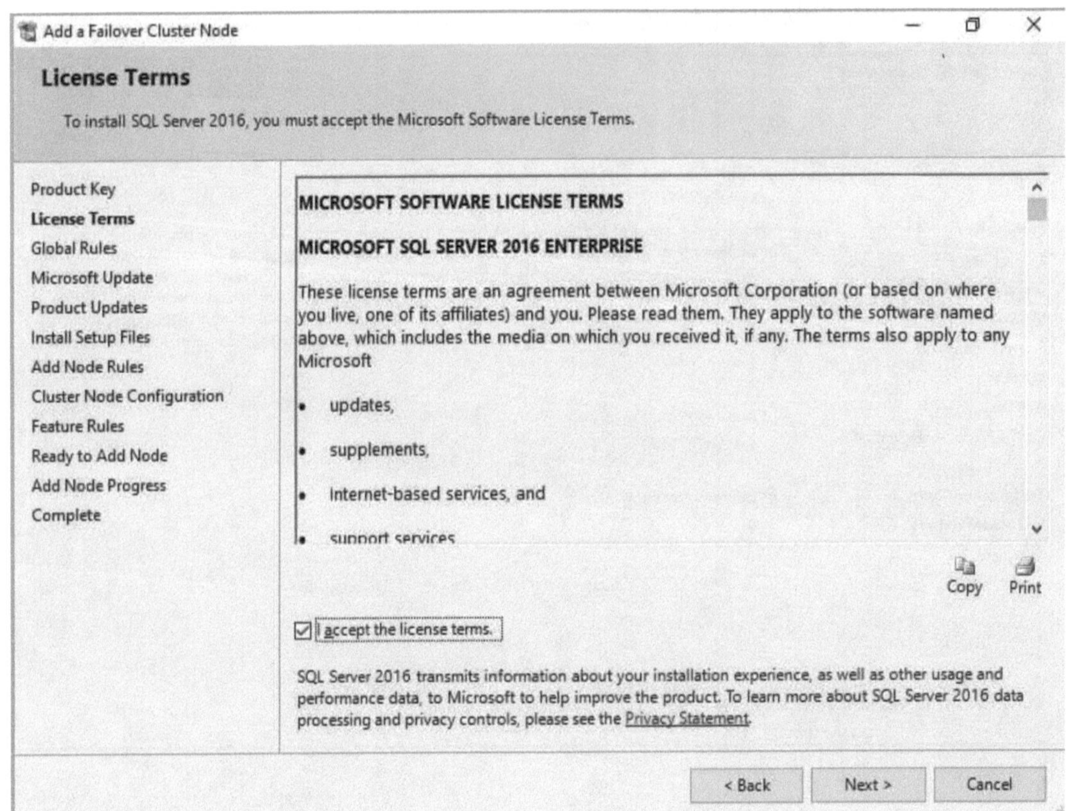

Figure 6-25. *Add a failover cluster node*

25. In the **Global Rules** dialog box, validate that the checks return successful results and click **Next** (As shown in Figure 6-26).

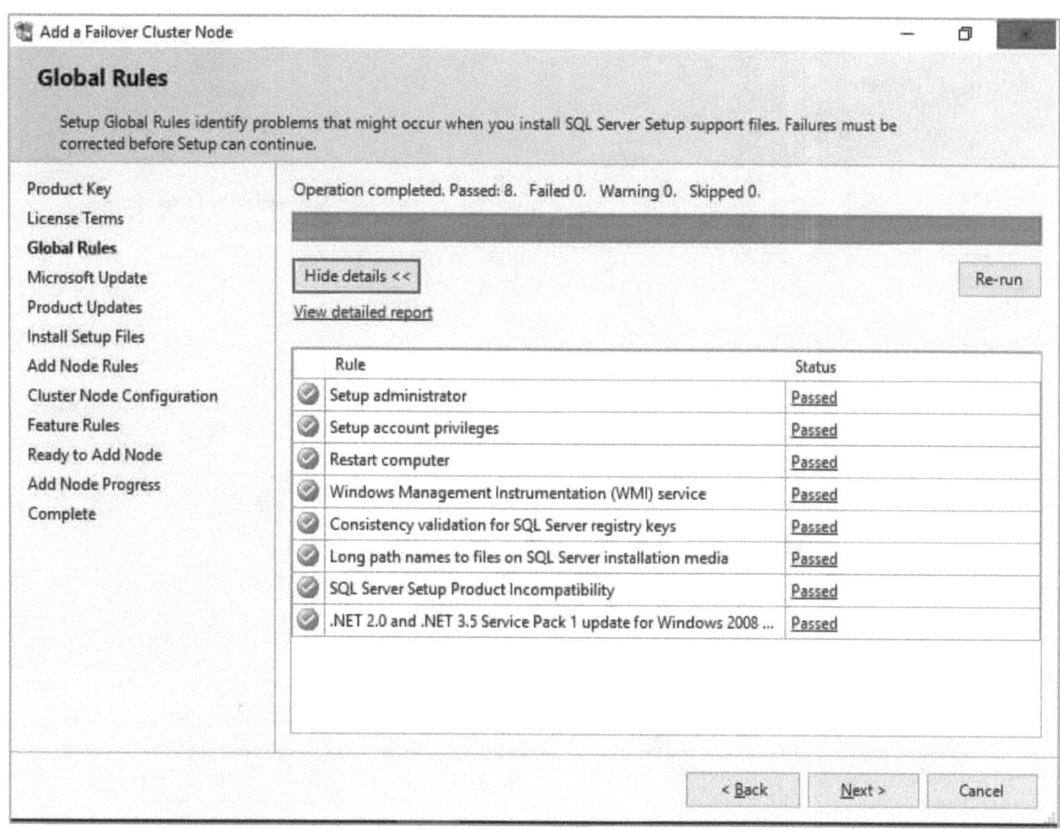

Figure 6-26. *Global rules*

26. In the **Microsoft Update** dialog box, click **Next** (As shown in Figure 6-27).

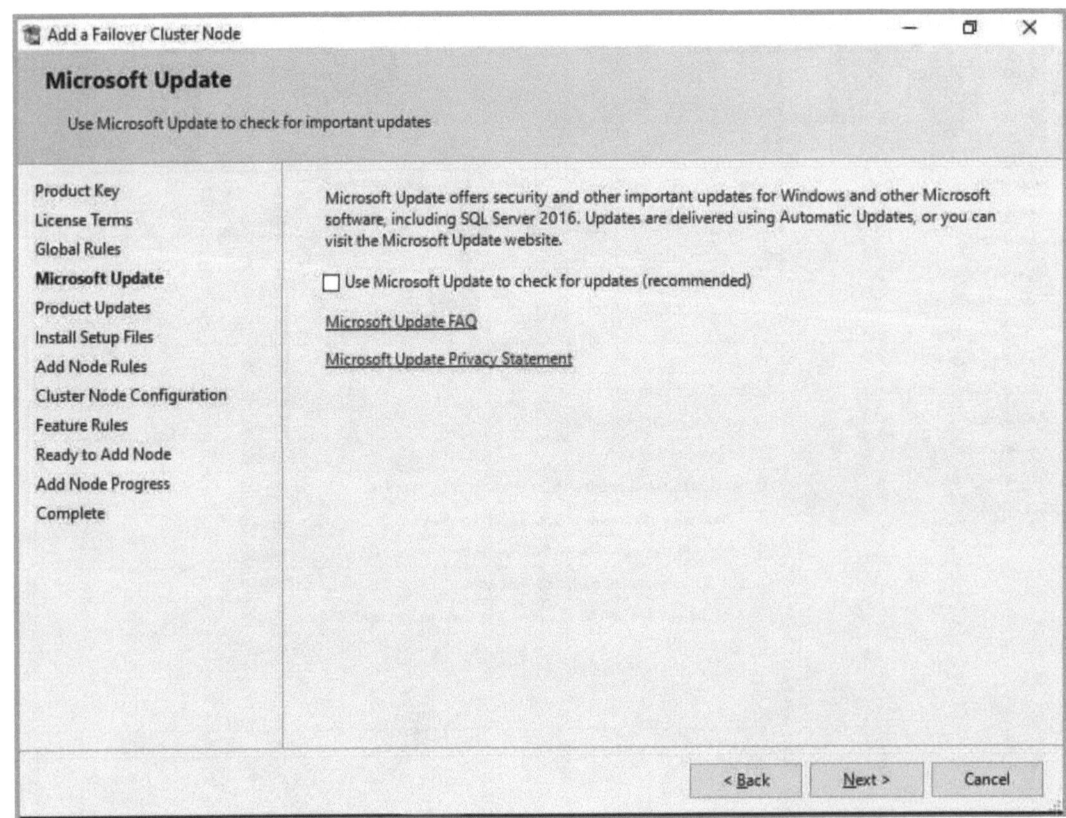

Figure 6-27. *Microsoft update*

27. In the **Add Node Rules** dialog box, validate that the checks return successful results. If the checks returned a few warnings, fix them before installing. Click **Next** (As shown in Figure 6-28).

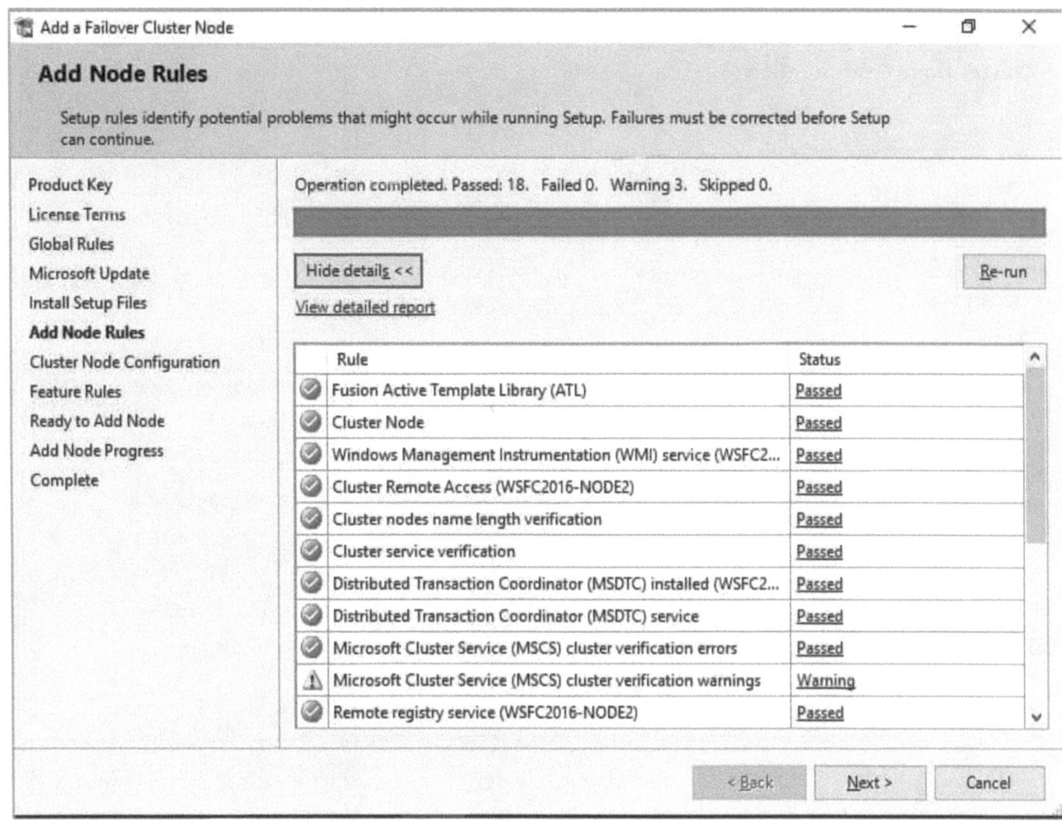

Figure 6-28. *Add node rules*

28. In the **Cluster Node Configuration** dialog box, validate that the existing SQL Server 2019 FCI information is correct. Click **Next** (As shown in Figure 6-29).

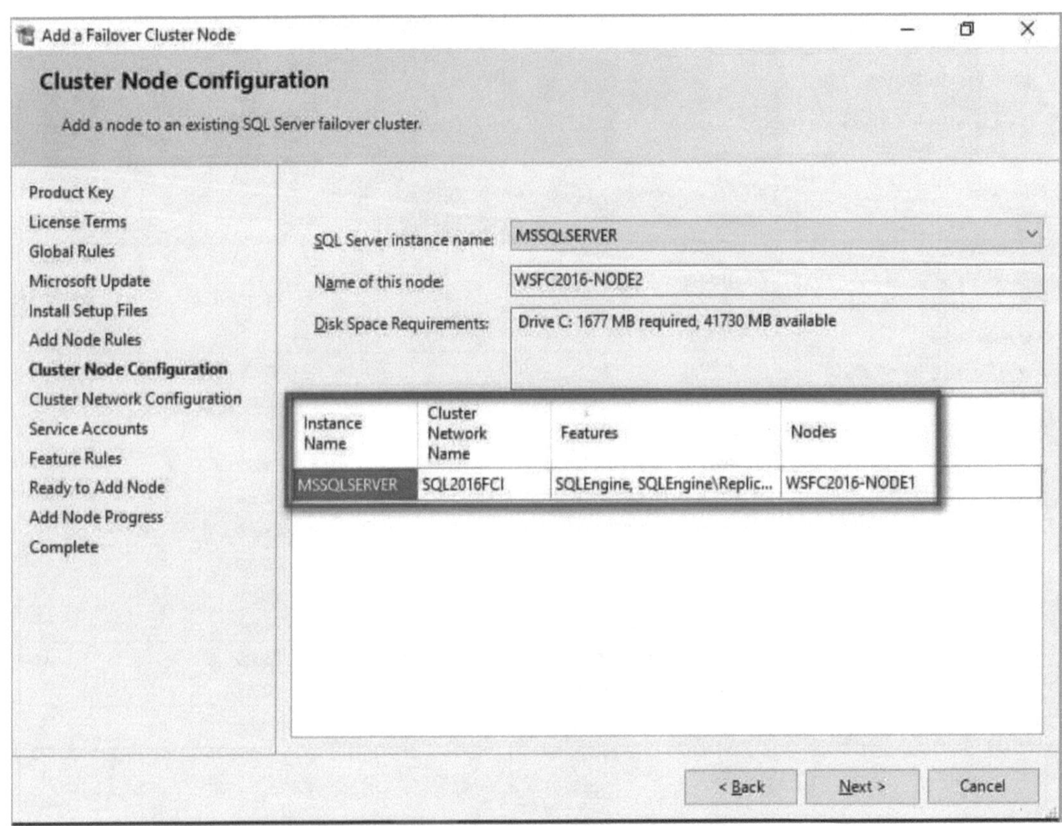

Figure 6-29. *Cluster node configuration*

29. In the **Cluster Network Configuration** dialog box, validate the IP address information (As shown in Figure 6-30).

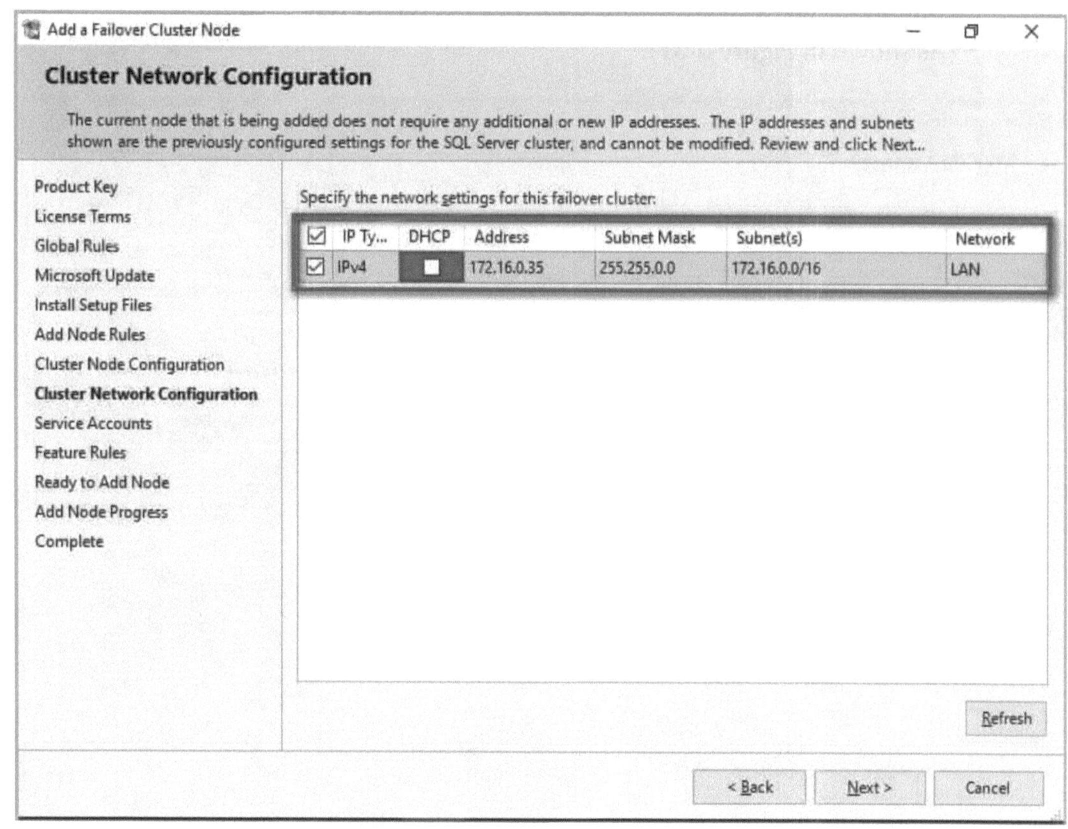

Figure 6-30. *Cluster network configuration*

30. On the **Service Accounts** page, confirm that the details match those used to set up the first node. Then, enter the correct credentials for each corresponding SQL Server service account (As shown in Figure 6-31).

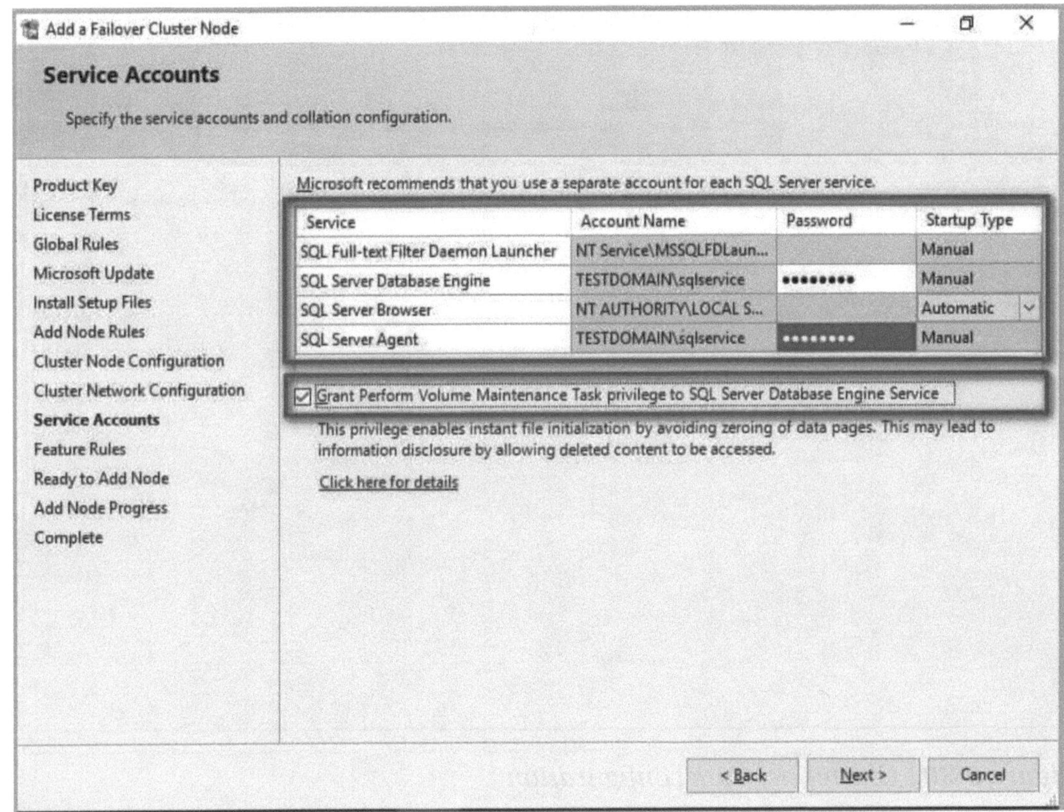

Figure 6-31. *Service accounts*

Note   Be mindful of the sequence in which the SQL Server services are listed, mainly when you use different service accounts. You see the SQL Server Agent service before the SQL Server Database Engine service. Here, it's the reverse—the SQL Server Database Engine service must be started before the SQL Server Agent service. Make sure not to confuse the two.

Check the option **Grant Perform Volume Maintenance Task privilege for the SQL Server Database Engine service** to enable Instant File Initialization, as shown here. Since this permission is assigned locally to a specific account, you'll need to configure it manually on each node in the SQL Server FCI.

Click **Next** to continue.

31. On the **Feature Rules** page, confirm that all validations pass successfully. Then, click **Next** (As shown in Figure 6-32).

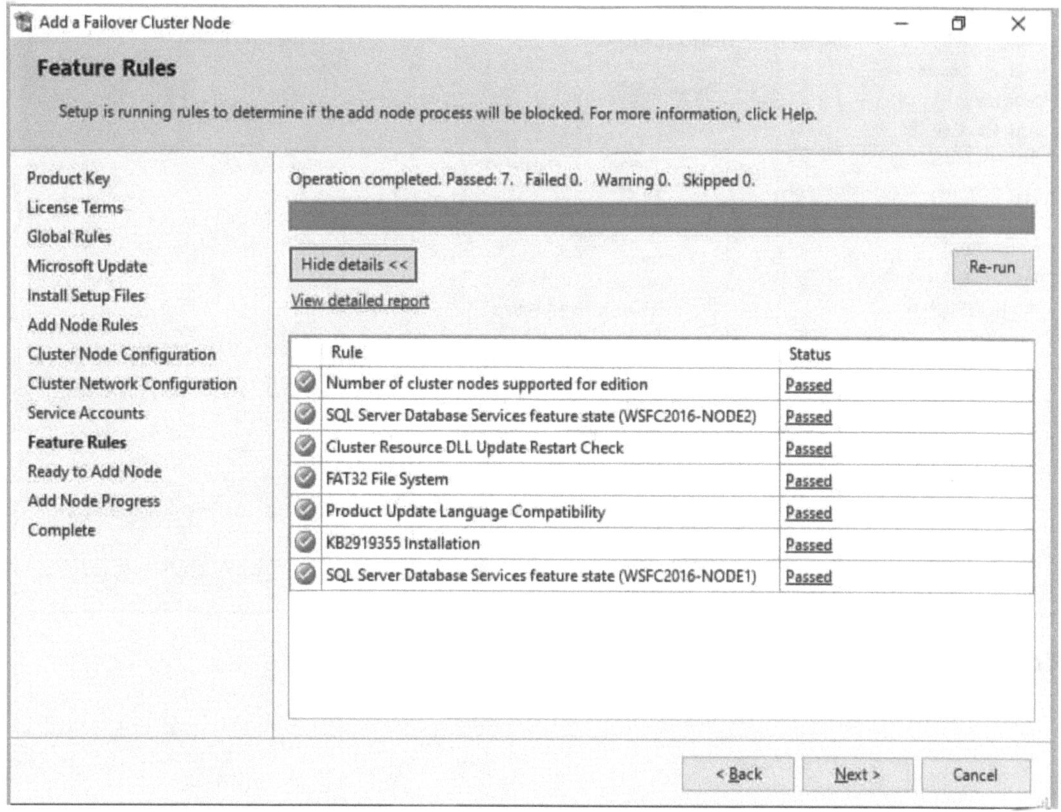

Figure 6-32. *Feature rules*

32. In the **Ready to Add Node** screen, review all configuration settings to ensure they are correct. Then, click **Install** to proceed with the setup (As shown in Figure 6-33).

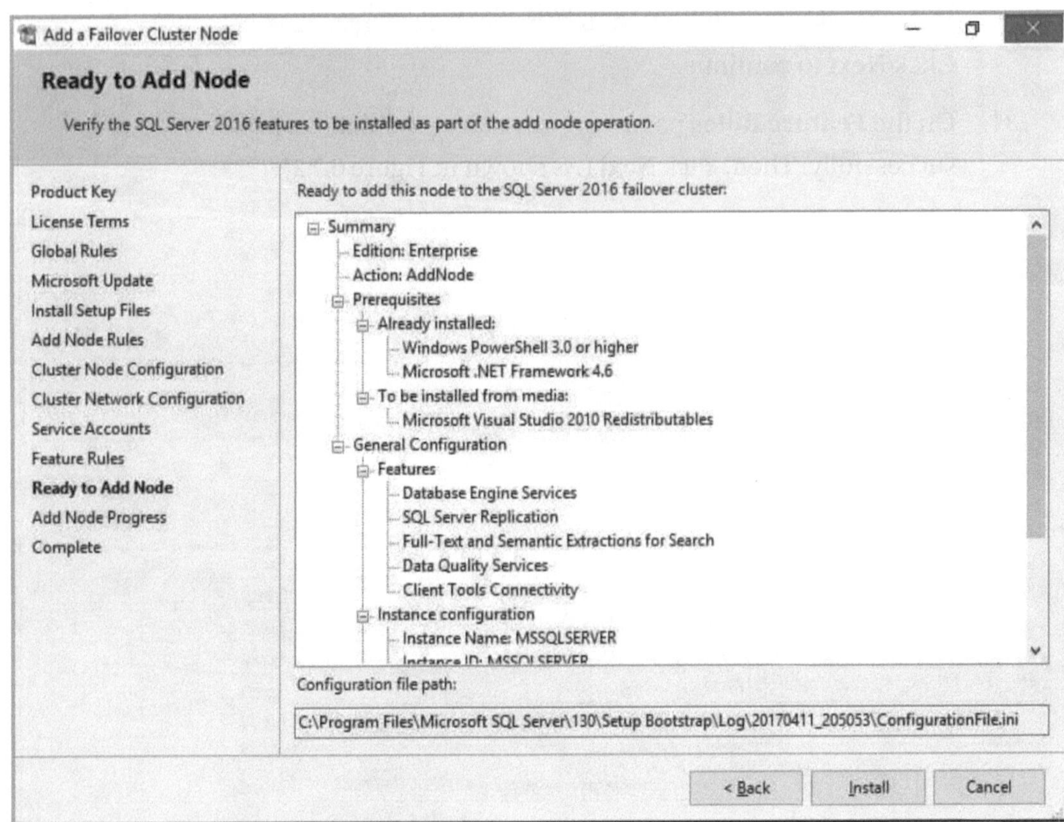

Figure 6-33. *Ready to add node*

33. Once the process is completed, the **Complete** dialog box will appear. Click **Close** to finish by adding a node to an existing SQL Server 2019 FCI (As shown in Figure 6-34).

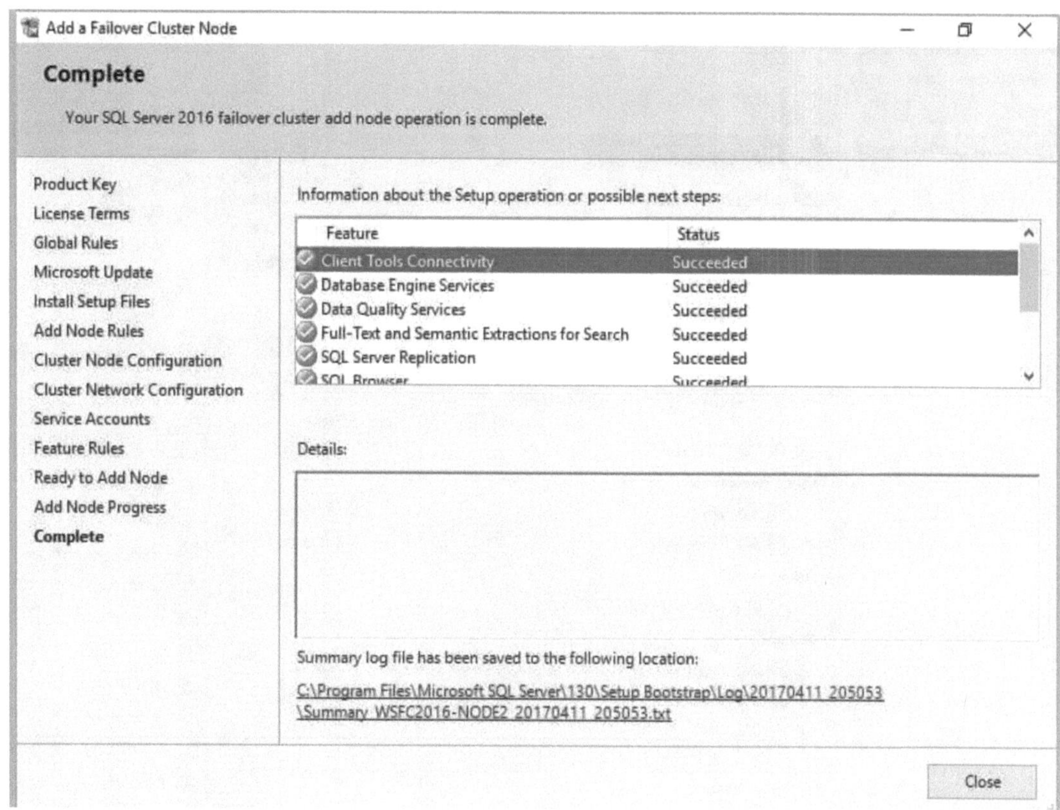

Figure 6-34. *Complete*

Once the node installation and configuration are completed, you should validate whether the SQL Server 2019 FCI can automatically or manually failover to all available nodes.

Testing SQL Server 2019 FCI Manual Failover

A simple way to test whether or not One way to test how the SQL Server 2019 FCI functions is by performing a manual failover. This procedure involves transferring the resource group or role of the SQL Server cluster from one node to another.

To test the failover process using the **Failover Cluster Manager** console:

1. Expand **Roles** and select **SQL Server (MSSQLSERVER)**
    (As shown in Figure 6-35).

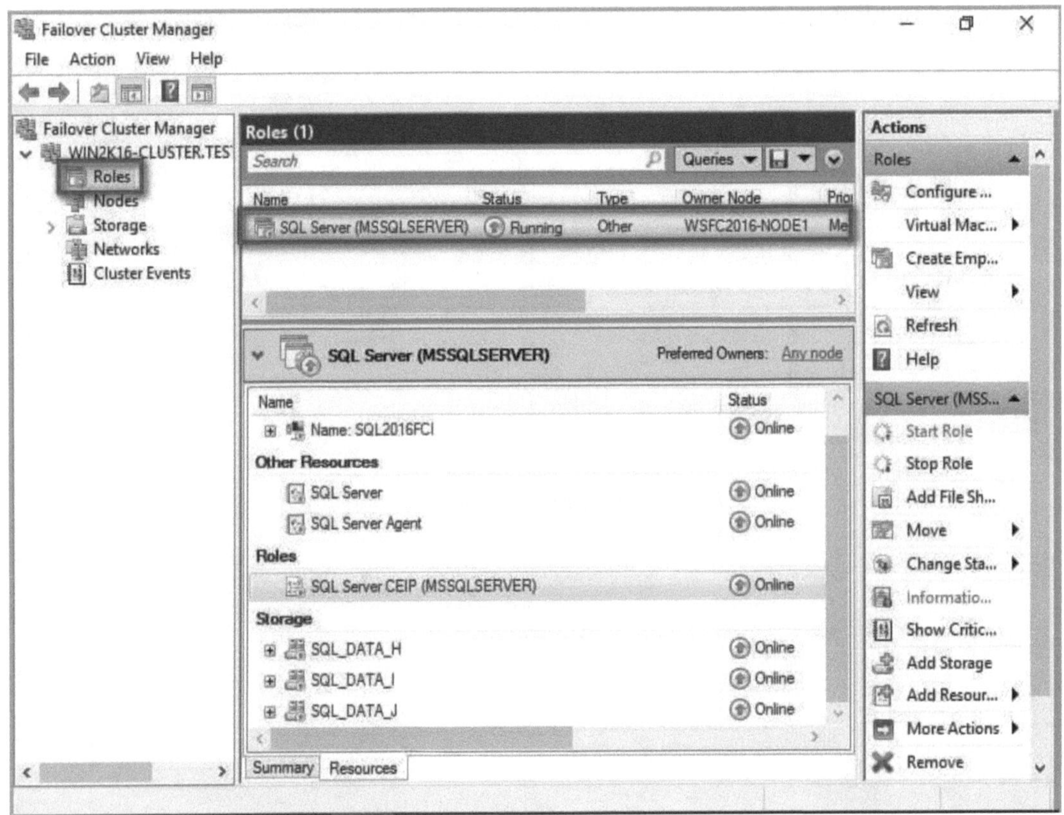

Figure 6-35. *Failover cluster manager*

2. Right-click on the **SQL Server (MSSQLSERVER)** role, choose **Move** and select **Node** (As shown in Figure 6-36).

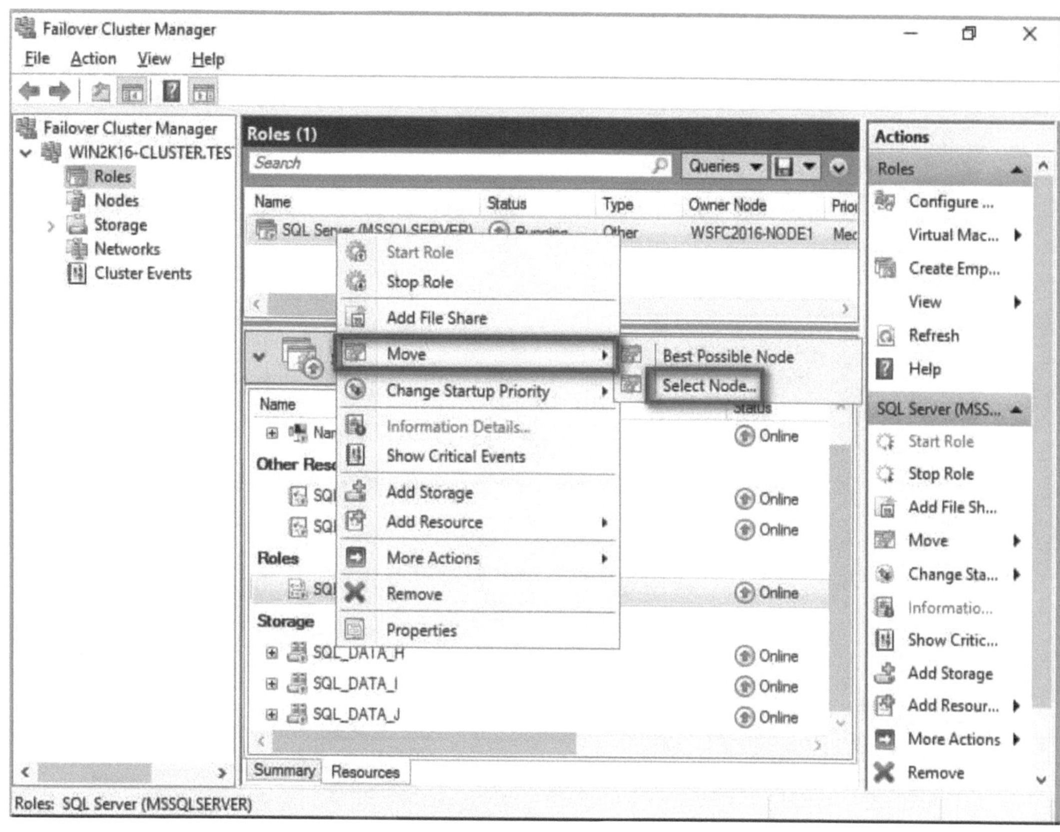

Figure 6-36. *Failover cluster manager*

3. In the **Move Clustered Role** dialog box, choose the node to which you want the SQL Server FCI to failover, then click **OK** (As shown in Figure 6-37).

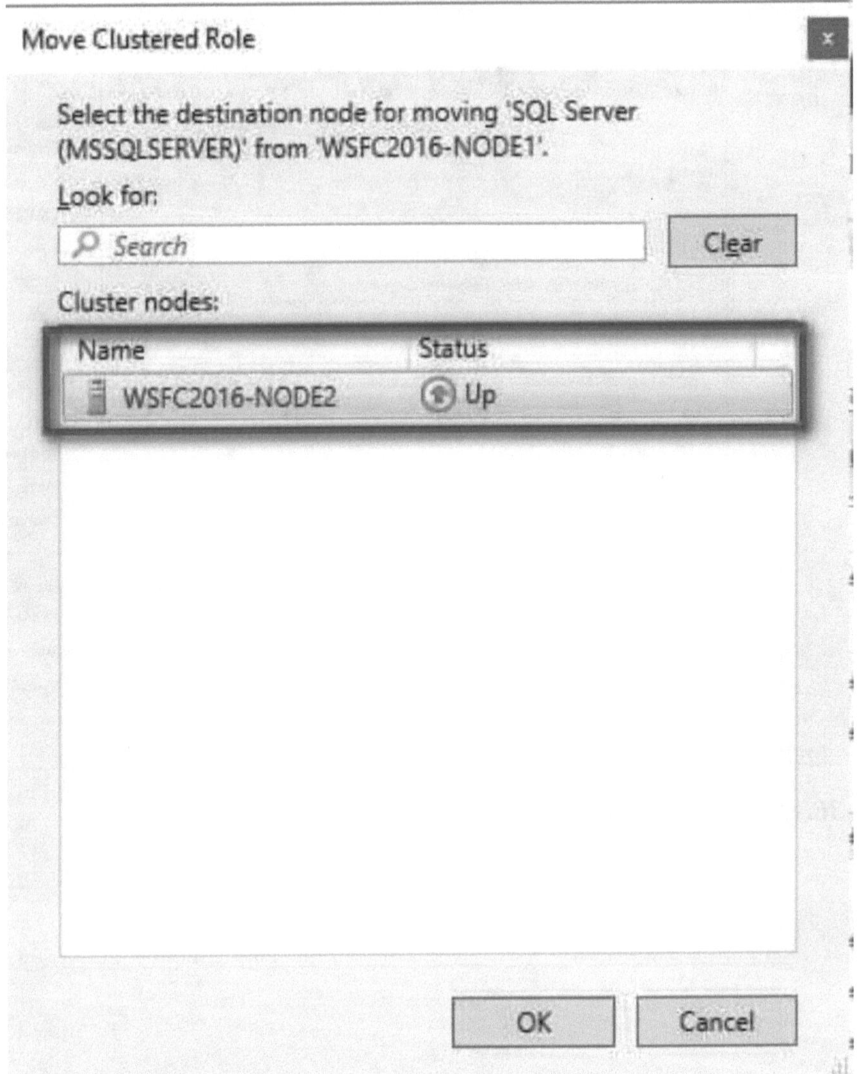

Figure 6-37. *Move clustered role*

4. Once the failover process is complete, rerun the query to confirm that the SQL Server FCI is running on the other node.

Conclusion

This chapter has thoroughly explored the intricacies of SQL Server clustering, beginning with understanding the underlying architecture and key components of a SQL Server cluster. We then examined the benefits and advantages of utilizing SQL Server clustering for high availability before delving into various cluster modes, comparing their functionality and performance implications. A practical guide to installing a SQL Server 2019 failover cluster instance was provided, followed by a discussion on the procedures for manually testing failover, a crucial validation step in a cluster environment. The core takeaway is that SQL Server clustering, when properly designed and implemented, provides a robust solution for maintaining high availability and business continuity by understanding the architecture, planning for failovers, and proactively validating these failovers, enabling organizations to safeguard against downtime and data loss.

CHAPTER 7

AlwaysOn Availability Groups

This chapter represents a shift in our learning. After establishing a robust foundation in SQL Server's internal workings, performance improvements, and protective measures, we will now turn our attention to a vital element for ensuring both high availability and effective disaster recovery: AlwaysOn Availability Groups (AGs). Over the coming sections, we'll explore the intricacies of AGs, including how to deploy them, administer them, and what factors are essential for their success.

We will begin with the core concepts behind AlwaysOn AGs, illustrating their importance in reducing downtime. We will then examine the necessary requirements for establishing a functioning AG, covering vital aspects such as network setups and security authorizations. Building on this foundation, we'll walk through the practical steps of setting up AlwaysOn AGs. This will include looking at different setup choices, such as defining primary and secondary copies of the database, and examining how to perform both controlled and forced failovers. We will also explore the crucial recovery procedure following a disaster, providing a step-by-step approach for initiating a forced failover. The chapter then outlines the actions needed for an unplanned disaster recovery event, including the steps that must be taken afterward. Finally, we will address the essential elements of AG management, such as monitoring health and performance and strategies for resolving problems.

By the conclusion of this chapter, you'll have a complete understanding of AlwaysOn AGs, from the initial planning stages all the way to the continuous maintenance required for a reliable SQL Server setup. This knowledge will allow you to effectively implement and manage this key technology, ensuring a high level of availability and solid protection from unexpected disruptions.

© Venkata Reddy Pasam and Petchikumar Andiappan 2026
V. R. Pasam and P. Andiappan, *The Expert's Guide to SQL Server*, https://doi.org/10.1007/979-8-8688-2451-7_7

What Is an AlwaysOn Availability Group?

An **AlwaysOn Availability Group (AG)** is a high-availability (HA) and disaster recovery (DR) solution in Microsoft SQL Server. It allows groups of databases (known as **availability databases**) to fail together as a single unit, ensuring their high availability. AGs also enable multiple copies of the databases to be maintained across different servers for redundancy and workload distribution.

Through SQL Server AlwaysOn Availability Groups, organizations can access a robust, high-availability disaster recovery solution for mission-critical databases. This feature also allows offloading read workloads to secondary replicas and enables backups to be configured on secondary instances.

Prerequisites of AlwaysOn Availability 2019

Implementing AlwaysOn Availability Groups in SQL Server 2019 (take an example) involves several steps. This feature ensures high availability and disaster recovery by allowing multiple database copies to be synchronized and available across different servers. Let's set it up using a step-by-step guide below:

Prerequisites

1. **Infrastructure Requirements**

   Windows Server Version:

   Windows Server 2016, 2019, or later is required to support AlwaysOn Availability Groups.

   Failover Cluster:

   A Windows Server failover cluster (WSFC) must be created and configured.

   All participating servers must be joined to the same domain.

   Network Configuration:

   Ensure low-latency and high-bandwidth connectivity between nodes.

   Use static IP addresses or DHCP reservations for reliability.

Configure DNS appropriately for the Availability Group Listener.

Domain Controller and Active Directory:

Active Directory Domain Services (AD DS) must be available.

All nodes must be joined to the same AD domain.

Quorum Configuration:

Proper quorum configuration is essential for the WSFC to avoid split-brain scenarios.

Depending on your setup, you can use quorum types like Node Majority, File Share Witness, or Cloud Witness.

Storage:

Shared storage is not required for AlwaysOn Availability Groups, unlike SQL Server Failover Cluster Instances (FCI).

Each node should have sufficient local storage for its copy of the database.

2. **SQL Server Instance Requirements**

SQL Server Edition:

AlwaysOn Availability Groups require SQL Server Enterprise Edition.

Basic Availability Groups are offered in the Standard Edition but with restricted functionality.

(It supports only one database per group and has no readable secondaries.)

SQL Server Installation:

SQL Server 2019 must be installed on all participating nodes with the same version and patch level.

Enable AlwaysOn Feature:

The AlwaysOn Availability Groups feature must be enabled on each SQL Server instance via SQL Server Configuration Manager.

Authentication:

Configure the SQL Server service account with appropriate permissions for AlwaysOn and cluster operations.

3. **Database Requirements**

Full Recovery Model:

All databases added to an Availability Group must use the Full Recovery Model.

Ensure no databases in the group are set to simple or Bulk-Logged Recovery Model.

Backup:

Perform a full database backup and a transaction log backup before adding the database to the Availability Group.

Readiness:

Databases must be in a synchronized state before failover or availability group creation.

4. **Account and Permission Requirements**

Cluster Service Account:

The WSFC service account must have sufficient permissions to manage the cluster.

The account should also have access to the quorum witness (if used).

SQL Server Service Account:

The SQL Server service account must be domain-based and have the necessary permissions to communicate with the cluster and replicas.

Listener Permissions:

Ensure permissions are configured to allow the Availability Group Listener to register with DNS.

5. **Availability Group Listener (Optional)**

   If using an Availability Group Listener for seamless application failover:

   Reserve an IP address for the listener.

   Ensure client applications can reach the IP address.

6. **Other Considerations**

   Synchronous vs. Asynchronous Commit Mode:

   Determine the appropriate commit mode based on requirements for performance and data loss tolerance.

   Synchronous commit ensures zero data loss, while asynchronous commit offers better performance for geographically distant replicas.

   Readable Secondary:

   Decide if secondary replicas will be configured for read-only workloads.

   Cluster Validation:

   Use the Windows Failover Cluster Validation Wizard to ensure the cluster is configured correctly before proceeding.

   Firewalls:

   Open the required ports (the default SQL Server port is 1433, and WSFC-related ports) to ensure communication between nodes.

Checklist Summary

Ensure all prerequisites are satisfied to seamlessly configure and deploy AlwaysOn Availability Groups in SQL Server 2019.

Process of Configuring AlwaysOn Availability

Step 1: Configure Windows Server Failover Clustering (WSFC)

Install Failover Clustering Feature:

Open Server Manager.

Go to Manager ➤ Add Roles and Features.

Follow the wizard to install the Failover Clustering feature on all servers that will be part of the AlwaysOn Availability Group.

Create a Failover Cluster:

Open the Failover Cluster Manager.

Click on Create Cluster and follow the wizard to create a new cluster. You need to specify the cluster name and IP address.

Validate the configuration and complete the creation.

Step 2: Configure SQL Server for AlwaysOn

Step 3: Enable AlwaysOn Availability in All the Nodes

1. From the **Start** screen, launch **SQL Server Configuration Manager**.

2. In the browser tree, choose **SQL Server Services**, right-click the **SQL Server (MSSQLSERVER)** service, and select **Properties**.

3. Go to the **AlwaysOn High Availability** tab and check the box to **enable AlwaysOn availability groups**.

Step 4: Take the full backup of databases

You must back up the new database to start the log chain. It cannot be added to an availability group without backing up the new database.

1. In Object Explorer, right-click the database, go to Tasks, and select Back Up.

2. Click OK to perform a full backup to the default backup location.

Step 5: Start the AlwaysOn High Availability Wizard

To do this, open Managment Studio, expand AlwaysOn High Availability, right-click Availability Group, and choose New Availability Group Wizard (As shown in Figure 7-1).

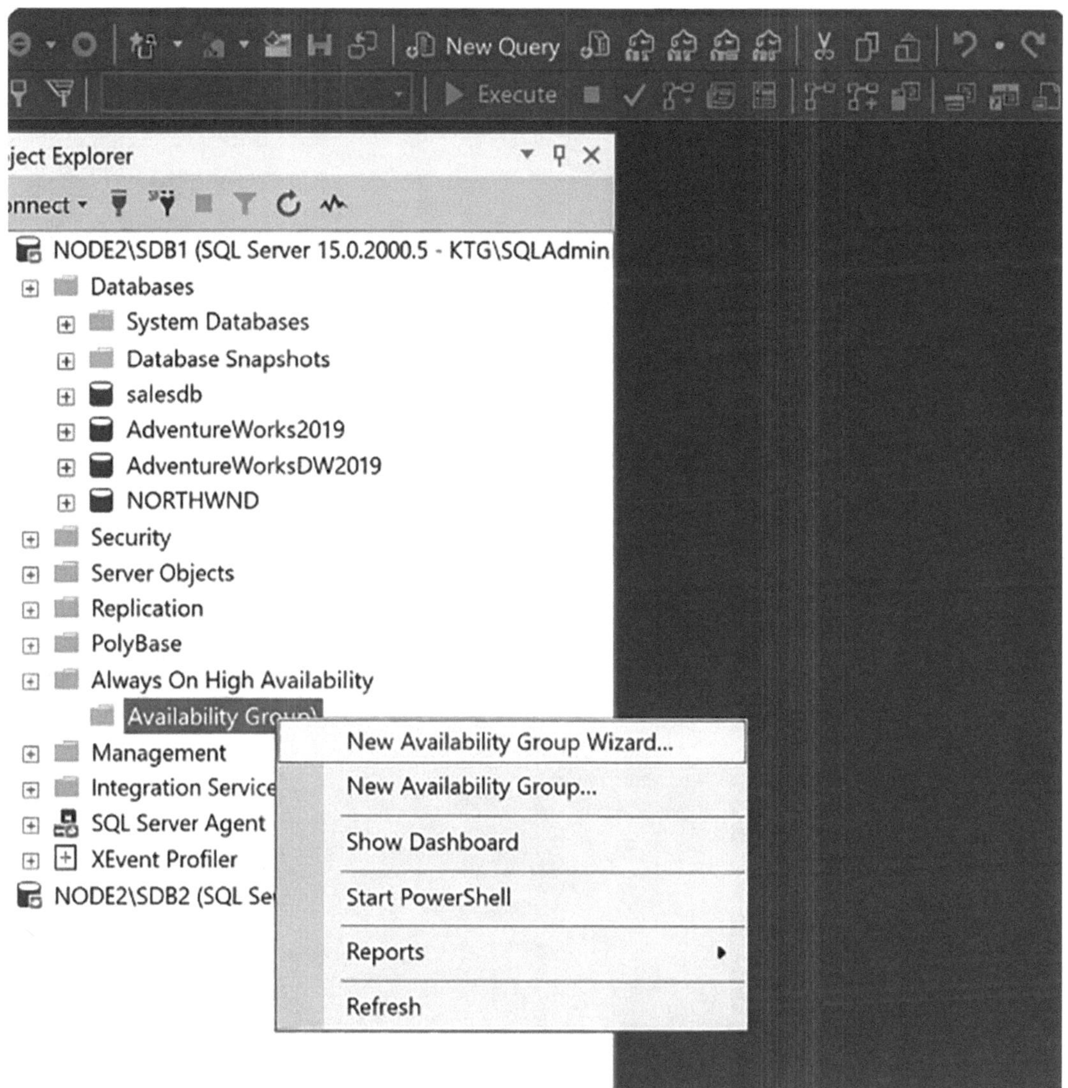

Figure 7-1. *Object explorer*

Start New Availability Group Wizard

Step 6: Click next on the wizard to provide the availability group's name.

(As shown in Figure 7-2).

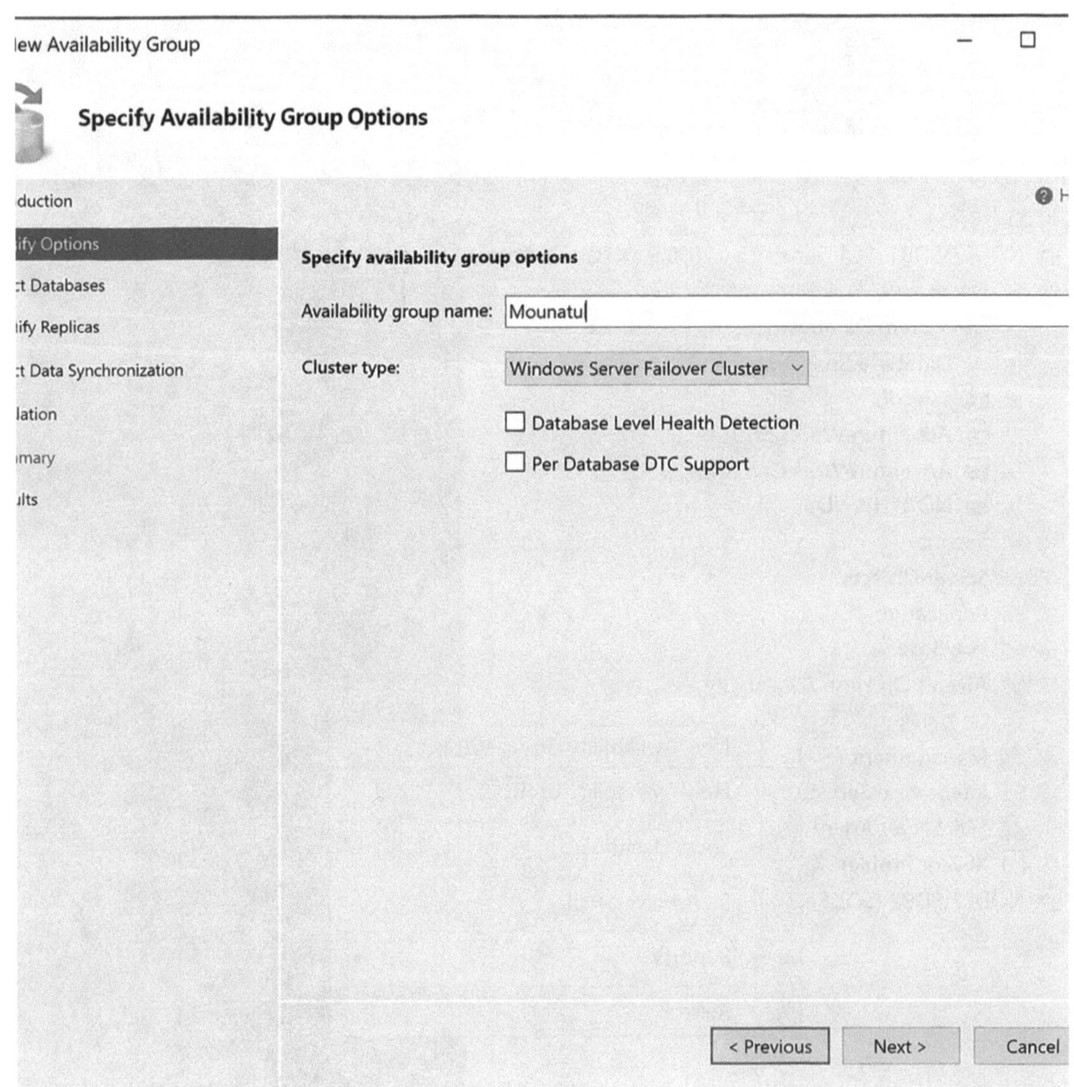

Figure 7-2. *Specify availability group options*

Name the Availability Group

Step 7: Select the databases you want to use for the Availability Group

(As shown in Figure 7-3).

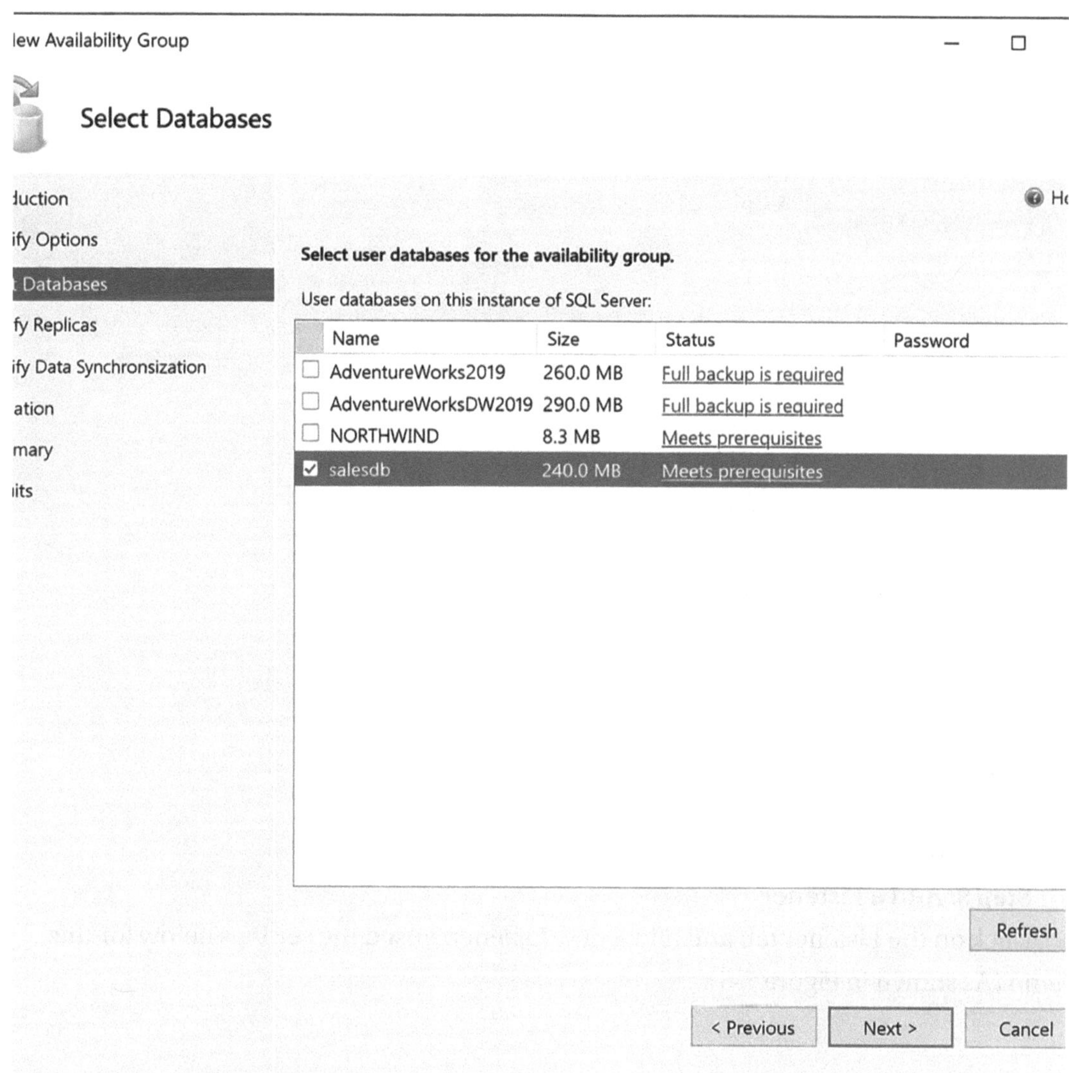

Figure 7-3. *Select database*

Select Databases That Meet the Prerequisite

Step 8: On the following screen, include the secondary replication using the button Add Replication. I added one more for this demo (As shown in Figure 7-4).

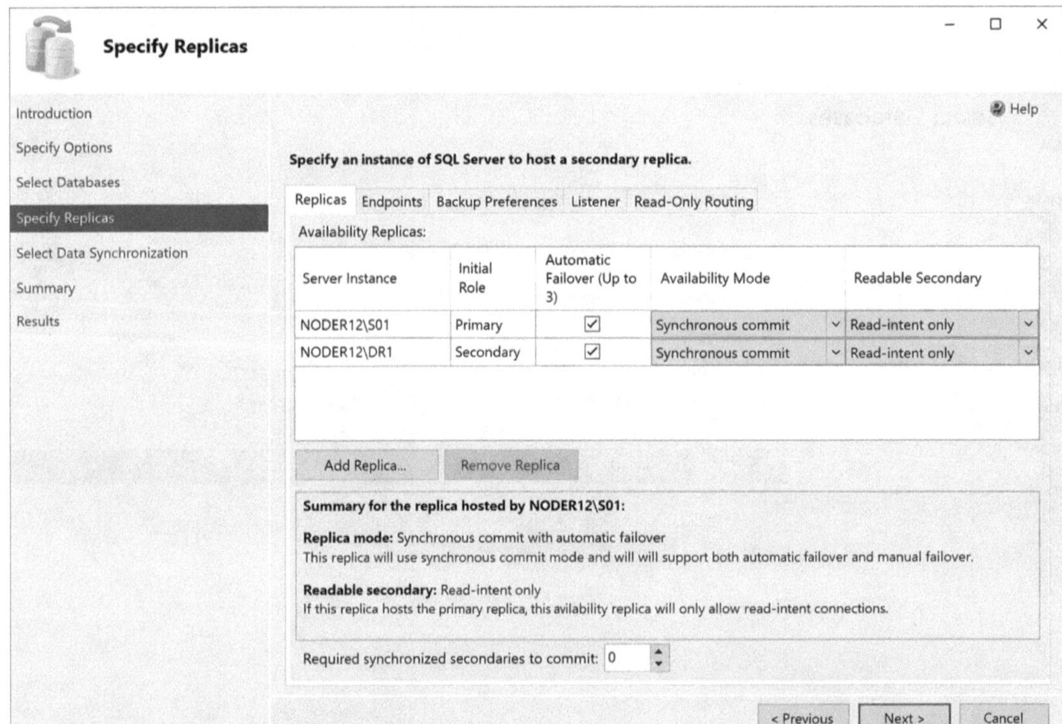

Figure 7-4. *Specify replicas*

Add Replicas

Step 9: Add a Listener

Click on the Listener tab and add a new Listener. I used the settings below for this demo (As shown in Figure 7-5).

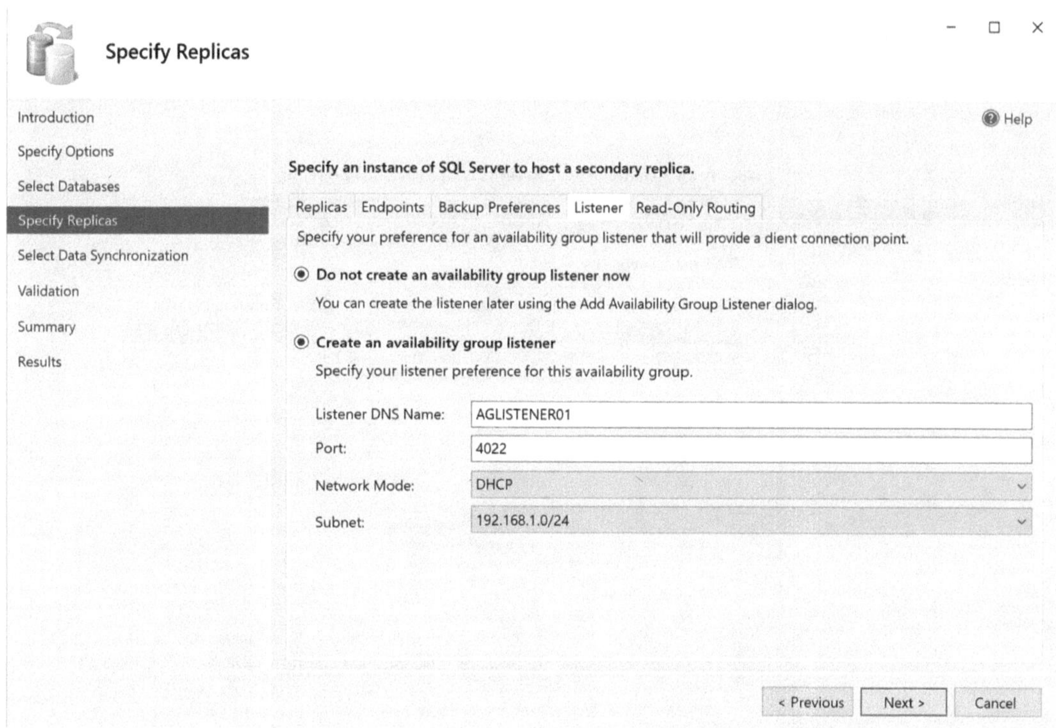

Figure 7-5. *Add a listener*

Add Availability Group Listener

Step 10: Read-Only Routing

The final tab on the Specify Replicas page is **Read-Only Routing**. This feature directs read-only connections to a secondary replica. A *routing URL* and a *read-only routing list* are required to enable it (As shown in Figure 7-6).

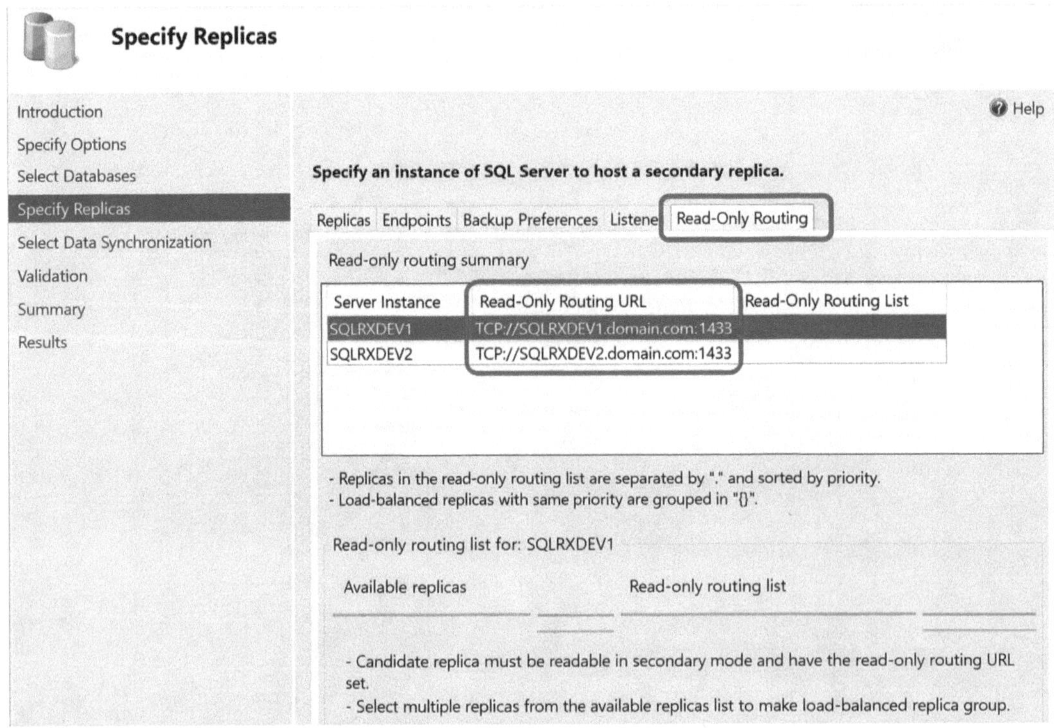

Figure 7-6. *Read-only routing*

Step 11: Select Initial Data Synchronization

This step is when you will add your databases to the Availability Group. Choose
the **Automatic Seeding** option to allow SQL to create the databases on your secondary
replicas automatically. Ensure the data and log file paths are the same across all replicas.
Automatic seeding operates on a single thread and can manage up to **five databases.**
(As shown in Figures 7-7 to 7-9)

Select Initial Data Synchronization

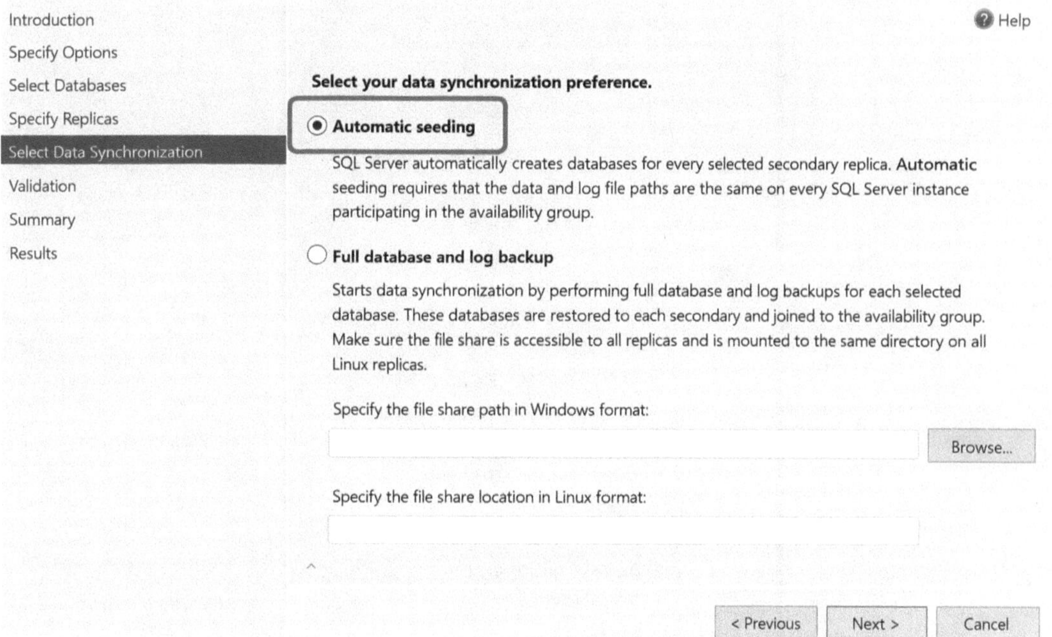

Figure 7-7. Select initial data synchronization

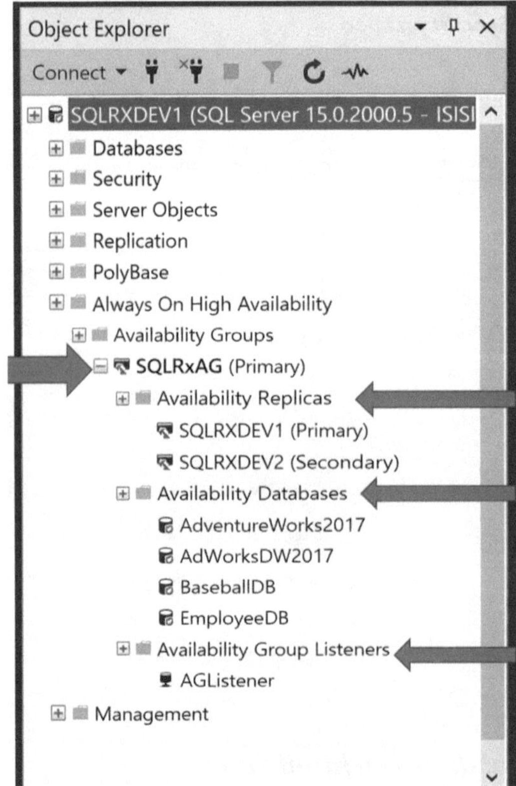

Figure 7-8. *Object explorer*

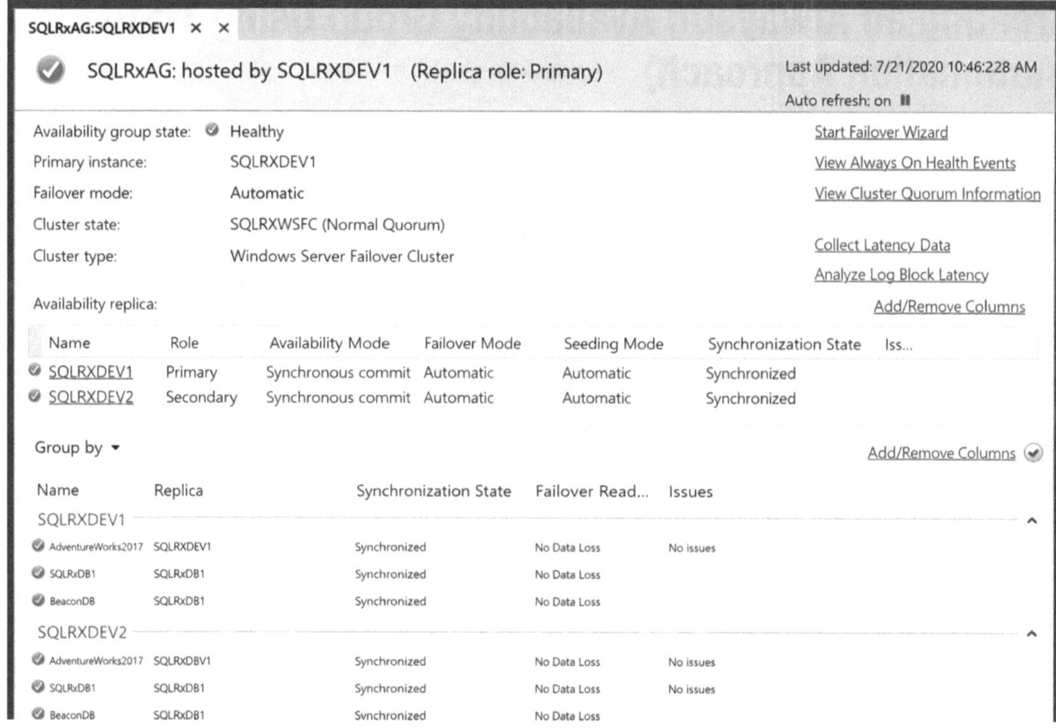

Figure 7-9. *SQLRxAG, hosted*

Creating an AlwaysOn Availability Group Using T-SQL

It should include:

- Enabling AlwaysOn (note: this part can only be done in Configuration Manager, not T-SQL)

- Database preparation (FULL + LOG backups)

- Creating the endpoints

- Granting endpoint CONNECT permissions

- Creating the Availability Group (CREATE AVAILABILITY GROUP)

- Joining secondary replicas

- Joining the databases to the AG

- Creating the listener

Creating an AlwaysOn Availability Group Using T-SQL (Automation Approach)

While SQL Server Management Studio provides a user-friendly wizard, many enterprises automate AlwaysOn configuration using T-SQL scripts. Below is an end-to-end example of creating an Availability Group entirely through T-SQL.

Step 1: Prepare the Databases

Each database must have a full backup and a log backup before being added to an AG.

```
USE master;
GO
BACKUP DATABASE AdventureWorks
TO DISK = 'C:\Backup\AdventureWorks_full.bak';
GO

BACKUP LOG AdventureWorks
TO DISK = 'C:\Backup\AdventureWorks_log.trn';
GO
```

Restore these backups on each secondary replica:

```
RESTORE DATABASE AdventureWorks
FROM DISK = 'C:\Backup\AdventureWorks_full.bak'
WITH NORECOVERY;
GO

RESTORE LOG AdventureWorks
FROM DISK = 'C:\Backup\AdventureWorks_log.trn'
WITH NORECOVERY;
GO
```

Step 2: Create Database Mirroring Endpoints (Required for AG Communication)

Run this on each replica:

```
CREATE ENDPOINT Hadr_Endpoint
STATE = STARTED
AS TCP (LISTENER_PORT = 5022)
FOR DATA_MIRRORING (ROLE = ALL);
GO
```

Grant permissions:

```
GRANT CONNECT ON ENDPOINT::Hadr_Endpoint TO [DOMAIN\SQLServiceAccount];
GO
```

Step 3: Create the Availability Group on the Primary Replica

```
CREATE AVAILABILITY GROUP SQLRxAG
WITH (AUTOMATED_BACKUP_PREFERENCE = PRIMARY)
FOR DATABASE AdventureWorks
REPLICA ON
'SQLNODE1' WITH
( ENDPOINT_URL = 'TCP://SQLNODE1:5022',
AVAILABILITY_MODE = SYNCHRONOUS_COMMIT,
FAILOVER_MODE = AUTOMATIC ),
  'SQLNODE2' WITH (
ENDPOINT_URL = 'TCP://SQLNODE2:5022',
 AVAILABILITY_MODE = SYNCHRONOUS_COMMIT,
FAILOVER_MODE = AUTOMATIC );
GO
```

Step 4: Join Secondary Replicas to the AG

Run on each secondary node:

```
ALTER AVAILABILITY GROUP SQLRxAG JOIN;
GO
```

Step 5: Join Databases to the AG

Run on each secondary replica:

```
ALTER DATABASE AdventureWorks
SET HADR AVAILABILITY GROUP = SQLRxAG;
GO
```

Step 6: Create an Availability Group Listener (Optional but Common)

Run on the primary replica:

```
ALTER AVAILABILITY GROUP SQLRxAG
ADD LISTENER 'SQLRXLISTENER'
(
    WITH IP ((N'10.10.10.50', N'255.255.255.0')),
    PORT = 1433
);
GO
```

Step 7: Configure Read-Only Routing (Optional)

On Primary

```
ALTER AVAILABILITY GROUP SQLRxAG MODIFY REPLICA ON 'SQLNODE1' WITH (READ_
ONLY_ROUTING_URL = 'TCP://SQLNODE1:1433');
ALTER AVAILABILITY GROUP SQLRxAG MODIFY REPLICA ON 'SQLNODE2' WITH (READ_
ONLY_ROUTING_URL = 'TCP://SQLNODE2:1433');
```

Define routing lists:

```
ALTER AVAILABILITY GROUP SQLRxAG MODIFY REPLICA ON 'SQLNODE1' WITH (READ_
ONLY_ROUTING_LIST = ('SQLNODE2'));
ALTER AVAILABILITY GROUP SQLRxAG MODIFY REPLICA ON 'SQLNODE2' WITH (READ_
ONLY_ROUTING_LIST = ('SQLNODE1')); GO
```

Availability Modes and Failover

Failover is switching roles between the availability replicas in an AlwaysOn Availability Group (AG) configuration. During a failover, the designated target replica (currently a secondary) assumes the primary role, bringing the database online to handle client connections. In a failback operation, the original primary replica (now secondary) regains its role as the primary replica in the AG configuration.

In an AlwaysOn Availability Group, one primary replica and one or more secondary replicas exist. The number of replicas depends on the SQL Server version. These replicas can operate in either Synchronous or Asynchronous commit modes:

Synchronous Commit Mode: The primary replica waits for an acknowledgment from the secondary replica before committing a transaction. This guarantees that the data on both replicas remain consistent.

Asynchronous Commit Mode: The primary replica commits transactions without waiting for confirmation from the secondary replica. This provides faster transaction processing but may lead to data latency.

The failover behavior in SQL Server AlwaysOn Availability Groups depends on the configured commit mode. SQL Server supports the following types of failovers:

1. **Planned Manual Failover:**

   Requires synchronous commit mode.

   Used for maintenance or testing, ensuring no data loss as the secondary replica is fully synchronized.

2. **Forced Failover (Manual):**

   Available in asynchronous commit mode or when synchronous replicas are not synchronized.

   This may lead to data loss, forcing the secondary replica to assume the primary role without verifying full synchronization.

3. **Automatic Failover:**

   It requires a synchronous commit mode and a healthy secondary replica configured for automatic failover.

   It occurs without manual intervention when the primary replica becomes unavailable.

These failover options provide flexibility and control in maintaining high availability and disaster recovery for SQL Server databases.

Manual Failover to DR (Planned Manual Failover)

Initiate Manual Failover (all nodes are still running and up—mainly used for DR testing)

Set the DR replica to synchronous availability mode to ensure no data loss during failover.

In Object Explorer, connect to the server instance hosting the primary replica and expand the server tree.

Then, expand the AlwaysOn High Availability node, followed by the Availability Groups node.

Click the availability group whose replica you want to change.

Right-click the replica and choose Properties.

In the Availability Replica Properties window, use the Availability mode drop-down list to change the availability mode of this replica (As shown in Figure 7-10).

Replica Name	Availability Mode	Failover Mode	Readable Secondary	Endpoint URL
PrimaryNode	Synchronous Commit	Automatic	Yes	TCP://PrimaryNode:5022
SecondaryNode1	Synchronous Commit	Automatic	Yes	TCP://SecondaryNode1:5022
SecondaryNode2	Asynchronous Commit	Manual	Yes	TCP://SecondaryNode2:5022

Figure 7-10. *Availability replicas*

In the Availability Replica Properties dialog box, use the Availability mode drop-down list to change the availability mode of this replica.

In Object Explorer, connect to a server instance that hosts a secondary replica of the availability group that needs to be failed over. Expand the server tree.

Expand the AlwaysOn, High Availability, and Availability Groups nodes. Then, right-click the availability group you wish to fail over and choose failover.

Select New Primary Server (DR) (As shown in Figure 7-11)

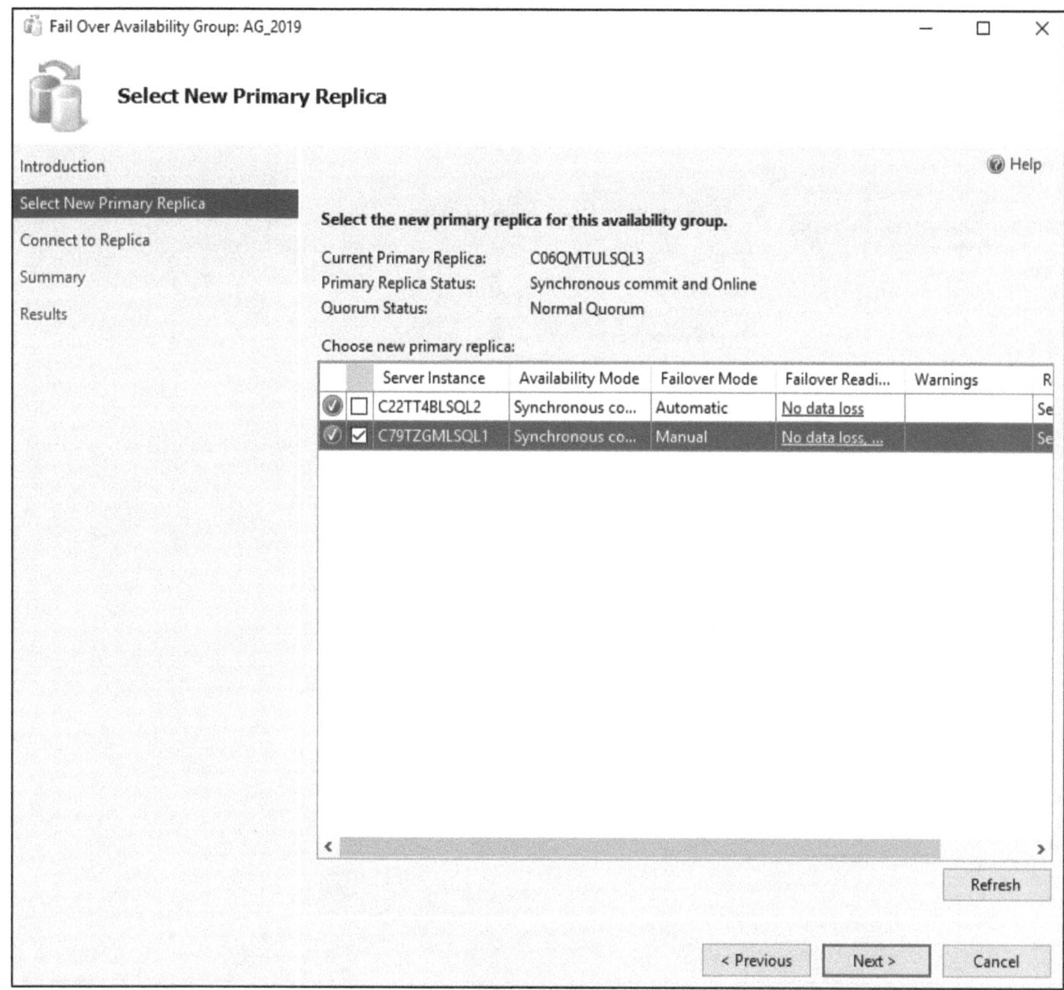

Figure 7-11. *Select new primary replica*

Connect the new primary server and finish the failover (As shown in Figures 7-12 and 7-13).

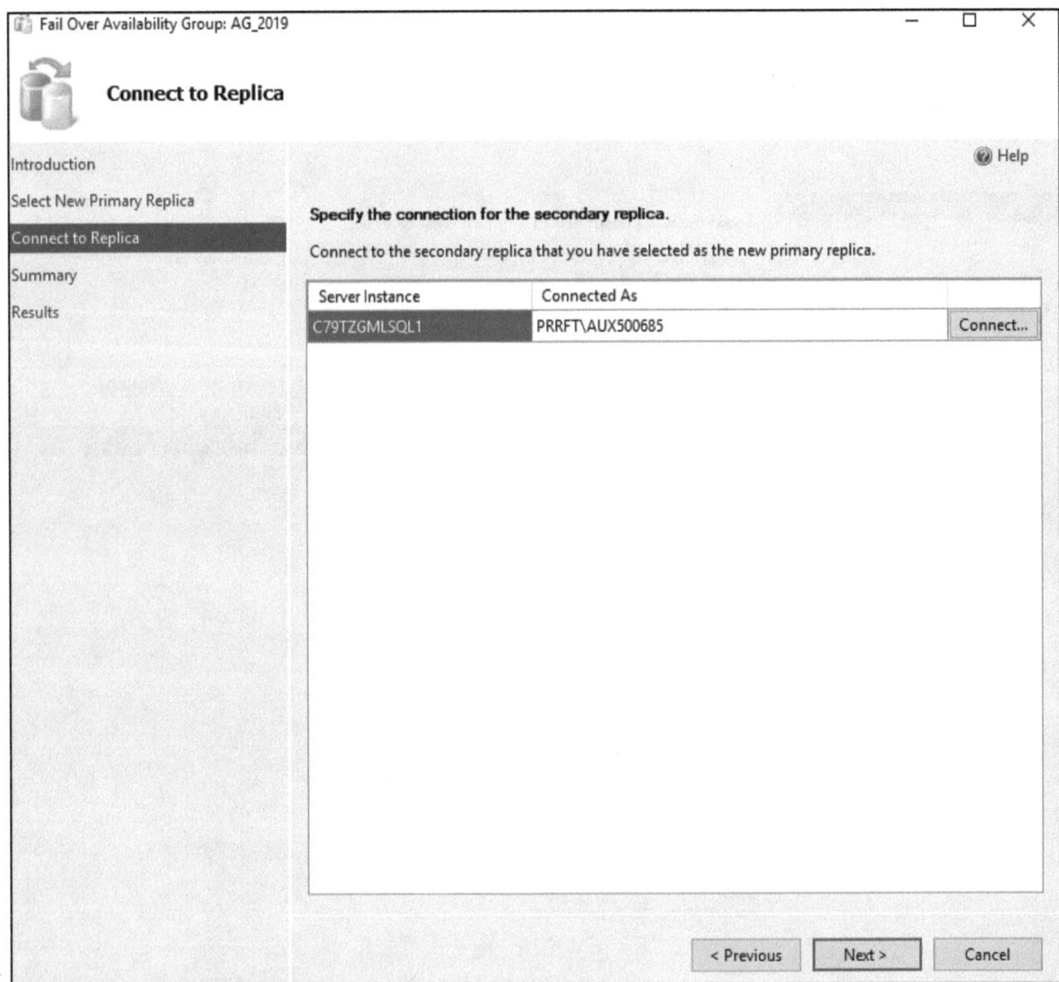

Figure 7-12. *Connect to replica*

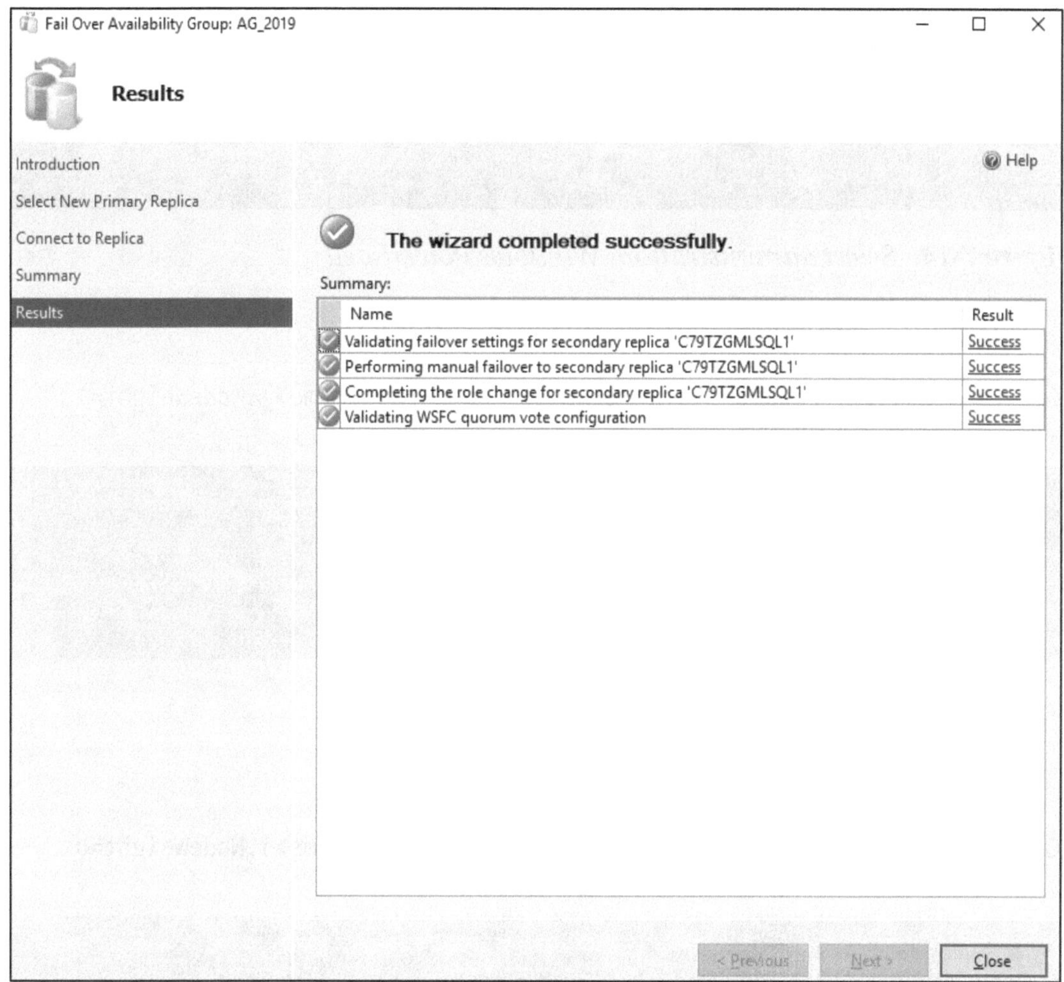

Figure 7-13. *Results*

After a successful failover, set the Primary and Secondary Replicas availability mode
to **Asynchronous mode** while testing on the DR Node and **make sure to Change the
Quorum Settings on the New Primary Node (in DR DC) and the Old Primary and
Secondary Node (in PROD DC).** If you fail to set the quorum setting, AG will return to
primary and bring down the DR cluster. AG Databases will not be accessible, which will
cause an application outage.

Check NodeWeight for a cluster.

Get-ClusterNode | ft name, dynamicweight, nodeweight, state -AutoSize

You will see that the NodeWeight for the DR Node is 0 (As shown in Figure 7-14)

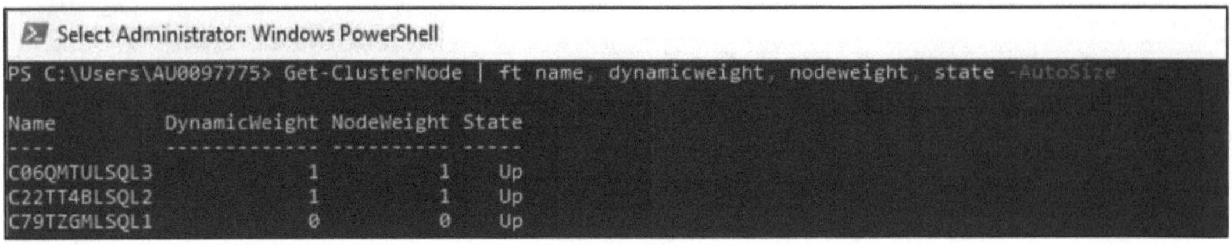

Figure 7-14. *Select administration: Windows PowerShell*

Set the DR Node voting to 1 (As shown in Figure 7-15)

```
(Get-ClusterNode -Cluster <ClusterName> -Name <NodeName>).NodeWeight=1
```

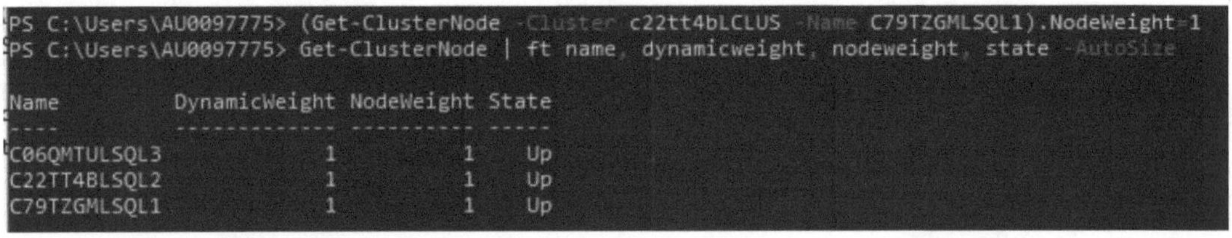

Figure 7-15. *Select NodeWeight*

Set the PROD Nodes voting to 0 (As shown in Figure 7-16)

```
(Get-ClusterNode -Cluster <ClusterName> -Name <NodeName>).NodeWeight=0
```

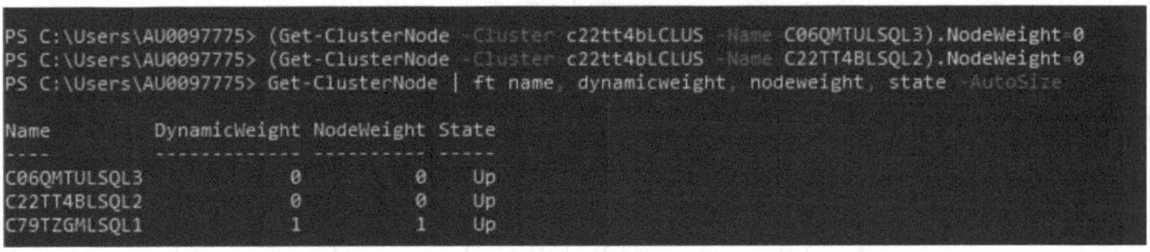

Figure 7-16. *PowerShell*

Manual Failback to PROD After DR Test

After a successful DR test, follow the **precheck** steps in the DR server and start the failback on the PROD server.

Perform a manual failover to the PROD node.

In Object Explorer, connect to a server instance hosting a secondary replica of the availability group that requires failover. Then, expand the server tree to the AlwaysOn High Availability node and the Availability Groups node.

Right-click the availability group to be failed over and select failover.

Select the old primary server (PROD).

Connect the old primary server and finish the failover.

After Successful Failover, set the

failover mode of the primary and secondary replicas to automatic with synchronous commit.

Set the DR replica to Asynchronous availability mode.

In Object Explorer, connect to the server instance that hosts the primary replica and expand the server tree.

Expand the AlwaysOn High Availability node and the Availability Groups node.

Click the availability group whose replica you want to change.

Right-click the replica and click Properties.

In the Availability Replica Properties dialog box, use the Availability mode drop-down list to change the availability mode of this replica.

After failover, Change the Quorum Settings on the Old Primary Node, Secondary Node (in PROD DC), and DR Server.

Set the DR Node voting to 0

```
Get-ClusterNode -Cluster <ClusterName> -Name <NodeName>).NodeWeight=0
```

Set the Prod Nodes voting to 1 (As shown in Figure 7-17)

```
(Get-ClusterNode -Cluster <ClusterName> -Name <NodeName>).NodeWeight=1
```


Figure 7-17. *PowerShell*

Forced Failover to DR

After a planned failover, if we fail to set the quorum settings, AG might fail back to Primary and bring down the DR cluster. AG Databases will not be accessible, which will cause an application outage. In some cases, Primary may not be accessible or unable to RDP. Follow the steps below to bring the DR Replica online with the Forced Failover option (As shown in Figure 7-18).

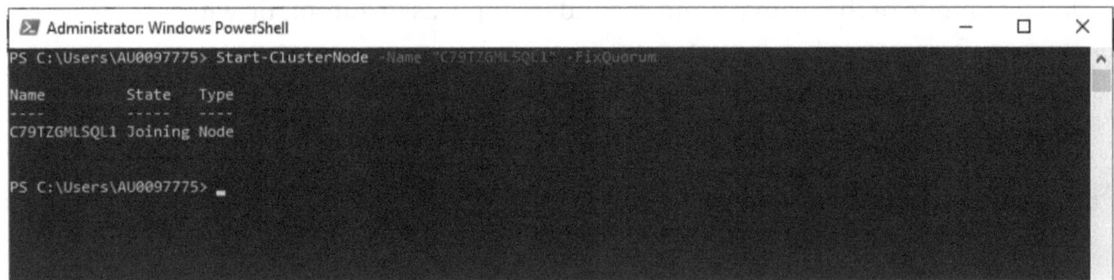

Figure 7-18. *PowerShell*

In the DR node, execute the PowerShell script to fix the quorum issue. Start-ClusterNode –Name "DRNODE" -FixQuorum

Check the node status (As shown in Figure 7-19).

```
Get-ClusterNode –Name "DRNODE"
```

Figure 7-19. *Node Status*

Once the node is up, the failover manager will be accessible, and the AG Resource will be in a failed state (As shown in Figure 7-20).

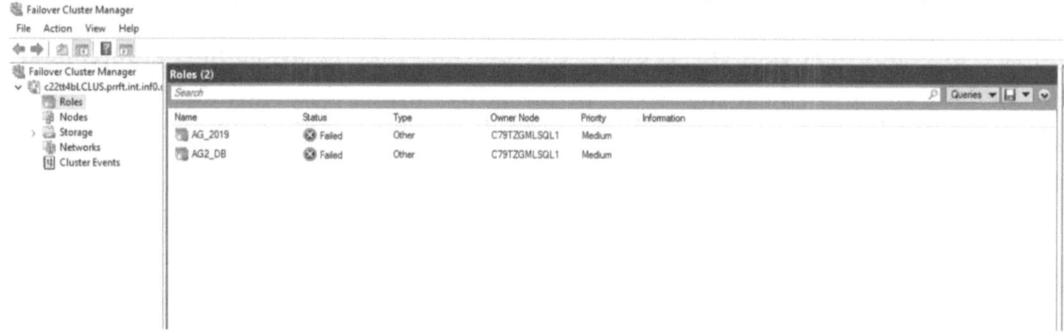

Figure 7-20. *Failover cluster manager*

Update the Quorum Settings, DR Node to 1, and Prod Nodes to 0.

Set the DR Node voting to 1 (As shown in Figure 7-21)

```
(Get-ClusterNode -Cluster <ClusterName> -Name <NodeName>).NodeWeight=1
```

```
PS C:\Users\AU0097775> (Get-ClusterNode -Cluster c22tt4bLCLUS -Name C79TZGMLSQL1).NodeWeight=1
PS C:\Users\AU0097775> Get-ClusterNode | ft name, dynamicweight, nodeweight, state -AutoSize

Name           DynamicWeight NodeWeight State
----           ------------- ---------- -----
C06QMTULSQL3               1          1    Up
C22TT4BLSQL2               1          1    Up
C79TZGMLSQL1               1          1    Up
```

Figure 7-21. *PowerShell*

Set the PROD Nodes voting to 0 (As shown in Figure 7-22)

```
(Get-ClusterNode -Cluster <ClusterName> -Name <NodeName>).NodeWeight=0
```

```
PS C:\Users\AU0097775> (Get-ClusterNode -Cluster c22tt4bLCLUS -Name C06QMTULSQL3).NodeWeight=0
PS C:\Users\AU0097775> (Get-ClusterNode -Cluster c22tt4bLCLUS -Name C22TT4BLSQL2).NodeWeight=0
PS C:\Users\AU0097775> Get-ClusterNode | ft name, dynamicweight, nodeweight, state -AutoSize

Name           DynamicWeight NodeWeight State
----           ------------- ---------- -----
C06QMTULSQL3               0          0    Up
C22TT4BLSQL2               0          0    Up
C79TZGMLSQL1               1          1    Up
```

Figure 7-22. *PowerShell*

After updating Quorum Settings, execute the below script to check the AG Sync status. If the value of **is_failover_ready** is 1, it indicates that the availability group failed; the database was synced because it can be brought online without any data loss. If the value is 0, the database was not synchronized when the availability group went offline, and getting the database online would result in data loss.

Execute the following query to retrieve the replica server name, failover readiness, database name, recovery LSN, and truncation LSN:

SQL

```
Choose dharcs.replica_server_name, dhdrcs.is_failover_ready, dhdrcs.
database_name, dhdrcs.recovery_lsn, dhdrcs.truncation_lsn
FROM sys.dm_hadr_database_replica_cluster_statesdhdrcs join sys.dm_hadr_
availability_replica_cluster_statesdharcson(dhdrcs.replica_id = dharcs.
replica_id) order by dharcs.replica_server_name,dhdrcs.database_name
```

Connect to the SQL Server on the DR node and issue the following query to bring the availability group online.

```
ALTER AVAILABILITY GROUP <availability group> FORCE_FAILOVER_ALLOW_
DATA_LOSS
```

Important   When issuing the failover command, "FORCE_FAILOVER_ALLOW_
DATA_LOSS" must be issued because the cluster service was started with a force
quorum, even if the secondary was set up to be a synchronous commit.

The availability replica is online in the primary role, and the availability databases should be available on the DR node.

If there is no data loss and once the PROD and Secondary Nodes are online, execute the below command to resume the data synchronization on each server by running the following T-SQL on each database.

Alter database dbname set had resumed.

Once you have force-started the cluster on a node, you must start any remaining nodes in your cluster with a configuration that prevents quorum. Starting a node with this setting signals the cluster service to join the active cluster rather than creating a new cluster instance. This helps avoid the formation of a split cluster with two competing cases.

In some multisite disaster recovery scenarios, you must recover your cluster after force-starting it on your DR site. To join the force-started cluster in the DR site, the nodes in your primary site must be started with the quorum prevented.

Use the below command to start the cluster service with the quorum prevented on primary nodes.

Start-ClusterNode –Node "Nodename" –PQ

To fail back to the PROD server, follow the steps in **Manual Failback to PROD After the DR Test.**

Unplanned DR Failover

If both primary and secondary SQL nodes are lost in PRDO DC, an unplanned DR failover will be needed. Follow the steps below to bring the DR Replica online with the Forced Failover (forced quorum) option.

In the DR node, execute the PowerShell script to fix the quorum issue. Start-ClusterNode –Name "DRNODE" -FixQuorum (As shown in Figure 7-23).

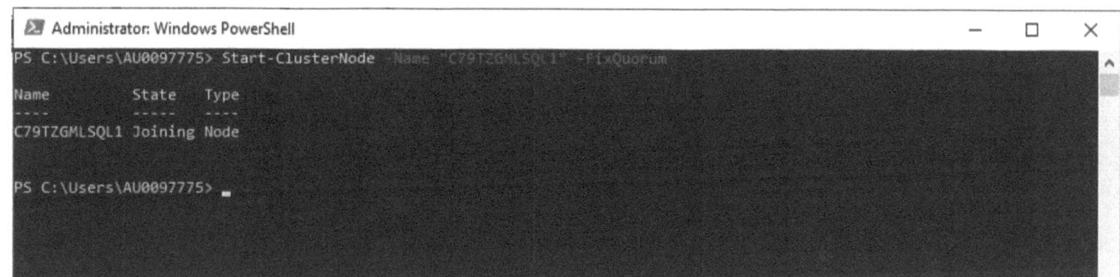

Figure 7-23. *Administrator: Windows PowerShell*

Check the node status (As shown in Figure 7-24).

```
Get-ClusterNode –Name "DRNODE"
```

Figure 7-24. *Administrator: Windows PowerShell*

Once the node is up, the failover manager will be accessible, and the AG Resource will be in a failed state (As shown in Figure 7-25).

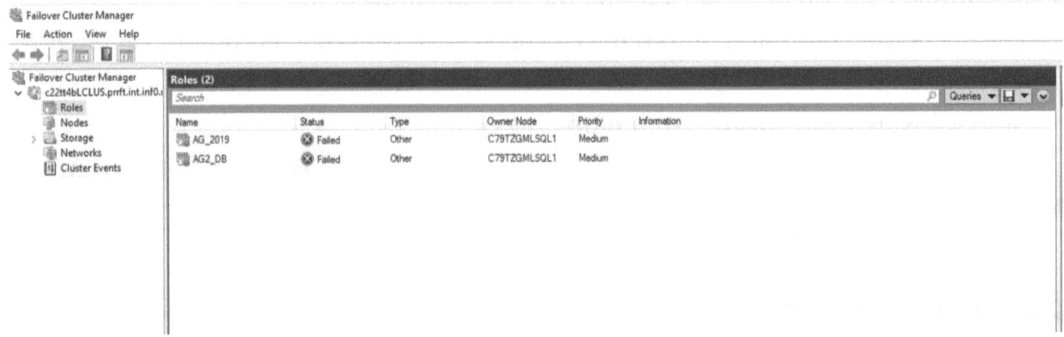

Figure 7-25. *Roles*

Update the Quorum Settings, DR Node to 1, and Prod Nodes to 0.

Set the DR Node voting to 1 (As shown in Figure 7-26)

```
(Get-ClusterNode -Cluster <ClusterName> -Name <NodeName>).NodeWeight=1
```

```
PS C:\Users\AU0097775> (Get-ClusterNode -Cluster c22tt4bLCLUS -Name C79TZGMLSQL1).NodeWeight=1
PS C:\Users\AU0097775> Get-ClusterNode | ft name, dynamicweight, nodeweight, state -AutoSize

Name            DynamicWeight NodeWeight State
----            ------------- ---------- -----
C06QMTULSQL3                1          1 Up
C22TT4BLSQL2                1          1 Up
C79TZGMLSQL1                1          1 Up
```

Figure 7-26. *Administrator: Windows PowerShell*

Set the PROD Nodes voting to 0 (As shown in Figure 7-27)

```
(Get-ClusterNode -Cluster <ClusterName> -Name <NodeName>).NodeWeight=0
```

```
PS C:\Users\AU0097775> (Get-ClusterNode -Cluster c22tt4bLCLUS -Name C06QMTULSQL3).NodeWeight=0
PS C:\Users\AU0097775> (Get-ClusterNode -Cluster c22tt4bLCLUS -Name C22TT4BLSQL2).NodeWeight=0
PS C:\Users\AU0097775> Get-ClusterNode | ft name, dynamicweight, nodeweight, state -AutoSize

Name            DynamicWeight NodeWeight State
----            ------------- ---------- -----
C06QMTULSQL3                0          0 Up
C22TT4BLSQL2                0          0 Up
C79TZGMLSQL1                1          1 Up
```

Figure 7-27. *Administrator: Windows PowerShell*

After updating Quorum Settings, execute the below script to check the AG Sync status. If the value of the **is_failover_ready**. If the value is 1, it means following the availability group's offline period, the database was synchronized and can be brought online without data loss. If the value is 0, the database was not synchronized when the availability group went offline, and getting it online would result in data loss.

Run the following query:

SQL

```
SELECT dharcs.replica_server_name, dhdrcs.is_failover_ready, dhdrcs.
database_name, dhdrcs.recovery_lsn, dhdrcs.truncation_lsn FROM sys.dm_hadr_
database_replica_cluster_states AS dhdrcs JOIN sys.dm_hadr_availability_
replica_cluster_states AS dharcs ON dhdrcs.replica_id = dharcs.replica_id
ORDER BY dharcs.replica_server_name, dhdrcs.database_name;
```

On the DR node, connect to SQL Server and run the following query to bring the availability group online:

```
ALTER AVAILABILITY GROUP <availability group> FORCE_FAILOVER_ALLOW_
DATA_LOSS
```

Important   The FORCE_FAILOVER_ALLOW_DATA_LOSS command must be used when performing the failover because the cluster service was started with force quorum, even if the secondary replica was configured for synchronous commit.

Once executed, the availability replica will be activated primarily, and the availability databases should become accessible.

On the DR node, after you have force-started the cluster on a node, it is necessary to start any remaining nodes in your cluster with a setting to prevent a quorum. A node started with a setting that prevents quorum indicates to the cluster service to join an existing running cluster instead of forming a new cluster instance. This prevents the remaining nodes from forming a split cluster that contains two competing cases.

This is essential when recovering your cluster in certain multisite disaster recovery situations after force-starting the cluster on your DR site. To join the force-started cluster in the DR Site, the nodes in your primary site must be started with the quorum prevented.

Use the below command to start the cluster service with the quorum prevented on primary nodes. For more information, refer to the MS Article.

Start-ClusterNode –Node "Nodename" –PQ

If there is data loss and a need to recover the data from the old Primary, remove the original primary database from the availability group once the PROD and Secondary Nodes are online. This results in the database entering the RESTORING state. At this stage, it is recommended that the tail log be attempted again. After removing the database's log, you can update the new Primary (previously the secondary database) by exporting the data you wish to recover from the initial central database and transferring it into the new primary database.

After recovering and importing the data to the DR server, clean up the database in the old Primary to fail back to the PROD server. Follow the steps in the Manual Failback to PROD after DR Test section.

Automatic failover

This type of failover happens automatically when the primary replica goes down.

For automatic failover to work, the primary and at least one secondary replica must be configured with Synchronous commit and Automatic failover.

Both replicas should be synchronized.

To confirm if your Availability Group (AG) supports automatic failover, right-click the availability group and open its properties. The configuration will appear as follows:

Availability Mode: Synchronous commit

Failover Mode: Automatic (As shown in Figure 7-28)

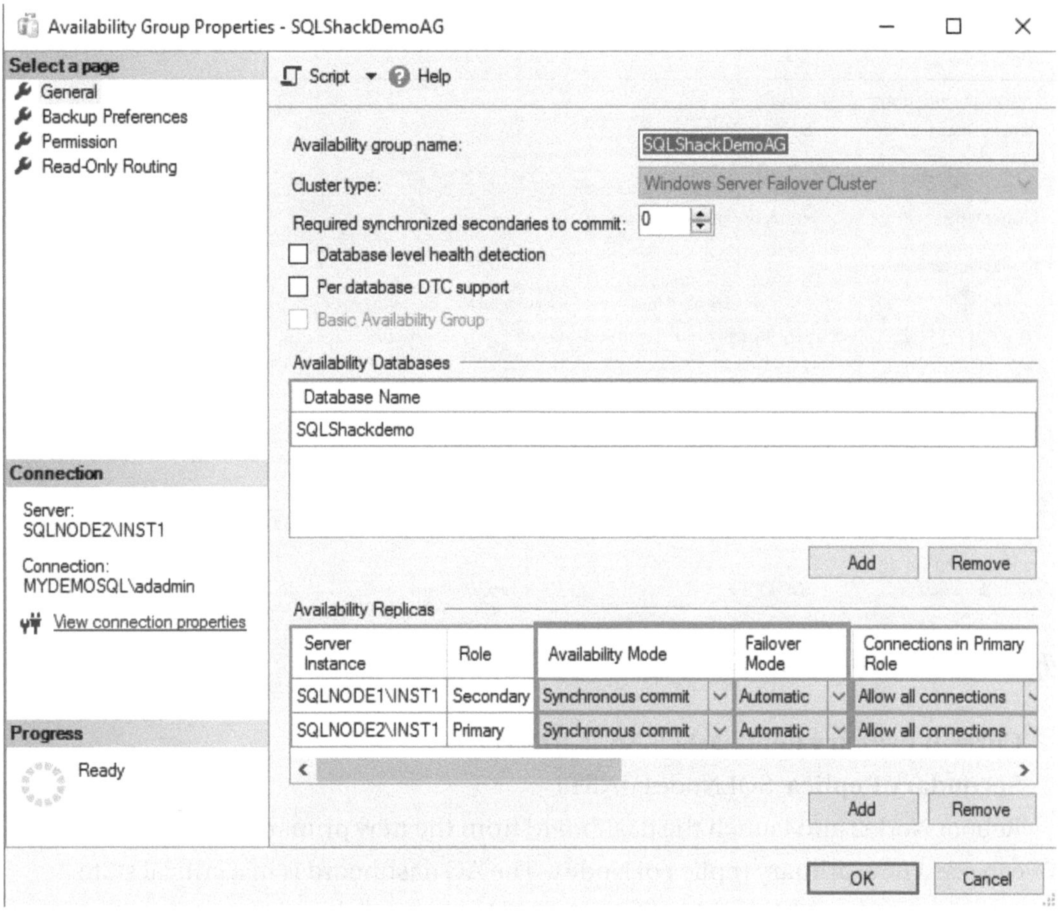

Figure 7-28. *Automatic failover*

Let's demonstrate automatic failover in action. To trigger an automatic failover, I intentionally rebooted the primary replica. Before shutting down the primary replica, ensure your AG databases are synchronized and that loss is displayed on the dashboard (As shown in Figure 7-29).

Note   Avoid performing these steps in a production environment for testing purposes.

SQLShackDemoAG: hosted by SQLNODE2\INST1 (Replica role: Primary)

Availability group state: Healthy
Primary instance: SQLNODE2\INST1
Failover mode: Automatic
Cluster state: SQLAGCLU (Normal Quorum)
Cluster type: Windows Server Failover Cluster

Availability replica:

Name	Role	Availability Mode	Failover Mode	Seeding Mode	Synchronization State	Issues
SQLNODE1\INST1	Secondary	Synchronous commit	Automatic	Automatic	Synchronized	
SQLNODE2\INST1	Primary	Synchronous commit	Automatic	Automatic	Synchronized	

Group by ▾

Name	Replica	Synchronization State	Failover Readi...	Redo Queue Si...
SQLNODE1\INST1				
SQLShackdemo	SQLNODE1\INST1	Synchronized	No Data Loss	
SQLNODE2\INST1				
SQLShackdemo	SQLNODE2\INST1	Synchronized	No Data Loss	

Figure 7-29. *SQL ShackDemoAg: Hosted*

Current Primary Replica: SQLNode2\INST1

Secondary Replica: SQLNode1\INST1

Reboot Node2 and launch the dashboard from the new primary replica, Node1.
We can see a new primary replica of Node1. The AG dashboard is in a critical state
because the previous Primary is still down, and its status is shown as Not Synchronizing
(As shown in Figure 7-30).

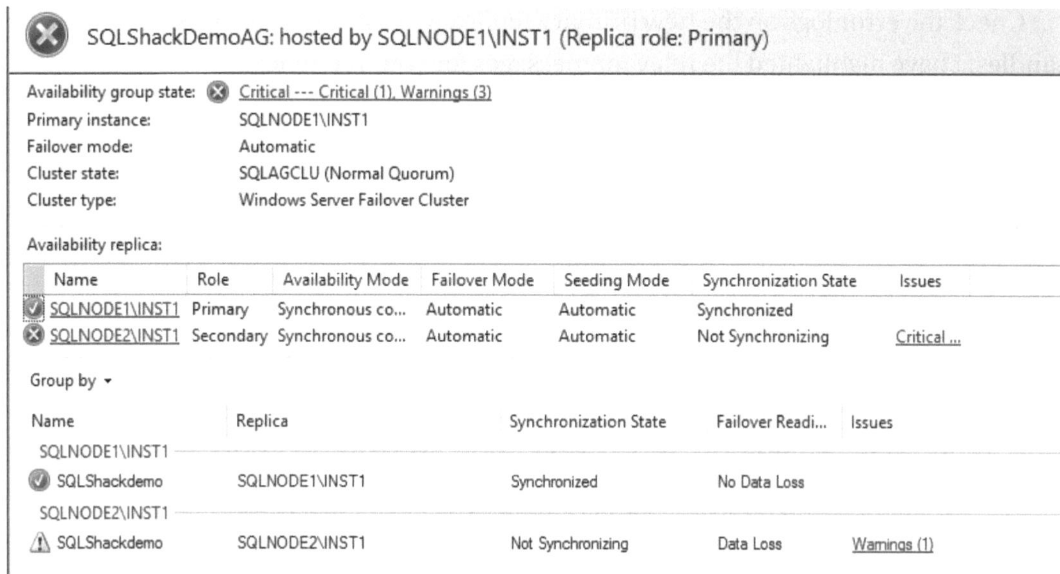

Figure 7-30. *SQL ShackDemoAG: hosted By SQLNoDe1*

Once the server (SQLNode2\INST1) is back online and capturing the transaction logs, the status will be updated to Synchronized (As shown in Figure 7-31).

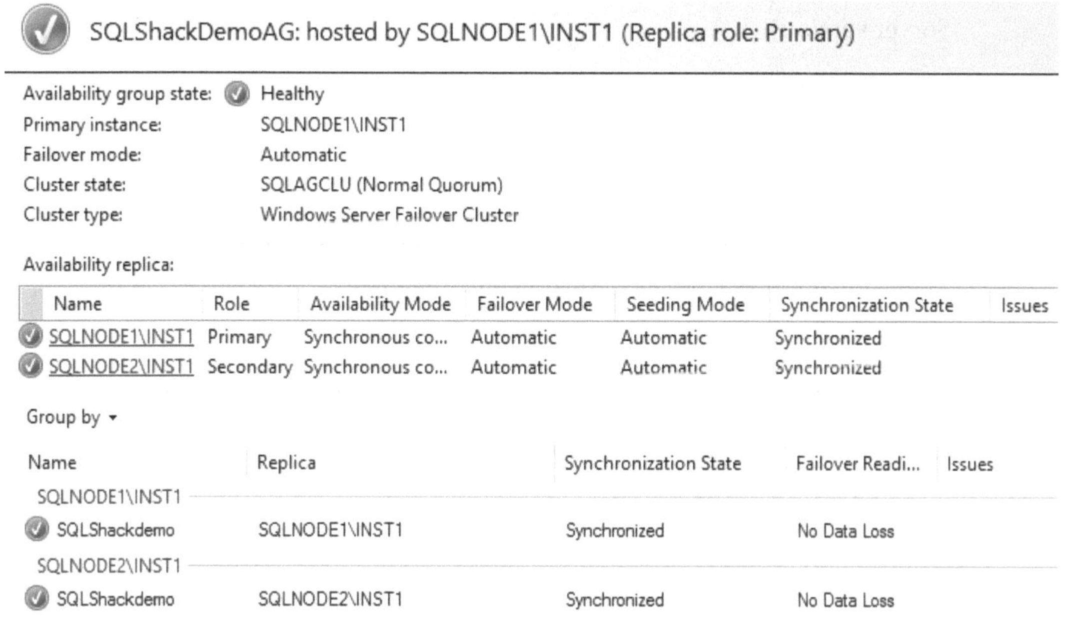

Figure 7-31. *Replica role: Primary*

Check the error logs on the new primary replica to examine the processes SQL Server handles. I have highlighted the relevant messages for your reference.

Advantages of AlwaysOn Availability Groups in SQL Server

AlwaysOn Availability Groups (AG) is a solution in SQL Server designed for high availability and disaster recovery that offers several benefits for enterprise applications. Here are the key advantages:

1. **High Availability and Disaster Recovery (HADR)**

   Provides automatic failover to secondary replicas, ensuring minimal downtime during hardware or software failures.

   It supports synchronous replication for zero data loss, making it a robust disaster recovery solution.

2. **Multiple Secondary Replicas**

   Allows up to eight secondary replicas (depending on the SQL Server version).

   Enables flexible deployment with both synchronous and asynchronous commit modes.

3. **Readable Secondary Replicas**

   Secondary replicas can be configured to be readable for offloading read-only queries, such as reporting and analytics.

   Reduces the workload on the primary replica, enhancing overall performance.

4. **Transparent Client Redirection**

   Provides seamless client redirection during failovers using **Listener** configuration.

   Applications automatically connect to the primary replica without manual intervention.

5. **Automatic Page Repair**

   Automatically repairs corrupted pages detected in the primary or secondary replicas.

   Prevents downtime due to page corruption.

6. **Backup Offloading**

   Backups can be performed on secondary replicas, reducing the impact on the primary replica's performance.

   Enhances overall resource utilization and availability.

7. **Support for Multi-Subnet Clustering**

   Enables deployment across geographically dispersed data centers.

   Provides disaster recovery solutions for large-scale enterprise environments.

8. **Database-Level Failover**

   Supports failover at the database level rather than at the server instance level.

   It offers granular control, allowing other databases on the instance to remain unaffected.

9. **Improved Performance for Maintenance Tasks**

   Maintenance tasks such as backups, reporting, and querying can be distributed across replicas.

   Minimizes the impact on the primary replica, ensuring smooth operations.

10. **Integration with SQL Server Features**

    Works seamlessly with features like Transparent Data Encryption (TDE), SQL Server Agent, and database snapshots.

    Enhances security, scheduling, and debugging options.

11. **Enhanced Monitoring and Troubleshooting**

    Includes built-in dashboards in SQL Server Management Studio (SSMS) for real-time monitoring of AG health.

    Generates detailed diagnostic data to aid in troubleshooting.

12. **Scalability**

    Enables load balancing of read-only workloads across multiple readable replicas.

    Supports hybrid deployments, combining on-premises and cloud-based replicas for scalability.

Conclusion

This chapter provided an in-depth exploration of AlwaysOn Availability Groups (AG) in SQL Server, beginning with an understanding of their purpose as a key solution for high availability and disaster recovery. The chapter then covered the necessary prerequisites for configuring an AG, delving into the practical steps for setting up and configuring them. We explored various failover modes and their implications, detailing the procedures for both manual and automatic failover, as well as planned and unplanned disaster recovery scenarios. The chapter concluded with a review of the advantages of using AlwaysOn AGs, including high availability, multiple secondary replicas, readable secondaries, and transparent client redirection during failovers. The essential takeaway is that AlwaysOn Availability Groups offer a comprehensive set of features for enhancing the resilience of SQL Server databases, providing robust protection against various types of outages and enabling continuous operations through thoughtful planning and diligent configuration.

CHAPTER 8

Performance Tuning and Optimization

This chapter focuses on enhancing SQL Server performance—an essential aspect of effective database management. The goal is not to chase theoretical maximum speeds but to strike a balance between efficient query execution, optimal resource utilization, and acceptable response times. We will explore various techniques that drive performance improvements while considering real-world resource constraints.

The chapter begins by covering fundamental query optimization principles, outlining core concepts that underpin efficient data retrieval. Next, we will examine partitioning strategies that intelligently divide data to accelerate query processing, along with techniques for optimizing tempdb, ensuring temporary resources are used efficiently.

A dedicated section will explore tempdb performance optimization, highlighting its significance and methods to enhance its speed. The discussion will then shift to SQL Server wait statistics and troubleshooting, equipping you with the skills to identify performance bottlenecks by analyzing wait events and applying targeted solutions.

The primary focus is finding the optimal balance between speed and resource efficiency. Real-world scenarios will illustrate these techniques, allowing you to proactively enhance SQL Server performance without unnecessary resource consumption. By the end of this chapter, you will be equipped to refine your queries and optimize performance while maintaining system stability.

Introduction to Query Optimization

Performance tuning is an essential component of SQL Server management. It ensures efficient query execution, optimal resource utilization, and reduced response time. This chapter delves into essential SQL Server optimization strategies, including query tuning,

© Venkata Reddy Pasam and Petchikumar Andiappan 2026
V. R. Pasam and P. Andiappan, *The Expert's Guide to SQL Server*, https://doi.org/10.1007/979-8-8688-2451-7_8

indexing best practices, partitioning strategies, TempDB optimization, and wait statistics analysis. These ideas are demonstrated through case studies from the real world.

When optimizing a query, we must balance performance improvements with resource constraints. Instead of striving for absolute maximum speed, a practical approach is to optimize until the query runs efficiently and remains sustainable over time. This balance is both a technical and a business decision. While unlimited resources could theoretically solve any performance problem, real-world constraints require us to determine when an optimization effort is "good enough."

Several Key Checkpoints Help Guide This Process:

The query now runs efficiently within acceptable limits.

Further optimization would require excessive resources.

Any additional improvements yield minimal benefits.

A better alternative makes the current approach obsolete.

While optimization is essential, excessive fine-tuning can be wasteful. For example, creating an extensive index with little benefit can introduce long-term overhead. Rewriting already efficient code may consume unnecessary time and effort. Sometimes, a small performance gain may not justify the extensive work required.

Ultimately, the goal is to solve the problem efficiently without unnecessary over-engineering.

Understanding the Query

Before optimizing a query, it's crucial to define its purpose. Key questions to consider:

What is the expected result set?

What generates this query—code, reports, or a UI?

How large is the result set—millions of rows or just a few?

Are parameters fixed or variable?

How frequently is it executed—once a day or every second?

Are there invalid input values that indicate an issue?

What level of performance is acceptable?

Jumping into optimization without understanding these factors wastes time. Sometimes, a new index isn't needed—breaking a query into smaller parts or fixing a parameter issue might be a better solution. Caching data may be more effective for reports running infrequently than optimizing for real-time execution. Asking the right questions upfront leads to more innovative, more effective improvements.

Tools for Optimization

We'll focus on a few key tools.

Execution Plans

Visual representation of how the query optimizer executes a query (As shown in Figure 8-1).

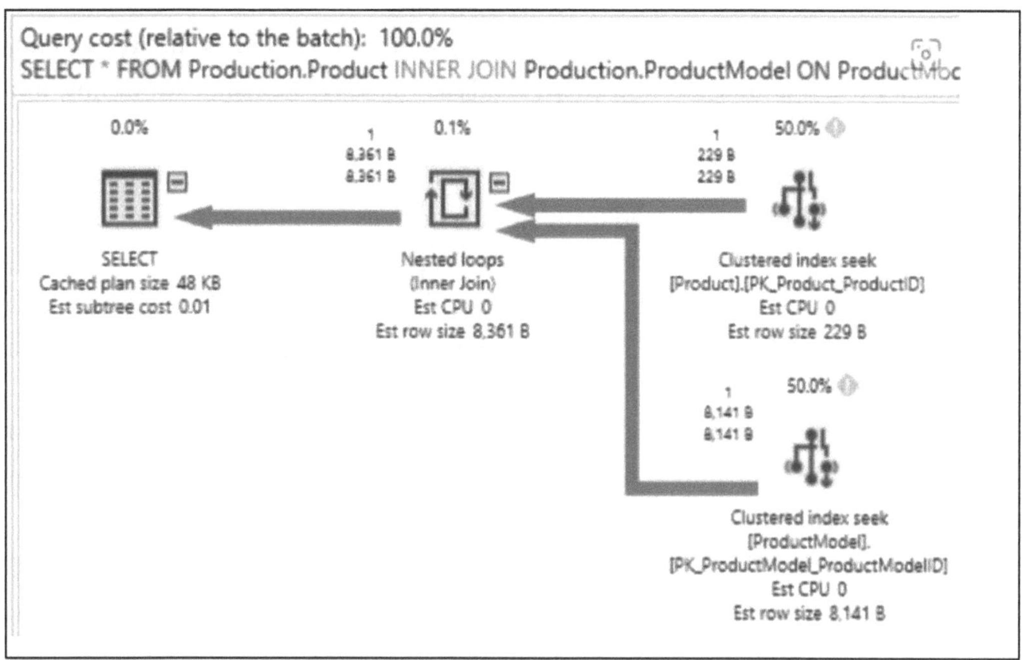

Figure 8-1. *Tools for optimization*

Execution plans reveal how queries access and join tables, detailing query costs, row sizes, CPU and I/O usage, and index utilization. The key is identifying operations processing excessive rows. By pinpointing high-cost components, we can focus on optimizing their performance.

STATISTICS IO

This allows us to see how many logical and physical reads are made when a query is executed and may be turned on interactively in SQL Server Management Studio by running the following T-SQL (As shown in Figure 8-2):

```
SET STATISTICS IO ON;
```

```
Results  Messages  Execution plan
    Table 'ProductModel'. Scan count 0, logical reads 2, physical reads 0.
    Table 'Product'. Scan count 0, logical reads 2, physical reads 0, rea
```

Figure 8-2. *Results appear in the messages panel*

Logical reads tell us how many reads were made from the buffer cache. We will refer to this number when we discuss how many reads a query is responsible for or how much IO it is causing.

Physical reads tell us how much data was read from a storage device, as it was not yet in memory. If data is frequently read from storage devices rather than memory, this can be a valuable indication of buffer cache/memory capacity problems.

IO will be the primary cause of latency and bottlenecks when analyzing slow queries. The unit of measurement of STATISTICS IO is one read, a single 8kb page, or 8192 bytes.

Query Duration

Typically, the #1 reason we research a slow query is that someone complained and told us it was too slow. The time it takes a query to execute will often be the smoking gun that leads us to a performance problem that needs a solution.

For our work here, we will measure duration manually using the timer found in the lower-right-hand corner of SSMS:

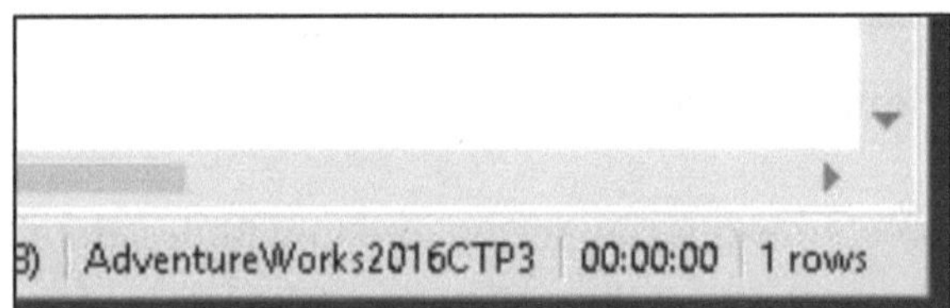

There are other ways to accurately measure query duration, such as setting STATISTICS TIME. Still, we'll focus on queries that are slow enough that such a level of accuracy will not be necessary. We can easily observe when a 30-second query is improved to run in sub-second time. This also reinforces the user's role as a constant source of feedback as we try to improve an application's speed.

Index Scans

Data may be accessed from an index via a scan or a seek. A seek is a targeted selection of rows from the table based on a (typically) narrow filter. A scan is when an entire index is searched to return the requested data. If a table contains a million rows, then a scan will need to traverse all million rows to service the query. A search of the same table can traverse the index's binary tree quickly to return only the data needed without inspecting the entire table.

If there is a legitimate need to return a great deal of data from a table, an index scan may be the correct operation. For example, an index scan makes sense if we need to return 950,000 rows from a million-row table. However, a search would be far more efficient if we only needed to return 10 rows.

Index scans are easy to spot in execution plans (As shown in Figure 8-3):

```
SELECT*
FROM Sales.OrderTracking
INNER JOIN Sales.SalesOrderHeader
ON SalesOrderHeader.SalesOrderID = OrderTracking.SalesOrderID
INNER JOIN Sales.SalesOrderDetail
ON SalesOrderDetail.SalesOrderID = SalesOrderHeader.SalesOrderID
WHERE OrderTracking.EventDateTime = '2014-05-29 00:00:00';
```

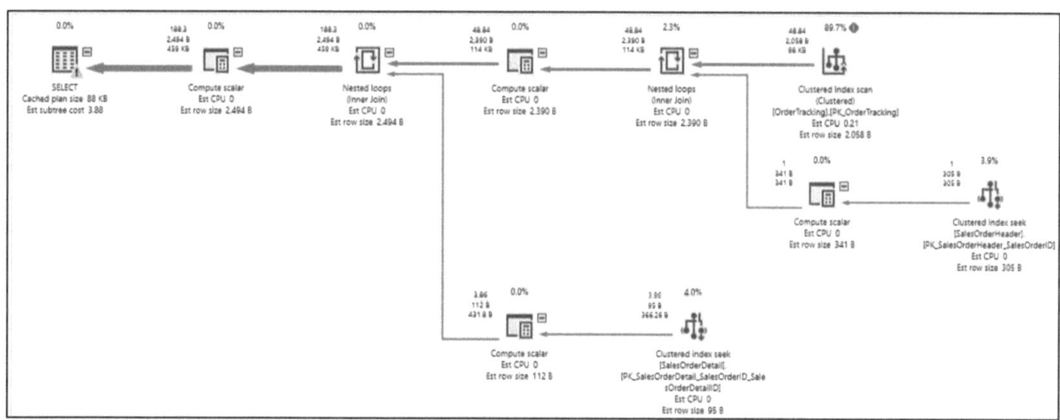

Figure 8-3. *Index scans*

We can quickly spot the index scan in the top-right corner of the execution plan. Consuming 90% of the resources of the query and being labeled as a clustered index scan quickly lets us know what is going on here. STATISTICS IO also shows us a large number of reads against the *OrderTracking* table (As shown in Figure 8-4):

```
Results  Messages  Execution plan
    Table 'SalesOrderDetail'. Scan count 89, logical reads 508, physical reads 1,
    Table 'SalesOrderHeader'. Scan count 0, logical reads 370, physical reads 1,
    Table 'OrderTracking'. Scan count 1, logical reads 4437, physical reads 0, re
```

Figure 8-4. *Order tracking table*

Many solutions are available when we have identified an undesired index scan. Here is a quick list of some thoughts to consider when resolving an index scan problem:

Is there any index that can handle the filter in the query?

In this example, is there an index on *EventDateTime*?

Should we create one to improve query performance if no index is available?

Is this query executed often enough to warrant this change? Indexes improve read speeds on queries but will reduce write speeds, so we should add them with caution.

Is this a valid filter? Is this column one that no one should ever filter on?

Should we discuss this with the app's developers to determine a better way to search for this data?

Is there some other query pattern that is causing the index scan that we can resolve? We will attempt to answer this question more thoroughly below. If there is an index on the filter column (*EventDataTime* in this example), other shenanigans that require our attention may be here!

Is the query one for which there is no way to avoid a scan?

Some query filters are all-inclusive and must be searched in the table. In our demo above, if *EventDateTIme* happens to equal "5-29-2014" in every row in *Sales. OrderTracking*, then a scan is expected. Similarly, if we performed a fuzzy string search, an index scan would be complex to avoid without implementing a Full-Text Index or similar feature.

Reviewing more examples will discover numerous additional methods for determining and resolving undesired index scans.

Joins and WHERE Clauses

A theme in optimization is a constant focus on joins and the WHERE clause. Since IO is generally our highest cost, and these query components can limit IO the most, we'll often find our worst offenders here. The faster we can slice down our data set to only the rows we need, the more efficient query execution will be!

When evaluating a WHERE clause, any expressions must be resolved before turning out our data. These functions must also be resolved if a column contains tasks around it, such as DATEPART, SUBSTRING, or CONVERT. If the function must be evaluated before execution to determine a result set, then the entirety of the data set will need to be scanned to complete that evaluation.

Consider the following query:

```
SELECT
Person.BusinessEntityID,
Person.FirstName,
Person.LastName,
Person.MiddleName
FROM Person.Person
WHERE LEFT(Person.LastName, 3) = 'For';
```

This will return any rows from *Person. The Person* that has a last name beginning with "For." Here is how the query performs (As shown in Figures 8-5 and 8-6):

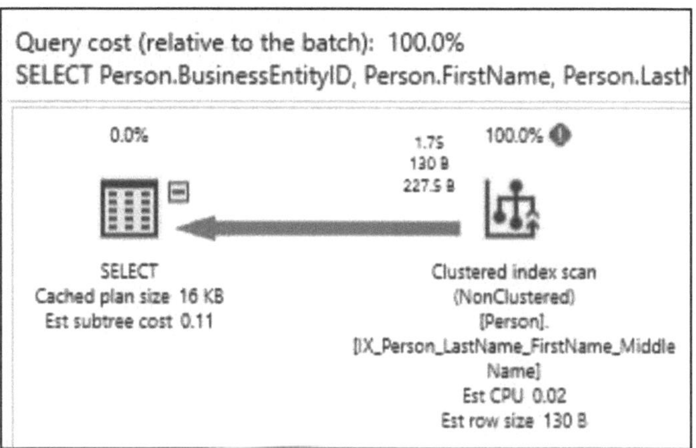

Figure 8-5. *Joins and WHERE clauses*

Figure 8-6. *Messages*

Despite only returning four rows, the entire index was scanned to return our data. The reason for this behavior is the use of LEFT on *Person.LastName.* While our query is logically correct and will return the desired data, the SQL Server must evaluate LEFT against every row in the table before determining which rows fit the filter. This forces an index scan, but luckily, it's one that can be avoided!

When faced with functions in the WHERE clause or a join, consider ways to move the function onto the scalar variable instead. Also, think of ways to rewrite the query so that the table columns can be left clean (without functions attached to them!).

The query above can be rewritten to do just this:

```
SELECT
    Person.BusinessEntityID,
    Person.FirstName,
    Person.LastName,
    Person.MiddleName
FROM Person.Person
WHEREPerson.LastName LIKE 'For%'
```

By using LIKE and shifting the wildcard logic into the string literal, we have cleaned up the *LastName* column, allowing SQL Server full access to seek indexes against it. Here is the performance we see on the rewritten version (As shown in Figures 8-7 and 8-8):

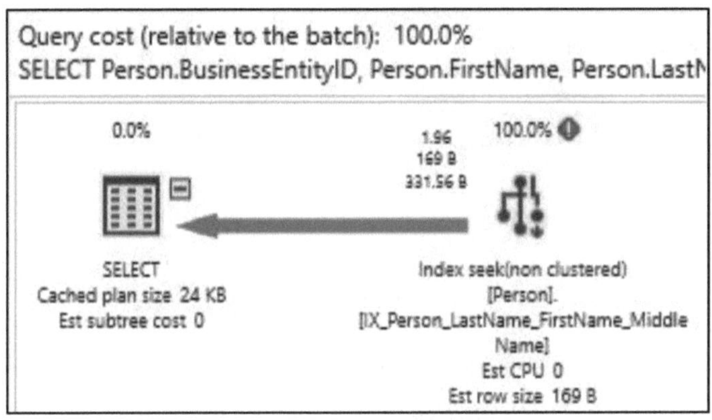

Figure 8-7. *Query cost*

Figure 8-8. *Messages*

The relatively minor tweak allowed the query optimizer to utilize an index seek and pull the data we wanted with only two logical reads instead of 117.

The theme of this optimization technique is to ensure that columns are left clean! When writing queries, feel free to put complex string/date/numeric logic onto scalar variables or parameters but not on columns. If you are troubleshooting a poorly performing query and notice functions (system or user-defined) wrapped around column names, think of ways to push those functions off into other scalar parts of the query. This will allow SQL Server to seek indexes rather than scan, making the most efficient decisions possible when executing the query!

Conclusion

Query optimization is a vast topic, but focusing on key areas can simplify the process. Instead of analyzing an entire query or procedure, identifying high-cost operations allows for targeted improvements. A single line in a lengthy script could be the root cause of performance issues.

This manual offers a place to start when diagnosing and resolving query latency. While some optimizations may require additional resources, such as indexing, many performance gains come from simply rewriting queries—reducing resource usage without added costs. Optimizing queries improves efficiency and leads to cost savings and a smoother user experience.

Indexing Best Practices

Introduction

Indexing is one of the most crucial aspects of database performance optimization in Microsoft SQL Server. Properly designed indexes can drastically improve query performance, while poorly designed indexes can degrade it. This guide explores best practices for indexing in SQL Server, covering different index types, strategies, and maintenance tips to ensure optimal performance.

1. **Understanding Indexes**

    Indexes in SQL Server work similarly to an index in a book, allowing the database engine to locate data quickly. Without indexes, SQL Server must scan the entire table to retrieve results, leading to poor performance for large datasets.

Types of Indexes

The clustered index determines the physical arrangement of the data in a table. Each table can have only one clustered index.

Non-clustered Index: This index stores a separate structure with pointers to the actual data. A table can have multiple non-clustered indexes.

Unique Index: Ensures uniqueness of values in a column.

Filtered Index: Optimized index that covers only a subset of rows, improving performance for specific queries.

Columnstore Index: Designed for analytical queries and data warehousing.

Full-Text Index: Supports text-based searches across large datasets.

2. **Best Practices for Indexing**

   a. **Choosing the Right Index**

      Use clustered indexes on columns frequently in range-based queries and sorting (e.g., dates, identity columns).

      Create non-clustered indexes on columns used in WHERE, JOIN, and ORDER BY clauses.

      Use filtered indexes for queries that retrieve specific subsets of data.

      Implement covering indexes to include all columns a query requires, reducing lookups.

   b. **Avoid Over-Indexing**

      Due to additional maintenance overhead, too many indexes can slow down DML (INSERT, UPDATE, DELETE) operations.

      - Regularly review and drop unused indexes using DMVs (sys. dm_db_index_usage_stats).

c. **Indexing for Joins and Searches**

Create indexes on foreign key columns to speed up join operations.

Use composite indexes for queries that filter on multiple columns.

Consider FULLTEXT indexes for complex text-based searches.

d. **Index Order and Column Selection**

Place the most selective column first in multi-column indexes to maximize efficiency.

Index columns are used in GROUP BY and ORDER BY clauses.

Use included columns for frequently queried non-key columns to avoid key lookups.

e. **Index Fragmentation and Maintenance**

Monitor fragmentation using sys.dm_db_index_physical_stats.

Rebuild indexes (ALTER INDEX ... REBUILD) when fragmentation exceeds 30%.

Reorganize indexes (ALTER INDEX ... REORGANIZE) when fragmentation is 10%-30%.

Schedule index maintenance jobs during off-peak hours.

3. **Advanced Indexing Strategies**

a. **Partitioning and Indexing**

Use partitioned indexes for large tables to improve query performance.

Align indexes with table partitions for better efficiency.

b. **Indexed Views**

Use indexed views for frequently executed complex queries.

Ensure all underlying tables are used WITH SCHEMABINDING.

   c. **Optimizing for OLTP vs. OLAP Workloads**

     OLTP Workloads: Use narrow indexes, keep indexes lightweight, and avoid redundant indexes.

     OLAP Workloads: Leverage column store indexes for large aggregations and analytical queries.

4. **Monitoring and Performance Tuning**

   Use SQL Profiler and Extended Events Indexing:monitoring and performance tuning to identify slow queries.

   Analyze execution plans (SET SHOWPLAN_XML ON) to determine if indexes are utilized efficiently.

   Utilize Database Engine Tuning Advisor for recommendations on index improvements.

   Regularly review missing index DMVs (sys.dm_db_missing_index_details) to create necessary indexes.

5. **Common Mistakes to Avoid**

   Not using indexes on large tables leads to full table scans.

   Over-indexing, causing performance overhead.

   Ignoring index maintenance leads to fragmentation and performance degradation.

   Creating redundant indexes, increasing storage usage, and slowing down writes.

   Not testing index impact, potentially slowing down other queries.

Conclusion

Effective indexing is essential for maintaining optimal SQL Server performance. By following best practices, monitoring usage, and continuously refining indexing strategies, databases can run efficiently and handle queries with minimal resource consumption. Regular maintenance and careful index design will ensure long-term database performance and scalability.

Partitioning Strategies

Introduction to Partitioning

Partitioning in SQL Server enables dividing big tables and indexes into smaller, easier-to-manage pieces called partitions. This enhances query performance, improves manageability, and reduces maintenance overhead.

Types of Partitioning

1. **Horizontal Partitioning**: Distributes rows across partitions based on column values (e.g., range-based partitioning).

2. **Vertical Partitioning**: Splits a table into multiple tables based on columns to improve performance for specific queries.

3. **Partitioned Views**: Uses UNION ALL queries across multiple tables to simulate partitioning when native partitioning is unavailable.

Partitioning Methods in SQL Server

1. **Range Partitioning**

   - It splits data into partitions according to specified value ranges.

   - Commonly used for time-series data (e.g., monthly or yearly sales data).

   - Implemented using Partitioned Tables with a Partition Function and Partition Scheme.

   Example: Partitioning sales data by year:

```
CREATE PARTITION FUNCTION SalesPartitionFunction (INT)
AS RANGE LEFT FOR VALUES (2019, 2020, 2021);

CREATE PARTITION SCHEME SalesPartitionScheme
AS PARTITION SalesPartitionFunction
ALL TO ([PRIMARY]);

CREATE TABLE Sales (SaleID INT PRIMARY KEY,SaleDate DATE, Amount
DECIMAL(10,2)ONSalesPartitionScheme(SaleDate);
```

2. **List Partitioning**

- Categorizes data into specific partitions based on predefined values.

- Ideal for datasets with well-defined categories (e.g., regions, departments).

Example: Partitioning orders by region:

```
CREATE PARTITION FUNCTION RegionPartitionFunction (VARCHAR(10))
AS RANGE LEFT FOR VALUES ('North,' 'South,' 'East,' 'West');
```

3. **Hash Partitioning**

- Distributes data evenly across partitions using a hash function.

- It is practical when there is no clear range-based partitioning criterion.

Example: Distributing user accounts across partitions:

```
CREATE PARTITION FUNCTION UserPartitionFunction (INT)
AS HASH WITH (BUCKET_COUNT = 4);
```

4. **Composite Partitioning**

Combines two partitioning strategies, such as Range-Hash.

Useful for massive datasets with multiple dimensions (e.g., partitioning by year and hashing by user ID).

Performance Benefits of Partitioning

1. **Query Performance Optimization:**

Queries can only contain relevant partitions (partition elimination).

Reduces index and table scan overhead.

2. **Improved Data Load and Maintenance:**

Partition switching enables faster data archiving and loading.

It is easier to manage large tables by focusing on specific partitions.

3. **Reduced Index Fragmentation:**

Indexes can be rebuilt at the partition level rather than the entire table.

Case Studies

Case Study 1: Enhancing Performance in a Large E-Commerce Database

Problem:

A large e-commerce platform faced slow query performance due to a growing Orders table (100+ million rows).

Solution:

Implemented range partitioning by order date.

Created a partition scheme that stored recent orders on SSDs and older orders on slower HDDs.

Result:

Queries for recent orders ran 70% faster due to reduced data scans.

Archiving old data was simplified using partition switching.

Case Study 2: Multi-Tenant SaaS Application Optimization

Problem:

A SaaS platform serving multiple clients stored all customer data in a single user table, leading to slow queries and maintenance challenges.

Solution:

Implemented Hash Partitioning on CustomerID.

Spread data across multiple partitions, enabling better parallelism and load distribution.

Result:

Query execution time improved by 50%.

Evenly distributed workload across database nodes, preventing hotspots.

Case Study 3: Financial Transactions Processing

Problem:

A banking application is needed to optimize transaction retrieval for audit and compliance reports.

Solution:

Used Composite Partitioning (Range-Hash).

Partitioned by transaction year (Range) and then hashed by AccountID.

Result:

80% reduction in query execution time.

Improved maintainability with efficient archiving strategies.

Best Practices for Partitioning in SQL Server

1. **Choose the Right Partitioning Strategy**: Use range partitioning for time-series data, list partitioning for categorical data, and hash partitioning for uniform data distribution.

2. **Indexing Considerations**: Use aligned indexes to ensure indexes benefit from partition elimination.

3. **Monitor Partition Performance**: Use sys. Partitions and sys.dm_db_partition_stats will be used to analyze partition health.

4. **Minimize Partition Count**: Avoid excessive partitions to prevent metadata overhead.

5. **Leverage Partition Switching**: Use ALTER TABLE SWITCH for fast data movement between tables.

Conclusion

One practical SQL Server approach is partitioning.

That enhances query performance, improves manageability, and optimizes storage. Organizations can achieve significant performance gains by implementing the right strategy based on data access patterns while reducing maintenance overhead.

Optimizing TempDB Performance

Introduction

TempDB is a critical system database in SQL Server that handles temporary objects, internal work tables, and version store data. Since it is shared across all databases in an instance, performance issues in TempDB can cause system-wide slowdowns. This article outlines effective practices and approaches for optimizing TempDB performance for better overall SQL Server efficiency.

Understanding TempDB Usage

TempDB is used for

1. **Temporary Tables (#TempTables, ##GlobalTempTables)**: Stores temporary data within a session.

2. **Table variables (@TableVariable)**: Uses TempDB for internal storage.

3. **Work Tables and Work Files**: Created by SQL Server for sorting, hashing, and spooling operations.

4. **Version Store:** Required for Snapshot Isolation and Read Committed Snapshot Isolation (RCSI).

5. **Sorting and Hashing Operations**: Large result sets or queries with ORDER BY, GROUP BY, and JOINs often use TempDB.

TempDB Performance Bottlenecks

TempDB performance issues often result from the following:

- Heavy contention on allocation pages (PFS, GAM, SGAM)

- Inadequate TempDB disk I/O performance

- Improper sizing and autogrowth settings

- Excessive workload from temporary objects and version store

Best Practices for Optimizing TempDB Performance

1. **Configure Multiple Data Files**

   To reduce contention on system pages (PFS, GAM, SGAM), create multiple TempDB data files. The recommended approach:

   Match the number of data files to the number of logical processors (up to 8 files initially).

   Ensure all TempDB data files are of equal size to balance I/O distribution.

   Example:

   SQL

```
ALTER DATABASE TempDB
MODIFY FILE (NAME = tempted, SIZE = 4GB, FILEGROWTH = 512MB);
```

2. **Place TempDB on High-Performance Storage**

   Use SSDs or NVMe disks for TempDB to reduce disk latency.

   Separate TempDB onto dedicated storage (avoid placing it with user databases).

   Use a RAID 10 configuration for better I/O performance.

3. **Set Optimal Initial Size and Autogrowth Settings**

   Pre-size TempDB to avoid frequent autogrowth events.

   Disable auto growth if TempDB is properly pre-sized and monitored.

   If autogrowth is needed, set it to a fixed MB size instead of a percentage.

   Example:

   SQL

```
ALTER DATABASE TempDB
MODIFY FILE (NAME = tempted, SIZE = 8GB, FILEGROWTH = 1GB);
```

4. **Minimize TempDB Contention**

   Use table variables instead of temp tables when possible (for small datasets).

   Avoid frequent creation and deletion of temp tables inside loops.

   Enable Read Committed Snapshot Isolation (RCSI) cautiously to control version store usage.

   SQL

```
ALTER DATABASE MyDB
SET READ_COMMITTED_SNAPSHOT ON;
```

5. **Monitor and Optimize Queries Using TempDB**

   Identify heavy queries consuming TempDB using DMV queries:

   SQL

```
SELECT session_id, database_id, task_alloc, task_dealloc
FROM sys.dm_db_task_space_usage
ORDER BY task_allocDESC;
```

   Use sp_WhoIsActive to track real-time TempDB usage.

   Optimize queries by reducing unnecessary sorts, joins, and temporary table usage.

Case Studies: Real-World Optimizations

Case Study 1: Reducing TempDB Contention in a High-Traffic System

Issue:

A financial application experienced severe performance degradation during peak hours. Queries with heavy sorting and hashing operations were causing contention with TempDB.

Solution:

1. Increased TempDB data files from 1 to 8 (equal to CPU cores).

2. Placed TempDB on a dedicated SSD RAID 10 storage.

3. Optimized query logic to use indexed temp tables instead of prominent sorts.

Outcome:

Query execution time dropped from 12 seconds to 3 seconds, and system-wide blocking was significantly reduced.

Case Study 2: Fixing TempDB Disk Latency in an E-Commerce Database

Issue:

An online store using snapshot isolation experienced frequent TempDB disk stalls. Monitoring showed excessive version store growth, which caused disk I/O bottlenecks.

Solution:

1. Moved TempDB to NVMe SSDs, improving disk throughput

2. Enabled version cleanup monitoring to alert users of excessive version store usage automatically

3. Tuned auto-growth settings to avoid fragmentation

Outcome:

Transaction response time improved by 40%, and version store cleanup reduced excessive TempDB usage.

Conclusion

TempDB is critical to SQL Server's performance, and poor configuration can lead to significant bottlenecks. You can significantly enhance SQL Server performance by configuring multiple data files, optimizing storage, tuning autogrowth settings, and monitoring TempDB usage.

SQL Server Wait Statistics and Troubleshooting

SQL Server Wait Statistics are crucial for understanding SQL Server performance. They provide insight into where SQL Server sessions are waiting, helping identify potential bottlenecks in the system.

SQL Server operates as a multi-threaded system, and threads often have to wait for various resources (like I/O, CPU, or locks) to become available. Analyzing wait statistics can identify areas where performance tuning is needed.

In this detailed explanation, we'll cover the following:

1. What are Wait Statistics?

2. Types of Waits

3. Common Wait Types and Their Meaning

4. Analyzing Wait Statistics

5. Using DMV to View Wait for Statistics

6. Resetting Wait Statistics

7. Best Practices for Interpreting Wait Statistics

1. **What Are Wait Statistics?**

   Wait statistics in SQL Server track the time that SQL Server tasks (threads) spend waiting for a resource to become available. When a thread cannot proceed because it is waiting for a resource, the SQL Server records the type of wait and the duration of that wait. This information is accumulated over time and can be analyzed to detect potential performance bottlenecks.

   - **Wait Time**: A thread spends waiting for a resource.

   - **Signal Wait Time**: The time a thread spends waiting to get access to the CPU after its resource becomes available.

   Why Waits Occur:

   - **CPU Bottleneck**: Threads waiting to be scheduled on the CPU.

   - **I/O Bottleneck**: Waiting for disk I/O operations to complete

   - **Lock Contention**: Waiting for locks held by other transactions

- **Memory Pressure**: Waiting for memory resources

- **Networking**: Waiting for network-related operations to complete

By examining these wait times, DBAs can gain insight into where SQL Server is experiencing delays.

2. **Types of Waits**

SQL Server waits can be broadly classified into several categories, each corresponding to a different type of resource or condition:

1. **I/O Waits:**

   - Threads waiting for disk I/O tasks to finish, like writing or reading data to a disk.

   - Common I/O-related waits include PAGEIOLATCH_*, WRITELOG, and ASYNC_IO_COMPLETION.

2. **Lock Waits:**

   - Threads waiting for locks on database objects (like tables, rows, etc.).

   - Common lock-related waits include LCK_M_* waits (e.g., LCK_M_S, LCK_M_X, LCK_M_U).

3. **Memory Waits:**

   - Threads waiting for memory resources, such as the buffer pool, to become available.

   - Common memory-related waits include RESOURCE_ SEMAPHORE and MEMORY_ALLOCATION_EXT.

4. **CPU Waits:**

   - Threads waiting for CPU resources, particularly when there is high CPU contention.

   - Common CPU-related waits include SOS_SCHEDULER_ YIELD and CXPACKET (which can also relate to parallelism).

5. **Network Waits:**

   - Threads waiting for network communication to complete, such as sending or receiving data over the network.

   - Common network-related waits include NETWORK_IO and ASYNC_NETWORK_IO.

6. **Other Waits:**

   - Miscellaneous waits that don't fall into the above categories, such as RESOURCE_GOVERNOR_QUEUE, BROKER_RECEIVE_WAITFOR, and CLR_SEMAPHORE.

3. **Common Wait Types and Their Meaning**

Below are some of the most common wait types and what they indicate:

4. **Analyzing Wait Statistics**

When analyzing wait statistics, you are essentially trying to answer these questions:

- Where is SQL Server spending the most time waiting?

- Which resources are causing delays?

- Are these waits normal for the workload or indicative of a performance problem?

Wait statistics can help pinpoint system bottlenecks related to CPU, I/O, memory, locks, or other resources.

Steps for Analyzing Wait for Statistics:

1. **Look at the Most Significant Waits:** Focus on the waits that consume the most time. Some waits are normal in any system, but excessive waits can point to a problem.

2. **Consider the Wait Types in Context:** Some are expected under specific workloads. For example, CXPACKET waits are common in systems that heavily use parallel queries. These waits don't always indicate a problem, but excessive amounts might.

3. **Check for Symptoms of Resource Bottlenecks**:

   I/O Bottlenecks: Excessive PAGEIOLATCH_* waits to suggest that the disk subsystem might not meet demand.

   CPU Bottlenecks: High SOS_SCHEDULER_YIELD waits suggest CPU contention.

   Memory Pressure: RESOURCE_SEMAPHORE waits to suggest that SQL Server is under memory pressure and is waiting to allocate memory for queries.

4. **Look for Lock Contention**: If you observe high LCK_M_* waits, it may indicate that other transactions are blocking transactions due to lock contention.

5. **Using DMV to View Wait for Statistics**

   SQL Server provides a Dynamic Management View (DMV) called sys.dm_os_wait_stats, which contains cumulative information about all the wait types experienced by SQL Server since the last restart or since the wait stats were last cleared.

   Query to Retrieve Wait for Statistics:

```
SELECT
wait_type,

SUM(wait_time_ms) AS wait_time_ms,

SUM(waiting_tasks_count) AS waiting_tasks_count,

SUM(max_wait_time_ms) AS max_wait_time_ms,

SUM(signal_wait_time_ms) AS signal_wait_time_ms FROM sys.dm_os_
wait_stats

WHERE wait_type NOT IN (

  'BROKER_TO_FLUSH',

  'BROKER_TRANSMITTER',

  'CHECKPOINT_QUEUE',
```

```
'FT_IFTS_SCHEDULER_IDLE_WAIT, '

'LAZYWRITER_SLEEP',

'SLEEP_TASK',

'SQLTRACE_BUFFER_FLUSH',

'WAIT_FOR',

'LOGMGR_QUEUE',

'REQUEST_FOR_DEADLOCK_SEARCH',

'XE_TIMER_EVENT',

'XE_DISPATCHER_WAIT',

'SLEEP_SYSTEMTASK',

'BROKER_EVENTHANDLER',
'DIRTY_PAGE_POLL'

GROUP BY wait_type

ORDER BY SUM(wait_time_ms) DESC;
```

This query filters out background waits that are generally irrelevant to performance analysis, such as waits associated with the SQL Server's internal processes (e.g., lazy writer, checkpoint).

Important Columns:

wait_type: The type of wait (e.g., CXPACKET, PAGEIOLATCH_SH, etc.).

wait_time_ms: SQL Server has spent waiting on this wait type (in milliseconds).

waiting_tasks_count: The number of tasks on this type of wait.

6. **Resetting Wait Statistics**

Wait statistics accumulate over time, so resetting them when troubleshooting specific issues is sometimes helpful. This allows you to track waits from a particular point in time.

You can reset wait statistics using the following command:

```
DBCC SQLPERF('sys.dm_os_wait_stats', CLEAR);
```

This will clear the wait statistics, and SQL Server will begin accumulating new data from that point.

7. **Best Practices for Interpreting Wait Statistics**

    - **Monitor Regularly**: Wait statistics should be monitored regularly, especially during peak loads, to identify trends and anomalies.

    - **Correlate with Other Metrics**: Wait statistics should be considered alongside other performance metrics like CPU usage, memory utilization, I/O throughput, and query execution times.

    - **Look for Patterns**: Focus on the top wait types that are consuming the most time and compare them with the expected behavior for your workload.

    - **Analyze Wait Ratios**: Calculate the ratio of wait time to signal wait time. If the signal wait time is high, it indicates that threads are waiting for CPU resources.

    - **Consider Workload Characteristics**: Some wait types may be expected depending on your workload. For example, systems that execute parallel queries will naturally have some CXPACKET waits.

Summary:

SQL Server Wait Statistics provide valuable insight into where SQL Server tasks are spending time waiting, helping you identify performance bottlenecks. DBAs can optimize query performance, tune the server, and resolve resource contention issues by understanding the types of waits and the resources involved.

Regularly monitoring and correctly interpreting wait statistics are essential for maintaining a well-tuned SQL.

Conclusion

This chapter has explored a suite of vital practices for optimizing SQL Server performance, emphasizing that achieving efficiency requires a holistic approach. Starting with the foundational principles of query optimization, we explored how careful query design and proper indexing dramatically improve data retrieval and manipulation. This segued into discussions on the strategic application of partitioning to enhance manageability and performance in large databases. We then focused on the often-overlooked importance of optimizing the TempDB database, acknowledging its impact on the entire SQL Server environment. Finally, and perhaps most crucial, we examined the significance of understanding SQL Server wait statistics to proactively identify and resolve performance bottlenecks. Through these combined strategies—from query optimization and data partitioning to TempDB management and wait analysis—database professionals can ensure the robustness, responsiveness, and overall optimal health of their SQL Server systems, ultimately providing a better user experience.

CHAPTER 9

SQL Server Advanced Monitoring and Troubleshooting

This chapter delves into the essential realm of advanced monitoring and troubleshooting within SQL Server environments. As databases become increasingly critical to business operations, proactive performance analysis and rapid issue resolution are paramount. This chapter provides a deep dive into various advanced techniques and tools that enable database administrators to not only maintain system health but also to optimize performance for peak efficiency.

We will begin by examining extended events for deep monitoring capabilities, moving beyond basic diagnostics to capture granular information on system activity. We'll then explore the power of query store for gaining valuable performance insights and understanding the execution plans of queries. Further, we'll turn our attention to automated performance baselines and alerts, which are crucial for identifying anomalies and proactively addressing potential problems before they impact users. Central to any troubleshooting toolkit, we'll dedicate a section to the complexities of deadlocks and blocking, investigating their root causes and preventative measures.

Collectively, the knowledge shared in this chapter equips database professionals with skills and expertise to effectively monitor, diagnose, and optimize their SQL Server instances. Mastering these advanced techniques will ensure stable, high-performing database systems capable of supporting the demanding needs of modern applications.

© Venkata Reddy Pasam and Petchikumar Andiappan 2026
V. R. Pasam and P. Andiappan, *The Expert's Guide to SQL Server*, https://doi.org/10.1007/979-8-8688-2451-7_9

Extended Events for Deep Monitoring

What Is SQL Server Extended Events?

SQL Server **Extended Events** is a robust performance monitoring and troubleshooting tool that collects and analyzes database engine activities to diagnose issues in **SQL Server**. Introduced in **SQL Server 2008**, Extended Events was designed to replace **SQL Profiler**, which had several performance drawbacks.

One of SQL Profiler's main limitations was its **high resource consumption**, which negatively impacted database performance. In contrast, **Extended Events** offers a lightweight, efficient, and highly customizable event-tracing mechanism without significantly affecting system performance.

Extended Events provides **a wide range of events** that assist in troubleshooting **query performance issues, deadlocks, and other database problems**. Due to its minimal overhead and comprehensive insights into the underlying issue, Extended Events should be the first choice when dealing with deadlocks.

Identifying Long-Running Queries in SQL Server

Long-running queries are among the most frequent issues with **SQL Server** performance and can significantly impact database efficiency. The first step in effectively troubleshooting these queries is **identifying and analyzing them**.

Defining a query as **problematic** depends on establishing a **threshold value** based on the specific database environment. Some systems require responses within microseconds, while others can tolerate longer execution times. Since waiting tolerance varies, setting an appropriate benchmark is crucial.

Several tools are available to detect slow-running queries, but **SQL Server Extended Events** is one of the most efficient methods for identifying performance bottlenecks. The key challenge is selecting the **right event**, as SQL Server provides numerous options.

One of the most valuable events for tracking query execution is **sql_statement_ completed**, which captures all queries executed in the database and provides critical performance metrics, including:

CPU time used by the query

Query execution duration

Logical and physical reads were performed

Number of writes

SQL text and execution details

Client hostname

Client application name

By leveraging **Extended Events**, database administrators can gain deeper insights into query performance, detect inefficiencies, and optimize execution times effectively.

Creating an Extended Event Session to Identify Long-Running Queries

The **SQL Server Management Studio (SSMS)** application allows you to develop **Extended Events sessions** to capture and analyze long-running queries. Follow these steps to set up a session:

1. Open **SSMS** and connect to the SQL Server instance.

2. Expand the **Management** folder.

3. Right-click on **Sessions** and select **New Session** to begin configuring the event session (As shown in Figure 9-1).

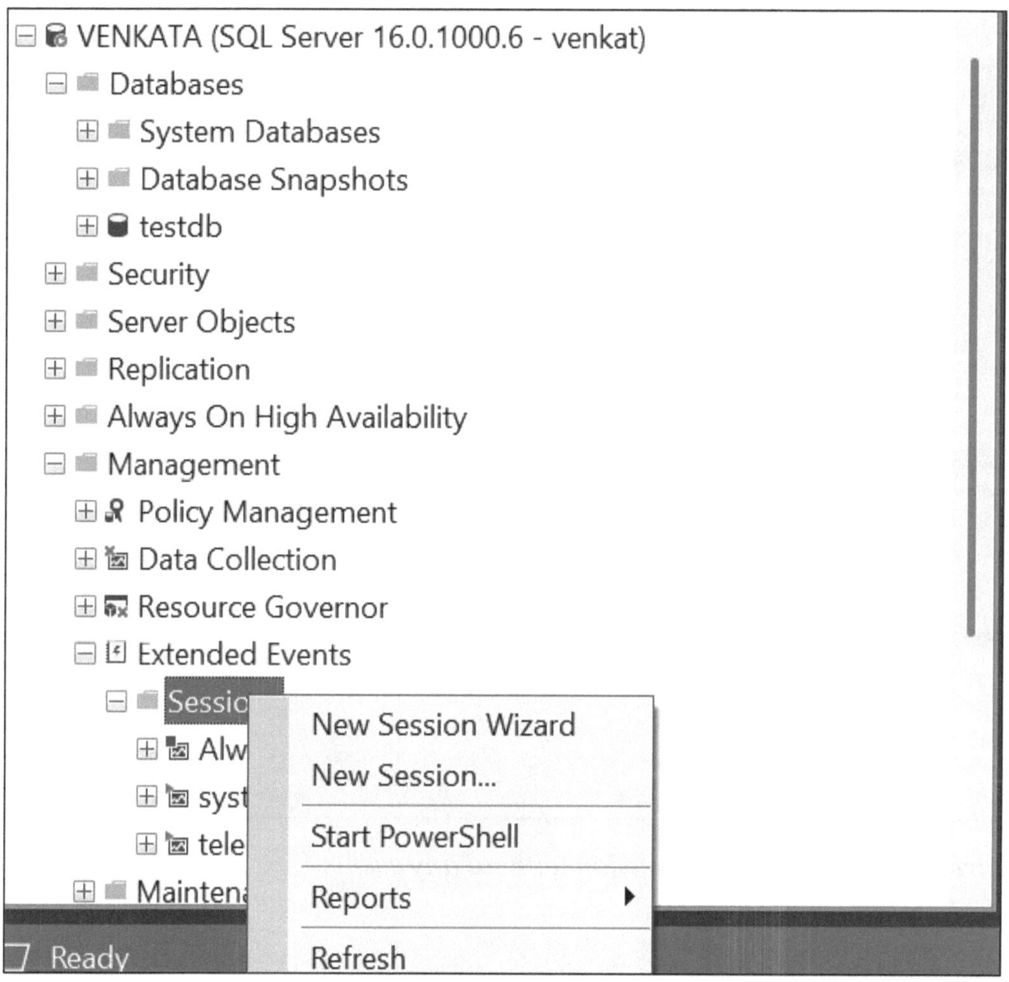

Figure 9-1. Creating an Extended Event session to identify long-running queries

To create a new Extended Events session in SQL Server Management Studio (SSMS), take the following actions:

1. Click on the New Session option from the menu.

2. The New Session window will appear.

3. Enter a descriptive name for the event session.

4. Enable the following options for automated session management:

   - Start the event session at server startup (ensure the session begins when the SQL Server service is restarted).

   - Begin the event session as soon as it is created. (Data collection starts right after the session is created. As shown in Figure 9-2.)

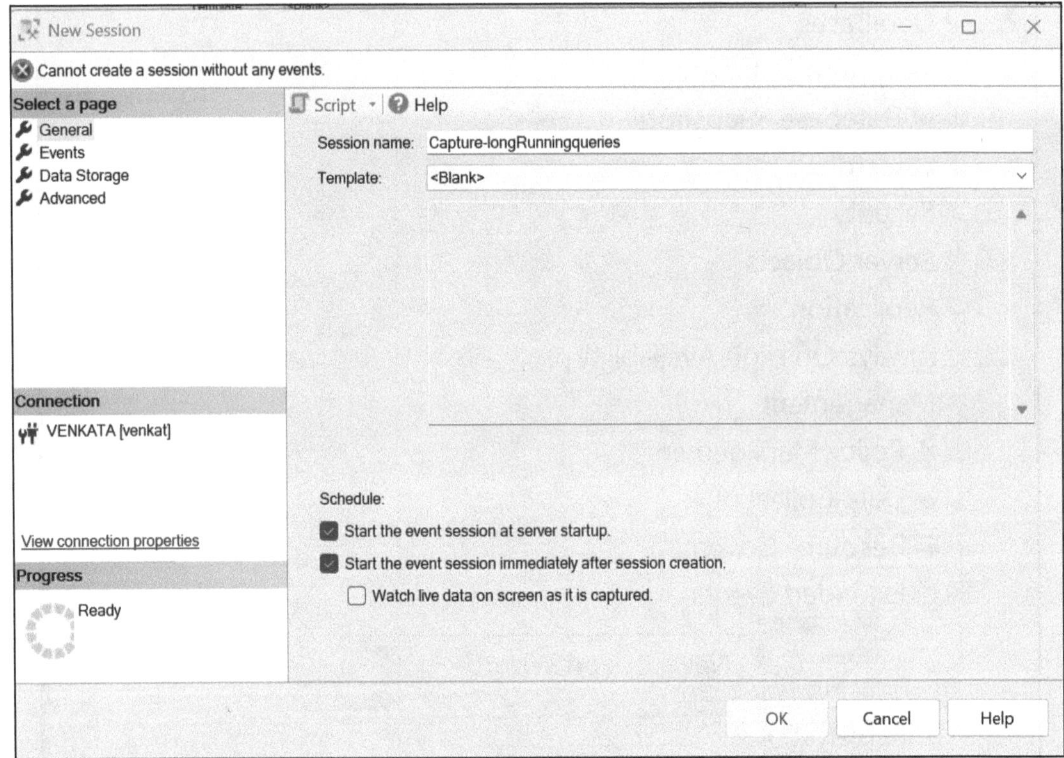

Figure 9-2. Cannot create a session without any events

After naming the session, we proceed to the **Events** tab. Events are triggered when specific actions take place within SQL Server. On this screen, we can browse all available events and apply a filter to locate the **sql_statement_completed** event. Once identified, we add it to the **Selected events** list by clicking the **Configure** button to choose the global event fields, which provide details about specific aspects of the events. For example, to identify the application name that triggered the event, select the client app name field. Select the client app name and hostname in the Global Fields (Action) list (As shown in Figures 9-3 and 9-4).

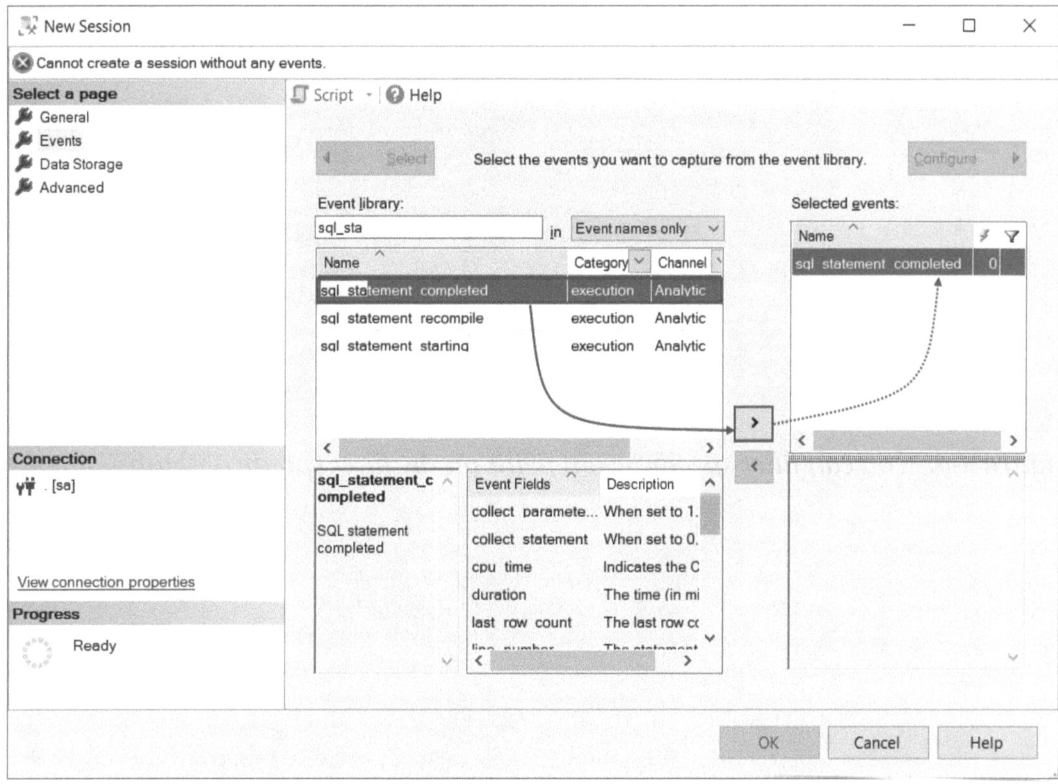

Figure 9-3. *New session*

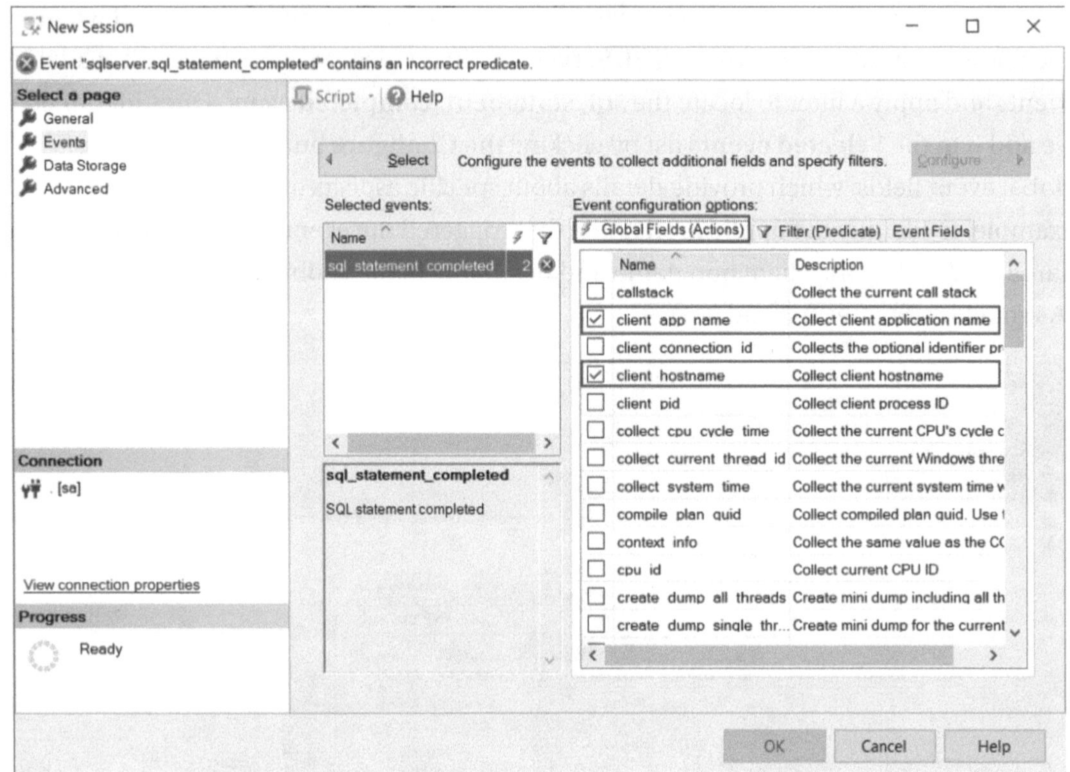

Figure 9-4. *You can filter specific event fields on the filter (predicate) tab*

You can filter specific event fields on the **Filter (Predicate)** tab. For our example with the SQL Server extended events session, we'll filter by database name to track only SQL statements executed within that database (As shown in Figure 9-5).

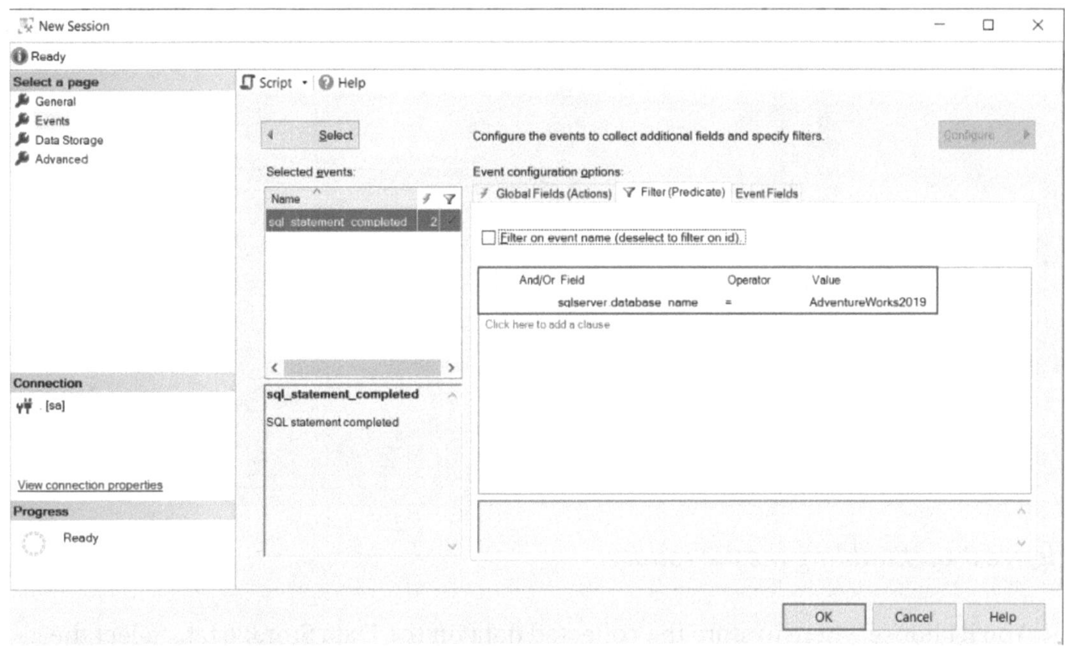

Figure 9-5. *New session.*

Additionally, if you've set a threshold for poor-performing queries, you can filter by duration to help troubleshoot query performance issues (As shown in Figure 9-6).

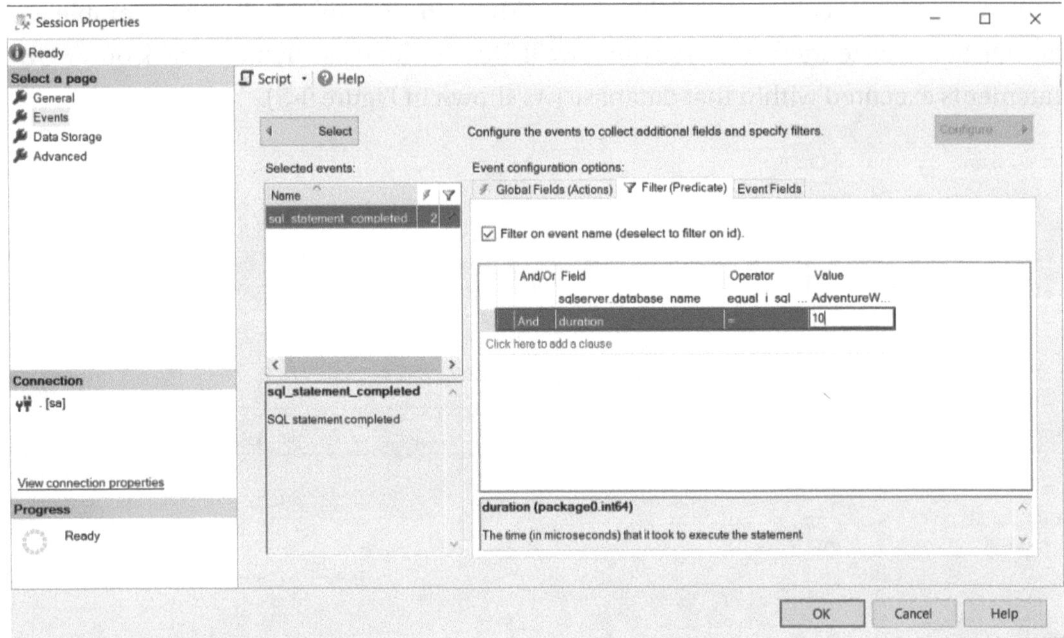

Figure 9-6. *Enabling the file rollover*

You'll choose where to store the collected data on the Data Storage tab. Select the event file option to write data to an **XEL** file. Once selected, define the file location and set a maximum file size. **Enabling the file rollover** option ensures that when the XEL file reaches the size limit, a new file is created with the same name, appending a sequence number to the filename (As shown in Figure 9-7).

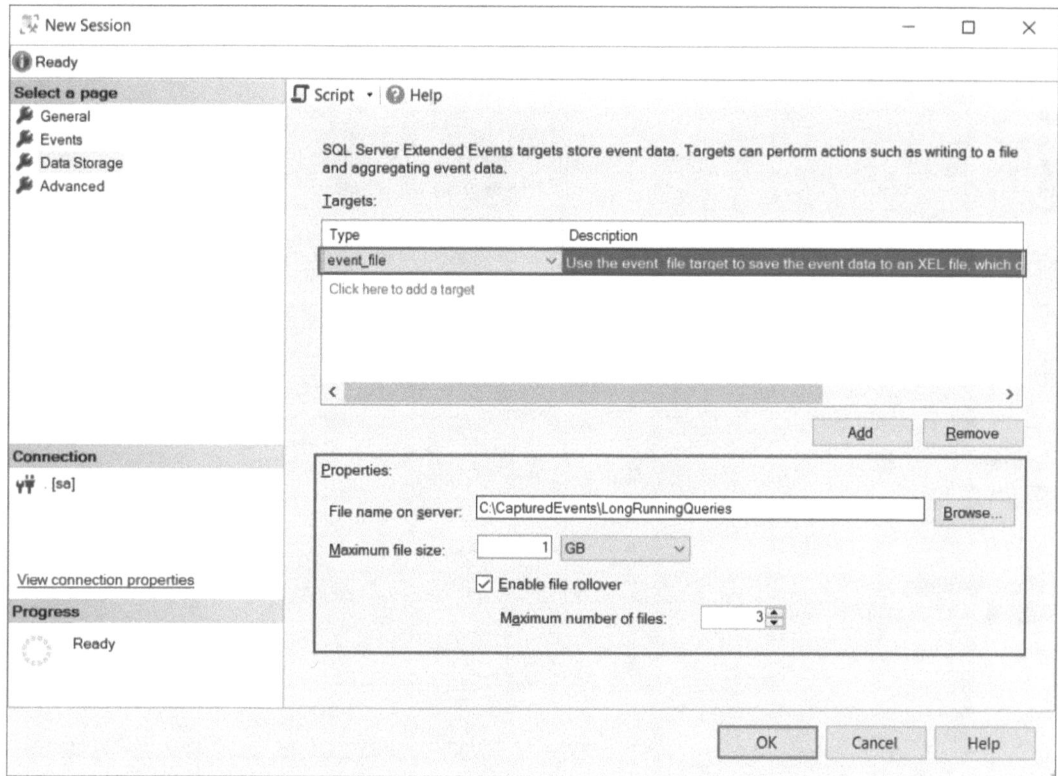

Figure 9-7. *SQL server*

The **Advanced** tab offers more detailed settings, such as specifying the tolerance for data loss in the session's event storage mode. You can choose "No event loss," but this option may impact system performance on databases with heavy workloads. Another option is **maximum dispatch latency**, which sets the maximum time an event can remain in the buffer before being written to the target. After making your selections, click **OK** to create the extended event session (As shown in Figure 9-8).

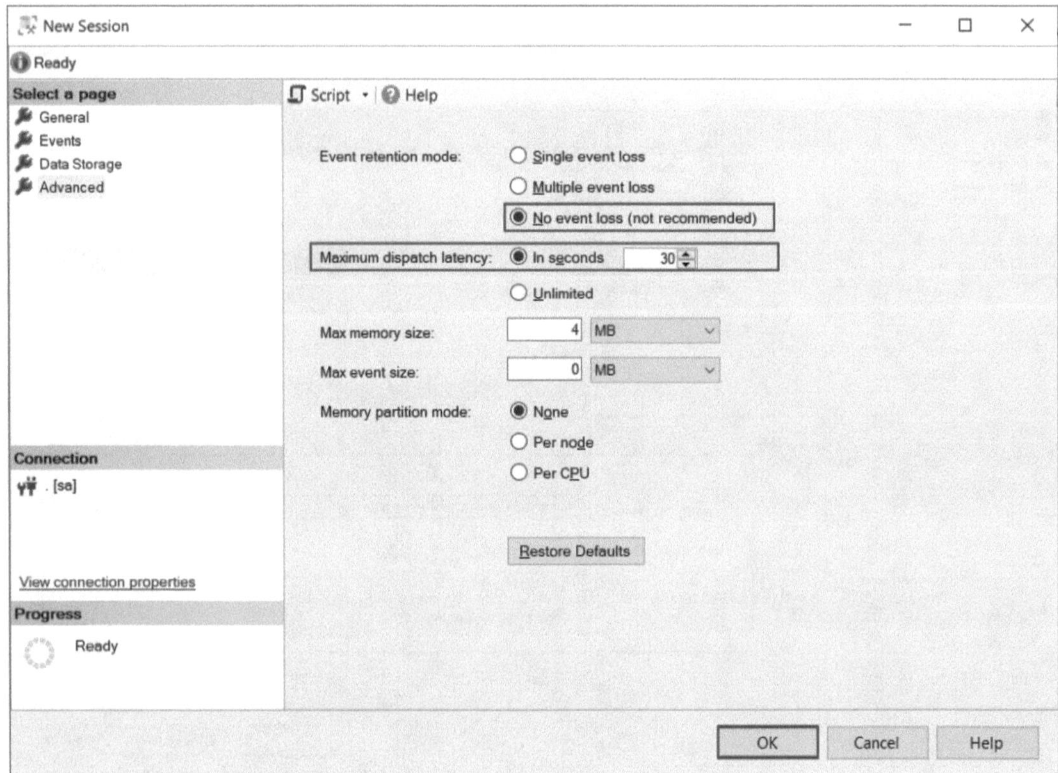

Figure 9-8. *No event loss*

Once the extended event session is created, it will be included in the list of expanded events (As shown in Figure 9-9).

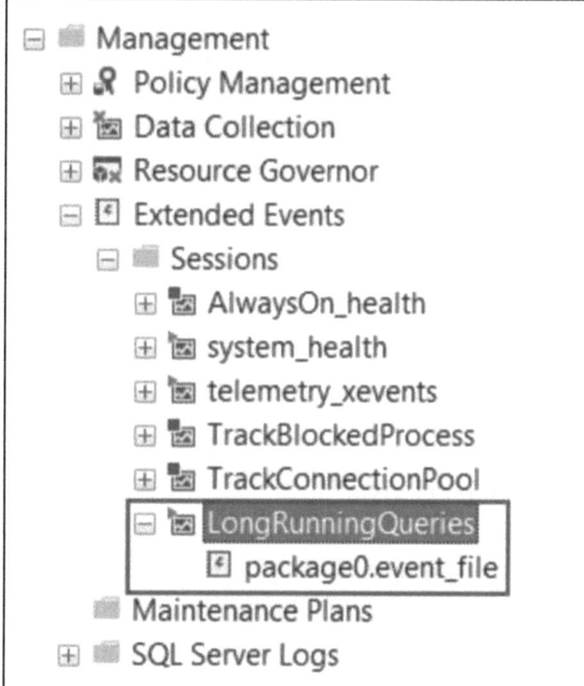

Figure 9-9. *Long-running queries*

Analyzing the Collected Data

Once the extended event session has been created, it will start automatically and collect data. You can use the "Watch Live Data" option to analyze the data. For instance, executing a query in the AdventureWorks database will capture the query in the extended event (As shown in Figure 9-10).

```
SELECT  SO.AccountNumber FROM
Sales.SalesOrderHeader SO
INNER  JOINSales.SalesOrderDetail SD
ON SO.ModifiedDate = SD.ModifiedDate
```

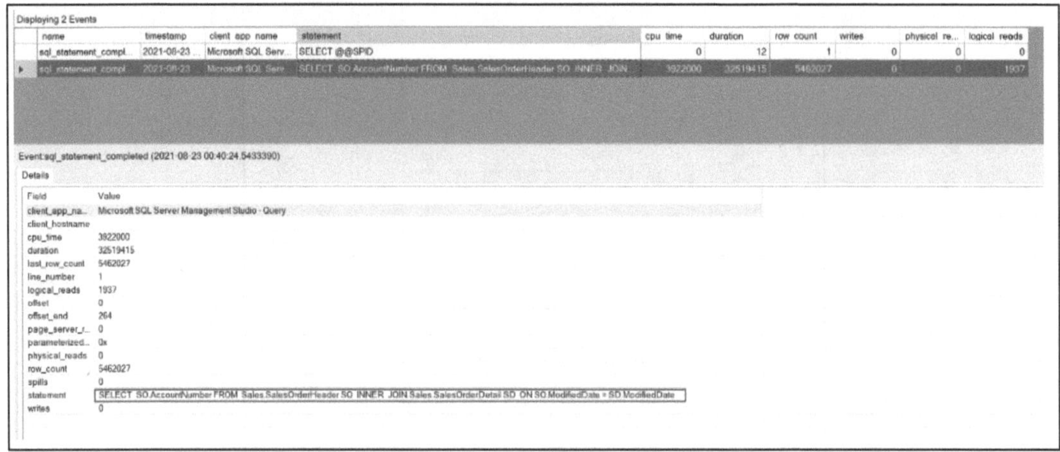

Figure 9-10. *Displaying two events*

A query can more effectively analyze query performance and resolve performance issues. To do this, the first step is to identify the location of the XEL files and then read the file using the fn_xe_file_target_read_file (As shown in Figure 9-11)

```
function.SELECT s.name,
CAST(t.target_data AS XML).value('(EventFileTarget/File/@name)[1]',
'VARCHAR(MAX)') AS fileName
FROM sys.dm_xe_sessions AS s
INNER JOIN
sys.dm_xe_session_targets AS t
    ON s.address = t.event_session_address
WHERE t.target_name = 'event_file'
    AND name = 'LongRunningQueries';

SELECT CAST(event_data AS XML) AS event_data
FROM sys.fn_xe_file_target_read_file('C:\CapturedEvents\
LongRunningQueries_0_132741419843740000.xel', NULL, NULL, NULL);
```

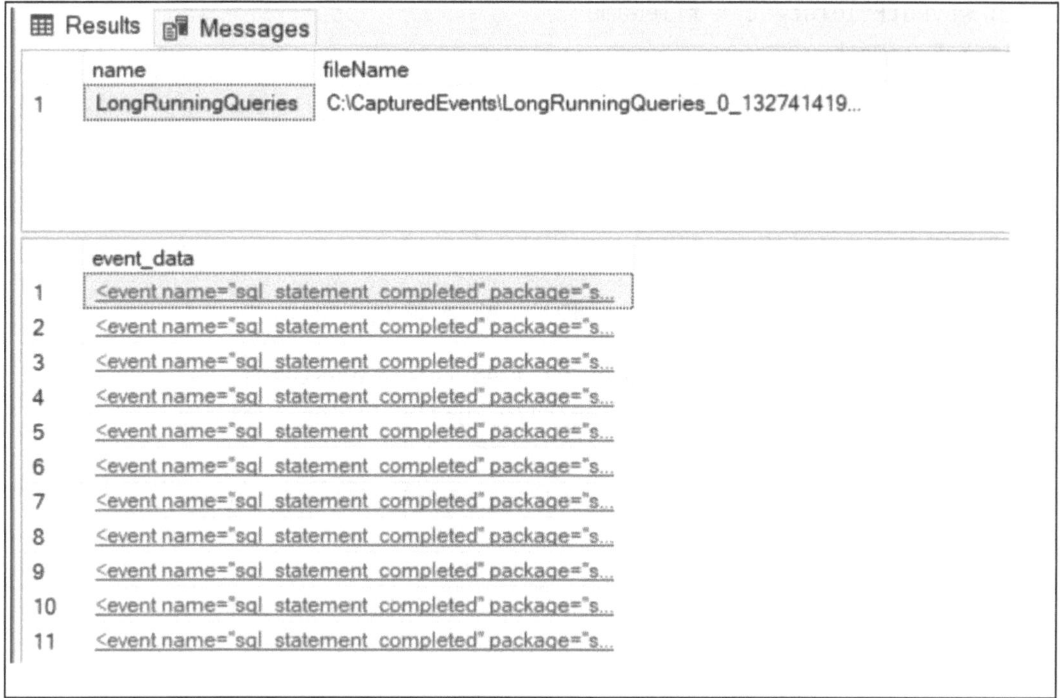

Figure 9-11. *XML format*

- The data is captured in XML format; we must convert it into a relational format.

- The following query retrieves the TOP 10 queries causing the highest I/O load on the database (As shown in Figure 9-12).

```
DROP TABLE IF EXISTS #EX_FilePath;
DROP TABLE IF EXISTS #AnalyzeTable;

SELECT s.name,
CAST(t.target_data AS XML).value('(EventFileTarget/File/@name)[1]',
'VARCHAR(MAX)') AS fileName
INTO #EX_FilePath
FROM sys.dm_xe_sessions AS s
INNER JOIN
sys.dm_xe_session_targets AS t
    ON s.address = t.event_session_address
WHERE t.target_name = 'event_file';

DECLARE @EventFileTarget AS NVARCHAR(500);
```

```
SELECT @EventFileTarget = fileName
FROM #EX_FilePath
WHERE name = 'LongRunningQueries';

SELECT * INTO #AnalyzeTable
FROM
    SELECT n.value('(@name)[1]', 'varchar(50)') AS event_name,

n.value('(@package)[1]', 'varchar(50)') AS package_name,

n.value('(@timestamp)[1]', 'datetime2') AS [utc_timestamp],
n.value('(data[@name="physical_reads"]/value)[1]', 'bigint') AS
physical_reads,
n.value('(data[@name="logical_reads"]/value)[1]', 'bigint') AS
logical_reads,

n.value('(data[@name="writes"]/value)[1]', 'bigint') AS writes,

n.value('(data[@name="row_count"]/value)[1]', 'bigint') AS row_count,

n.value('(action[@name="client_app_name"]/value)[1]', 'varchar(max)') AS
client_app_name,
n.value('(data[@name="cpu_time"]/value)[1]', 'bigint') AS cpu_time,

n.value('(data[@name="duration"]/value)[1]', 'bigint') / 1000 AS
duration_ms,

n.value('(data[@name="statement"]/value)[1]', 'varchar(MAX)') AS sql_text
FROM
    SELECT CAST(event_data AS XML) AS event_data
    FROM sys.fn_xe_file_target_read_file(@EventFileTarget, NULL,
NULL, NULL)
AS ed
CROSS APPLY
ed.event_data.nodes('event') AS q(n)
AS TMP_TBL;

SELECT TOP 10
sql_text AS SQL;
```

Note   This SQL query code is already in a structured and precise format, so it's best left unchanged as it's specific to SQL Server's functionality and syntax.

```
COUNT(*) AS NumberOfQueries,
SUM(logical_reads) AS TotalLogicalReads
FROM #AnalyzeTable
GROUP BY sql_text
ORDER BY 3 DESC;
```

	Sql_Statment	NumberOfQueries	TotalLogicalReads
1	SELECT SO.AccountNumber FROM Sales.SalesOrderHea...	1	1937
2	select @UserOption=convert(int, c.value) from sys.configur...	5	860
3	SELECT * FROM Sales.CreditCard	4	756
4	[uspGetEmployeeManagers] 12	1	239
5	SELECT ISNULL(actual_state, -2) FROM sys.database_qu...	1	150
6	[uspGetEmployeeManagers] 13	1	103
7	select * from Production.BillOfMaterials	3	66
8	[uspGetEmployeeManagers] 16	1	25
9	[uspGetEmployeeManagers]	1	2
10	[uspGetBillOfMaterials]	1	2

Figure 9-12. *Select SO.AccountNumber*

Query Store and Performance Insights

Understanding and Utilizing SQL Server Query Store for Performance Optimization

SQL Server 2016 introduced **Query Store**, a valuable feature designed to help database administrators and developers analyze query performance over time. By capturing query execution details, including execution plans and performance trends, Query Store simplifies diagnosing slow-running queries and optimizing database performance.

What Is Query Store?

Query Store functions like a **black box recorder** for SQL Server, continuously gathering a historical record of query executions, performance metrics, and associated execution plans. Unlike **Dynamic Management Views (DMVs)**, which lose data after a server restart, Query Store retains this information, making it an excellent tool for **long-term query performance tracking**.

Key Benefits of Query Store:

Tracks **query performance trends** over time.

Stores multiple execution plans for a query.

Detects **performance regressions** when query execution slows down.

Provides visibility into execution plan changes.

Enabling Query Store:

By default, Query Store is disabled on SQL Server databases. You can activate it with the following command:

```
ALTER DATABASE [YourDatabaseName] SET QUERY_STORE = ON;
```

To configure settings like **data retention period, storage limits, and collection intervals**, use:

```
ALTER DATABASE [YourDatabaseName]
SET QUERY_STORE (OPERATION_MODE = READ_WRITE,
MAX_STORAGE_SIZE_MB = 1000,
INTERVAL_LENGTH_MINUTES = 15);
```

Components of Query Store:

1. **Runtime Statistics:**

   Tracks execution details such as **query duration, execution count, CPU usage, and I/O operations**.

2. **Execution Plans:**

   Stores every execution plan a query has used, allowing comparisons of past and present plans to detect inefficiencies.

3. **Wait Statistics:**

   Identifies where queries spend the most time waiting, helping diagnose performance bottlenecks.

Analyzing Query Performance:

Once Query Store is enabled, you can retrieve performance insights using system views.

Query Store System Views:

Sys.query_store_query: Holds query-specific details

Sys.query_store_plan: Contains execution plans for queries

Sys.query_store_runtime_stats: Stores runtime statistics like duration, CPU time, and I/O

To find the **slowest queries by average execution time**, run:

```
SELECT
q.query_id,
qsqt.query_sql_text,
rs.avg_duration,
rs.avg_cpu_time,
rs.avg_logical_io_reads
FROM sys.query_store_query AS q
JOIN sys.query_store_plan AS qp ON q.query_id = qp.query_id
JOIN sys.query_store_runtime_stats AS rs ON qp.plan_id = rs.plan_id
JOIN sys.query_store_query_text AS qsqt ON q.query_text_id = qsqt.
query_text_id
ORDER BY rs.avg_durationDESC;
```

This helps pinpoint queries that take the longest time to execute.

Query Store Reports in SSMS

SQL Server Management Studio (**SSMS**) provides built-in Query Store reports for more straightforward analysis:

> **Top Resource-Consuming Queries:** Identifies queries using the most resources.
>
> **Regressed Queries:** Highlights queries that have worsened in performance.
>
> **Tracked Query Plans:** Displays queries with multiple execution plans for comparison.

Handling Query Plan Regressions

One significant advantage of Query Store is that it captures **multiple execution plans for a single query**. If SQL Server unexpectedly switches to a less efficient plan, you can **force a better-performing execution plan**.

To force a query to use a specific plan:

```
EXEC sp_query_store_force_plan @query_id = 1, @plan_id = 3;
```

To remove the forced plan:

```
EXEC sp_query_store_unforce_plan @query_id = 1;
```

Optimizing Performance with Query Store

You can **proactively tune query performance** using Query Store through:

1. **Identifying Slow Queries:** Locate long-running queries and optimize them.

2. **Tracking Execution Plan Changes:** Monitor plan alterations and ensure SQL Server always picks the most efficient one.

3. **Fixing Performance Regressions:** Force an efficient plan if query performance deteriorates.

4. **Historical Analysis:** Review past performance data to evaluate long-term database health.

Best Practices for Query Store

To maximize the effectiveness of Query Store, follow these **best practices**:

Monitor Storage Usage: Set a reasonable storage limit (e.g., 1000 MB) to prevent excessive space consumption.

Review Query Performance Regularly: Periodically check regressed queries and resource-heavy queries.

Enable Automatic Cleanup: Prevent Query Store from storing outdated data by configuring auto-cleanup:

```
ALTER DATABASE [YourDatabaseName]
SET QUERY_STORE (CLEANUP_POLICY = (STALE_QUERY_THRESHOLD_
DAYS = 30));
```

Conclusion

Query Store monitors **query behavior, execution plans, and database performance trends**. By leveraging its insights, **database administrators and developers** can proactively optimize SQL Server workloads, troubleshoot performance issues faster, and maintain consistent query efficiency. Enabling Query Store and following best practices ensures a **well-optimized SQL Server environment**, reducing troubleshooting time and improving overall database performance.

Automated Performance Baselines and Alerts

The Importance of Monitoring and Alerts in Performance Optimization

SQL Server performance is influenced by dynamic workloads, hardware constraints, and system configurations, making it essential to monitor and adjust proactively. Tracking performance trends and detecting anomalies early helps prevent issues before they escalate. Alerts serve as a proactive notification system for problems like high CPU usage, long-running queries, or low disk space, enabling timely intervention.

Best Practices for SQL Server Monitoring and Alerts

1. **Identify Key Performance Indicators (KPIs)**

   Before setting up a monitoring system, define the critical metrics that reflect SQL Server's health and efficiency. These should include CPU, memory, disk activity, and SQL Server-specific performance indicators.

   Best Practices:

   Track CPU usage, memory allocation, disk I/O, query wait times, and buffer cache efficiency.

   For I/O-intensive databases, monitor page life expectancy (PLE) to gauge buffer cache retention.

   Observe transaction log space usage and growth patterns to detect inefficient queries or oversized transactions.

2. **Leverage Dynamic Management Views (DMVs)**

   DMVs provide real-time insights into SQL Server's performance, helping pinpoint problems such as inefficient queries, memory bottlenecks, and indexing issues.

   Best Practices:

   Use sys.dm_exec_query_stats to identify resource-heavy queries and sys.dm_os_wait_stats to analyze wait types.

Assess index usage through sys.dm_db_index_usage_stats to determine optimization opportunities.

Automate DMV data collection for historical trend analysis.

3. **Configure Performance Alerts**

   SQL Server Agent facilitates alerts for various performance conditions, such as excessive CPU or memory usage, job failures, and connection problems. These notifications may be sent by email or logged for later review.

   Best Practices:

   Establish alerts for CPU usage above 80%, blocked processes, disk space thresholds, and job failures.

   Set up alerts for critical wait types, such as PAGEIOLATCH (disk issues) and LCK_M_* (locking delays).

   Avoid unnecessary alerts by fine-tuning thresholds and focusing on high-priority performance indicators.

4. **Utilize Extended Events for Advanced Diagnostics**

   Extended Events offers a lightweight, customizable monitoring framework that captures detailed information on query execution, wait times, deadlocks, and system events.

   Best Practices:

   Design custom Extended Events sessions to track long-running queries and performance anomalies.

   They monitor deadlocks, capture session details, and identify affected resources for troubleshooting.

   Retain Extended Events data for long-term performance trend analysis.

5. **Implement Specialized Monitoring Tools**

   Built-in SQL Server tools can be supplemented with third-party monitoring solutions (e.g., SolarWinds, Redgate SQL Monitor, and Idera SQL Diagnostic Manager) that provide in-depth performance tracking, dashboards, and automated diagnostics.

Best Practices:

Select a tool that offers real-time monitoring, historical trend analysis, and comprehensive alerting.

Look for visualization features that make it easier to diagnose performance bottlenecks.

Choose tools with customizable alerts and integration with incident management systems.

6. **Track Query Performance**

Slow queries can severely impact SQL Server efficiency, making query performance monitoring crucial.

Best Practices:

Continuously analyze query execution times, CPU, and I/O usage.

Utilize the Query Store feature to monitor query plans and execution statistics.

Configure alerts for high-duration queries or those with frequent execution, indicating potential inefficiencies.

7. **Monitor tempdb Usage**

The tempdb database is vital for temporary storage, query sorting, and intermediate processing. However, using it at high temperatures can lead to contention and performance degradation.

Best Practices:

- Use DMVs like sys.dm_db_task_space_usage to track tempdb utilization.

- Set up alerts for sudden growth or excessive usage, which may indicate inefficient queries.

- Address contention issues by adding more tempdb data files and distributing workloads effectively.

8. **Create Custom Alerts for Specific Resource Metrics**

   Different applications have unique performance demands, and
   SQL Server allows the creation of tailored alerts for specific needs.

   Best Practices:

   - Configure alerts for lock escalations, deadlocks, and prolonged
     blocking sessions.

   - Set up security-related alerts for excessive login attempts or
     unusual access patterns.

   - Monitor query execution plan changes, which can signal
     suboptimal indexing or outdated statistics.

9. **Automate Responses to Critical Alerts**

   Manual intervention for every alert can be time-consuming.
   Automating responses helps mitigate issues promptly.
   Best Practices:

   - Configure SQL Server Agent to execute predefined actions, such
     as restarting services or optimizing resource allocation.

   - Implement automated scripts to collect diagnostic data when an
     alert is triggered.

   - Establish escalation protocols to ensure critical issues reach the
     appropriate teams.

10. **Maintain Long-Term Log Monitoring**

    Consistent log monitoring aids in detecting performance trends,
    recurring issues, and system changes over time.

    Best Practices:

    - Regularly review SQL Server Error Logs for I/O warnings, login
      failures, and deadlocks.

    - Monitor Windows Event Logs for system-related warnings that
      could affect SQL Server.

    - For streamlined log analysis, use centralized log aggregation tools
      like Elasticsearch, Splunk, or Azure Monitor.

Conclusion

Proactive monitoring and well-configured alerts ensure that the SQL Server remains efficient and reliable. Defining key metrics, leveraging built-in and third-party monitoring tools, tracking query performance, and automating responses help maintain optimal performance. Organizations can detect and resolve issues by adopting a structured approach to SQL Server monitoring before they impact operations.

Deadlocks and Blocking Analysis

Overview of Blocking and Deadlocks

In any database management system, locks ensure data integrity during concurrent access. Effectively managing concurrent transactions is essential, but improper lock usage can lead to challenges like blocking and deadlocks, which can severely affect database performance and cause operations to fail. Blocking and deadlocks are locking mechanisms that ensure transactional consistency and manage access to shared resources. A thorough understanding of these mechanisms is crucial for database administrators and developers, as adequately managing them can optimize performance while maintaining data integrity and consistency.

What Is Blocking in SQL Server?

In SQL Server, blocking occurs when a process holds a resource needed by another method, forcing the second process to wait until the resource is released. SQL Server enforces exclusive access to resources to maintain data consistency and accuracy. While blocking is a normal part of database operation, excessive blocking can lead to performance slowdowns and delays.

For example, consider two transactions—Transaction 1 and Transaction 2— attempting to access the same row in the Accounts table. If Transaction 1 updates the row and hasn't committed, it holds a lock on the row. Meanwhile, Transaction 2 attempts to read the same row but must wait for Transaction 1 to release its lock. The lock is removed once Transaction 1 commits or rolls back, allowing Transaction 2 to proceed.

If the database has the READ COMMITTED SNAPSHOT option enabled, which activates snapshot isolation, read operations won't experience blocking. In this scenario, Transaction 2 will not be blocked by Transaction

Typical Reasons for Blocking

Blocking in SQL Server can result from several factors:

Resource contention occurs when multiple transactions request conflicting access to the same resource. For example, *Transaction 1* might update a record while holding a lock, while *Transaction 2* wants to read or update the same record and must wait.

Long-Running Transactions: Transactions that hold resources for an extended period, causing delays for other transactions. This can happen with complex queries or uncommitted transactions left open.

Lack of Proper Indexing: Missing indexes can lead to inefficient queries, requiring full table scans or page-level locks.

Excessive Use of Locks: A transaction affecting a large volume of data may escalate from row- or page-level locks to locking entire tables.

Explicit Locking Hints: Developers may use locking hints like HOLDLOCK or TABLOCK, causing additional locks.

Poor Application Logic: Applications that unnecessarily open transactions may keep them open longer than necessary because of subpar transaction handling or delays in client-side processing.

Transaction Isolation Levels: Higher isolation levels, like SERIALIZABLE, can increase blocking since they enforce stricter access rules, such as preventing phantom reads.

Detecting Blocking in SQL Server

SQL Server offers various methods for identifying and troubleshooting blocking, mainly focusing on system process IDs (speeds) involved. These methods include:

System Stored Procedures

You can use the built-in sp_who2 system stored procedure to view blocking information. Running the following query will display active transactions and indicate if they are blocked:

SQL

Copy

```
EXEC sp_who2;
```

This query returns all active transactions on the ServerServer. A transaction holds a lock if its status is RUNNABLE or SUSPENDED. The *BlkBy* column shows the session ID of the blocking process. For example, a value of 53 in the *BlkBy* column refers to the blocking transaction's session ID (SPID) (As shown in Figure 9-13).

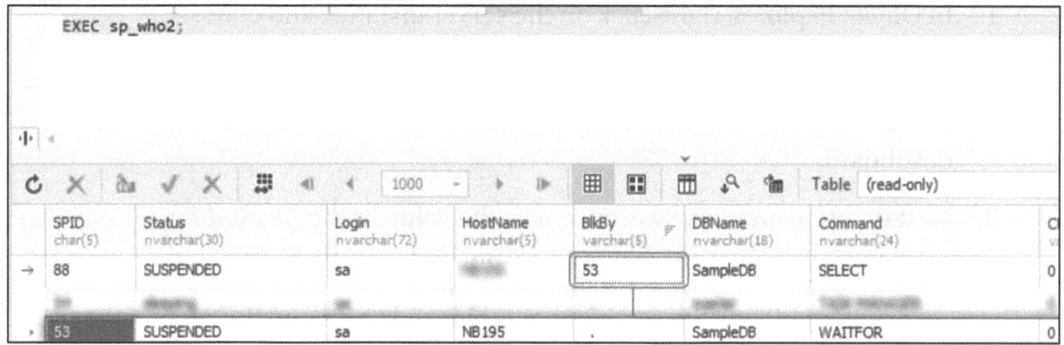

Figure 9-13. *Dynamic management views (DMVs)*

Dynamic Management Views (DMVs)

Dynamic Management Views (DMVs) allow you to monitor workload performance and identify blocked or long-running queries. For example, you can query the sys.dm_exec_requests DMV to return only blocked processes:

SQL

Copy

```
SELECT * FROM sys.dm_exec_requests WHERE blocking_session_id> 0; <> 0; GO
```

The sys.dm_os_waiting_tasks DMV allows you to see processes waiting for resources. To execute this DMV, the user must have permission from either the administrator or VIEW SERVER STATE on the instance.

SQL

```
SELECT session_id, wait_duration_ms, wait_type, blocking_session_id
FROM sys.dm_os_waiting_tasks
WHERE blocking_session_id> 0;> 0
GO
```

Activity Monitor

You prefer using SQL Server Management Studio (SSMS) rather than running queries for system objects or stored procedures. In that case, you can use the SSMS monitoring tool Activity Monitor, which lets you view blocking sessions to check server activity:

1. In Object Explorer, right-click on the server instance and choose Activity Monitor.

2. Expand the Processes pane to see all active sessions on the dashboard.

3. Next to the suspended session, check the value in the *Blocked By* column (it displays the session ID responsible for the block).

The screenshot highlights the session that is blocked (#58) and the session that is causing the block (#62) (As shown in Figure 9-14).

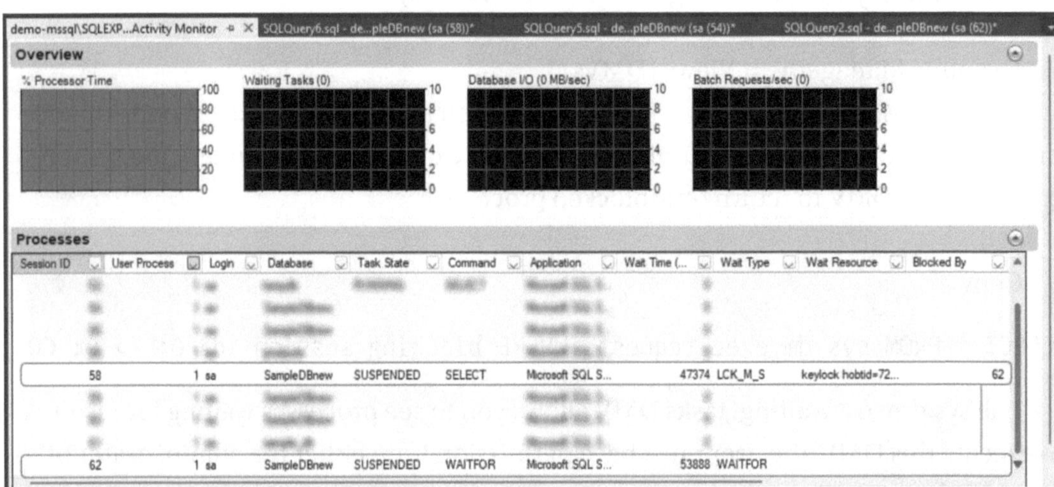

Figure 9-14. *Check server activity*

Reports

SSMS also offers the ability to monitor blocking transactions using the Reports feature. It can generate a report displaying all blocking transactions on the server instance.

To access the report, right-click the desired instance name and select Reports ➤ Standard Reports ➤ Activity—All Blocking Transactions (As shown in Figure 9-15).

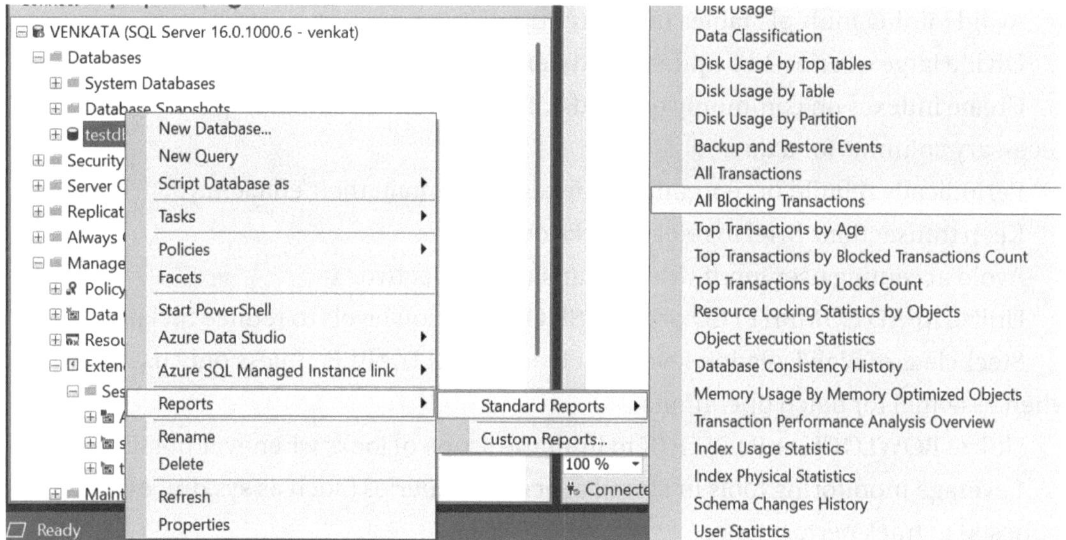

Figure 9-15. *Reports*

This will open the generated report in a new SQL document (As shown in Figure 9-16).

Activity - All Blocking Transactions
on DEMO\SQLEXPRESS01 at 12/16/2024 4:45:20 PM   SQL Server

This report provides information about each transaction on the Instance which is blocking one or more other transactions.

All Blocking Transactions
The description of transactions which are blocking other transactions.

Transaction ID	# Directly Blocked Transactions	# Indirectly Blocked Transactions	Transaction Name	State	Transaction Type	Start Time	Resource Type	Session ID	Blocking SQL Statement
⊞									⊞ WAITFOR DELAY '00:01:00'; -- Hold the lock for 1 minute
1203890	1	0	user_transaction	Active	Full Transaction	12/16/2024 4:44:45 PM	KEY	62	-- Commit the transaction after the delay

Figure 9-16. *Activity-All Blocking Transactions*

We have already covered the causes of blocking and the scenarios that might have led to these events. Now, let's discuss minimizing or preventing blocking in SQL Server databases.

Strategies to Reduce Blocking

To minimize blocking, enhance concurrency, enhance overall performance, use optimizing queries, use appropriate indexes, and minimize long-running transactions, it is recommended to mitigate. For long-running transactions, here are some practical steps to maximize performance:

Select only the necessary columns instead of using SELECT *.

Apply specific filters with indexed columns in the WHERE clause.

Avoid joining multiple tables unless required.

Divide large queries, like updates and deletes, into smaller batches.

Create indexes on commonly queried columns or those containing only the necessary columns for a query.

Periodically rebuild or reorganize indexes to maintain their efficiency.

Keep transactions brief to release locks quickly.

Avoid accepting user input while a transaction is active.

Utilize READ COMMITTED or SNAPSHOT isolation levels to reduce locking.

Steer clear of high isolation levels, such as SERIALIZABLE, unless only use TABLOCK when essential for batch operations.

Utilize ROWLOCK or PAGLOCK to limit the scope of locks whenever possible.

Leverage monitoring tools or stored procedure queries (such as sys.dm_exec_ requests) to track performance.

Identify and terminate long-running or stalled transactions as needed.

What Are Deadlocks in SQL Server?

Unlike blocking, deadlocks happen when simultaneous transactions are stalled because each one holds a lock on a resource that the others require and waits for the other to free it. This forms a cycle of dependency, causing the process to potentially run indefinitely. In such cases, none can proceed until the SQL Server aborts one transaction with an error, allowing the other transactions to be completed.

For instance, two transactions are attempting to transfer money between two accounts at the same time.

Transaction A is transferring funds from *Account1* to *Account2, while Transaction B* is transferring funds from *Account2* to *Account1*.

A deadlock can occur if both transactions try to lock the accounts in different orders.

Common Causes of Deadlocks

As mentioned, deadlocks occur when two or more transactions are waiting on each other in a cycle of dependencies, preventing any of them from proceeding. The most common causes of deadlocks are conflicts in resource ordering and high contention.

Resource Order Conflicts

Deadlocks frequently happen when queries involving multiple tables or resources do not follow a consistent locking order. For *instance, transaction A* locks Resource X and then attempts to lock Resource Y, while *Transaction B* locks Resource Y and tries to lock Resource X. In this case, both transactions wait for the other to release its lock, leading to a deadlock.

High Contention on Shared Resources

Deadlocks may also arise due to frequent updates on rows, long-running queries or transactions holding locks for extended periods, or many row-level locks being converted into a single table-level lock.

How Can Deadlocks Be Resolved?

SQL Server has a built-in mechanism—a lock monitor thread—that automatically detects and resolves deadlocks to ensure system stability.

The SQL Server Database Engine continuously monitors for transactions that may cause deadlocks in the background. Once a deadlock is detected, SQL Server determines which transaction will be chosen as the "victim" and terminated based on factors like transaction cost or deadlock priority. For instance, a transaction with the lowest price will be selected as the victim over the others because terminating it will have the least effect on system performance.

By default, all transactions have the same deadlock priority. However, developers can manually assign a deadlock priority to a transaction, such as low, normal (which is the default), or high, by using the SET DEADLOCK_PRIORITY command. Developers can also assign a specific deadlock priority value within the range of -10 to 10.

SQL

```
SET DEADLOCK_PRIORITY HIGH;
```

If the sessions involved in the deadlock cycle share the same priority level and the exact if there is no specific priority set, SQL Server randomly selects a victim based on cost, choosing the least costly transaction to terminate.

Once the deadlock "victim" is terminated, when a transaction is rolled back, SQL Server releases any locks held by the terminated transaction, allowing the other transactions to continue.

Ways to Prevent Deadlocks

We have discussed how and why deadlocks happen in SQL Server and the approaches to resolve them. While deadlocks cannot be eliminated, they can be minimized in SQL Server. Below is a brief checklist to help reduce deadlocks when working with SQL databases:

Access resources in a consistent order.

Divide large transactions into smaller parts.

Avoid user interactions during a transaction.

Use appropriate indexes and the lowest necessary isolation level.

Avoid using overly strict isolation levels like SERIALIZABLE unless required.

Track and improve query performance.

Key Differences Between Blocking and Deadlocks

In summary, the primary distinction is that a deadlock involves a harmful cycle in which two or more processes hinder each other by retaining resources required by the others and preventing any progress. On the other hand, blocking happens when one process is a resource needed by another process, causing the blocked process to wait until the blocking process completes its task.

Conceptual Differences

The table below highlights the conceptual differences between blocking and deadlocks in SQL Server.

Aspect	Blocking	Deadlocks
Definition	The Process Holds a Resource; Another Waits	Processes are in a cyclic waiting pattern.
Nature	Temporary and solvable	Persistent unless addressed
Cause	Contention for a single resource	Circular wait conditions involving multiple resources
Resolution	Releases automatically once completed	SQL Server must terminate one process (the victim)
Severity	This leads to delays but doesn't result in failure	Causes transaction failure

Transaction Impact

While blocking is a regular aspect of SQL Server concurrency control, blocking can significantly negatively affect performance if it persists for extended periods or happens frequently. Transactions waiting for a resource are held in a queue, leading to delays in execution and a decline in overall system performance. Furthermore, blocking transactions involving lengthy queries or ongoing transactions can trigger cascading delays, impacting several transactions. This will further degrade the database performance.

Deadlocks have a more critical effect as they fail one or more transactions. When a deadlock occurs, SQL Server identifies the circular dependency and ends one of the transactions, marking it as the *deadlock victim*, to allow the remaining transactions to continue. This rollback consumes processing time and resources, as the failed transaction must be retried. Consequently, deadlocks cause transaction delays, impacting system reliability and the user experience.

Detection and Resolution Techniques

The following table outlines the detection and resolution method differences between blocking and deadlocks in SQL Server.

Aspect	Blocking	Deadlocks
Detection Techniques	Activity Monitor	SQL Server Error Log
	Sys.dm_exec_requests, sys.dm_tran_locks, and sys.dm_os_waiting_tasks are dynamic management views used to monitor requests, transaction locks, and tasks waiting for resources, respectively.	system_health session
Resolution Techniques	Identify and kill blocking sessions	The ServerServer will automatically select a victim to end the transaction.
	Reduce transaction period	Access resources consistently
	Reduce lock contention	Shorten transaction duration
	Break long transactions into smaller ones.	Use snapshot isolation levels.
Impact on Performance	Delays in transaction processing	Transaction rollback and failure

Conclusion

This chapter has equipped us with advanced techniques for maintaining a healthy and performant SQL Server environment, extending beyond basic monitoring to address more complex scenarios. Beginning with extended events, we explored how these flexible mechanisms capture granular data for detailed performance analysis and incident investigation. The chapter then shifted focus to the practical application of query store for identifying and resolving query performance regressions. We learned about utilizing baselines and alerts for proactive performance management, helping us stay ahead of issues before they impact users. Finally, we tackled the challenging realm of deadlock and blocking analysis, providing insights into the root causes of these complex concurrency problems. By mastering extended events, query store analysis, performance baselines, and deadlock resolution, administrators and developers can confidently handle advanced performance issues, ensuring high availability and responsiveness within their SQL Server ecosystems.

CHAPTER 10

Machine Learning and AI in SQL Server

This chapter explores the powerful capabilities that enable data scientists and machine learning practitioners to integrate their workflows seamlessly with SQL Server. It focuses on performing advanced data analytics directly within the database environmental strategy essential for efficiency and speed. The discussion follows two key approaches:

First, the section "Running R and Python in SQL Server" introduces the integration of these popular programming languages within SQL Server. This section covers how to execute code directly where the data resides, leveraging tools like Visual Studio Code and Jupyter Notebooks for efficient data exploration, model training, and deployment. By processing data within the database, this approach minimizes the need for large data transfers and optimizes computational performance.

Next, the section "Integrating AI Models with SQL Server" explores how trained machine learning models can be operationalized within SQL Server. This section demonstrates how to apply AI-driven insights directly to business operations, enhancing decision-making and automating complex data processes.

Together, these sections provide a comprehensive guide to harnessing machine learning and AI within SQL Server, empowering organizations to maximize the efficiency of data-driven workflows and decision-making.

Running R and Python in SQL Server

Introduction

R and Python are two of the most widely used programming languages. Used by data scientists, data engineers, and machine learning practitioners. The ability to execute Python scripts directly within SQL Server opens up numerous possibilities for data processing, including in-database machine learning for handling large datasets

© Venkata Reddy Pasam and Petchikumar Andiappan 2026
V. R. Pasam and P. Andiappan, *The Expert's Guide to SQL Server*, https://doi.org/10.1007/979-8-8688-2451-7_10

efficiently. While IDEs such as VS Code and Jupyter Notebooks are commonly used for machine learning experimentation due to their interactive nature, they can become less effective when dealing with massive data volumes or when deploying models into production. This has created a strong demand for executing and training models directly within the database environment. In this guide, you will explore various approaches to achieve this seamlessly.

MS SQL Server Machine Learning Services

SQL Server Machine Learning Services enables the execution of Python and R scripts directly within the database, allowing for seamless integration with relational data. It supports open-source libraries and Microsoft-provided Python and R packages, making it a powerful tool for predictive analytics and machine learning. This feature ensures that scripts run within the database environment, eliminating the need to move data outside SQL Server or across a network.

With SQL Server Machine Learning Services, users can perform data preparation, cleansing, feature engineering, model training, evaluation, and deployment, all within the database. Running scripts where the data resides enhances efficiency, minimizes data movement, and optimizes the performance of large-scale analytics and machine-learning workloads.

Python and R Versions Supported in SQL Server

The versions of Python and R supported in SQL Server depend on the SQL Server version you are using. Below is an overview of the supported versions:

SQL Server 2017

R: Microsoft R Open 3.3.3

Python: Python 3.5.2

SQL Server 2019

R: Microsoft R Open 3.5.2

Python: Python 3.7.1

SQL Server 2022

R: Microsoft R Open 4.0.2

Python: Python 3.9.5

Small Python Code runs in SQL Server

As a first step, during SQL Server installation, navigate to the Features section and ensure that Python is selected under Machine Learning Services and Language Extensions. A machine learning server should also be included to enable advanced analytics and scripting capabilities within the database (As shown in Figure 10-1).

Instance Features
☑ Database Engine Services
  ☐ SQL Server Replication
  ☑ Machine Learning Services and Language Extensions
    ☑ R
    ☑ Python
    ☐ Java
  ☐ Full-Text and Semantic Extractions for Search
  ☐ Data Quality Services
  ☐ PolyBase Query Service for External Data
  ☐ Java connector for HDFS data sources
☐ Analysis Services
Shared Features
  ☑ Machine Learning Server (Standalone)
    ☑ R
    ☑ Python
  ☐ Data Quality Client
  ☑ Client Tools Connectivity
  ☐ Integration Services

Figure 10-1. *Small Python code runs in SQL Server*

After completing the installation, you must enable script execution for the instance by modifying its configuration settings. To do this, run the following command on your SQL Server instance:

```
EXEC sp_configure' external scripts enabled,' 1;
RECONFIGURE;
GO
```

This configuration allows script execution through the **Launchpad service**, enabling the use of the sp_execute_external_script stored procedure for running Python and R scripts within SQL Server.

Running Your First Python Script in SQL Server

After configuring SQL Server to support external scripting, you can execute Python code within the database. Instead of working with files, Python scripts are passed as string variables and executed using the sp_execute_external_script stored procedure.

This procedure accepts multiple parameters, but for now, we will focus on two key ones:

@language: Specifies the programming language (e.g., "Python").

@script: Contains the actual Python script as a string.

Before running our first Python script, let's create a database in a **SQL Server 2019 instance** using the following command:

```
CREATE DATABASE PythonDemo;
GO
USE PythonDemo;
GO
```

Now that the database is set up, create and run a basic Python script for the SQL Server.

The following script iterates through a range of numbers and prints only the odd values:

Python

```python
for i in range(1, 10, 2):
print(i)
```

To run this script in SQL Server, we pass it as a string parameter to

```sql
EXEC sys.sp_execute_external_script
@language = N'Python',
@script = N'
for i in range(1, 10, 2):
print(i)
';
GO
```

This approach enables Python execution within SQL Server, allowing data processing and analysis without moving data outside the database.

Passing Data into Python Scripts in SQL Server

Executing a script without input data is rarely helpful. SQL Server allows data to be passed into a Python script using sp_execute_external_script. This is achieved through the @input_data_1 parameter, which inputs a SQL query. The data from this query is then accessible in Python as InputDataSet, while the default output is stored in OutputDataSet.

Basic Example of Passing Data

Let's pass a simple dataset into a Python script and verify that it is being received correctly:

SQL

CopyEdit

```sql
EXEC sp_execute_external_script
@language = N'Python',
@script = N'OutputDataSet = InputDataSet',
```

```
@input_data_1 = N'SELECT value FROM (VALUES (5), (10), (15)) AS
Data(value)';
GO
```

This execution confirms that the data is successfully passed to the Python script, as the result set will mirror the input values.

Using a Declared Query for Better Readability

To improve clarity and maintainability, it is recommended to declare the SQL query separately and pass it as a variable:

SQL

```
DECLARE @Query NVARCHAR(2000) = N'
SELECT value FROM (VALUES (5), (10), (15)) AS Data(value)
EXEC sp_execute_external_script
@language = N'Python',
@script = N'OutputDataSet = InputDataSet',
@input_data_1 = @Query;
GO
```

Defining Output Metadata with Result Sets

By default, the output does not include column names. Using the WITH RESULT SETS clause, we can explicitly define the metadata, making the output more readable:

SQL

CopyEdit

```
DECLARE @Query NVARCHAR(2000) = N'
SELECT number, extra_value
FROM (VALUES (2, 20), (4, 40), (6, 60)) AS Data(number, extra_value)

EXEC sp_execute_external_script
@language = N'Python',
@script = N'OutputDataSet = InputDataSet',
@input_data_1 = @Query
WITH RESULT SETS
( [PrimaryNumber] INT NOT NULL,
  [AdjustedValue] INT NULL )
GO
```

This ensures the output is well-structured and readable.

Storing Output in a Table

Sometimes, we want to store the output of a Python script in a SQL Server table for further processing. We can use the INSERT INTO statement along with EXEC sp_execute_external_script:

SQL

CopyEdit

```
CREATE TABLE ProcessedData
(   Number INT,  MultipliedValueDECIMAL(10,2)
DECLARE @Query NVARCHAR(2000) = N'
SELECT number, CAST(value * 1.5 AS DECIMAL(10,2))
FROM (SELECT 1, 10 UNION ALL SELECT 2, 20 UNION ALL SELECT 3, 30), (4, 40))
AS Data(number, value)
WHERE number <= 3
INSERT INTO ProcessedData
EXEC sp_execute_external_script
@language = N'Python',
@script = N'OutputDataSet = InputDataSet',
@input_data_1 = @Query;

SELECT * FROM ProcessedData;
```

This approach enables the storage of processed results in a SQL table for further analysis.

Utilizing Python Libraries in SQL Server

SQL Server allows the use of Python libraries for advanced computations. Below is an example of performing a sum operation using the NumPy package:

SQL

CopyEdit

```
DECLARE @Query NVARCHAR(2000) = N'
SELECT number FROM (VALUES (5), (10), (15), (20)) AS Data(number)
EXEC sp_execute_external_script
@language = N'Python',
@script = N'
import the numpy library as np
```

```
import the panda's library as pd
total = np.sum(InputDataSet["number"])
OutputDataSet = pd.DataFrame({"TotalSum": [total]})
@input_data_1 = @Query;
GO
```

NumPy is used to compute the sum of all numbers, and pandas ensure the result is formatted as a data frame before returning it to SQL Server.

Conclusion

By integrating Python scripts within SQL Server, we can perform powerful data manipulations, analytics, and machine learning without moving data outside the database. Whether passing input queries, defining structured outputs, storing results in tables, or leveraging Python libraries, sp_execute_external_script provides a robust framework for in-database analytics.

Running R Code in SQL Server 2016 R Services

Overview: SQL Server 2016 introduces integration with the R programming language, allowing users to run R scripts directly within the database engine. This feature enables advanced analytics and data processing without moving data outside SQL Server.

Prerequisites: For those who want to execute R scripts within a client environment, refer to the relevant guide on setting up a data science workstation. This approach allows R code to run locally or within the SQL Server database. To execute R scripts directly in the SQL Server database engine using stored procedures, the **Advanced Analytics Extensions** feature and the required R packages must be installed. The installation and configuration process is detailed in the SQL Server R Services setup guide.

Using sp_execute_external_script, SQL Server 2016 introduces a new stored procedure, sp_execute_external_script, which allows executing scripts written in supported languages from an external source. This procedure operates under SQL Server's control and must be enabled before use:

```
sp_configure' external scripts enabled,' 1;
```

The stored procedure takes the following parameters:

> **@language**: Specifies the scripting language. Currently, only "R" is supported.

> **@script**: Contains the R script to be executed. This can be a literal string or a variable of type varchar (max).

@input_data_1: Defines the dataset passed to the R script. It accepts a T-SQL query and returns a result set. If no input data is required, an empty string must be used.

@input_data_1_name: Assigns a variable name to the dataset in the R script. Defaults to inputDataSet if unspecified.

@output_data_1_name: Specifies the variable name in the R script that holds the output dataset. Defaults to outputDataSet if omitted.

Certain SQL Server data types, such as a cursor, timestamp, datetime2, datetimeoffset, time, SQL variant, text, image, XML, hierarchyid, geometry, geography, CLR types, and all Unicode types, are not supported in the input query. These must be converted to compatible types beforehand. Additionally, SQL Server's datetime range is broader than R's, so any out-of-range values will be converted to NA. Conversely, R-specific float values (+Inf, -Inf, and NaN) are not supported and should be converted to NULL.

The WITH RESULT SETS clause must be included if an R script returns a dataset.

Examples

The following example calculates quantiles for customer ages. You may use any table that contains a birth date field. For illustration, this example uses the generic AdventureWorks sample database, but you can substitute any equivalent table.

```
SELECT Ages = DATEDIFF(YEAR, BirthDate, GETDATE())
FROM Person.Person
WHERE BirthDate IS NOT NULL;
```

Executing this query inside sp_execute_external_script:

```
EXEC sp_execute_external_script
@language = N'R',
@script = N'
result <- quantile(inputDataSet$Ages);
 print(result);
',
 @input_data_1 = N'
SELECT Ages = DATEDIFF(YEAR, BirthDate, GETDATE())
FROM Person.Person
```

```
WHERE BirthDate IS NOT NULL;
';
```

To return results as a SQL result set, format the R output as a data frame:

```
EXEC sp_execute_external_script
@language = N'R',
@script = N'
 result <- quantile(inputDataSet$Ages);
 df <- data.frame(result);
 ',
@input_data_1 = N'
SELECT Ages = DATEDIFF(YEAR, BirthDate, GETDATE())
 FROM Person.Person
WHERE BirthDate IS NOT NULL;
',
@output_data_1_name = N'df'
WITH RESULT SETS (("result" FLOAT NOT NULL));
```

To insert results into a table

```
INSERT INTO QuantileResults
EXEC sp_execute_external_script
@language = N'R',
 @script = N'
result <- quantile(inputDataSet$Ages);
 df <- data.frame(result);
',
@input_data_1 = N'
SELECT Ages = DATEDIFF(YEAR, BirthDate, GETDATE())
FROM Person.Person
WHERE BirthDate IS NOT NULL;
',
@output_data_1_name = N'df';
```

Additional Features

The WITH RESULT SETS clause allows defining complex outputs, such as machine learning models or graphical representations. SQL Server documentation provides examples of integrating R-generated plots into SQL Server Reporting Services (SSRS).

Conclusion

The sp_execute_external_script stored procedure enables executing R scripts within SQL Server, allowing advanced analytics without exporting data. While there are some limitations in data type compatibility, this functionality provides a seamless way to leverage R's analytical power within SQL Server.

Integrating AI Models with SQL Server

Introduction

The world of data is rapidly evolving, and artificial intelligence (AI) is no longer confined to large technology companies. Today, organizations of all sizes leverage AI to enhance their data-driven decision-making processes. One of the most potent combinations in this landscape is AI integrated with SQL Server, a platform trusted for years to store, manage, and analyze massive amounts of data.

This post will examine valuable strategies for integrating AI into SQL Server, walk through real-world use cases, and provide hands-on examples to show how you can utilize AI's possibilities directly within your database environment.

1. **The Synergy Between AI and SQL Server**

   AI and SQL Server may seem like separate worlds, but they complement each other perfectly. AI thrives on data, and SQL Server is often the primary data storage and management system in many organizations. By embedding AI into SQL Server, businesses can move beyond traditional analytics and reporting to predictive modeling, optimization, and automation of data-driven tasks.

   Why SQL Server + AI?

   - **AI in Your Database**: With SQL Server's Machine Learning Services, you can directly integrate machine learning models in Python or R, execute them from within SQL Server, and return the results to your database.

- **Efficiency**: Instead of exporting data to external AI tools, SQL Server enables in-database machine learning, making the process more efficient and secure.

- **Scalability**: SQL Server supports both on-premise and cloud-based deployments, allowing you to scale your AI-driven solutions quickly across your infrastructure.

2. **Real-World Applications of AI in SQL Server**

AI integrated into SQL Server opens numerous opportunities to solve complex business challenges. Let's explore a few practical applications:

a. **Predictive Maintenance in Manufacturing**

Use case: Manufacturing systems generate a wealth of sensor data that can be stored in SQL Server. Based on this historical data, AI models can predict when equipment will fail, allowing for preemptive maintenance and reducing downtime.

SQL Server Integration: You can train a predictive model using Python or R, and then embed it within SQL Server to monitor real-time sensor data for anomalies.

b. **Customer Segmentation in Marketing**

Use Case: Understanding customer behavior is key for marketing teams. SQL Server can store demographic and purchase data, which AI models can analyze to identify customer segments.

SQL Server Integration: Train clustering models in SQL Server's ML services to segment your customer base and use this information to inform tailored advertising campaigns.

c. **Fraud Detection in Financial Services**

Use Case: Financial transactions are often stored in SQL databases. AI models can be trained to detect fraud by analyzing transaction patterns and flagging anomalies in real time.

SQL Server Integration: Build AI models within SQL Server that monitor incoming transactions and trigger alerts for suspicious behavior.

3. **Step-by-Step Python Code for SQL Server Machine Learning**

For this code example, we'll focus on student dropout predictions based on experience with academic registry systems.

Step 1: Enable SQL Server to Run External Scripts

Before running any Python code within SQL Server, ensure that sp_execute_external_script is enabled:

```
EXEC sp_configure' external scripts enabled,' 1;
RECONFIGURE WITH OVERRIDE;
```

Step 2: Prepare Data in SQL Server

Assume student data is stored in a table named Students, with columns like student_id, age, gender, attendance, grades, and dropout_status.

```
SELECT
CAST(SUBSTRING(student_id, 2, LEN(student_id)) AS INT) AS
student_id,
age,
CASE
WHEN gender = 'Male' THEN 1
WHEN gender = 'Female' THEN 0
ELSE NULL
END AS gender,
attendance,
CAST(grades AS FLOAT) AS grades,
dropout_status
INTO #tempStudentData
FROM Students;
```

Step 3: Run Python Script in SQL Server

```
EXEC sp_execute_external_script
@language = N'Python',
@script = N'
import pandas as PD
from sklearn.linear_model import LogisticRegression
from sklearn.model_selection import train_test_split
input_data = pd.DataFrame(InputDataSet)
X = input_data.drop(columns=["dropout_status"])
y = input_data["dropout_status"]
```

The dataset is split into training and testing sets using the following code: X_train, X_test, y_train, y_test = train_test_split(X, y, test_size=0.2, random_state=42), where 20% of the data is reserved for testing, and the split is randomized with a fixed seed value of 42.

```
model = LogisticRegression()
model.fit(X_train, y_train)
predictions = model.predict(X_test)
output = pd.DataFrame({
"student_id": input_data.loc[X_test.index, "student_id"],
  "PredictedDropout": predictions
})
OutputDataSet = output
',
@input_data_1 = N'SELECT student_id, age, gender, attendance,
CAST(grades AS FLOAT) AS grades, dropout_status FROM
#tempStudentData',
@input_data_1_name = N'InputDataSet',
    @output_data_1_name = N'OutputDataSet'
WITH RESULT SETS ((student_id INT, PredictedDropoutBIT))
```

4. **Best Practices for AI and SQL Server Integration**

To ensure that your AI models run efficiently and provide valuable insights, consider these best practices:

Data Quality Matters: AI models depend on high-quality, clean data. Use SQL Server's data cleaning capabilities to remove duplicates, handle missing values, and ensure consistency.

Automate AI Workflows: Use SQL Server Agent to schedule model training and predictions, automating the entire process for real-time applications like fraud detection.

Monitor Performance: AI models can be resource-intensive. Optimize SQL Server by indexing key columns, partitioning large datasets, and monitoring system resources.

Key Tools and Technologies for AI in SQL Server

Several tools and platforms extend the capabilities of AI within SQL Server:

SQL Server Data Tools (SSDT): Used for database development and deployment.

Microsoft Machine Learning Server: Enables advanced analytics within SQL Server.

Azure Machine Learning Services: Offers cloud-based AI model training and deployment.

5. **Saving a Trained Model and Using It for Predictions in SQL Server**

A key advantage of SQL Server Machine Learning Services is the ability to train AI models directly inside the database and persist them for future use. This eliminates the need to retrain models each time you want to score new data and allows SQL Server to serve as a centralized model repository.

Below is a complete example demonstrating:

- Training a Python machine learning model inside SQL Server

- Saving the trained model into a SQL table

- Loading that saved model

- Using it to generate predictions on new student records

This is a real-world workflow used in fraud detection, churn prediction, risk scoring, student retention systems, and more.

Step 1: Create a Table to Store Saved Models

```
CREATE TABLE ML_Trained_Models
(
model_name NVARCHAR(100) PRIMARY KEY,
 model VARBINARY(MAX) NOT NULL,
 created_on DATETIME DEFAULT GETDATE()
);
This table stores serialized (pickled) Python models.
```

Step 2: Train a Model and Save It into the Table

```
EXEC sp_execute_external_script
@language = N'Python',
 @script = N'
import pandas as pd
import pickle
from sklearn.linear_model import LogisticRegression
 #Load training data
df = InputDataSet
X = df.drop(columns=["dropout_status"]) y = df["dropout_status"]
#Train model
model = LogisticRegression() model.fit(X, y)
#Serialize with pickle
model_bytes = pickle.dumps(model)
#Return as binary for SQL Server to store
OutputDataSet = pd.DataFrame({"model": [model_bytes]})
', @input_data_1 = N'
SELECT student_id, age, gender, attendance, grades, dropout_status
FROM #tempStudentData;
',
@input_data_1_name = N'InputDataSet',
@output_data_1_name = N'OutputDataSet'
WITH RESULT SETS ((model VARBINARY(MAX)));
```

Store the model:

```
INSERT INTO ML_Trained_Models(model_name, model) SELECT
'DropoutPredictionModel', model;
```

Step 3: Load the Saved Model and Score New Data

```
EXEC sp_execute_external_script @language = N'Python', @script = N'
import pandas as pd
import pickle

#Incoming data

new_df = InputDataSet

#Load saved model
model_bytes = ModelData.iloc[0]["model"]
model = pickle.loads(model_bytes)
#Run predictions
pred = model.predict(new_df)
OutputDataSet = pd.DataFrame({
"student_id": new_df["student_id"],
"PredictedDropout": pred
})
    ',
    @input_data_1 = N'
        SELECT student_id, age, gender, attendance, grades
        FROM NewStudents;
    ',
    @input_data_1_name = N'InputDataSet',

    @input_data_2 = N'
        SELECT model FROM ML_Trained_Models
        WHERE model_name = ''DropoutPredictionModel'';
    ',
    @input_data_2_name = N'ModelData',

    @output_data_1_name = N'OutputDataSet'

WITH RESULT SETS ((student_id INT, PredictedDropout BIT));
```

Conclusion

This chapter has demonstrated the powerful integration of machine learning and artificial intelligence capabilities directly within the SQL Server environment, showcasing how these tools are transforming data management practices. We began by understanding how to run and utilize R within SQL Server, bringing advanced statistical capabilities to our database environment. The chapter then extended into the world of Python, highlighting its versatility and widespread use for creating sophisticated AI models and machine learning operations, all from within SQL Server. We concluded with a look at the practical integration of AI models, underscoring the power of leveraging these advancements for tasks like predictive analytics, automation, and sophisticated data insights. Through these explorations of R, Python, and AI model integration, this chapter has unveiled how SQL Server is evolving into a more powerful, data-driven platform capable of handling the complex demands of the modern era.

CHAPTER 11

Common Mistakes in SQL Server You Need to Fix

Ensuring a well-optimized SQL Server environment requires avoiding common pitfalls that can hinder performance, compromise data integrity, and create inefficiencies. This chapter highlights frequent mistakes and provides practical solutions to help you build a more reliable and high-performing SQL Server system.

We begin with the section "The Pitfalls of Using SELECT," which explains why retrieving all columns can degrade performance and increase resource consumption. In the section "Neglecting Indexes," we explore how overlooking indexing strategies can lead to slow query execution and inefficient data retrieval.

Next, the section "Optimizing SQL LIKE Queries" addresses the impact of missing or misused wildcards on query performance. The section "Overusing Subqueries" discusses how excessive reliance on subqueries can complicate queries and reduce efficiency, along with strategies for improvement.

Handling NULL values correctly is another challenge, covered in the section "Managing NULLs Effectively." This section explains the unintended consequences of improper NULL handling and how to mitigate potential errors. In the section "Misusing DISTINCT in Queries," we examine when the DISTINCT keyword is unnecessary and how to refine queries for better efficiency.

For those dealing with complex SQL queries, the section "Simplifying Query Logic" offers techniques to make queries more readable and efficient. Finally, the section "Analyzing Query Performance" emphasizes the importance of assessing execution plans and using performance tuning tools to identify bottlenecks.

By understanding these common SQL Server mistakes and applying the recommended best practices, you can enhance query efficiency, maintain data integrity, and optimize system performance.

© Venkata Reddy Pasam and Petchikumar Andiappan 2026

V. R. Pasam and P. Andiappan, *The Expert's Guide to SQL Server*, https://doi.org/10.1007/979-8-8688-2451-7_11

You've likely faced SQL database performance challenges as a database developer or administrator. Are you aware of common missteps subtly impairing your database performance? This article explores a few SQL mistakes that slow queries and risk data integrity.

Why SELECT * Is a Bad Habit

Using SELECT * can significantly affect performance and maintenance in SQL Server. Always specify the required columns explicitly for better efficiency, maintainability, and security. Many users commonly use SELECT * instead of specifying the columns they need.

Bad practice `SELECT * FROM TABLE1;`
Good practice `SELECT column1, column2, column3, column4 FROM TABLE1;`

Why it's terrible: Retrieving unnecessary columns, higher disk I/O usage, slower query execution time, more network bandwidth consumption, especially with large tables, and uses more memory in the client application.

Ignoring Indexes

SQL Server performs a full table scan without an index, reading every row to find matches, which is inefficient for large tables.

Slow Query Without Proper Indexing

```
SELECT * FROM transactions WHERE transaction_date = '2024-11-27';
```

Without an index on transaction_date, SQL Server scans the entire transactions table.

Create an Index to Speed Up the Query

```
CREATE INDEX idx_ transaction_date ON transactions (transaction_date);
```

With an index on transaction_date, SQL Server directly looks up the rows for "2024-11-27", reducing execution time significantly.

Key Points:

Always analyze queries and identify frequently filtered or sorted columns for indexing.

Monitor the impact of indexes to avoid over-indexing.

Regularly review unused or underperforming indexes to optimize storage and performance.

It is possible to improve query performance significantly. With indexes, particularly for big tables.

Hidden Cost of Misusing Wildcards in SQL-Like Clauses

Using wildcard characters incorrectly in LIKE clauses can severely degrade query performance, particularly when wildcards are placed at the start of the search pattern. This practice prevents SQL Server from using indexes effectively, forcing it to perform a full table scan to locate matching rows.

Bad practice `select * FROM transactions WHERE cust_nameLIKE '%venkat';`

The % at the beginning of the pattern ('%venkat') means SQL Server must evaluate every row in the transactions table to check if cust_name ends with "Venkat."

Indexes cannot be used because the search starts with a variable character, making it impossible for the database engine to use an ordered index for optimization.

Better practice `select * FROM transactions WHERE cust_name LIKE 'venkat%';`

The search pattern starts with a fixed string ("venkat%"). SQL Server can use an index on the cust_name column to perform an index search, retrieving matching rows much faster than scanning the entire table.

Key Points:

Avoid using % at the start of LIKE patterns unless essential.

Design queries and indexes to leverage fixed starting characters for faster lookups.

Consider advanced indexing techniques or additional filters for unavoidable wildcard scenarios.

Overusing Subqueries

While subqueries can be helpful in specific scenarios, overusing them, particularly in the SELECT or WHERE clause, can lead to inefficient query execution and slow performance.

Potentially Slow Subquery (Bad Practice)

```
SELECT student_id,
(SELECT course_name
FROM courses
WHERE courses.course_id = enrollments.course_id) AS course_name
FROM enrollments;
```

The query retrieves each student_id from the enrollments table and uses a subquery to fetch the corresponding course_name from the courses table based on the course_id column. If we use the above queries, we can see many performance issues, like table scans, poor query optimization, and resource incentives.

Often Faster JOIN (Better Practice)

```
SELECT enrollments.student_id, courses.course_name
FROM enrollments
JOIN courses ON enrollments.course_id = courses.course_id;
```

Key Points:

Avoid Subqueries in the SELECT Clause: They often lead to redundant execution and inefficiency.

Use JOINs: They allow the database to combine tables more effectively, leveraging indexing and optimized execution plans.

Analyze Execution Plans: Check how the query is processed and ensure indexes are used effectively.

Indexes Matter: Ensure columns used in the JOIN condition are indexed (courses.course_id).

Ignoring NULL Values

When working with SQL queries, it's essential to handle NULL values properly to avoid unexpected results. Failing to account for NULL can lead to incomplete or misleading query outcomes, especially when the data you're querying might contain missing or undefined values.

Bad practice `select * FROM sales_transactions WHERE discount = 0;`

This query assumes that the discount column is either zero or a valid non-NULL value. However, if some rows contain NULL values in the discount column, they will not be included in the result set, even if you might expect to retrieve all transactions with a zero discount.

Better practice `select * FROM employees WHERE commission_pct = 0 OR commission_pct IS NULL;`

Key Points:

Always Consider NULL: Never assume that columns contain only valid data, such as zero or an empty string. Always explicitly handle NULL values when querying databases.

NULL != Zero or Empty String: Understand the difference between NULL, 0, and empty strings in SQL. NULL means unknown, whereas zero and empty strings are valid values.

Use IS NULL for NULL Handling: Use the IS NULL condition to check for missing values. This ensures that rows with NULL values are not unintentionally excluded from your results.

Query Accuracy: Account for all possible values (0, empty string, NULL, etc.) to ensure your queries return the complete set of expected data.

Avoiding the Unnecessary Use of DISTINCT in SQL Queries

Using DISTINCT in SQL queries is a common practice to remove duplicate rows from a result set. However, overusing DISTINCT unnecessarily, especially when better alternatives exist, can negatively impact query performance. Here's an example to understand the impact and the alternatives.

Inefficient Query Using DISTINCT (Bad Practice)

```
SELECT DISTINCT category_id FROM products;
```

The DISTINCT keyword forces the database engine to evaluate all product table rows, sort the results to identify duplicates, and then return unique category_id values. This sorting operation can be computationally expensive for large datasets.

Optimized Query Using GROUP BY (Better Practice)

```
SELECTcategory_id FROM products GROUP BY category_id;
```

The GROUP BY clause also retrieves unique values but avoids the sorting step often required by DISTINCT. For specific execution plans, GROUP BY can use hashing or other optimized algorithms to reduce computational overhead.

Key Points:

Avoid Overusing DISTINCT: Only use DISTINCT when necessary, as it may lead to slower performance due to sorting operations.

Consider GROUP BY for Better Performance: GROUP BY can efficiently retrieve unique values, especially for large datasets.

Understand Your Query's Needs: Use DISTINCT for simplicity and GROUP BY for versatility and performance, especially if you plan to compute aggregates.

Analyze Execution Plans: Check the query execution plan to see if the database performs expensive operations like sorting when using DISTINCT.

Simplifying Complex SQL Queries: Why and How

Overly complex SQL queries can be challenging to read, optimize, and maintain. Breaking them into smaller, modular parts makes them easier to understand and often improves performance by allowing the database to optimize each part more effectively.

Complex Query (Bad Practice)

```
SELECT o.*, c.*, p.*
FROM orders o
JOIN customers c ON o.customer_id = c.customer_id
JOIN products p ON o.product_id = p.product_id
WHERE o.status = 'shipped'
AND c.regionIN ('North', 'South')
AND p.stock_date> '2023-06-01';
```

It's tough to read and maintain and has optimization challenges.

Better Practice

```
WITH shipped_orders AS (
SELECT *
FROM orders
WHERE status = 'shipped'
),
filtered_customers AS (
SELECT *
FROM customers
WHERE region IN ('North', 'South')
),
recent_products AS (
SELECT *
FROM products
WHERE stock_date> '2023-06-01'
)
SELECT o.*, c.*, p.*
FROM shipped_orders o
JOIN filtered_customers c ON o.customer_id = c.customer_id
JOIN recent_products p ON o.product_id = p.product_id;
```

Key Points and Why This Is Better

Improved Readability:

Each logic part (filtering orders, customers, and products) is separated into sections, making the query more straightforward.

Ease of Maintenance:

You can update individual CTEs without modifying the entire query. For example, changing the filter on products is straightforward.

Modular Debugging:

Testing individual CTEs allows for easier debugging. If the final results are incorrect, you can isolate issues in one CTE at a time.

Performance Benefits:

The database optimizer can evaluate and reuse intermediate results from CTEs, potentially improving execution time.

The Importance of Query Performance Analysis

Neglecting to analyze query performance using tools like EXPLAIN is a missed opportunity to identify and fix inefficiencies. Query performance analysis helps you understand how the database executes a query, revealing bottlenecks like full table scans, unoptimized joins, or missing indexes.

Query Without Analysis: (Bad Practice)

```
SELECT * FROM transactions WHERE account_id = 5678;
```

Potential Issues Without Analysis:

- **Full Table Scans**: If the account_id column lacks an index, the database might scan the entire transactions table, causing delays for large datasets.

- **Suboptimal Execution Plans**: Without understanding the execution plan, you might miss opportunities to optimize the query or database structure.

Example of Query with Analysis: (Better Practice)

```
EXPLAIN SELECT * FROM transactions WHERE account_id = 5678;
```

Output:

```
Seq Scan on transactions (cost=0.00..150.00 rows=100 width=50)
Filter: (account_id = 5678)
```

Key Points:

Understand Query Execution: EXPLAIN shows whether the database uses indexes, performs joins efficiently, or scans rows sequentially.

Identify Bottlenecks: Detect expensive operations like full table scans or inefficient joins.

Iterate and Enhance: Use the knowledge to improve your queries, add indexes, or adjust table design.

Following best practices optimizes performance, makes our code easier to maintain, and safeguards data integrity.

Conclusion

This chapter has served as a crucial guide to navigating common pitfalls in SQL Server development and administration, emphasizing that avoiding these errors is as important as implementing best practices. The chapter highlighted the risks associated with seemingly innocent habits like using SELECT * and ignoring index usage. We explored the insidious costs of using wildcards inappropriately and how to avoid potential subquery issues. The importance of null value handling and careful use of DISTINCT was also addressed, along with the complexities of over-complicating SQL queries and the often overlooked need for query performance analysis. By recognizing and actively addressing these frequent mistakes, database professionals can foster more efficient, maintainable, and ultimately more robust SQL Server systems, ensuring data integrity and performance across their entire data landscape.

Next time you craft a SQL query, consider these tips.

Have you encountered other SQL pitfalls in your projects? Please share your experiences and solutions in the comments!

Concluding Remarks

We appreciate your participation in this in-depth exploration of the world of SQL Server. Throughout this book, we have journeyed through the core concepts, best practices, and advanced techniques necessary to harness SQL Server's full power. From the fundamentals of database design to the complexities of high availability, performance tuning, and disaster recovery, we've covered a broad spectrum of topics to help you become a proficient SQL Server professional.

However, as with any field in technology, the world of SQL Server is constantly evolving. New features, tools, and methodologies continue to emerge, reshaping how we approach database management. Yet, the foundational principles of relational database design, efficient query optimization, and effective data management will remain timeless pillars of best practice.

In this guide, we have focused not only on the technical expertise required to build, maintain, and optimize SQL Server databases but also on the softer skills crucial to success. Clear communication, meticulous documentation, and collaborative problem-solving are as vital as writing efficient queries or configuring backup strategies. These skills will set you apart in a rapidly changing environment and help you work more effectively with your teams and stakeholders.

Our goal is to equip you with a comprehensive skill set that empowers you to scale your SQL Server environments effectively, whether working with on-premises or cloud-based systems. The ever-increasing demand for data-driven decisions means that your role as a SQL Server professional will continue to grow in importance. As the industry adapts, so will the tools and technologies you use, but the principles we've explored in this book will always provide a solid foundation on which to build.

Beyond the technical and tactical aspects, we've also emphasized the significance of solution architecture, problem-solving, and the philosophy of continuous improvement. With a focus on simplicity, clarity, and thoughtful decision-making, you can confidently solve even the most complex challenges in SQL Server.

Finally, as you continue your journey, remember that the broader SQL Server community is an invaluable resource. Contributing to forums, sharing knowledge through blogs or articles, attending conferences, and networking with fellow professionals can accelerate your growth and keep you ahead of the curve. Adopt the mindset of lifelong learning and continue to explore, experiment, and evolve with the technology.

We wish you the best of luck in your SQL Server endeavors. May your databases be continually optimized, your queries be lightning-fast, and your troubleshooting be consistently effective. The adventure is only beginning, and we look forward to seeing you thrive in the world of SQL Server!

This conclusion reflects on the book's technical content, emphasizes the importance of ongoing learning, and encourages readers to engage with the community while maintaining the same inspiring tone.

Index

A

Access control, 113, 131

Access control lists (ACLs), 143

Accuracy, 279

Accurate execution, 90

ACID properties, 10

Active-active cluster, 154–155

Active Directory, 101

Active Directory Domain Services
(AD DS), 195

Active node, 151

Active-passive cluster, 153–154

Additional full backup, 38

Add Node Rules, 181

Administrators, 114

Advanced analytics extensions, 295

AdventureWorks sample database, 296

AES_256 encryption, 53

Alerts in performance optimization, 275–279

AlwaysOn Availability Groups (AGs),
124–126, 193

   advantages, 228–230

   availability group listener, 210

   databases, 193, 201, 208, 210

   failovers, 211–212

   forced failover to DR, 217–221

   group options, 200

   group wizard, 199

   infrastructure requirements, 194

   Listener tab, 202

   mirroring endpoints, 209

   primary replica, 209

   process of configuring, 197–207

   read-only routing, 203, 204, 210

   secondary replicas, 209

   SQL Server, 194

   SQL Server instance
requirements, 195–196

   synchronous commit mode, 211

   T-SQL, 207

   unplanned DR failover, 221–228

Amazon RDS, 145

Application connection strings, 137

Application services, 116

Application testing, 143, 146

Artificial intelligence (AI)

   real-world applications, 299

   and SQL Server integration, 301–303

   step-by-step Python, 300–301

   synergy, 298–299

   valuable strategies, 298

Asymmetric key encryption, 48

Asynchronous commit mode, 197, 211

Asynchronous mode, 215

Atomicity, consistency, isolation, and
durability (ACID), 10

Auditing, 114

Aurora PostgreSQL, 146

   applications, 144

   Babelfish environment, 146

   features, 144

   migration, 144–146

   size and complexity, 144

   SQL Server setup, 144

M

N

O

P

R

Range partitioning, 243–244

Reading data, 117

Read-only access, 116

Read-only routing, 203, 204

Read-only workloads, 197

Ready to Add Node screen, 186

Real-world scenarios, 231

Regulatory compliance, 131

Relational engine, 1, 2, 4, 11
    command (CMD) parser, 7
    optimizer, 8
    query executor, 9

Replica, 214

Resetting, 254

Resolution, 287

Resource metrics, 278

Restorations, 114, 142
    backups, 69
    database, 61, 62, 65, 68, 70, 75
    differential backups, 64–65, 76, 77
    large-scale disasters, 61
    operation, 71
    pre-restoration preparations, 62
    process, 72, 78, 79
    transaction log, 65
    wizard, 67, 74

RESTORE command, 61

RESTORE operation, 34

Restoring, 56–58

Right event, 258

Role-based access control (RBAC), 146

R programming, 289–298

Row identifier (RID) lock, 13

Row-level locks, 10

Row-level security (RLS), 91
    benefits, 131
    best practices, 133

    control access, 131
    predicates, 131
    security policy, 132
    SQL Server, 130
    testing, 132–133

S

Scalability, 152, 230, 299

Secondary data files (PDF), 11

Secondary Nodes, 215, 217, 220

Secondary replicas, 125, 228

Securables tab, 98

SecureDB database, 55

SecureDB_Cert, 53

Security, 91
    folder, 94
    row-level security (RLS), 130–134
    Windows authentication, 92–102

Security admin, 119

Security policies, 114, 132

Security teams, 114

SELECT *, 308

SELECT clause, 310

Selected events, 261

Separation of duties, 115

Sequence of operations, 8

Server configuration, 165–166

Server configuration settings, 119

Server-level roles, 91, 96, 104, 117–121

Server Network Interface (SNI), 3–4

Server-wide settings, 119

Service Accounts, 165, 184

setup.exe, 156, 175

Shared memory, 3, 5

Shared storage, 148, 195

Shared storage subsystem, 151

Side-by-side migration, 136, 137

V

W, X, Y, Z